Orion on the Dunes

Orion on the Dunes

A Biography of Henry Beston

by DANIEL G. PAYNE

DAVID R. GODINE, PUBLISHER

Boston

First published in 2016 by
David R. Godine, Publisher
Post Office Box 450
Jaffrey, New Hampshire 03452
www.godine.com

LIBRARY OF CONGRESS CATALOGING-IN-PUBLICATION DATA
Payne, Daniel G., 1958–
Orion on the dunes : a biography of Henry Beston / Daniel Payne.
pages cm
Includes bibliographical references and index.
ISBN 978-1-56792-549-4 (alk. paper)
1. Beston, Henry, 1888–1968.
2. Naturalists—Massachusetts—Biography.
3.Authors—United States—Biography.
I. Title.
QH31.B48P39 2015
508.092—dc23
[B]
2015024975

First edition
Printed in the United States of America

This book is lovingly dedicated to my parents,
Herbert D. Payne and Helen J. Payne,
with humility, gratitude, and respect.

WHATEVER attitude to human existence you fashion for yourself, know that it is valid only if it be the shadow of an attitude to Nature. A human life, so often likened to a spectacle upon a stage, is more justly a ritual. The ancient values of dignity, beauty, and poetry which sustain it are of Nature's inspiration; they are born of the mystery and beauty of the world. Do no dishonor to the earth lest you dishonour the spirit of man.

HENRY BESTON
The Outermost House

Contents

Acknowledgments

THE ORIGINS OF THIS PROJECT go back many years, and have taken several fortuitous turns to reach fruition. One day back in the 1970s, while I was working as a young clam digger on Long Island's Great South Bay, I had just sold my catch at the Maple Avenue docks and was walking along Main Street in Bay Shore when I happened to see a paperback copy of Henry Beston's *The Outermost House* in the window of a second-hand store. The cover photo of a lonely shack on the dunes attracted my attention, and so, on a whim, I walked into the shop, paid my fifty cents, and brought the book home. It was love at first read. In the book Beston described, in prose more beautiful than I thought possible, a landscape very similar to that where I had been raised—the south shore of Long Island, the bay, the great barrier beach of Fire Island, and the Atlantic Ocean. Most important to my young mind, the depiction of the land, the waters, and the human and animal inhabitants of Cape Cod rang true. It seemed to me not just a beautiful account of, as Beston wrote, "a year of life on the great beach of Cape Cod," but an honest one. Infused as I was with the philosophy of Emerson and Thoreau (as Thoreau writes in the conclusion to *Walden*, "Say what you have to say, not what you ought. Any truth is better than make-believe."), I thought then—and still do—that this made Beston's philosophy one worth full and careful consideration.

About fifteen years later when one of my dissertation advisors, John Elder at Middlebury College, offered me the opportunity to write an article about Henry Beston for *American Nature Writers* (New York: Scribners, 1996) I eagerly accepted. I soon realized, however, that there was no biography about Beston (and unexpectedly little biographical information about him

Acknowledgments

generally) available, which surprised me, considering how prominent a writer he was. While this made the task of writing the article about him more challenging, it also presented me with an opportunity to make up for what I saw as an astonishing omission. I owe John Elder many thanks for his kindness and mentorship over the years, and I thank him in particular here for getting me started on this project.

My deepest thanks go also to Barry Lopez, who was kind enough to put me in touch with his friend Kate Beston Barnes—Henry Beston's younger daughter and literary executor. From the beginning, Kate gave her full support to my efforts to chronicle her father's life and career, giving me not only full access to extensive archival materials, but also emphasizing that there were no restrictions on how I would use those resources to tell Beston's story. I will always be very grateful to Barry and to Kate for their unfailing generosity of spirit.

From the beginning, the best part of what has sometimes been an arduous endeavor has been developing relationships and, in many cases lasting friendships, with the people who have been so cordial and generous throughout the time spent researching and writing this book. My deepest thanks go to Gary Lawless and Beth Leonard—words cannot express how much their help and friendship have meant to me over the past several years. I am also profoundly grateful to Marie Sheahan and Joanie Sheahan Schwab, Henry Beston's nieces; John Neff, the son of J. Luther Neff, one of Henry Beston's dearest friends; Henry Beston's godson, Richard Beston Day and his wonderful family; Don and Nita Wilding, founders of the Henry Beston Society; Brett and Rebecca Barry, who produced a superb audiobook edition of Beston's *The Outermost House* for Silver Hollow Audio; William F. Brabenec for sharing his collection of correspondence between Beston and Clayton and Hazel Smith of Windsor, Ontario; Jeff and Sharon Prostovich; Elizabeth, Isabella, Henry, and Harold Barnes; John Nash; Dr. Gerald Landry; Kathy Meeker from the Grants Development Office at SUNY College at Oneonta; my colleagues at SUNY Oneonta, most especially Gwen Crane, Patrick Meanor, Jim Mills, Richard Lee, Eileen Morgan-Zaycheck, Amie Doughty, Bill Simons, and Julie Freeman; and Anne McDonald Diers, for sharing her "Hold Your Hands Out Over the Earth," a musical piece

Acknowledgments

putting Beston's words to music. Many thanks also go to Terri Rowe from the Milne Library at SUNY Oneonta, who did a remarkable job of finding countless, often hard to find, articles by Henry Beston.

As befits a family of writers, there is a remarkable amount of archival material that had to be examined before writing this biography. In particular I would like to thank the Boston Athenaeum, Boston Massachusetts; the Eastham Historical Society, Eastham, Massachusetts; the Maine Women Writers Collection, University of New England, Portland, Maine; Raymond H. Fogler Library, University of Maine at Orono Special Collections; the Widener and Houghton Library Special Collections, Harvard University Library, Cambridge, Massachusetts; Rauner Special Collections Library, Dartmouth College Library, Hanover, New Hampshire; Sara Georgini, Library Assistant at the Massachusetts Historical Society, Boston, Massachusetts; Bill Burke, Hope Merrill, Bob McCormack, and Jenna Sammartino at the Cape Cod National Seashore, Eastham, Massachusetts; the Quincy Historical Society, Quincy, Massachusetts; the Catskill Center for Conservation and Development in Arkville, New York; the Provincetown Community Compact; Bethany S. Rutledge, Director of Collections & Exhibits, and Mary Beers, Director of Education at the Thornton W. Burgess Museum, East Sandwich, Massachusetts; and Leatrice Armstrong, Education Coordinator, and Mary Katherine Ellis, Collections Manager at the Wheelwright Museum of the American Indian in Santa Fe, New Mexico. I am particularly grateful to the staff at the George J. Mitchell Department of Special Collections and Archives at the Bowdoin College Library, where the Beston Family Archives are located—Director Richard Lindemann and archivists Caroline Mosely, Kathy Petersen, and Daniel Hope are consummate professionals whose gracious and friendly assistance with this project has been deeply appreciated.

Last, but certainly not least, I would like to thank David R. Godine, Heather Tamarkin, and my editors Aaron Kerner and Chelsea Bingham at David R. Godine, Publisher, who took this work to completion. I also owe a great debt to the support of my family: Helen, Herbert, Anne, Rebecca, Emily, and Jake Payne, Michele Payne, and Dave Nixon, whose patience and encouragement were vital and everlastingly appreciated.

Introduction

If industrial man continues to multiply his numbers and expand his operations he will succeed in his apparent intention, to seal himself off from the natural and isolate himself within a synthetic prison of his own making. He will make himself an exile from the earth and then will know at last, if he is still capable of feeling anything, the pain and agony of the loss.

EDWARD ABBEY, *Desert Solitaire*

IN FEBRUARY 1916 Henry Sheahan, a twenty-seven-year-old volunteer ambulance driver with the American Field Service, was stationed with his unit, Section Sanitaire Américaine No. 2, just outside the French fortress city of Verdun. Several weeks earlier the French military command—which up to that time had considered the city and the imposing circle of forts around it to be nearly impregnable—had noted increased activity in the German lines near Verdun, and began belatedly to prepare for the possibility of a German offensive directed at this crucial bulwark in the French line. On February 21 the attack began. Sheahan and several other drivers were working on their ambulances in the parking area outside their barracks when the first bombs hit: "A whistling scream, a kind of shrill, increasing shriek, sounded in the air and ended in a crash. Smoke rolled heavily in another direction. Another whistle, another crash, another and another and another. The last building shot up great tongues of flame. . . . Across the yard a comrade's arm beckoned me, 'Come on, we've got to help put out the fires!'"[1] For twenty minutes, the drivers desperately worked to extinguish the fires while the attack continued, diving for cover whenever the whistle of the shells indicated a nearby strike. That night the town was

Introduction

blacked out as Verdun was pounded by German artillery. Before retiring to the barracks and a fitful sleep, Sheahan stood outside, listening to the ceaseless thunder of the bombardment: "One great nation, for the sake of a city valueless from a military point of view, was preparing to kill several hundred thousand of its citizens, and another great nation, anxious to retain the city, was preparing calmly for a parallel hecatomb . . . all one's faculties of intellect are revolted by the stark brutality of death *en masse.*"[2]

The American Field Service volunteers performed heroically, risking their own lives to transport wounded soldiers to makeshift field hospitals behind the lines, working almost without sleep until the worst of the fighting ended several weeks later. On one such trip, Sheahan was ordered to transport three injured men to the barracks. The road had been churned into thick mire, and was crowded with troops and horse-drawn supply wagons headed to the front, and a funereal procession of dead and wounded being transported to the interior. His ambulance was just behind a two-horse wagon carrying medical supplies and another wagon drawn by a single horse, when he heard the thunder of anti-aircraft fire behind him, followed by the sound of an approaching German warplane:

> A few seconds later, there sounded the terrifying scream of an air-bomb, a roar, and I found myself in a bitter swirl of smoke. The shell had fallen right between the horses of the two-horse wagon, blowing the animals to pieces, splintering the wagon, and killing the driver. Something sailed swiftly over my head, and landed just behind the ambulance. It was a chunk of the skull of one of the horses. The horse attached to the wagon in front of me went into a frenzy of fear and backed his wagon into my ambulance, smashing the right lamp. In the twinkling of an eye, the soldiers dispersed. Some ran into the fields. Others crouched in the wayside ditch. A cart upset. Another bomb dropped screaming in a field and burst; a cloud of smoke rolled away down the meadow.[3]

After several weeks of savage fighting the French army succeeded in holding Verdun, but the victory came at a staggering cost—they lost approximately 377,000 men in the battle; the Germans lost almost the same number.[4] Although Henry Sheahan's six-month long tour of duty had ended shortly after the onset of the battle, he remained with his unit until the worst of the

Introduction

fighting was over, unwilling to leave France during its moment of greatest need: "I am very happy to be able to do something here," he wrote in a chapter on his experience at Verdun included in *Friends of France: The Field Service of the American Ambulance Described by its Members* (1916), "very proud to feel that I am doing something . . . To half jest, I am enduring war for peace of mind."⁵ That April, after seven months of valiant service on the western front, Sheahan finally boarded a ship heading home to Quincy, Massachusetts.

Whatever peace of mind Henry Sheahan may have felt as a result of his wartime service did not endure; in fact, as was the case with many of his contemporaries, the war called into question fundamental beliefs that had been inculcated in him since childhood. When the conflict in Europe broke out in 1914 many young Americans—politically and culturally disposed to favor the Western democracies of France and Britain against the autocracies of the central European powers—were eager to aid the British and French war effort. Furthermore, news reports of German atrocities in Belgium and U-boat predations against ostensibly neutral shipping on the high seas fueled anti-German sentiment. Although it would be nearly three years before the United States entered the war on the side of the Allies, thousands of young Americans, driven in no small part by romantic notions that would soon be dispelled by the realities of modern industrial warfare, volunteered to serve in France. Many of these volunteers served as ambulance drivers; as Arlen J. Hansen writes in *Gentlemen Volunteers: The Story of the American Ambulance Drivers in the Great War*, "The number of those who drove ambulances in Europe and subsequently became famous literary figures is astonishing."⁶ These literary volunteers included Louis Bromfield, Malcolm Cowley, John Dos Passos, E.E. Cummings, Ernest Hemingway, and Archibald MacLeish, among many others. Like most other chroniclers of this phenomenon, however, Hansen only mentions Henry Sheahan in passing, unaware that the young volunteer who described his experiences on the western front in *A Volunteer Poilu* (1916) later gained far greater literary acclaim under the *nom de plume* of Henry Beston, author of several outstanding works including *The Outermost House*, one of the undisputed masterpieces of American nature writing.

Introduction

By the time the guns fell silent on November 11, 1918, the Great War—the "war to end all wars," as Woodrow Wilson had hopefully prophesied—had transformed the world. A new era of industrial, mechanized warfare had been ushered in, and many of the old regimes, the despotic monarchies of Germany, Austria-Hungary, the Ottoman Empire, and Russia, had collapsed. As many of the "Lost Generation" now saw it, millions of their comrades had been led to the slaughter by the inept and corrupt leadership of the previous generation, and they now bitterly renounced the national, cultural, and religious institutions that had initiated the cataclysm. The widespread loss of faith in these institutions spawned a revolution in arts and literature as the rejection of traditional rules and codes led to a need, as Ezra Pound wrote, to "make it new." Some of these new ideas, such as those of the Dadaists, for instance, rejected the notion that there *was* an inherent order to things. Other creative artists, such as Hemingway, believed that in the absence of an objective standard of moral conduct each individual should develop his own, subjective code. Still others, after a spasm of rebellion, returned to the familiar, timeworn comforts of religion, nationalism, or alcohol, often with sad, predictable results.

Henry Beston took a different path. Even before the war, he had experienced heart wrenching personal losses, including the untimely death of his mother and then that of his father a few years later, that caused him to reassess many of the foundational teachings of his youth. After his father, a devout Roman Catholic, died in 1906, Henry stopped attending Catholic services. Not long afterwards he began using "Beston" as a middle name, beginning the transition (for reasons that aren't entirely clear) toward dropping the use of Sheahan as his last name. His wartime experiences exacerbated his sense that there was something fundamentally wrong with modern industrial civilization and its effect on the human spirit. On the western front, Beston observed how the war had transformed the French countryside into a morass of barbed wire, trenches, and shell-holes, and in the desolation he detected a link between modern industrial society, war, and the human spirit. The war had transformed the landscape into something sinister, and he fully agreed with a "distinguished French artist" with whom he served, who told him that "Nature as Nature is never sinister; it is when there is a disturbance of the relations between Nature and human life that you have the sinister . . . Here Man is making Nature unlivable for Man. This will all end when the peasants plant again."[7] Long after the war ended, this idea would form one of the key tenets of Beston's worldview, and often appeared in his writing, where he contended that modern industrial society worked in insidious ways to distance man from nature and undermine the human spirit.

After the war Beston began to write fairy tales in an attempt to counter the effect of his wartime experiences.[8] Although these stories were immensely popular with young readers, including those of his close friend Theodore Roosevelt Jr., Beston still felt that he had something more than journalism and children's stories to offer as a writer. Beston found himself at midlife working as an editor for *Living Age* magazine but he soon became dissatisfied with the daily routine of the job, writing to his friend Maurice "Jake" Day (who had illustrated two of his children's books), "this steady downpour of newspapers, reviews, books and magazines is slowly crazing me. I am beginning to think that I shall have to get out for my soul's sake. I don't know whether I'm lazy or just bored. Probably both. But I'm beginning to crave a little time all to myself."[9] Beston resigned his editorial position a short time later, and embarked upon a career as a full-time writer, saying, "If you *can* write and *don't*, something within you withers & dies, and with its death envenoms the soul."[10]

In early September of 1926 Beston arrived on Cape Cod to spend a few weeks in a cottage he'd built on the dunes overlooking the Atlantic Ocean near Eastham. As he later wrote, "The fortnight ending, I lingered on, and as the year lengthened into autumn, the beauty and mystery of this earth and outer sea so possessed and held me that I could not go."[11] During his sojourn on the great beach Beston experienced an epiphany, a dawning realization that the sense of order and vital meaning that he and many of his generation had been searching for was to be found not in human institutions but in the elemental and eternal rhythms of nature. On the Cape he developed and refined his ideas regarding the harmful effects that industrial civilization had on the human spirit—dulling our senses, increasing our proclivity towards violence, and disconnecting us from the vital rhythms

[xix]

of the earth. Twenty years before Aldo Leopold set out his famous "land ethic" in *A Sand County Almanac*, arguing that humankind should cease to see itself as a conqueror of the land-community but rather as a "plain member and citizen of it," Henry Beston had come to a similar conclusion. His time on Cape Cod led him to the realization that the antiquarian notion that humans were of a different order than the rest of creation was fundamentally flawed: "We need another and a wiser and perhaps a more mystical concept of animals . . . They are not brethren, they are not underlings; they are other nations, caught with ourselves in the net of life and time, fellow prisoners of the splendour and travail of the earth."[12]

Rachel Carson was one of many readers who have appreciated the enduring insight and exquisite prose of *The Outermost House* since it was first published in 1928, writing that it was "among the books that I have loved best and that have influenced me the most."[13] It has never been out of print and has justly earned a reputation as one of the great classics of American nature writing. Even before Beston donated his dune shack, the Fo'castle, to the Massachusetts Audubon Society in 1961, a number of outstanding writers and visual artists had the opportunity to stay there including Ted Hughes and Sylvia Plath, who paid tribute to Beston in her poem "The Hermit at Outermost House." Thomas Lyon, the editor of *This Incomperable Lande: A Book of American Nature Writing*, compares *The Outermost House* to Thoreau's *Walden* and Edward Abbey's *Desert Solitaire* as a "talismanic book of solitude."[14] It was one of the inspirations behind the creation of the Cape Cod National Seashore in 1961 and, three years later, the Fo'castle, located a short distance from the park's new visitors center, was designated a National Literary Landmark.

Several months after the publication of *The Outermost House* Beston married Elizabeth Coatsworth, a widely published poet and children's author. After an idyllic honeymoon spent at the Fo'castle and on a walking tour in England, they returned home and began their lives as a married literary couple. Favorable reviews and word of mouth steadily increased sales of *The Outermost House*, and it soon went into a second printing. The book's success presented Beston with numerous writing opportunities; John Farrar, publisher and co-founder of Farrar and Rinehart Publishing, suggested that he write a novel and offered him an advance if he chose to do so. Houghton Mifflin was eager for Beston to write a companion book to *The Outermost House*, and when he casually mentioned that he was thinking of writing a book about the inner Cape, the bay side, they quickly sent him a contract on far more favorable terms than they had offered for his previous book. For the first few years of their marriage Henry and Elizabeth lived in Hingham, an old south shore village approximately thirteen miles south of Boston. They soon had two children, Margaret and Catherine (Kate Beston Barnes went on to be named the first poet laureate of the state of Maine), and in 1931 Elizabeth won the prestigious Newberry Award for *The Cat Who Went to Heaven*. Even as the nation entered into a devastating economic depression that would last a full decade, it appeared that Henry Beston was on a remarkable roll, personally and professionally.

Beston enthusiastically began work on the book about the inner Cape, but it was soon evident that something had changed—it was as if during his year on Cape Cod he had caught a glimpse of nature's holy grail, but was unable to recapture it once he left the Cape. He found it difficult to write at Hingham, complaining, "there was no nature for a naturalist to see, save 'the spotted Chevrolet and the Greater and Lesser Buick.'"[15] He took frequent short trips to Cape Cod to work on the book, but the inspiration of place that had been a constant with him during the period when he was writing *The Outermost House* was gone; "I'm pretty well exploded as a hermit, dear," he wrote despairingly to Elizabeth at one point.[16] Frustrated, he finally abandoned the project and destroyed much of what he had written, convinced that, whatever its merits, the book would not measure up to *The Outermost House*. Beston grew dispirited, both about his writing and about the toxic effects of a modern industrial civilization that he felt was "without a truly human past and may be without a human future."[17] In stark contrast to Henry, Elizabeth, even while busy with two young children, was astonishingly prolific. She wrote and published over one hundred books during her lifetime, which was occasionally a source of some anxiety for them both.

One day over lunch, shortly after returning from a visit to Maine to see Jake Day and his family, Beston surprised his wife with a question from out of the blue: "How would you like to have us buy a Maine farm?" he asked.

Introduction

Without missing a beat, Elizabeth answered, "It sounds fine," and a few weeks later they were the owners of an old farm in Nobleboro, Maine.[18] Chimney Farm, as they named it, soon became nearly as important to Beston and his writing as Cape Cod had been, although it never quite equaled Cape Cod in his literary imagination. As he wrote to his young Eastham friend Truesdell Fife in 1932: "there is always a door in my inner spirit from behind whose panels rises a great sound, a sound which is part of life for me, the great roar of the October ocean beyond the dunes. No high wild cry of evergreens shall ever drown it, no sound of other waters confuse it, that vast and memorable cry."[19] In 1935, seven years after the publication of *The Outermost House*, Beston's next book, *Herbs and the Earth* was finally published. He described it as "part garden book, part musing study of our relationship to Nature," and while it is a quieter, more intimate study of nature than was *The Outermost House*, in many ways it is a profound and wholly appropriate if somewhat belated successor. Beston believed that the physical and spiritual connection with the land and nature's elemental presences and cycles that were such an integral part of farm life might provide a vital counterweight to "a civilization obsessed with power." As he writes in *Herbs and the Earth*, "it is this earth which is the true inheritance of man, his link with his human past, the source of his religion, ritual and song, the kingdom without whose splendor he lapses from his mysterious estate of man into a baser world."[20]

In later years Beston's work consistently found an appreciative critical and popular audience, and in books such as *The St. Lawrence* (1942) and *Northern Farm* (1948) he continued to explore the theme of humankind's vital and necessary connection with the land. His old children's stories also enjoyed a renaissance when they were collected and republished as *Henry Beston's Fairy Tales* in 1952. Despite a series of honors and literary successes, however, Beston became increasingly concerned about his literary legacy, fearing that he would be remembered for just one book. In a development that was not without a certain sad irony, he also become somewhat fixated on his family legacy; when his beloved nephew George Sheahan died in a tragic automobile accident on Cape Cod, Henry—who had long ceased using his patronymic surname—grieved both for his nephew and for the end

Introduction

of the Sheahan line. After a series of debilitating strokes, Henry Beston died at Chimney Farm in 1968. Ten years later—fifty years after the publication of *The Outermost House*—the Fo'castle was washed out to sea during an immense winter storm, a fate that would undoubtedly been seen as fitting by the man who had written, "To understand this great outer beach . . . one must have a sense of it as the scene of wreck and elemental disaster."[21]

While *The Outermost House* is, as Robert Finch writes, a work "established on imperishable foundations," Beston's fear that he would be remembered for that book alone has proven to be unfounded.[22] The continued appeal of Beston's other work has been borne out by the recent reissue of several of his books, including *Herbs and the Earth*, *Northern Farm*, *The St. Lawrence*, and *Chimney Farm Bedtime Stories*, and by the designation of Chimney Farm as a Literary Landmark in August 2012. At times, Beston's take on the link between humankind and the land can seem elegiacally agrarian in its romantic appreciation of rural life (he sometimes referred to himself as a Virgilian in his outlook) but more often his critique of modern civilization is still remarkably current, even prescient, in a world where political and religious extremism, and corporate industrialism on a global scale have spawned a more violent, materialistic, and pessimistic humankind that searches—often in very odd places—for hope and spiritual solace. The keystone to our well-being as individuals and as a species, Beston believed, is in the elemental presences of the world: the cycles of the seasons, the sky above us, the waters around us, and the beloved earth beneath our feet. As he wrote in the foreword to the 1949 edition of *The Outermost House*:

> Once again, I set down the core of what I continue to believe. Nature is a part of our humanity, and without some awareness and experience of that divine mystery man ceases to be man. When the Pleiades and the wind in the grass are no longer a part of the human spirit, a part of very flesh and bone, man becomes, as it were, a kind of cosmic outlaw, having neither the completeness and integrity of the animal nor the birthright of a true humanity. As I once said elsewhere, "Man can either be less than man or more than man, and both are monsters, the last more dread."[23]

It is, in a sense, unfortunate for Henry Beston's literary reputation that he is so strongly identified with this one classic book, for it has overshadowed

Introduction

his other works, several of which are also outstanding. As Sherman Paul writes in *For Love of the World: Essays on Nature Writers*, "Beston should figure for us as a writer of several works, not just *The Outermost House*."[24] In 1960, when Beston became the third recipient of the Emerson-Thoreau Medal awarded by the American Academy of Arts & Sciences—the first two writers to be so honored were Robert Frost and T. S. Eliot—the award was, as always, given in honor of the writer's total literary achievement, not just one work. It should also be emphasized that while Beston's most well-known works are generally associated with Cape Cod or Maine, his work transcends local or regional significance. Henry Beston is clearly a product of New England's great literary tradition, however, he can only be considered a local or regional writer in the same sense that Emerson, Thoreau, Hawthorne, *et al.* are local writers; they are writers in whose work close observations about a specific place build into universal truths concerning humankind and the world around us. Robert Finch, another outstanding writer about Cape Cod, stated in his introduction to the 1988 edition of *The Outermost House* that it is astonishing that no biography on Beston has yet been written. When one considers how many great modern writers were admirers of Beston—including Rachel Carson, Sylvia Plath, Kurt Vonnegut, and John Hay, to name just a few—this does seem to be rather surprising to say the least. Perhaps this is due in part to the fact that Beston was not a prolific writer. He wrote slowly, taking great pains to create prose where "sound and sense" work together seamlessly. What Beston may have sacrificed in quantity, however, he made up with quality—as a prose stylist, his work is exemplary; his books and essays are models of clear, concise writing. Few writers have managed to capture the rhythms of the English language as lyrically as did Beston. As one of his contemporaries, the literary critic and essayist Van Wyck Brooks states in *From the Shadow of the Mountain*, if modern literary critics truly appreciated the aesthetics of writing "there would be no writers more critically esteemed than Henry Beston or Rachel Carson or Loren Eiseley."[25]

In addition to his literary accomplishments, Beston should also be recognized as a key figure in the development of modern environmentalism who, along with Aldo Leopold, shifted the focus of early twentieth century

Introduction

conservation to a more expansive gaze. His influence on Rachel Carson—an author whose work is often cited as the fountainhead of the twentieth-century environmental movement—in itself makes him a figure of note. Paul Watson, a founder of Greenpeace and the Sea Shepherd Conservation Society, also identifies Beston as one of the inspirations behind his activism.[26] Many of the primary themes in Beston's work, such as challenging anthropocentric perspectives concerning nature; the importance of establishing a connection with place; the link between the cycles of nature and humankind's yearning for a spiritual bond with the world; and the dangers presented by our industrial, consumerist culture—all maintain their relevance today and are evident in the work of many outstanding contemporary writers, including Edward Abbey, Wendell Berry, Terry Tempest Williams, and Barry Lopez. Beston's words from the conclusion of *The Outermost House* resonate more powerfully than ever: "A human life, so often likened to a spectacle upon a stage, is more justly a ritual. The ancient values of dignity, beauty, and poetry which sustain it are of Nature's inspiration; they are born of the mystery and beauty of the world. Do no dishonour to the earth lest you dishonour the spirit of man."[27]

A Sense of Place

Look underfoot. You are always nearer to the true sources of your power than you think. The lure of the distant and difficult is deceptive. The great opportunity is where you are. Don't despise your own place and hour. Every place is the center of the world.

JOHN BURROUGHS

IN RECALLING HIS CHILDHOOD Henry Beston would later say that his boyhood years in Quincy, Massachusetts were not a significant influence in fostering the love of nature that permeates his work. "Nature," as he wrote in a letter to his wife Elizabeth, "was in a suburban mood there; she went yachting in a catboat on Saturday afternoons and arranged the tides as if they had to take trains. There was no poetry. Fugitive glimpses, perhaps, but no deep, underlying mood."[1] However, while it certainly took many years before Beston's response to nature coalesced into a cohesive philosophical framework, his "New England boyhood of sea and shore" had a far more profound and lasting influence on his work than he seemed to have realized. His lifelong love of the ocean, the shoreline's constant reminder of nature's endless process of destruction and creation, and his joy in the panoramic and cyclical changes of New England's four distinct seasons all contribute to a perspective that in an ecocritical sense is both "green" and "blue." Beston's love of the New England landscape and the sea, as well as the region's cultural legacy (including that of the American Indians, who were a lifelong interest of his) are clearly evident in his work. Beston is a literary descendant of the great New England writers before him, particularly Ralph Waldo Emerson and Henry Thoreau with whom he

[xxvii]

shared not only a love of nature but also a conviction that a spiritual, "poetic" relation with nature was vitally important to humankind. As Beston wrote in *Herbs and the Earth*, "It is only when we are aware of the earth and the earth as poetry that we truly live. Ages and people that sever the earth from the poetic spirit, or do not care, or stop their ears with knowledge as with dust, find their veins grown hollow and their hearts an emptiness echoing to questioning."[2]

Henry Beston's birthright, therefore, was not just his family history, but also the environmental and cultural history of his native New England. This is reflected many times in his literary works—in the opening pages of *The Outermost House* where he begins with a lengthy description of the geology of Cape Cod; throughout his Maine books, *Herbs and the Earth* and *Northern Farm*; in *The St. Lawrence*; and in his remarkable historical compendium, *American Memory*. His literary imagination extends far back into the distant reaches of New England's past when a vast sheet of ice thousands of feet deep covered much of North America, carving and shaping the topography. When the glaciers finally retreated they left behind a landscape that had been transformed into what was now a genuinely "new world." The coast-line of the land that the aboriginal people called Massachusett, or "great hills place," was now punctuated with bays and harbors carved out by the glaciers. Numerous islands, including Nantucket, Martha's Vineyard, and the Boston Harbor Islands were formed by the sand and rock deposited by the retreating glaciers, as was Cape Cod, a sixty-five-mile-long peninsula that juts out from the mainland like a flexed arm, partially enclosing and sheltering Cape Cod Bay from the tempestuous Atlantic Ocean.

After the retreat of the glaciers, groups of Paleolithic hunter-gatherers roamed northward into the region. By the time European adventurers began their explorations of the area in the sixteenth century, Algonquian-speaking tribes were well-established in the coastal areas of New England. In 1614, the English explorer John Smith estimated the population of the Algonquians at upwards of 4,000 people, which was probably a significant underestimate of the actual number.[3] In the summer, the Massachusetts Indians coalesced along the shore in small communities where they would cultivate the land—maize, beans, and squash were primary crops—and take advantage of the rich variety of fish and shellfish found in the bays and estuaries of the coast. In the fall, they traveled inland, toward the wooded hills to the west where they spent the winter hunting. They were skilled pottery makers, and quarries in the Blue Hills furnished them with the material they needed for implements used in agriculture and hunting, although by the mid-sixteenth century commerce with European traders brought them manufactured goods as well.[4] Unfortunately for the Indians, trade goods were not all the Europeans brought with them. In 1616 a ravaging illness, probably smallpox, brought over by European traders spread along a corridor extending from Maine to Rhode Island; by 1619 up to ninety percent of the natives had succumbed to disease.

In November 1620 a ship that had sailed from England two months earlier arrived at Cape Cod. The *Mayflower* carried about one hundred passengers, most of whom were Puritan separatists planning to establish a colony, as their future governor William Bradford wrote, "derived out of the Virginia patent and wholly secluded from their government, viz., New England."[5] A group of sixteen well-armed men led by Captain Miles Standish formed a scouting party and landed near the site of present day Provincetown. Upon arriving on shore, they saw "five or six persons with a dog coming toward them, who were savages," but these fled at the sight of the armed party. Standish's party followed the natives, and while they did not catch up with them, they did find some fields of Indian corn that had recently been harvested and a cache where many baskets of corn were buried. They returned to the *Mayflower* bearing several baskets of the corn, and a subsequent party found another place where the Indians had buried corn and beans. This was also taken with the intent, as William Bradford averred in his history of Plymouth Plantation, "to give [the Indians] full satisfaction when they should meet with any of them as, about six months later they did, to their great content."[6] In early December, the Puritans sent a small shallop and ten men to reconnoiter the partially sheltered bay of the inner Cape, hoping to find a promising location for their colony. One of the areas they explored was near present-day Eastham, where Henry Beston would build his dune shack on the beach some three hundred years later. They failed to find a suitable place to settle on Cape Cod, and after a brief skirmish with some of the native inhabitants, they opted to sail for a sheltered harbor on the western shore of the bay recommended by the *Mayflower's* pilot. This place became the site of the settlement they named Plymouth Plantation.

Five years after the establishment of the Plymouth colony, Captain Richard Wollaston established a small trading post and settlement about twenty-seven miles up the coast from Plymouth. Daunted by the frigid New England winter, Wollaston didn't stay long. The following year he returned to Virginia, leaving his settlement in charge of one of his subordinates, Lieutenant Filcher. Filcher was apparently an inept manager, and when an adventurer and free spirit named Thomas Morton arrived that spring, discord ensued. Morton inspired the other settlers, most of whom were servants still indentured to Captain Wollaston, to cast off their bonds of servitude and join him in a plantation and trading post he dubbed "Mare-Mount" (or Merry Mount), which Bradford snidely referred to as a "school of atheism." Among Morton's many offenses, according to the Puritans, was the erection of a maypole (which they saw as rank idolatry), the quaffing of strong spirits, and his cordial relations with the local Indians—most particularly the women.

What undoubtedly alarmed the Puritans most, however, was Morton's success in trading with the Indians, due in no small measure to the fact that he, unlike the Puritans, was perfectly willing to sell them muskets, shot, and powder. A party of armed men from the Plymouth Plantation under the command of Miles Standish was sent to arrest Morton. They shipped him back to England for what the Puritans assumed would be a speedy trial and lengthy term of imprisonment. Instead, he was promptly acquitted, the authorities in London being no admirers of the Puritans. Morton soon returned triumphantly to New England to resume trade with his Indian friends. Still determined to rid themselves of Morton, this time the Puritans seized all his goods and burned down his house before summarily deporting him to England. Morton returned to New England once more several years later, but by this time he was old and broke, and he died shortly thereafter in what is today the state of Maine. Morton left behind an account of his ecstatic response to the American landscape published as *New English*

A Sense of Place

Canaan in 1637, which Beston drew upon in the sympathetic portrayal of Morton he wrote in his engaging collection of biographical sketches *The Book of Gallant Vagabonds* (1925).

After the banishment of Morton, Mare-Mount was annexed by the town of Boston in 1634 and renamed Braintree. In Puritan New England, a parish had to be created prior to the incorporation of a town, so Braintree remained a part of Boston until 1640. The rocky soil of the area made for difficult farming, and so the population grew slowly throughout the seventeenth and eighteenth centuries. Eventually, however, there were enough settlers for two more parishes to be created. The north precinct of Braintree was renamed Quincy in 1797 in honor of its leading citizen, Colonel John Quincy (1689–1767).[7] Braintree was also the birthplace of two of the leaders of the American Revolution, John Hancock and John Adams. The Adams Academy, the school that Henry Beston attended as a boy, was built on the site of the old Hancock house.

On October 25, 1764, two of the leading families of Braintree were joined when Abigail Smith (her mother was Elizabeth Quincy) married John Adams, who became the second President of the United States in 1797. In 1824 their son, John Quincy Adams, was elected the nation's sixth President. The role of the Adams family in American political history over the first hundred years of the republic was so prominent that Henry Adams, grandson of John Quincy and son of Charles Francis Adams (Congressman and Ambassador to England during the Civil War), wrote in his Pulitzer Prize winning autobiography *The Education of Henry Adams* (1919), that as a boy he naturally assumed that he would in due course become President too. When the paternal grandparents of Henry Beston emigrated from Ireland to Massachusetts, they settled in Quincy; for a time his grandmother was employed as a domestic by the Adamses, and when her son Joseph was admitted to medical school in Paris, his passage to France was paid for by Charles Francis Adams Jr.

Although it may have seemed like it at times, politics was not the only business of Quincy. Shipbuilding, fishing, and maritime trade were Quincy's most important commercial enterprises until the early 1800s. Until then the copious amounts of granite in the Quincy soil had been little more than a nuisance to farmers, although it came in useful for foundations, quays, and the stonewalls endemic to New England. Quincy granite was notoriously hard, and difficult to cut and shape, but when a new method of stone cutting—drilling holes into the stone and then driving in wedges until the stone split cleanly—was developed in the early nineteenth century, Quincy granite became highly prized for its strength and durability. In 1825 it was selected as the building material for the new Revolutionary War monument planned for Bunker Hill. America's first railway was constructed to bring the granite mined from the quarries in Quincy to the Neponset River, where it would be loaded onto ships and transported to the building site in Charlestown. Quincy granite was in great demand for much of the nineteenth century and was a major source of employment in the region; several of Boston's other landmarks, including Quincy Market, the Custom House, and the Charlestown Navy Yard were constructed using this long-lasting stone.

Many of the laborers (later to include Beston's grandfather) for these building projects were the Irish immigrants who made up a substantial part of Boston's population by the 1820s. The relationship between the Protestant Yankees and the Irish-Catholic newcomers was a perennially uneasy one. In 1834 there was an anti-immigrant riot directed at the Irish in Charlestown; the Ursuline convent was burned to the ground, and only the intervention of the Catholic clergy prevented reprisals by the outraged Irish immigrants. The Irish-Catholics were clustered in segregated communities surrounded by people who feared and despised them. As historian Marjorie R. Fallows described one such community, "South Boston emerged as an urban slum, a congested and frightening district soon deserted by native Americans. Crime soared by as much as 400 percent, and the death rate among the Irish climbed to 37 per 1,000."[8]

In the mid-1840s, Irish immigration to Boston and other East Coast cities soared as a result of an ecological catastrophe in the mother country. Irish tenant farmers grew crops such as wheat, oats, and barley to pay their rent, but potatoes were the basis of their own sustenance. In early August of 1845 there were reports from the Isle of Wight, off the southern coast of England, that the potato crop had been stricken by blight. By

A Sense of Place

September, reports came in from Ireland that the blight was destroying the potato crop and was spreading from county to county at a terrifying rate. The first sign of trouble was a white mold appearing on the leaves of the potato plant that spread to the tuber itself, causing it to turn black and pulpy. Ironically, the potato blight, caused by a fungus called *phytophthora infestans*, probably spread from spores released from the cargo holds of ships arriving from North America, where the blight had also appeared in the previous few years. Entire fields of potatoes withered and died, and when farmers hastily harvested their crop in an attempt to head off the disease, seemingly healthy potatoes transformed overnight into a mass of nauseating pulp unfit for consumption. The result was devastating. Over the next several years in Ireland, as the potato blight returned again and again to destroy the harvest, over a million people died, and twice that number fled the country, most heading to Canada and the United States. Many of the emigrants were poor tenant farmers who were summarily evicted by their landlords, some of whom were so anxious to clear their properties of tenants that they paid for their passage to North America, albeit without supplying the provisions they would need to sustain them during the voyage. The ships that transported the destitute Irish were often over-crowded, unsanitary, and the passengers were often reduced to starvation rations during their voyage. Malnutrition and disease were rife, and many of these "coffin ships" had to be quarantined or even turned away by the authorities once they arrived in port.

In 1847 the United States Congress passed the Passenger Acts, which increased the cost of passage in an attempt to discourage ships bearing the most destitute of the immigrants from landing in the United States. Many of these ships were then diverted to Canada, which as a British colony was obligated to accept them. Still, American ports such as New York and Boston were inundated with new arrivals, many of whom were weakened by starvation and disease. Native-born Americans did not view their arrival favorably. When the Irish potato famine began in 1845, the city of Boston had about 114,000 inhabitants, and over the previous decade had absorbed somewhere on the order of 5,500 immigrants annually. In a single year, 1847, it is estimated that 37,000 emigrants arrived in Boston, three-quarters of them Irish. Many Bostonians were outraged, with one declaring that their city was being turned into "the moral cesspool of the world."[9] More than 100,000 Irish emigrants would eventually settle in the Boston area, transforming the culture and politics of Massachusetts. It was against this backdrop that Maurice Sheahan, the paternal grandfather of Henry Beston, sailed in 1848 from Cobh, Ireland, bound for America and a new life.

Orion on the Dunes

Doctor Joseph Maurice Sheahan (rear) and George, Henry, and Marie Louise Sheahan, 1889. The Sheahan home at 12 School Street in Quincy, Massachusetts, also served as Doctor Sheahan's medical offices.

CHAPTER ONE

A New England Boyhood
of Sea and Shore
1888–1915

O you will take whatever's offered
And dream that all the world's a friend,
Suffer as your mother suffered,
Be as broken in the end.
But I am old and you are young,
And I speak a barbarous tongue.

WILLIAM BUTLER YEATS
"To a Child Dancing in the Wind" (1916)

A NATIVE OF THE TOWN of Knocklong in County Limerick, Ireland, Henry Beston's grandfather, Maurice Sheahan, was one year older than his wife, Catherine Beston Sheahan, when in the early spring of 1848 he boarded the *Laurel*, a ship departing from the port of Cobh (Queenstown) on the southern coast of Ireland and bound for Boston.[1] Many of the immigrants who arrived from Ireland after 1847 were tenant farmers who, through hard work, astute planning, youthful vigor, or simply good luck, had managed to eke out a living during the first few years of the potato famine but had finally decided that it was unlikely things in Ireland were going to improve any time soon. This was almost certainly the case with Maurice Sheahan; he was physically robust and so youthful in appearance that his age was recorded in the ship's manifest as "about twenty," even though he had been born in 1816 and was therefore in his early thirties. He arrived in Boston Harbor on June 2, 1848, and soon found employment as

[3]

a laborer. Sheahan was undoubtedly a hard-working and thrifty man, for he brought some money overseas with him and by the following summer he had accrued enough additional capital to pay the passage for his wife Catherine and their children, who left Cobh for Boston on the ship *Wakefield*. She arrived in Boston on July 19, 1849, accompanied by the couple's two young daughters, three-year-old Eliza and two-year-old Mary.

The massive influx of poor Irish immigrants into Boston during this period infuriated many Bostonians and inspired a nativist backlash. The Boston City Census, for example, classified the children of immigrants as "foreigners" even if they were born in the United States, stating that "subject as they are to the control, instruction and associations of their parents, they properly belong to, and are under the influence of the foreign element." All young children, of course, are subject "to the control, instruction and associations of their parents"; the objectionable "foreign element" referred to in connection with the Irish immigrants was Roman Catholicism and the pope. Furthermore, many job openings were posted with the stipulation "Irish Need Not Apply." The anti-foreigner, anti-Catholic "Know Nothing" party dominated Massachusetts state politics throughout much of the 1850s, enacting numerous restrictive laws aimed primarily at the Irish.

Whether due to overt anti-Irish bigotry in Boston or simply to a desire to seek economic opportunity in a less urban setting, Maurice and Catherine Sheahan soon moved to Braintree, ten miles south of Boston. There they had two more children, both sons: Thomas F. Sheahan, born on December 11, 1849, and Joseph Maurice Sheahan, born on November 25, 1851. Shortly after the birth of Joseph, the family moved from Braintree to the nearby municipality of Quincy, where they bought a small house, which was valued at approximately $1800 in the 1870 census.[2] It was in Quincy that their fifth and final child, George A. Sheahan was born on March 8, 1857. Like most male Irish immigrants, Maurice Sheahan was initially employed as a manual laborer, first as a road builder and then as a stonecutter in the Quincy stone quarries, where he worked his way up to a foreman's position before taking a municipal job building roads for the city of Quincy. Catherine, as was typical of many Irish women, became a domestic, employed for a time as kitchen help (probably the family's cook) by Charles Francis Adams, Jr., grandson of former United States President John Quincy Adams.[3] Within a short time, the Sheahans became pillars of the rapidly growing Irish-Catholic community in Quincy. By the early 1850s the first Catholic church in Quincy, St. Ann's, was no longer sufficient to serve the needs of the parish, and a second church, St. John the Baptist, was built to accommodate worshippers from the central and northern portions of the city. Maurice Sheahan was among the principal donors contributing to the construction of the new church.

Unlike many of the recent immigrants from Ireland, both Maurice and Catherine were literate and impressed upon their children the value of obtaining an education. The eldest, Eliza, became a schoolteacher, and all of their children attended school in Quincy. It was Joseph, however, who was soon recognized as an exceptionally promising student. A perennial source of debate within the Irish-American community was whether to remain segregated in Catholic parochial schools or to seek integration with an often-hostile Protestant community by sending their children to secular public or private schools. The Sheahans chose integration. Joseph was admitted to Quincy High School at the age of ten, excelling in mathematics (his father had also been adept at math and encouraged his son's talent) and he graduated with high honors when he was just fourteen. He was then admitted to the Boston Latin School, Boston's premier public exam school. Founded in 1635, Boston Latin had educated many of Boston's Protestant, "Brahmin" elite since its inception, including Cotton Mather, Samuel Adams, John Hancock, Henry Ward Beecher, and Ralph Waldo Emerson. The school's headmaster, Francis Gardner (who served as headmaster from 1851 until his death in 1876) was one of New England's most prominent educators, and the school's curriculum emphasized the study of the classics, a hallmark of the Latin-school movement of the eighteenth-century. Declamation, the delivery of a memorized piece such as a famous speech, or soliloquy from a play was also emphasized, and with his remarkable poise and phenomenal memory Joseph excelled in this skill. As one of the school's best athletes—he had a particular talent and fondness for baseball—he was also able to overcome many of the social barriers that stood in the way of Irish-Catholics during this period. Joseph Sheahan won high honors at Boston Latin School, and after graduation matriculated at Harvard University in 1869.

Even into the early twentieth century, Harvard University was not welcoming to the Irish, so many Irish-Catholics chose instead to send their children to Jesuit institutions such as Boston College and Holy Cross. Charles Eliot, president of Harvard from 1869 to 1909, was unabashedly anti-Catholic, stridently declaring that he was "an enemy of all that the Catholic Church inwardly stands for."[4] While Joseph Sheahan's acceptance to Harvard was a remarkable accomplishment in itself, he was not content merely to be admitted to this bastion of Yankee privilege; he was driven to excel, to prove that the Irish belonged. He won high honors academically, was a member of Pi Eta (a literary and theatrical club), and placed second in the 1872 Boylston competition in elocution. The unwavering support of his family (and indeed, the Irish-Catholic community of Quincy generally, which took pride in the scholastic achievements of one of their own) was crucial in providing the emotional support Joseph needed to meet the social and academic challenges of his undergraduate years. He often walked the several miles from Harvard to Quincy and back again to see his family and friends on weekends and holidays, even during winter. Two other things also helped Joseph overcome the sectarian divide: his sense of humor (clearly evident in some of his later class notes) and sports. Joseph once again won acclaim and social acceptance for his skill at baseball, playing catcher for Harvard's varsity team and for the Beacons, one of Boston's finest amateur baseball teams. There were very few young men from Quincy—particularly young Irishmen—who attended college in those days, and Joseph Sheahan's Ivy League success made him the pride of Quincy's Irish-Catholic community.[5]

Shortly after graduating from Harvard in 1873, Sheahan was accepted at the Ecole de Médecine at the Université de Paris, which was widely recognized as one of Europe's leading medical schools. Charles Francis Adams Jr., who served as a financial benefactor to a number of Quincy's brightest young students, paid for Sheahan's passage to France, but upon his arrival in Paris Joseph faced the daunting prospect of supporting himself while taking a full schedule of medical classes, all of which were taught in French. He rose to the challenge and so impressed one of his professors—the famed Claude Bernard—that Bernard became a mentor to the young Irish-American. Bernard was a brilliant but controversial figure in the scientific world of the late nineteenth century. He had come to Paris at the age of twenty-one with intentions of becoming a playwright, but was persuaded by the respected literary critic Saint-Marc Girardin that his talents lay elsewhere. Bernard took up the study of medicine and went on to become one of the preeminent physicians and medical researchers of the nineteenth century, stressing the use of the scientific method in medical research.

Although Bernard's work led to some important medical breakthroughs, his use of vivisection in his research was controversial even in his own time. In 1875 a British physician who had taken a position in Bernard's laboratory wrote a letter describing the practice in horrifying detail to the London newspaper *The Morning Post*. While the letter did not name Bernard directly it was widely known that he was the "experimental physiologist" described. The exposé ignited a public outcry against the practitioners of vivisection and led to the establishment of a Royal Commission to investigate the procedure. On another, earlier, occasion one of the dogs that had been subjected to vivisection managed to escape from Bernard's laboratory; its pitiable condition so enraged the local residents that Bernard was forced to relocate the facility. Bernard's employment of vivisection eventually led to an estrangement from his wife and daughter who became active campaigners against the use of live animal subjects in medical research. In an interesting literary connection, several critics have suggested that Bernard was the inspiration for the character of Doctor Moreau in H. G. Wells's *The Island of Doctor Moreau*. While there is no record of what Joseph Sheahan himself thought about his mentor's research experiments performed on living creatures, given his love of animals it is doubtful that he would have approved—although his appreciation for Bernard's mentorship would have made any overt opposition unlikely. It appears that some years later Joseph Sheahan may well have discussed vivisection with his son Henry, perhaps even in such vivid terms that it left a lasting impression in the boy.[6] As an adult, Beston displayed a strong antipathy toward live animal research and supported the work of the American Anti-Vivisection Society.

[7]

Tall and broad-shouldered, with thick auburn hair, and a strong chin, Sheahan cut an impressive figure, and while attending medical school in Paris he met Marie Louise Maurice, a petite, quiet woman seven years his junior.[7] Beston later claimed that his mother was from "an old military and Bonapartist family," but this may have been a romantic embellishment on his part; at any rate, her mother's maiden name was Behrman and she may well have been of German or German-Jewish descent. The Maurices were originally from Burgundy, but Marie Louise's father probably moved to Paris for professional reasons; both he and later his son were first violinists with the Paris Opera. After earning his medical degree in 1879, Sheahan remained in the city to serve his residency and became engaged to Marie Louise. Sheahan loved Paris and apparently planned to stay in France— after receiving his degree in medicine he served as an intern with hospitals in Paris and was appointed a reserve surgeon in the French army—but his parents beseeched their dutiful son to return to Quincy. Sometime in 1881, Sheahan left France to return to Massachusetts where, not without some regrets about the bright future that appeared to stretch before him in Europe, he established a general medical practice in Quincy. After the medical practice was set up, Marie Louise sailed from France to join her fiancé in Quincy where they were married on February 16, 1882.

The life of a general practitioner in the late nineteenth-century was very demanding, but Dr. Sheahan's energy and devotion to his work became legendary. House calls to sick patients were the norm, not the exception, and doctors were expected to be both physician and surgeon and to work under sometimes challenging circumstances. Sheahan's skill as a surgeon was considerable, and he might well have chosen to specialize in this field in any of the large medical hospitals in Boston, but a strong sense of responsibility for his hometown and to his patients, many of whom were friends and neighbors, kept him in Quincy. The sight of Doctor Sheahan and his horse-drawn carriage became a familiar one to the residents. He loved horses, and even after most other Boston area doctors made the transition to automobiles after the turn of the century, he traveled by horse-drawn carriage (it was said that he could harness it in less than three minutes) to his appointments.[8] In addition to his medical practice he was an attending physician at several local hospitals, and served as a member of the Norfolk South District Medical Society, and the local Board of Health.

Doctor Sheahan's dedication to the Irish-Catholic community of Quincy, including those who were too poor to pay for his services, was remarkable. He was attracted to the Catholic modernist movement and to the efforts of writers such as Pierre Teilhard de Chardin to reconcile science and religion.[9] He was a firm believer in the doctrine of good works and was active in numerous fraternal and charitable organizations, including the Knights of Columbus and the St. Francis Court of the Massachusetts Catholic Order of Foresters, a chapter of the Ancient Order of Foresters, a non-sectarian charitable organization founded in 1834.[10] The primary mission of the Order was to provide help to families that had need of assistance due to the death or incapacity of the family's breadwinner. Dr. Sheahan not only provided medical services without cost to families in need, but as an act of fraternity waived medical fees for his fellow members of the Order.

On December 2, 1882 Joseph and Marie Louise Sheahan celebrated the birth of their first child, a boy they named George Maurice Sheahan. They bought a house located at 12 School Street in Quincy, a short walk from their parish church, that served as both the family's residence and as Doctor Sheahan's medical offices.[11] From an early age George showed himself to be intellectually gifted, and even as a young boy was determined to follow in his father's footsteps as a physician. One morning when George was not more than four or five years old, he woke up early, marched into his parents' bedroom and climbed up onto the bed, proudly announcing, "Now there's two doctors in bed!"[12] As a student George also followed in his father's footsteps, attending Adams Academy in Quincy from 1894–1898, distinguishing himself both as an athlete and as a student, winning the Adams Gold Medal for excellence in elocution in his senior year. He matriculated at Harvard University in the fall 1898 semester, earning his A.B in 1902. While at Harvard he continued to excel as a scholar-athlete, winning a trophy for sculling. After graduating from Harvard he entered Harvard Medical School in the fall of 1902, although he lost a year of study when he came down with typhoid fever that December.

On June 1, 1888, Joseph and Marie-Louise had their third and last child, who they named Henry Edouard Sheahan. A second child, Joseph Louis, had been born on March 31, 1885, but was just two years old when he died May 16, 1887. Henry was extremely close to his mother, and from childhood was as fluent in French as he was in English, which he said was a vital factor in the development of his concise but elegant writing style: "Mine was a French childhood, my mother a Parisian . . . Literature, I learned, was an art. I admired the swiftness and lucidity, the *clarité* of French style, and strove constantly for a smooth rhythm. Sentences should flow like ocean breakers."[13] Like his father and brother George, Henry loved sailing, and he would later state that, along with his French upbringing, living near the sea had the greatest influence on him during his formative years: "we enjoyed a New England boyhood of sea, and shore, enriched with a good deal of the French spirit."[14] The family bought a summer cottage near the Quincy waterfront and Dr. Sheahan acquired a small catboat for his sons to use. George and Henry spent many happy afternoons sailing around Quincy Bay, exploring its islands and reveling in the many minor adventures that sailing afforded them. In sentiments that Henry shared, George later wrote, "I was lucky in being born near the sea, with a strong love for it, and parents who encouraged me therein as well as their means would allow. To me the ocean is neither hostile nor altogether friendly, but indifferent . . . to human fate. It is a relentless taskmaster, but richly rewards its pupils, and there is no better training for a boy than handling a sailboat."[15]

Despite the love of sailing and salt water shared by the Sheahan men, life at home was not idyllic. Oddly perhaps, for a writer who often uses the first person in his essays and books, Beston wrote very little about his boyhood. It seems likely that his circumspection when it came to writing about his early years was due at least in part to aspects that were still somewhat painful to recall even many years later. As is often the case with second-generation Americans, Doctor Sheahan drove himself mercilessly, and he expected much of his sons. As Beston later stated in an interview: "My father was a brilliant physician, but was awfully irritable at home."[16] While Henry had an athletic build he didn't share his father's interest in baseball and other organized sports, perhaps due in part to poor eyesight—by his teens he was already wearing eyeglasses to correct his nearsightedness and astigmatism. Instead, Henry had an aptitude and fondness for the arts and music, and his mother encouraged this interest. He didn't take music lessons, but he taught himself how to play the piano and concertina (an instrument similar to the accordion) by ear, eventually supplementing his innate talent with lessons that he paid for himself when he was in college. Many years later when he lived alone in his dune shack on Cape Cod, he brought his concertina with him.

Beston's other youthful passions were literature and the theater, and his aunt Eliza Sheahan shared in and fostered these interests: "I remember our aunt, a teacher, used to take us every now and then to Boston for lunch and the theatre . . . I had a little cardboard theatre and characters which I really loved, but my father would much have preferred to have me play baseball in the backlot."[17] Beston's fondness for the theater was a lifelong constant, and included both stage dramas and motion pictures, and during his college years he entertained dreams of becoming a playwright. As his wife Elizabeth Coatsworth Beston later recalled,

> The theatre! That has been the golden thread woven through all Henry's life. When he was a little boy his aunt used to take him and his older brother George to see all the British melodramas which in those far-off days came every year to Boston; and later he went to light operas and serious operas, to Shakespeare, to Shaw, to O'Neill, and the rest. He loved them all, but especially he loved that moment of sheer magic when the lights in the theatre grow dim, the footlights come on and the curtains open onto another world.[18]

Another lifelong fascination for Beston that began when he was still a boy was his avid interest in the night sky; as Don Wilding writes, "If there was anything that he loved more than the theater, it was the constellations of the stars—the theater of the natural world."[19]

Like his father and his brother, Beston attended Adams Academy in Quincy and he later recalled his time at the school with a marked ambivalence. He greatly respected the headmaster of the school, William Everett, calling him "a superb scholar and Victorian eccentric." Everett, Beston recalled, had "an arrogant integrity of the things of the mind and a fierce belief in their importance. He was quite a remarkable man." The school itself, however, Beston dismissed as a "forlorn school . . . in a commercial town."[20] He was a fine student, if not quite as academically outstanding in mathematics as his father and brother had been, but in his senior year he too won the Academy's prize for public speaking and was awarded the prestigious gold medal which bore a figure of Cicero on one side and the motto *"verbo animi proferre"*—to put forth the words of the soul—on the other. The honor meant a great deal to Beston, as did the inscription. In a letter to a friend many years later, he confided, "I have really tried to live by the beautiful phrase: I have never once been consciously false to it."[21] When Beston was awarded the Emerson-Thoreau Medal in 1954, he recalled the importance of Everett and the Adams Academy in his speech to the American Academy of Arts and Letters, saying "My high school years were spent at the old Adams Academy ruled over—and I mean ruled over!—by William Everett, who had had his education at Harrow and Trinity. He was a character and often a difficult character but I have always been grateful to him for teaching me a respect for a civilized point of view and the niceties of the language. With all his eccentricities he guided us safely into Harvard College."

Sometime in her early thirties, Marie-Louise Sheahan developed some troubling symptoms that did not escape the notice of her physician husband, and which proved to be uterine cancer.[22] During the summer months Doctor Sheahan sent his wife to stay at farms used as country boarding homes, hoping that the rural setting would bolster her health and spirits. Unwilling to be apart from her children for such an extended period, she would generally take Henry with her. Too young to fully appreciate how sick his mother really was, Henry enjoyed the trips to the countryside and the opportunity to spend time alone with her. Marie Louise's condition steadily worsened, however, and Henry was just twelve years old when she died on November 15, 1900 at the age of 41.

The untimely death of Marie Louise cast a pall over the entire Sheahan household, and the additional burden it cast on the hard-working Doctor Sheahan could not have made life at home any easier. Being so close to his mother, Henry must have been devastated by her death—however, it is striking that as an adult he referred to her only infrequently (and usually in the context of his French heritage and upbringing) in his writings and interviews, and rarely spoke directly of her death so far as we can tell. Instead, his deep and abiding love for his mother seems to have been sublimated into a love for France and all things French. It may well have been partially due to Doctor Sheahan's awareness of the enormous gap that the death of their mother had left in his son's lives that he took a new wife only two years after the death of Marie Louise. Mary Conway Sheahan was a Quincy schoolteacher who was kind-hearted and intelligent; she quickly formed a very close bond with her stepsons and her maternal affection for Henry often shielded him, as he later wrote to Elizabeth Coatsworth, from his father's frequent "irritable" periods.[23] Her love was unreservedly returned, and Henry always considered "Muz" to be his second mother rather than a stepmother. Shortly before his wedding to Elizabeth Coatsworth in 1929 Henry wrote to his bride-to-be: "I'm so glad you liked Mother's letter. She's a dear person, warm and loving, a wise and understanding one, too, for coming to us as a 'second mother' . . . a real mother, wise and kind (and the situation was not at all an easy one, dear, but one with very special cussedness and complications)."[24]

It was nearly two full years before Doctor Sheahan managed to find the time to take a honeymoon with his new wife, but in the spring of 1904 they finally left for a long-delayed voyage to Europe. Their vacation lasted barely as long as the voyage itself. He became very ill shortly after arriving in France with what was probably Bright's Disease, a nineteenth-century term for acute kidney inflammation or nephritis, a condition for which there was as yet no effective medical treatment. The symptoms of Bright's Disease include high fever, acute pain in the lower back, and edema, which was almost certainly the case with Doctor Sheahan, whose condition was so serious that his treating physicians in France believed that he would not survive a voyage home. He insisted on returning to Quincy, however, and not only survived the trip but for a time his family believed that his physical strength and sheer determination might enable him to pull through. After a series of setbacks his condition once again took a turn for the worse, however, and after remaining bedridden for several months he died on

September 21, 1905. Doctor Sheahan's funeral at St. John's church in Quincy was a testament to the enormous respect that his friends and neighbors had for him; the church was packed with mourners and no fewer than ten local priests were on hand to assist in the services. The obituaries for Dr. Sheahan noted his selfless devotion to his patients and suggested that his passing may well have been hastened by the grueling hours he put into his work.[25] The epitaph that he chose for his headstone was a verse from his favorite poem, "The Rubaiyat" by Omar Khayyam: "So when the Angel of the darker Drink/ At last shall find you by the river-brink,/ and, offering its cup, invite your soul/ Forth to your Lips to quaff—you shall not shrink." The choice of this epitaph was, perhaps, a final defiance of the conservative Catholic establishment, which had forbidden the reading of the poem due to its authorship by a poet they deemed a dangerous freethinker.[26]

George, who was attending Harvard Medical School when his father died, had long planned to get his medical degree and enter into practice with him, hoping to ease his father's burden. It was an effort for both brothers to remain focused on their academic work throughout their father's illness, but with the help of their stepmother Mary, they managed to persevere. Just prior to his death, Dr. Sheahan had asked George to make sure that Henry completed his education at Harvard, a charge that his eldest son was determined to honor. In many ways, George took on the role of surrogate father to his younger brother, assisting Henry financially with his college tuition and helping to maintain the family home in Quincy. When George received his M.D. in 1907 he took his residency at Massachusetts General Hospital, where he worked closely with Dr. Maurice H. Richardson, a man he referred to as "a genuine genius." In 1909 he finished his residency and took up the general practice of medicine in Quincy at the same home office, 12 School Street in Quincy, where his father had practiced. For Henry, his elder brother provided a measure of stability through some very unsettled years: "George is the salt of the earth, a philosopher, a fine mind, as a surgeon, exquisitely careful and skilful, his surgery an art practiced on a stage of the most blessed and rare *common sense*. His touch with human pain has . . . given him a very special and beautiful understanding and compassion, really a very deep and beautiful quality."[27]

A New England Boyhood of Sea and Shore

Beston had only just begun his undergraduate studies at Harvard a few weeks before his father died, and it was at this time that he began forging a new self-image, a metamorphosis that went beyond the usual transformation experienced by first year collegians. After the funeral rites for his father, he apparently never attended a Roman Catholic service again, although he always maintained a spiritual sensibility that tinges much of his later writing about nature. It was also at this time that he began using "Beston," abandoning the middle name "Edouard" he'd been given at birth and using instead the surname of his maternal grandparents on his father's side as a middle name. He later claimed that it was his friends in college who started calling him "Henry B," recalling: "for some reason or other [I] was always known in college as 'Henry B'—the initial being added and pronounced by [my] friends."[28] For a time in the early 1920s, after he'd started writing under the name Beston, he retained the "B" in his name and published as Henry B. Beston but he soon dropped the meaningless middle letter. The reason for his adoption of Beston as a surname remains unclear, although anti-Irish bias at Harvard may have contributed to it.[29] At least as late as 1940 he had not legally changed his name to "Henry Beston," and perhaps never got around to formally doing so, as his last will and testament identifies "Henry Beston" as an "alias."[30] Beston did, however, claim on at least one occasion that he had legally changed his name in the 1940s. The issue of his name change, therefore, remains ambiguous.

Beston's interest in writing and literature truly began to flourish while at college, and he joined a number of writing clubs and read voraciously. While he excelled in subjects such as literature, history, and languages, Beston had considerably more trouble with mathematics. He was unable to pass his entrance examinations in Algebra and Trigonometry, and had to return for two successive summers before Harvard quietly seems to have waived the requirement in recognition of his strong coursework in his other subjects. Fond of the King James Bible and Greek and Roman classics, he loved Sir James Frazer's *The Golden Bough: A Study in Magic and Religion,* which was first published in 1890 and analyzed mythology and religion from a modernist, comparative perspective that was not well received by many conservative Christians but was enormously appealing to Beston.

[15]

Shakespeare's plays were a perennial favorite (he could recite much of *Hamlet* by heart) as were the novels of Walter Scott and W. H. Hudson, Stowe's *Uncle Tom's Cabin,* and the work of many of the great New England writers such as Nathaniel Hawthorne, Ralph Waldo Emerson, and Henry Thoreau. Richard Jefferies was a particular favorite, and the sharp-eyed accounts of English rural life in his essays and books influenced Beston's own turn toward nature writing some years later. Another great favorite was the Irish writer Edward Plunkett, the eighteenth Baron of Dunsany, whose early stories of fantasy and wonder captivated Beston. He also joined the Pi Eta Society (his father and brother had also been members), a literary and theatrical organization founded in 1866 that had a reputation for being more open and diverse than many of the other clubs and fraternities on campus. Like its older and more famous Harvard counterpart, the Hasty Pudding Club, the highlight of the academic year for Pi Eta was the staging of a musical farce written, acted, and directed by its members. In the spring semester of his sophomore year Beston played the role of Selum Short, a Wall Street broker in the club's musical comedy, "The Financier."[31] In his senior year he co-wrote the book and lyrics for the club's annual musical, entitled *The Highflier*, which the *Harvard Graduates Magazine* declared was "comparable with the Hasty Pudding play for tunefulness and fun-provoking qualities."[32]

Throughout his undergraduate years at college, Beston sometimes displayed a rather careless attitude toward college rules pertaining to attendance, punctuality, and library privileges. He received several letters chastising him for accrued library fines and his failure to promptly pay them. In the fall semester of Henry's senior year George, in his role as his brother's guardian, was unpleasantly surprised by a letter from Professor B. S. Hurlburt that advised, "If Henry is with you during the recess I wish that you would impress upon him the importance of keeping all of his appointments. No less than twenty-two marks of absence or tardiness are recorded against him since the beginning of the year."[33] No disciplinary measures were taken against Henry, as it appears that he successfully pleaded that the absences were unavoidable, due to the long hours he was devoting to writing the Pi Eta Society's spring play and a back injury that he suffered while moving some heavy scenery and which kept him bedridden for several days.

A New England Boyhood of Sea and Shore

Cast and Crew from the "High Flier," a musical comedy put on by Harvard University's Pi Eta Club in 1909. Beston (bottom row, third from right) was one of the primary authors of the play.

The personable Beston had numerous close friends while at Harvard, including his future brother-in-law F. Morton Smith (who had also attended the Adams Academy in Quincy with him); Clarence Britten, who went on to have a distinguished career as an English professor and editor; and his closest "college amigo" Warren Butler, with whom he shared a room (Room 402) at Craigie Hall. Craigie was conveniently located near Harvard Square and the trolley line and boasted modern amenities including steam heat, gas and electric light in each room, swimming pool, elevator, and janitor service—all for one hundred dollars per semester. Warren's sister Katherine Butler, two years younger than her brother, also became a friend. Katharine suffered from a spinal disease that had confined her to bed for much of her childhood in the hope of preventing her back from becoming permanently deformed. The treatment was unsuccessful but she read voraciously while she was bedridden; her love of literature became a saving grace of the ordeal. She attended Radcliffe as a special case student from 1910 to 1912 and later became a writer of children's books such as *Mr. Muffet's Cat and Her Trip to Paris* (1934), although she is best remembered for two posthumously published books, a memoir of her difficult childhood entitled *The Little Locksmith* (1943) and *The Journals and Letters of the Little Locksmith* (1946). In *The Little Locksmith* she describes meeting Beston (then still known as Henry Sheahan) and Ben Hodges, another friend of her brother Warren.

> They were brilliant and talkative like my brother, but more strange and fascinating than he could ever be . . . They were tall and beautiful as well . . . I fell in love first with one and then with the other. The intense pleasure that I felt while I watched and listened and adored was equaled by the bewilderment and distress of knowing that I was locked and hidden away in a prison where they could never see me or know I was there; for I thought of myself as a responsive, gay and brilliant woman who was sitting in front of them disguised as a little oddity, deformed and ashamed and shy.[34]

In 1932 she married Daniel Rugg Hathaway and moved to Maine, where she died in 1942. Shortly after her death Beston wrote a heartfelt homage to her in the *Book of the Month Club* newsletter, celebrating her work and recalling that he never thought of her as "deformed" and disliked hearing that adjective applied to her: "Small, frail, yes, not like others in the harmony of the body, her head shrunken into her child's shoulders—this might be the first glimpse, but after that first glimpse, it was Katharine the person, the beautiful, bold spirit, and the friend."[35]

Another college classmate and close friend was Theodore Roosevelt Jr., who had the daunting challenge of attending Harvard while his father was President of the United States. Like his father, Ted Jr. was a great lover of the outdoors; and in the summer of 1900 he'd had the singular experience of staying for a few days with the nation's most famous and beloved nature writer, John Burroughs, at his Hudson Valley writing cabin, Slabsides. Burroughs, who was then in his early sixties, soon learned that spending time outdoors with Roosevelt *fils* was in some ways similar to experiencing it with Roosevelt *père*: "I had young Teddy Roosevelt with me three days, two weeks ago. What a chase he led me! We had some fine adventures. He is only twelve, but has the real stuff in him. He is like his father in miniature. He climbed trees and rocks so recklessly that I expected he would break his limbs or his neck, but he did not."[36] Over one break from classes Beston and some other college friends were invited by Ted Jr. to visit the Roosevelts; it is unclear whether the visit was to the White House or to the Roosevelt home at Sagamore Hill, Long Island, but it was a memorable occasion passed down through the family for many years. The first morning of the visit, the boys were gathered around the dining room table for breakfast when President Roosevelt strode in and boomed, "What's your favorite meal, boys?" When they all responded "Breakfast!" in unison, TR beamed and pronounced, "There's nothing wrong with a country where the boys' favorite meal is breakfast."[37] That evening while everyone was gathered at the dinner table, a monkey suddenly came bounding into the room and, as Beston later told the story, perched on his shoulder for much of the meal.

While Theodore Roosevelt Jr. was the most famous of Beston's classmates at Harvard, there were others who went on to gain public renown. T. S. Eliot and Van Wycks Brooks, who were a year behind Beston at Harvard became major figures in twentieth-century American literature. Others such as Robert Emmons Rogers, who was awarded the post of class poet at graduation, an honor for which Beston came in third, went on to a distinguished career as a writer and professor at M.I.T. and Hans von Kaltenborn (who came in second) became a well-known American radio commentator from 1928–1958. Other than Ted Roosevelt Jr., the most famous—or rather, infamous—member of the Harvard University class of 1909 was a student from Munich, Germany named Ernst "Putzi" Hanfstaengl. After graduation he moved to New York to manage the New York branch of his family's publishing business, where he became friendly with such celebrities as William Randolph Hearst, Charlie Chaplin, and the novelist Djuna Barnes, to whom he was briefly engaged. He returned to Germany after the First World War, where he heard an obscure Bavarian politician named Adolf Hitler deliver a speech at a Munich beer hall in 1922. Hanfstaegl became a friend and confidante of Hitler's until, in 1937, he fell out of favor with the dictator and defected to England, where he was imprisoned as a German spy after the war began. In a rather bizarre twist to the story, Hanfstaengl was turned over to the United States in 1942, where he provided details of Hitler's personality that were used to create a psychological profile of the Nazi leader. In 1957 Hanfstaengl published a memoir of his experiences in the upper echelons of the Third Reich entitled *Hitler: The Missing Years*.

After Beston received his bachelor's degree in June 1909 he entered the graduate program in English history and literature at Harvard for the fall 1909 semester. His attendance difficulties behind him, Beston successfully completed his first year of graduate courses, and his name was entered on the approved list of undergraduate instructors in English. In the fall 1910 semester he was assigned to teach English A, Harvard's course in freshman composition. Until 1885 freshman rhetoric and composition had not been a required course at the university, but the efforts of Professor Adams Sherman Hill were instrumental in finally convincing the faculty and administration that the writing skills of incoming students were so dismal that an entrance exam in writing and a freshman composition course were necessary requirements for undergraduate students. By the early twentieth century Hill had retired, but professors Charles Townsend Copeland and H. M. Rideout had taken up the cause, describing the goal of English A as being to drill "the habitual use of correct and intelligent English . . . into the Freshmen."[38] The establishment of Freshman English as a required course at Harvard and other American universities had far-reaching academic repercussions; as Sharon Crowley writes in *Composition in the University* (1998), "Freshman English had much to do with the establishment of English as a university discipline. The connection between Freshman English and the status of English studies was not lost on the authors of the 1897 *Harvard Reports*, who crowed that with the creation of English A, Harvard 'manifestly aims at nothing less than elevating the study of English to the same plane of dignity which has for centuries been the peculiar attribute of foreign tongues' (Adams et al. 423)."[39]

The following semester, Beston once again taught English A, which not only provided him with an instructor's salary but helped him to refine his own writing skills as he became increasingly expert in the fine points of composition. His graduate coursework and teaching were sufficiently impressive that the chair of the English Department, Professor F.N. Robinson, referred him to Professor Copeland, who was teaching a new course on Walter Scott (English 53) in the spring 1911 semester. Copeland named

Beston as his teaching assistant, and in that capacity he helped Copeland in the planning and development of the course in fall 1910. Beston's eagerness to assist Copeland caused him some trouble with the Harvard libraries once again. The English Department chair and Professor Copeland sent a note to the library requesting teaching assistant privileges for Beston. When he kept two books out past their due dates, he received a letter threatening him with expulsion. After a series of frustrating if sometimes comic efforts to straighten out the misunderstanding ("On my referring to 'Professor' Robinson the library calls up Secretary Robinson who knows nothing of the case!"), Beston finally regained his library privileges and resolved the case.[40] Beston—who was then living at Holyoke House—greatly admired Copeland and he and some of the other graduate students in literature often received invitations to visit "Copey" at his lodgings at 15 Hollis, where they engaged in long discussions of life and literature.

Copeland was Beston's most important teacher and mentor while at Harvard, and his encouragement and support meant an enormous amount to him—he always spoke of his former professor in glowing terms. After Beston received his master's degree in English history and literature in May 1911, Copeland encouraged him to pursue a career in teaching, and helped him to secure a position as Lecteur d'Anglais at the University of Lyon for the 1912–1913 academic year. Located on the Rhône River in central France, Lyon was an ancient Roman settlement and France's second largest city, after Paris. Beston was one of the youngest instructors to ever be appointed to the position at Lyon, although his students probably thought he was several years older; by his mid-twenties, Beston had an imposing stature. An American passport issued to Beston in 1918 stated that he was six feet, one and a half inches in height, but several people who knew him claimed that he was in fact taller than this—two or three inches taller, in fact; it may be that his broad shoulders and athletic build made him *seem* taller, or perhaps the passport information is simply incorrect. He had a high forehead, dark brown hair and brown eyes, and on his passport his nose was described as "aquiline." For at least part of his year in France, Beston also sported a chaplinesque moustache, although he soon realized that while the "toothbrush" style might fit the diminutive comedian Charlie

Chaplin, it did not look quite so suitable on him. At the university Beston taught a special course in English literature—"L'Etude d'Anglais"—and took a class on the fine arts with Professor Henri Lechat, a noted expert in Greek sculpture and antiquities.

During his time in France, Beston rented a room at a chateau owned by a titled family in Ste. Catherine, a farming community approximately forty kilometers southwest of Lyon. The only known photograph of Beston during his year in Lyon shows him with his landlord and the landlord's daughter, who appears to be in her mid to late twenties, and with whom he apparently had a brief love affair. The teaching position left Beston with plenty of free time to explore the rural landscape outside Lyon, and he later stated that this period was instrumental in developing his love of nature:

> I heard across the lovely, wet, sunlit autumn countryside the rumble of a farm cart's wheel and the fine challenge of a cock, and hearing them I thought of how all these earthy things carry me back to France, back to Ste. Catherines sous Riviere, the village in the Monts Lyonnais where I lived quite a fair share of my French year. The mountains were about twenty miles in from the Rhône, one side running parallel to the river, another facing south on the wide plain of an ancient sided valley tributary to the Rhone. I used to take a little train across the foothill country lying west of Lyons, get off at the end of the line at Mormant, a village-town at the foot of the massif (for it was a "massif" rather than a range) and then continue to Ste. Catherine on foot. The climbing road, some ten kilometers all together, went first up the Rhône-wards slope, then turned a steep grassy descent—almost a sort of grassy precipice—and then emerged on the southern flank, high, high above the wide valley and its scatter of red-roofed village huddles with the usual outlying few farms. Thirty or forty kilometers across was the superb solitary mountain *Le Mont Pilat* of the Cévennes, a glorious mountain which in winter across the "brume" of the morning hillside, rose distant and violet and chasmed with pure radiation of new snow. Ste. Catherine, if I forget the farm boarding houses Mother and I were sent to in the summer (places not unlike the Bennetts but a little bit better, not "run down") was the first place in which I encountered and knew and loved the earth. I hadn't had any true chance before. We had a cottage on Quincy bay . . . but Nature, as well as the very decent "comfortably-offs"—in the Quincy valuations—

Henry Sheahan [Beston], his landlord, and his landlord's daughter (with whom he apparently had a brief affair) at their chateau in Ste. Catherine, France. During the 1912–1913 academic year, Beston taught at the University of Lyon near rural Ste. Catherine. It was during his long walks in the surrounding countryside, Beston said, that he "first came to know and love the earth."

was in a suburban mood there; she went yachting in a cat boat on Saturday afternoons and arranged her tides as if they had to take trains. There was no *poetry*. Fugitive glimpses, perhaps, but no deep, underlying mood. Then came France, and the earth and the revelation of the earth.[41]

Beston was an indefatigable walker, and he spent many happy hours wandering through the French countryside, drinking in this new "revelation of the earth." After the academic year ended he went on a "vagabond journey," as he called it, spending several months traveling on foot through France, Corsica, Germany, and Switzerland.[42]

It was not until late 1913 or early 1914 that Beston finally returned to Massachusetts from his travels in Europe. After his year of independence in France, he was reluctant to live once again at the family home in Quincy, so he took rooms at the Parson Capen House, a landmark seventeenth-century minister's home in Topsfield, Massachusetts. With the help of Professor Copeland once again, Beston secured a teaching position at Harvard for the 1914–1915 academic year, and was in charge of the modern literature conferences for English 31. Well-read, poised, and an excellent lecturer, it appeared that Beston was on his way to a career as a college teacher, perhaps even as a professor at his alma mater. His year in France and the months he spent traveling through Europe, however, appear to have intensified the romantic side of Beston's nature, instilling a yearning for travel and adventure. In an ironic twist, this aspect of his character may have been an unconscious response to his father's unrequited yearning for an opportunity to test his talents and intellectual gifts in Europe rather than his hometown of Quincy, Massachusetts. In watching his father work himself into an early grave as a family doctor, limiting his horizons out of a sense of duty and responsibility but becoming irritable and perhaps even somewhat bitter in the process, Beston may well have determined that he would not share this fate; that there was be a larger stage, a greater set of possibilities for *him*.

During the summer of 1914, a series of events in Europe began to unfold that would change everything—for Beston, and for much of the world. In faraway Serbia, a young Slavic nationalist named Gavrilo Princip assassinated the crown prince of the Austro-Hungarian Empire, Archduke Franz Ferdinand, and his wife Sophie while they were on a tour of Sarajevo. A month later, Austria-Hungary declared war on Serbia; in response, Serbia's ally Russia announced a full mobilization of her massive army. The conflict then spread with breath-taking speed as Germany entered the war on the side of the Austro-Hungarians, and France joined Russia in an alliance against the central European powers. After some initial quick successes by the Kaiser's army, including a victory over the Russians at the Battle of Tannenberg and a surprise invasion of neutral Belgium that had the French scrambling to defend Paris, the possibility of a short decisive war was ended by a French victory in early September at the First Battle of the Marne that the French called the "Miracle of the Marne." The conflict then entered a long and bloody period of stalemate as trenches were dug all along the western front, Germany declared unrestricted submarine warfare to keep supplies from reaching Britain and France, and the Ottoman Empire entered the war on the side of Germany and Austria-Hungary.

Determined to keep the United States out of the war, President Woodrow Wilson steadfastly maintained American neutrality despite increasingly vociferous calls by political opponents such as Theodore Roosevelt for the United States to enter the war on the side of the Allies. While Germany's invasion of neutral Belgium delivered a temporary military advantage to the Kaiser's armies, it was a propaganda goldmine for the Allies, who gave full play to reports leaking out of occupied Belgium about German atrocities against civilians. After the sinking of the *Lusitania* on May 7, 1915, which claimed the lives of over 1,000 civilians, including 128 Americans, anti-German feeling reached new highs. On Ivy League campuses such as Harvard, students eagerly followed the war news from Europe, and many of them were in favor of joining America's sister democracies France and Britain in the conflict. Supporters of the Allies often stopped short of calling for an American entry into the war, but as Professor Copeland told Beston, America should help the British and French in any way possible. Despite his Irish heritage—many Irish and German-Americans opposed American intervention on behalf of the Allies—Beston was an ardent Francophile who was receptive to the call for volunteers to aid France in her hour of need. Sometime during the spring 1915 semester he decided that he would not return to Harvard to teach in the fall semester; he would instead volunteer to be among the first young Americans to assist in the Allied war effort.

CHAPTER TWO

A Volunteer Poilu
1915–1916

That flesh we had nursed from the first in all cleanness was given
To corruption unveiled and assailed by the malice of Heaven—
By the heart-shaking jests of Decay where it lolled on the wires—
To be blanched or gay-painted by fumes—to be cindered by fires—
To be senselessly tossed and retossed in stale mutilation
From crater to crater. For this we shall take expiation.
But who shall return us our children?

RUDYARD KIPLING
"The Children"
upon the death of his son, John Kipling,
at Loos, September 27, 1915.

IN APRIL 1915, A. Piatt Andrew, former Harvard Professor and Assistant Secretary of the United States Treasury, who had recently been appointed as Inspector of the Field Service of the American Ambulance (later shortened to American Field Service), persuaded the French authorities to permit ambulances from the Field Service to serve as independent Sanitary Sections, as the ambulance squads were designated by the French military. Three units of twenty light Ford ambulances each, along with support vehicles, were formed: Section Sanitaire Amèricaine N° 1 was stationed at Dunkirk, Section Sanitaire Amèricaine N° 2 was stationed in Lorraine, and Section Sanitaire Amèricaine N° 3 was stationed in the Vosges.[1] A fourth section was created in December 1915, and several more were created during the course of the war. The majority of volunteers serving in the Field Service were young American collegians, many of whom were drawn from Ivy League institutions, most notably Harvard, Yale, and Princeton. The usual term of service was six months, at which time volunteers could opt to reenlist.

At the outbreak of war in August 1914, the French army was still dependent primarily upon horse-drawn ambulances—they had only two sections of motorized ambulances, with just twenty cars in each. The ambulances were responsible for two primary tasks. The first was transferring wounded soldiers between hospitals and other recuperative facilities in the interior. The second task, near the front lines, was to transport the wounded from aid stations (*poste de secours*) located near the rear lines of the trenches to field hospitals which could be reached by motorized ambulances within about forty-five minutes. For the first several months of the war, American volunteers were limited (as citizens of a non-combatant nation) to serving behind the lines.[2] The French government offered the Field Service the use of an unfinished school building, the Lycèe Pasteur, which had been requisitioned for military purposes as their headquarters. The Lycèe Pasteur was located on the Boulevard d'Inkerman in the Paris suburb of Neuilly-sur-Seine, just a few blocks away from the American Hospital on Boulevard Victor Hugo. The Field Service began work in September 1914, using ten donated Ford chassis that a local carriage builder converted into makeshift ambulances; by the end of 1916, the hospital at Neuilly was the base for thirty-five ambulances.[3]

By the summer of 1915, sheer necessity compelled the French and British armies to permit the American volunteers to provide ambulance service near the front lines, and they proved to be a godsend. The light, mobile Fords were well-suited for the horrendous road conditions near the front lines, and they were far more comfortable for the wounded than were the slow, mule- or horse-drawn ambulances still in common use by the French army. The American drivers, enthusiastic and daring, also impressed the French with their élan. As Arlen J. Hansen, author of *Gentlemen Volunteers: The Story of the American Ambulance Drivers in the Great War*, writes, "Weaving around and through mule-train convoys, they scooted up and down roads so narrow that two vehicles could seldom pass, so exposed to enemy artillery that headlights and horns were prohibited, and so steep that the drivers wore holes in their shoes from depressing the low-gear pedal hour after hour. The French had never seen ambulance drivers like these before. They wanted more."[4] By mid-1915, the Field Services chief, A. Piatt Andrew, proudly observed, "the little American ambulances could be seen scurrying over the flat plains of Flanders, on the wooded hills of northern Lorraine, and in the mountains and valleys of reconquered Alsace."[5]

Even before the spring 1915 term at Harvard had drawn to a conclusion, Beston had decided to join the Field Service. When he let Professor Copeland know of his plans not to return in the fall, Copeland gave his full support and approval, as was the case with Beston's brother George (who joined the Canadian Medical Service as a field surgeon in 1916), and their stepmother, Mary, who told Henry that volunteering for the Ambulance service was "a noble thing to do."[6] Early in July, Beston wrote to William R. Hereford, a New York banker who also served as the stateside recruitment officer for the American Field Service, offering his services as an ambulance driver in France. Hereford immediately responded:

> Dear Mr. Sheahan:—
> I was very glad to get your note and I am pleased to say that you can go any time that you think you are ready. Of course, you understand that if you are not able to drive and make the ordinary repairs you will be in the way, and would be of harm instead of being of service, but I depend upon your good judgment as to when you are ready. It does not require expert knowledge. All that is necessary is that you can drive a Ford and can take care of the ordinary repairs. If you can get your passport in time, and if you are ready, you might sail next Saturday. The sooner the better.[7]

Somewhat surprised as to how quickly things were falling into place, Beston hastily wrote back to Hereford, saying that he would need a few weeks to get his affairs in order, but he was assured that this would be no problem, and that he could go just as soon as he was ready. By the end of July, Beston let Hereford know that he was prepared to leave for France. As was the custom with the ambulance service volunteers, it was expected that he would pay his own way for the voyage from New York City to Bordeaux. The *Espagne* was the only available ship that offered first class accommodations, which cost $75.00; the other ships—the *Chicago*, *Rochambeau*, *Niagara*, and *Touraine*—

only offered a single class of passage, but Hereford assured Beston that "ambassadors and others who generally travel luxuriantly, have found them quite convenient under the present conditions."[8] The arrangements for the voyage were straightforward; Beston would simply need to meet with Hereford at the New York offices of the American Ambulance at 14 Wall Street in Manhattan, pay for the ticket (which would already have been reserved for him by the Ambulance Service), bring a certificate showing that he had been inoculated for typhoid fever, and receive in turn the signed papers required of volunteers heading to France. Hereford recommended that Beston bring his birth certificate if this was possible, "as this may be required on the other side. If you cannot get your birth certificate, it does not greatly matter, but if you can get it, it is well to have it." He also advised Beston to travel light: "take with you good comfortable shoes, three or four khaki shirts (preferably without collars) summer and winter underwear, woolen socks—but do not take too much as it will merely be in your way. It is best to carry it all in a couple of bags and not try to manage a trunk."[9]

At midday on August 12, 1915, Beston stood on the enormous two-storied pier at the New York docks where the *Rochambeau*, a French liner owned by the Compagnie Générale Transatlantique, was taking on supplies and passengers destined for France. The hot summer sun glinted off the oil-slicked water of the docks and accentuated the pungent odors of the boat basin—horse manure, the distinctive fragrance of stagnant salt water, and the acrid stench from coal stacks billowing smoke from the engines of the waiting ships. The chaotic sounds of the docks, of the longshoremen, dray horses, and machines laboring to move cargo from the wharf to the ship's hold became at last a single unified roar, punctuated by an occasional burst of noise from one quarter or another or a distinct voice rising out over the general din, such as that of a young American longshoreman loading enormous bags of flour into the depths of the *Rochambeau*, singing out to a co-worker in the hold, "More dynamite, Joe, more dynamite!"[10] By late afternoon, all the cargo having been safely stowed aboard ship, Beston wandered about the deck as knots of passengers gathered with relatives, friends, and business associates to say their good-byes. There was a great deal of worried talk about German submarines, and reassurances from more experienced travelers that since the French terminus had been moved from the northern port of Le Havre to the more southerly port of Bordeaux, the route was now a comparatively safe one. Many of the ship's passengers had commercial interests at stake: American drummers selling wartime supplies to the Allies in Europe, French *commis voyageurs* hustling to sell French goods in place of German merchandise, and French officials working with American munitions plants. Shortly before sunset, the *Rochambeau* weighed anchor, and left the port of New York for Europe and the war.

The passengers on board the *Rochambeau* were a mixed lot. Like Beston himself, there were a number of American volunteers, including several planning to enlist in the French or British military. One, a powerfully built young Iowan, told Beston that he had been a salesman of machine tools, but due to the war, the firm for which he worked now had so many orders lined up, that they no longer needed salesmen: "they offered us jobs inside; but God, I can't stand indoor work, so I thought I'd come over here and get into the war. I used to be in the State Cavalry. You ought to have seen how sore those Iowa Germans were on me for going. Had a hell of a row with a guy named Schultz."[11] Another young man, about eighteen or nineteen years old, struck Beston as being somehow suspicious in appearance: "there was something psychologically wrong with his face; it had that look in it which makes you want to see if you still have your purse." Once Beston and the young man—who identified himself as Oscar Petersen—discovered that they were both headed to France as volunteers, Petersen told him something of his past, which included running away from home at fourteen (confiding to Beston, "my father was a Bible cuss, never got over my swiping the minister's watch"), spending a year in a reform school, and then becoming a minor hoodlum in Chicago. After tiring of that life, he "got the bug to go to war," and was headed over to join the French Foreign Legion. Several months later Beston learned from a friend that Petersen had been killed by a stray shell in a small French village—but not before stealing a fifty franc note from Beston's friend.[12]

On the fourth day out the weather turned gray, and by nightfall rough seas driven by a strong storm front had forced most of the *Rochambeau's* passengers to their cabins. Unfazed by the storm and too excited to sleep,

Beston made his way to the ship's salon, which was deserted save for a man reading an article in an old French magazine that examined the psychology of the "barbaric Germans." The man was a former officer in the *chasseurs à pied* who had been wounded in action and now worked for a weekly magazine in Paris. Beston and the French officer talked late into the night, comparing the French and German attitudes toward war. "You must remember," the Frenchman told him, "that the word 'barbarian' which we apply to the Germans, is understood by the French intellectually . . . to the Germans, war is an end in itself and in all its effects perfect and good. To the French mind, this conception of war is barbaric, for war is not good in itself and may be fatal to both victor and vanquished." The former soldier went on to describe how the writer Ernest Psichari and his book *L'Appel des Armes* (*The Appeal of Arms*), a mystical blend of Catholicism and militarism, had been instrumental in countering the appeal of pacifism current in France prior to the war when institutions such as the church, government, and army were losing their moral force and, as he recalled, "cries of 'A bas l'armée' were heard in the streets." It was Psichari, claimed the officer, who had saved French morale during the early months of the war by teaching the French people and the army that "war was no savage *ruée*, but the discipline of history for which every nation must be prepared, a terrible discipline neither to be sought, nor rejected when proffered." "Thus," he continued, "the Boches, once their illusion of the glory of war is smashed, have nothing to fall back on, but the French point of view is stable and makes for a good morale."[13] Months later while serving at Bois-le-Prêtre, Beston saw first hand how important Psichari's *L'Appel des Armes* was to the French soldiers when he was preparing to transport a wounded French sergeant. Before being loaded onto the ambulance, the sergeant anxiously asked his comrades to retrieve his muddy, worn copy of the book to take with him to the hospital.

The rather bleak vision of pre-war France as expressed by the former officer was one that resonated with Beston, who, at this time, was still essentially in agreement with Theodore Roosevelt's doctrine of national power: speak softly and carry a big stick. It also corresponded to the impressions of French politics he had formed during his year of teaching in France. Pre-war France, Beston believed, had failed to take the lessons taught by the Franco-Prussian war of 1870 to heart, and when war broke out between the two nations once again in 1914, France was "unprepared for war, torn by political strife, and in a position to be ruthlessly trampled on by the Germans. The France of 1900–1913 is not a very pleasant France to remember."[14] For this, Beston blamed the radicals of the Socialist-Labor party then in power and their policies, foremost among them their move to seize property held by the Roman Catholic Church (which, he said, led to an icy hatred between the socialists and the church), and their attempt to "extirpate all conservatism, whether Catholic or not, from the army."[15] The election of conservative Raymond Poincaré as French president in 1913 (to replace Armand Fallières, a socialist premier whom Beston frankly despised) was in Beston's opinion a "sign of better times."[16] Beston never mentions that French anti-militarism during this era was in part due to the notorious Dreyfuss Affair of 1894, where a French artillery officer of Jewish descent, Captain Alfred Dreyfuss, was convicted of treason and sentenced to serve a life term on Devil's Island in French Guyana. The charges were subsequently proven—thanks in part to the efforts of the famed novelist Émile Zola—to have been fabricated by other French officers. Dreyfuss was finally exonerated in 1899, but the tawdry nature of the affair, rank with anti-Semitism, led to a significant loss of public support for the French army in the years leading up to the war. By 1914, however, the anti-militarism of the pre-war period had largely given way to an upsurge of patriotic fervor, and the outbreak of war had caused may of the old political and class divisions to be set aside—at least temporarily—in favor of *l'Union Sacrée*, a sacred union of all France to meet and repel the menace of German expansionism.

Despite the omnipresent fear of German submarines, the voyage to France passed without incident, and nearly two weeks after leaving New York City, the *Rochambeau* reached the mouth of the Gironde and began the trip upriver to Bordeaux. The first glimpse of the war in Europe was the occasional sighting of German prisoners of war set to work in the fields of the French countryside. When the ship reached Bordeaux, one passenger observed that other than the presence of men in uniform and the lack of taxis, the city looked much the same as it had prior to the war. Beston, however, immediately noted an enormous difference, the absence of youth: "Not that youth was entirely absent from the tables and the *trottoirs*; it was visible, putty-faced and unhealthy-looking, afraid to meet the gaze of a man in uniform, the pitiable *jeunesse* that could not pass the physical examination of the army."[17] The next morning, a Saturday, Beston went down to the railroad station to board the train for the six-hour passage to Paris. By sunset, the train was rumbling through the farms and fields outside the Capital—"hamlet after hamlet closed and shuttered, though the harvests had been gathered and stacked. There was something very tragic in those deserted, outlying towns." As they entered the railroad yards on the outskirts of Paris, one of Beston's fellow passengers, a young farmhand turned soldier from Normandy exclaimed, "I never expected to see Paris. How the war sets one to traveling!"[18]

FOLLOWING THE "Miracle at the Marne" in September 1914, where Entente forces successfully halted the German sweep through Belgium and northern France (the German offensive had very nearly reached Paris, which the Germans had hoped would result in a quick end to the war), the western front had settled into a bloody stasis. The Allies and the Germans fortified their defensive lines, digging trenches and fighting a never-ending series of sharp skirmishes—a war of attrition. In fact, both sides had anticipated a swift, decisive end to hostilities; neither had expected to fight the type of war that developed. One of the few who had planned on a relatively long war—perhaps even as long as three years—was Britain's war minister, Field Marshall Lord Kitchener, and even he had foreseen a rapidly changing cavalry-type war of movement. He was dumbfounded when the initial German advances and Allied counterattacks bogged down and both sides dug in. The impression of Kitchener's grasp of the military situation given by one visitor to the London War Office in 1915 was scathing: "Kitchener seemed to me very ignorant of what is being done, and how trenches are attacked, and how bombarded. He admitted that the nature of the modern lines of defence was quite new to him, and he said he 'felt at sea on the subject'."[19] A British field general, Douglas Haig, told the British War Council in early 1915 that "The machine gun is a much over-rated weapon and two per battalion is more than sufficient."[20] Another one of Kitchener's generals, Field Marshal Sir John French, the commander of the British Expeditionary Force (BEF) at the onset of the war, later confessed, "I cannot help wondering why none of us realized what the modern rifle, the machine gun, motor traction, the aeroplane, and wireless telegraphy would bring about."[21]

This underestimation of the change wrought by the machinery of modern warfare was in part due to an emphasis on the power of what the French referred to as élan. In many ways, this was the primary doctrine of the French military—the inculcation of a warrior mentality in its men that would enable them to advance and continue to advance, whatever the odds or the number of comrades falling around them. As Charles de Gaulle, then a young officer, told a group of conscripts in 1913, "Everywhere, always, one should have a single idea: to advance. As soon as the fighting begins, everybody in the French army, the general in command, the officers and the troops have only one thing in their heads—advancing, advancing to the attack, reaching the Germans, and running through them or making them run away."[22] De Gaulle's speech was doctrinaire—French military strategy was based almost exclusively on all-out attack, and there was no provision governing retreat, tactical or otherwise, in then-current French military manuals. While such training might seem to run against the human instinct for self-preservation, at least in the early years of the war, it was surprisingly effective in motivating soldiers to attempt the impossible. As Alan Seeger, an American volunteer in the French Foreign Legion wrote shortly before the bloody offensive in Champagne in September 1915, "I expect to march right up the Aisne borne on an irresistible élan. It will be the greatest moment of my life."[23] Seeger survived the Champagne offensive but was killed in action less than a year later, on July 4, 1916. The appalling number of casualties suffered by both sides in the early years of the war was also, as Ian Ousby writes in *The Road to Verdun*, attributable to the slowness of the generals to realize that "modern weaponry had shifted the odds quite decisively in favor of defense rather than attack. No amount of willpower and discipline in the attackers, no warrior code carried to whatever extreme of zeal, could level the odds against defenders now equipped with (among other advantages) concrete, long-range rifles and machine guns."[24]

Shortly after arriving in France, Beston received a letter from an old friend and former student from Harvard, Pierre Gouvy. Gouvy was a native of Arc-les-Gray in Haute Saone, who had enlisted in the French army shortly after the war began. Upon hearing that Beston had volunteered for the Field Service, Gouvy wrote:

> Henry, old boy:
> These [sic] are splendid news—you are coming back to dear old France—no you *are* in France, for if you have boarded the Rochambeau on the 12th, you must be in Neuilly by this time. Why, of course we are going to see each other, for I shall leave the front for the "interieur" within a week or two. Explanation: the Interieur is all that part of the country which is not the front. . . .
> As to me, I am in a hospital on the front near Avras at Saint Pol, have been quite sick but shall be well very soon. About Sept. 1st I shall leave this ambulance for another one in the Interieur, but don't know which one. Never mind, I shall tell you about it in time, and will meet you very soon I hope.
> I am writing a word to your dear mother[.] Now permit me to congratulate you for your fine idea of coming over—it is really worth[y] of Henry B. Sheahan.[25]

Even the relative lull in the war during the late summer of 1915, however, permitted few opportunities for visiting with old friends or enjoying the many charms of Paris. Much of Beston's time was spent becoming familiar with his duties and with the operation and maintenance of the Ford ambulance assigned to him, which he referred to as "old number 53." The volunteers were housed in a garret of the hospital in Neuilly-sur-Seine that had been filled with beds for the Americans. At night, the dormitory room was pitch-black, as all the windows in the hospital were covered by dark blue cambric curtains to keep any light from drawing the attention of marauding zeppelins. Across the quadrangle of the hospital and behind the darkly curtained windows of the opposite wing, Beston could hear the sounds of the wounded soldiers and their caregivers, "the steps on the tiled corridors, the running of water in the bathroom taps, the hard clatter of surgical vessels, and sometimes the cry of a patient having a painful wound dressed."[26]

A Volunteer Poilu

Even when Beston did get an opportunity to walk through the beautiful gardens of the Tuileries, or down the broad thoroughfare of the Champs-Élysées in the golden early autumn of 1915, he saw frequent reminders that this was not the "Gay Paree" of the pre-war years. Furloughed soldiers strolled through the gardens and he occasionally saw recent amputees struggling clumsily on their new crutches. In the Place de la Concorde, he observed a crowd of children gathered around a Punch and Judy show that featured a doll dressed in the bright red and blue uniform of a French Zouave whacking a puppet wearing a Prussian helmet whose face bore an uncanny likeness to that of Germany's emperor, Kaiser Wilhelm. Still, he was surprised to find that wartime Paris seemed superficially similar in appearance to Paris before the war: "The normal life of the city was powerful enough to engulf the disturbance, the theaters were open, there were the same crowds on the boulevards, and the same gossipy spectators in the sidewalk cafés. After a year of war the Parisians were accustomed to soldiers, cripples, and people in mourning."[27] Even the occasional bombing raid on Paris mounted by the terrifying German war zeppelins had become almost routine.

Throughout late August and into September, Allied artillery bombardment of the German lines increased steadily, and fierce fighting once again erupted in the province of Artois in Flanders, one of the most hotly contested regions in Belgium. Fighting in Alsace also intensified, with the French infantry attacking German forces in strategic highlands of the Vosges. If taken, these elevated positions would have enabled French artillery to shell key German positions in the nearby valleys. In the north, large numbers of newly-enlisted British troops had arrived from England, thereby freeing the French commander in chief, General Joseph Joffre, to redeploy French forces to Artois and the vineyard region of Champagne in preparation for a long-awaited offensive on the western front. The Allied plan was for the British to attack the German trenches in the northern sector to keep the Kaiser's troops pinned down there while the French directed their main forces against the Germans in Artois and Champagne in an effort to break through their fortified lines.[28] On the morning of Wednesday, September 22, 1915 Allied artillery units began a ferocious bombardment of the German trenches. After three days, one German soldier wrote home: "all places have been bombarded to such an extent that no human being could stand against it. The railway line [to the interior] is so seriously damaged that the train service for some time has been completely stopped. We have been for three days in the first line; during those three days the French have fired so heavily that our trenches are no longer visible."[29] At 9:15 A.M. on Sunday, September 25, Joffre issued the order to advance; following a chlorine gas attack, hundreds of thousands of British and French soldiers climbed out of their trenches along a front of approximately ninety kilometers and hurled themselves at the German defenders.

On that Sunday night in Paris, Beston and the other ambulance drivers had fallen asleep to the sound of a heavy rain pounding on the slate roof of the dormitory. Just after two A.M., the lieutenant of the Paris volunteers, a "mining engineer with a picturesque vocabulary of Nevadan profanity," rousted the sleepy volunteers, announcing that the call had come in for them to report to report to the railroad station at La Chappelle. The Allies had finally launched their attack along the western front, and the wounded from the Champagne sector had begun to flood the aid stations outside Paris. Beston and the other drivers dressed hurriedly and dashed down to the hospital yard, where the ambulances were parked. Within minutes, a procession of ambulances headed out the gate of the hospital yard, turned onto the Boulevard d'Inkermann, and headed down the dark roads to La Chappelle.[30]

All through the suburbs of Neuilly and Montmartre, there were scarcely any lights on, but once the ambulances arrived at La Chappelle and approached the railroad yards where the military had built a receiving station for the wounded men arriving from the front, the station was flooded with hastily strung lights. The street was a frenzy of ambulances rushing to and from the receiving station in the pouring rain, the air filled with the sound of grinding gears, squealing brakes, and the shouts of men directing the ambulance drivers to their pick-up points. Beston and his Number 53 were directed up a ramp and into a huge shed that was being used to load the wounded into ambulances for transport to Paris where they would receive further medical attention for their wounds. Beston would later describe his first experience as a volunteer ambulance driver in his memoir of the American Field Service, *A Volunteer Poilu* (1916):

> We entered a great, high, white-washed, warehouse kind of place, about four hundred feet wide, built of wood evidently years before. In the middle of this shed was an open space, and along the walls were rows of ambulances. *Brancardiers* (stretcher-bearers; from *brancard*, a stretcher) were loading wounded into these cars, and as soon as one car was filled, it would go out of the hall and another would take its place. There was an infernal din; the place smelled like a stuffy garage, and was full of blue gasoline fumes; and across this hurly-burly, which was increasing every minute, were carried the wounded, often nothing but human bundles of dirty blue cloth and fouled bandages. Every one of these wounded soldiers was saturated with mud, a gray-white mud that clung moistly to their overcoats, or, fully dry, colored every part of the uniform with its powder. One saw men that appeared to have rolled over and over in a puddle bath of this whitish mud, and sometimes there was a sinister mixture of blood and mire. There is nothing romantic about a wounded soldier, for his condition brings a special emphasis on our human relation to ordinary meat. Dirty, exhausted, unshaven, smelling of the trenches, of his wounds, and of the antiseptics on his wounds, the soldier comes from the train a sight for which only the great heart of Francis of Assisi could have adequate pity.[31]

A makeshift operating room had been prepared for the soldiers who needed immediate attention; those whose wounds were stabilized sufficiently to permit travel were loaded into the ambulances. The driver would then be handed a slip of paper that had the address of a site in Paris—sometimes an actual hospital, but often a school, public building, or even a private residence that had been designated as a "hospital"—and the wounded soldiers would be rushed to their assigned destination for additional care and recuperation.

For the next three days and nights, the ambulance squads worked almost without pause; 20,000 wounded soldiers were brought daily to the facility at La Chappelle alone. In the initial attack, the Allied forces overran the first line of the German trenches and broke through the line at numerous points. As the French and British soldiers gained ground it appeared that Joffre's plan for a decisive breakthrough had the Germans on their heels.

However, the German commanders Falkenhayn and Von Einem had used the time provided by the delayed Allied offensive to shore up their secondary defenses. A few miles behind their front line of trenches, the Germans had constructed a secondary line out of range of the French artillery. The Allied attack bogged down, and a week after the initial assault, the Germans counter-attacked. By the time the offensive ground to a close in late October, the lines were more or less back where they had been at the beginning of the offensive, with the Allies having gained only a few square miles of territory. In one month, the British and French lost 250,000 men; the German losses stood at about 60,000. As historian Hew Strachan writes, "Foiled in his attempt at breakthrough, Joffre fell back on another rationale for his attack: 'We shall kill more of the enemy than he can kill of us.' It was to become a familiar justification for the failure to break through."[32]

On October 8th, even before the fighting in Champagne had drawn to an uneasy deadlock, Beston received word that he had been assigned to Section Sanitaire No. 2, which was stationed southeast of Paris in the province of Lorraine. Fighting in this section was continuous and heavy, and the American ambulance drivers would no longer be working in the relative safety of the *intérieur*, but on the front itself. Pierre Gouvy, who was now recuperating in Paris, wrote to Beston:

> Dear Henry
>
> Where and how are you? . . . Probably you are accustomed now to all the queer sounds of the front: whistling bullets, exploding bombs, bursting shells—and will be unable to sleep when there are no "coalboxes" falling all around your tent. Be sure and send news as soon as you may.
>
> I am writing to the AA at Neuilly, but hope they'll forward the letter— and you must give me your address there. I am not writing more because I am all tired out by the rushing of Parisian life.
>
> Now good luck to you. Keep your spirits up—and, as Ben Pitman would say, everything else down.
>
> As ever your brother at arms
> Pete[33]

Beston immediately wrote back to Gouvy to inform him that he had been posted to the province of Lorraine. Gouvy apparently regretted asking

Henry where he was in his prior letter—this time, he strongly urged his friend to refrain from giving any specifics about his whereabouts on the front in any of his letters lest he put himself and his unit in danger should the letter be intercepted by the enemy: "I suppose you are quite familiar with trenches, and shelters, and all these things. But please do not tell me where you are. First I know it well, and secondly you *must not do it*." As for himself, said Gouvy, he had recovered from his illness and rejoined his unit: "I am all right now. Tomorrow we shall start for the firing line, and I want to make the Boches know that I am here again. I'll write in a few days to tell you about our sector, and the kind of shells we get, and the gases we have to breath" [sic].[34]

Beston's first stop on his way to the front was the city of Nancy in Lorraine, from where he could see vast clouds of smoke billowing from the enormous munitions factories located in the towns of Frouard and Pompey, just west of the city. The war had, at least for the time being, brought a wave of prosperity to Nancy, and the city was jammed with soldiers and refuges from the frontier villages. As Beston wrote in *A Volunteer Poilu*, "The middle class was making money, the rich were getting richer, and Nancy, hardly more than eighteen or nineteen miles from the trenches, forgot its danger till, on the first day of January 1916, the German fired several shells . . . into the town, one of which scattered the fragments of a big five-story apartment house all over Nancy. And on that afternoon thirty thousand people left the city."[35]

The following morning, Beston left for the front, a vast swathe of territory averaging about twenty miles in width. The front encompassed the French and German support units in the rear of the lines, the network of trenches constructed by both sides, and "no-man's-land" located between the opposing armies. It might also be fairly said that the front included all areas, including any town or city, within range of the opposing side's artillery. The French and British had arranged the organization of their lines along the front into units called *secteurs*; each *secteur* was administered separately and supplied by railway lines that ran up to the edge of the enemy's artillery range. From the railway depot, supplies arriving via rail would be brought to the front lines and distributed throughout the trenches. In return, any wounded would be carried by the stretcher-bearers to a medical post in the rear lines of the trenches. From the medical post, the ambulance drivers would take the wounded to the surgical units located along the front. In some areas, such as Bois-le-Prêtre where Beston served, the roads traveled by the ambulances were often little more than trenches that had been made wide enough for the ambulances; they were often virtually impassable due to muddy conditions, and they were always under the threat of shelling by German artillery.

The Field Service of the American Ambulance was, at this time, under the command of the French army, and the lieutenant in charge of the American section arrived in Nancy to take Beston to the front, some thirty kilometers distant. They left the city and proceeded north, through the Moselle River valley; by the time they reached the village of Dieulouard, some twenty miles north of Nancy, the signs of war were starkly evident. The once-quiet farming village was filled with soldiers, and the damage from German shells was everywhere. The lieutenant pointed out the remains of a cottage that had been hit by a shell the previous day, killing two people. As Beston gazed out at the destruction, his romantic conceptions of war vanished, replaced by the realization that this was a new kind of war that had none of the terrible beauty and gallantry of the wars of classical antiquity:

> [L]ooking at the muddy village-town full of men in uniforms of blue, in blue that was blue-gray and blue-green from wear and exposure to the weather, I realized that the old days of beautiful, half-barbaric uniforms were gone forever, and that, in place of the old romantic war of cavalry charges and great battles in the open, a new, more terrible war had been created, a war that had not the chivalric externals of the old.[36]

After leaving Dieulouard, Beston noticed other ominous signs of the war; burlap screens had been erected atop each rise in the road to provide those traveling with some degree of protection from spotters for the German artillery units. When the guns were silent, an eerie, quiet stillness was prevalent and they passed through villages that had been shelled so heavily that they were now nothing but mounds of earth and debris. A century later, many of these once-thriving villages are still designated on French maps as *ruines*.

That afternoon, they arrived in the battered, all but deserted town of Pont-à-Mousson, less than half a mile away from the trenches of Bois-le-Prêtre. Here, wrote Beston, "The sense of the 'front' began to possess me, never to go, the sense of being in the vicinity of a tremendous *power* ... One sees villages of the swathes so completely blown to pieces ... seeing them thus, in a plain still fiercely disputed night and day between one's own side and the invisible enemy, the mind feels itself in the presence of force, titanic, secret, and hostile."[37] As is often the case, the landscape itself dictated the terms of engagement by the opposing armies. Pont-à-Mousson is situated on the banks of the Moselle River in a valley overlooked by wooded ridges, the highest of which is the Bois-le-Prêtre (the Priest's Woods) just north of the town. Continuing to the northwest, a great plateau, the Plaine de la Woëvre, rises from the river valleys of the Moselle and the Meuse. In the opening days of the war, the German armies had driven a wedge between the fortress city of Verdun and Pont-à-Mousson to the town of St. Mihiel; the Germans then fortified their lines and maintained a defensive position in the St. Mihiel salient (which the French called "the hernia") until 1918. From 1914 until the end of the war, the ridge of Bois-le-Prêtre on the southern edge of the St. Mihiel salient remained hotly contested for tactical reasons; the Alsatian city of Metz (less than fifteen miles north of Pont-à-Mousson) had become one of the most important rail transport and supply centers for the Germans on the western front. If the French could take the ridge and position their artillery on that elevated position, Metz would be within range of long-range French artillery. "The Bois-le-Prêtre," recalled Beston, "dominated at once the landscape and our minds. Its existence was the one great fact of some fifty thousand Frenchman, Germans, and a handful of exiled Americans; it had dominated and ended the lives of the dead; it would dominate the imagination of the future."[38]

Upon arrival at Pont-à-Mousson, Beston was assigned quarters on the third floor of an apartment house that had been abandoned by its civilian occupants and which now served as quarters for a unit of French engineers. That night, Beston was awakened by the concussion of a large shell, followed soon by another that rained debris upon the roof of the apartment house. Dressing quickly, he hurried into the cellar, where several other inhabitants of the house had taken shelter. The more experienced soldiers told him that the Germans were firing incendiary shells, which would be followed by shrapnel shells intended to hinder those fighting the fires. By the time the shelling stopped, several fires raged in the area of the apartment house, and a man in an adjoining house had been killed. "With the next day," wrote Beston, "I began my service at the trenches, but the war began for me that very night."[39] Beston jotted down his initial impressions of the front in a journal he sporadically kept while at the front:

The quarters are on the third floor, a kind of apartment house. Windows of stained glass on the back of the staircase. We creep up them in total darkness, hardly daring to light a match. Any sign of light might mean death.

I wonder if I shall ever get used to living under the constant menace of death.

The life of the town in times of peace seems to have centred round its arcaded market place. Now the arcades are closed with sand bags and the shops are open in the shady cold corridors behind them. Many of the shops are open—even the Réunis with its glass roof.

A little life lingers on in the town; the people keeping mostly to one side of the street.

Many quite deserted streets with the grass growing in the cracks of the pavements and along the gutters. Windows all closed. Walls shrapnel splattered.

At Montauville sparrows fly in and out of the shell holes in wooden steeple of the church tower.

The villages in Lorraine are extraordinarily dirty. They put their barn yard dirt right in the road. Hateful little flies are always flying in one's face. Dieulouard is nasty, Belleville dreadful.

A picture of men groaning, horses, slimy, muddy roads, old walls shell bespattered, children. A certain stench, too.

The women still wash in the brook at Dieulouard.

From Belleville, at night fall, I saw the pin points of light break in the sky as they drove away a hostile aeroplane.

Bitterly cold. The nights in the Moselle Valley are freezing cold, and the days are still warmish. At the front here one longs for any touch of domesticity; for an open fire, a warm lighted room and pleasant voices one would do a great deal. But we gave up all this gladly to do our work.[40]

A Volunteer Poilu

It was not long after arriving in Pont-à-Mousson that Beston saw his first man killed in action. He had been talking to a young French sentry, who was curious to learn whether the Americans thought the Germans were going to win the war. Beston had just finished assuring him that the American public believed that the Allies would prevail, and was walking away when he heard the sound of a "seventy-seven," one of the large German 77 millimeter artillery shells, overhead. He ducked for cover, and when he turned around, saw the sentry lying face down in the street less than ten feet away from him: "A chunk of the shell had ripped open the left breast to the heart. Down his sleeve, as down a pipe, flowed a hasty drop, drop, drop of blood that mixed with the mire."[41]

The volunteers of the American Field Service were headquartered in the cellar of a deserted summer home in Montauville, on the outskirts of Pont-à-Mousson, that they wryly dubbed "Wisteria Villa." Just one hundred yards from Wisteria Villa was the crossroad to the trenches; wounded soldiers would be carried from the front lines of the trenches to a *poste de secours* in the rear lines, where the ambulance drivers would pick up the wounded for transport to the field hospital. Although it was shielded with burlap screens, the German artillery shelled the road near Wisteria Villa almost daily in an attempt to disrupt operations. In just one week, Beston counted over one hundred shells directed at the crossroads and realized that there was a vital science to decoding the various sounds of the war zone: "After a certain time at the front the ear learns to distinguish the sound of a big shell from a small shell, and to know roughly whether or not one is in the danger zone. It was a grim jest with us that it took ten days to qualify as a shell expert, and at the end of two weeks all those who qualified attended the funeral of those who had failed. Life at the Wood had an interesting uncertainty."[42]

Beston was struck by how soldiers adjusted to the "interesting uncertainty" of life in the trenches. The French soldier was commonly referred to as a *poilu*, which literally means hairy or shaggy one, but which idiomatically conveyed a certain powerful, bear-like masculinity. At the outset of the war, the French had generally referred to the German soldiers as "Les Allemands," but as the war dragged on and attitudes hardened, they were more commonly referred to with the contemptuous word "Boche," which Beston believed may have originated from the Parisian slang word for ugly head, "caboche." Beston's admiration for the French soldiers—characteristic of many of the volunteers who served in the Field Service—is clearly evident in *A Volunteer Poilu*:

> Any Frenchman who has the requisite education can become an officer if he is willing to devote more of his time, than is by law required, to military service. Thus the French army is the soul of democracy, and the officer understands, and is understood by his men. The spirit of the French army is remarkably fraternal, and this fraternity is at once social and mystical. It has a social origin, for the *poilus* realize that the army rests on class justice and equal opportunity; it has a mystical strength, because war has taught the men that it is only the human being that counts, and that comradeship is better than insistence on the rights and virtues of pomps and prides. After having been face to face with death for two years, a man learns something about the true values of human life.[43]

Beston was deeply impressed by the camaraderie of the men, their stolid acceptance of discomfort and hardship, and the way in which they used dark humor to deal with the war and the ever-present possibility of death. After spending some time with the *poilus* at the front, many of the American volunteers adopted a similar fondness for gallows humor. Beston noted that even among the well-educated, life in the trenches tended to discourage any intellectual pursuits, and that the "rough, genial, and simple" prevailed. He cited the case of a sergeant who had been a distinguished scholar before the war and now was "always throwing messages wrapped round a stone into the German trenches; the messages were killingly funny, amiably indecent, and very *jejune*."[44] As amusing to one's comrades in arms as this may have been, Beston learned from a friend that having a sense of humor could be dangerous: "Martin says the Boches began a parley the other day by holding up a white flag, the French did the same, then the Germans asked them if they wanted any bread, the French replied no and asked if they wanted any. The Germans held up a big fat Boche for an answer. Big row in the French trenches because some wanted to shoot him."[45]

For the most part, life in the trenches consisted of an uncomfortable boredom, punctuated by moments of intense violence. The old horrors of the rifle, bayonet, barbed wire, and field artillery had now been joined by the new horrors of modern industrial warfare—machine guns, airplanes, grenades, mortars, flamethrowers, tanks, and poison gas. The paradox of digging one's own grave to preserve life brought an endless series of additional miseries, including the constant presence of mud, cold, lice, rats—and not infrequently, the remains of other soldiers. During the Champagne offensive in 1915, a French adjutant and his comrades had just finished digging their new trenches, when they noticed "a vile stench in the new trenches . . . Rain came down in torrents, and we used bits of canvas we had found stuck in the trench-walls. The next day, at dawn, we saw that the trench had been built in a veritable grave-yard—the bits of canvas had been put there to cover bodies and human remains."[46] An affliction common during the first two years of the war, until effective preventive measures were developed, was what came to be known as "trench-foot." As war correspondent Philip Gibbs (who along with his brother Arthur later became a friend of Beston) described it, after standing for days in water and mud, the men's feet would "begin to swell, and then go 'dead,' and then suddenly to burn as though touched by red-hot pokers."[47] The pain was so intense that the men would have to crawl or be carried to the medical stations for treatment, and many lost toes or feet to the affliction. For many soldiers, the most terrifying prospect of life in the trenches was being buried alive. Both sides employed the tactic of using mining engineers or "sappers" to dig tunnels under no man's land and under the enemy's trenches. The tunnel would then be filled with high explosives and detonated, causing the trenches above to cave in, burying the soldiers in them. As Allan Lloyd writes in *The War in the Trenches*:

> Horrified that the enemy might be burrowing underfoot, British troops went to frantic lengths in their attempts to detect miners. Men knelt in the squelching mud trying to discern vibrations by holding one end of a stick in their teeth, bedding the other end in the ground. Oil drums filled with water were sunk into the bottom of trenches, where freezing soldiers lay in the filth to dip their ears into the freezing liquid. A few units grew so jittery they had to be withdrawn from the line.[48]

The cumulative toll of life in the trenches was often debilitating, both physically and mentally, and as the war went on the numbers of "walking wounded" increased exponentially.

For Beston, as for many other observers of life on the front lines, the most compelling question was, "How do the soldiers stand it?" Once the horror of life on the front became more familiar, he reasoned, one's response tended to become more casual. This had much to do with the attitude of the veterans—soldiers new to trench warfare were "sustained by the attitude of the veterans. Violence becomes the commonplace; shells, gases, and flames are the thing that life is made of. The war is another lesson in the power of the species to adapt itself to circumstances."[49] Beston himself was an example of this phenomenon. "At the beginning of my service," he wrote in *A Volunteer Poilu*, "I thought Pont-à-Mousson, with its ruins, its danger, and its darkness, the most awful place on the face of the earth. After a while, I grew accustomed to the *décor*, and when the time came for me to leave it, I went with as much regret as if I were leaving the friendliest, most peaceful of towns."[50]

There may well have been a bittersweet and unintended irony in Beston's fond recollection of Pont-à-Mousson, one that he himself never fully realized. Tall, broad-shouldered, and personable, with impeccably accented French, it was easy for Beston to make friends wherever he went in France—and with his matinée idol good looks, this was certainly the case with many of the young Frenchwomen he met. During the months that Beston was stationed in Pont-à-Mousson it appears that he became romantically involved with a local woman that he lost touch with after he and his unit were shifted to Verdun. Several months later, the young Frenchwoman had a son who may well have been Beston's. He never learned of the boy's existence, which only came to light many years later as a result of a letter sent to Beston's daughter Kate by the grandson of the Frenchwoman. Given how Beston yearned for a son and namesake in later years the irony of this situation is particularly poignant.

For the ambulance service volunteers, as for the soldiers, letters and packages from family and friends were vital to maintaining morale as well as supplying them with items not readily available at the front. To support the war effort, civilians without family members at the front would often "adopt" soldiers and send them letters and packages, sometimes establishing friendships that lasted even after the war had ended. In mid-October of 1915, Mabel Davison, a native of New York City who was living in Paris when the war broke out, sent a letter and package to Beston that included knee-warmers, cocoa, and a newspaper; this was the beginning of an enduring friendship between Beston and Davison, to whom he later dedicated *The Outermost House*. Davison served as a volunteer for several organizations formed to help the wounded; in *American Women and the World War*, Ida Clyde Clarke wrote of Davison that she had "worked unceasingly to help the blind, both in the government institution and at Miss Holt's famous Light House. Miss Davison held the light for many stumbling feet over there in blood-stained France, and perhaps no individual has brought more comfort and more cheer to the desperate and the hopeless than she."[51] Beston wrote back to her on October 22, 1915, to thank her for the gifts, and to share with her some of his observations from the front lines. A few days later, Beston received a long letter and another package from her containing a knitted woolen vest and some preserves. He immediately wrote again to thank her: "I can never thank you enough for all your kindness, nor tell you how it has touched me. When one fares alone in war time through a mourning land, friendly interest means a great, great deal to heart and mind . . . I am looking forward to a visit to your studio. You are doing the noblest of work; dear France is worthy of your efforts. The *poilu* is [a] fine fellow, and is facing the prospect of another winter in the trenches with fine courage and determination."[52]

In his letters to Davison, whom he came to call *Marraine* (godmother; *marraine de guerre* is used to designate a female wartime pen pal), Beston often described life on the front, and the underlying paradox of modern warfare: "A curious life, here. In the trenches one takes to the earth like a cave man, you live like a troglodyte while the 'dernier cri' of modern science bursts over your head. A paradox, n-est-ce pas?"[53] Like many of the volunteers, when lulls in the fighting occurred it was easy for Beston to fall prey to loneliness and homesickness. This was often apparent in his letters to Davison: "Your constant kindliness has meant a great deal to a rather lonesome young philosopher, for we are all 'philosophes' here. We have to be. A thousand thanks for the jolly papers and the tea. If you have any warm socks on hand, I should very much like to have some. The mud is fearful, and my feet are nearly always moist."[54] Winter came early to the western front in 1915, with much rain, sleet, and snow. In early December Beston wrote to Davison that the trenches were now mud sluiceways, and that, to make things even more nerve-wracking,

> all along the front, orders have been given to have gas-masks handy—the result, I believe, of the information that the Boches are manufacturing monstrous quantities of this stuff. The other day I was sent up to a village on the line to try out my mask. I put it on, half smothering myself with the multicoloured compress, and then descended into a cellar full of thick chlorine fumes. I never felt a thing, tho [sic] I realized that the air I was breathing was of a different quality than is usually found. The masks dehumanize us in an ogre-ish sort of way.[55]

In the same letter, he rather sheepishly conveyed some happier news: "I am very glad to write that I am now brigadier or corporal of the section, and wear two humble broad blue stripes upon my sleeve. The soldiers call me "Caporal" which amuses me hugely."

UNLIKE CHRISTMAS 1914, there would be no spontaneous "Christmas Truce" in 1915; instead, hostilities continued virtually unabated. For the Entente, 1915 had been a discouraging year. Despite tremendous losses, the Allies had made little progress in reconquering lost territory on the western front; the Russians had suffered a staggering number of casualties on the eastern front in addition to losing vast swaths of land to the Germans; the British offensive at Gallipoli ended in ignominious defeat. At the beginning of 1916, the western front was essentially divided into two primary sectors. The northern salient, which extended for 114 miles from the English Channel through the tiny portion of Belgium not occupied by the German Army, and through northern France as far as the River Somme, was defended by sixty-three divisions of British, Belgian, and French troops, facing off against thirty-two German divisions. The southern sector, which extended south from the Somme for approximately three hundred miles, was defended by eighty-seven French divisions opposed by seventy German divisions. While the German army still held a considerable advantage in artillery, the front had devolved into a battle of attrition, and General von Falkenhayn had become convinced that a major breakthrough was neither possible nor necessary. A concentrated attack and breakthrough on one segment of the line, he reasoned, would be enough to keep the Allies off balance, and would permit him the freedom to pursue the attack or break it off as the situation dictated. The fortified city of Verdun, which had withstood the initial German offensive of August 1914 and which inhibited German operations in the southern part of the front was designated by Falkenhayn as the objective of the German offensive, and Crown Prince Wilhelm's Fifth Army was chosen to lead the attack. Falkenhayn's plan was brutally simple—surprise the French, gain the highlands of the Meuse River overlooking Verdun, and pulverize the city with heavy artillery, forcing the French to abandon their defensive positions.[56]

During much of 1915, the French had considered the Verdun sector to be a quiet one. Believing that the Germans would not dare attack the stronghold, General Joffre had stripped away much of Verdun's artillery and troops, sending them to other, more active sectors. During early 1916, however, the Allies noticed increased activity in the German lines near Verdun, and began to belatedly prepare for the possibility of a German offensive on Verdun and the ring of fortresses surrounding the city. In February, Beston's ambulance unit was relocated to the city of Bar-le-Duc, where the French army was frantically preparing for the defense of Verdun: "the city was in a feverish haste of preparation . . . Nobody knew when the Germans were going to strike."[57] On February 21, the attack began with an air raid on Bar-le-Duc. Beston and several other drivers were working on their ambulances in the parking area outside their barracks when the first bombs hit: "A whistling scream, a kind of shrill, increasing shriek, sounded in the air and ended in a crash. Smoke rolled heavily in another direction. Another whistle, another crash, another and another and another. The last building shot up great tongues of flame. . . . Across the yard a comrade's arm beckoned me, 'Come on, we've got to help put out the fires!'"[58] For twenty minutes, the drivers worked to extinguish the blaze while the attack continued, diving for cover whenever the whistle of the shells indicated a nearby strike. Save for the frenzied activity of the *poilus*, the streets were deserted, the citizens of the city peering out from their homes then "disappearing at the first whistle of a bomb, for all the world like hermit-crabs into their shells."[59] That night the town was completely blacked out, and before retiring to the barracks and a fitful sleep, Beston stood outside, listening to the distant thunder of the ceaseless artillery attack directed toward Verdun as "One great nation, for the sake of a city valueless from a military point of view, was preparing to kill several hundred thousand of its citizens, and another great nation, anxious to retain the city, was preparing calmly for a parallel hecatomb . . . all one's faculties of intellect are revolted by the stark brutality of death *en masse.*"[60]

Verdun was not, as Beston himself knew, completely valueless. From the Allied lines northeast of Paris that marked the limits of the German advance in 1914, the front followed a line that ran basically in an east-west direction as far as Verdun, where it pivoted sharply to the south, running along the highlands east of the Meuse River. In his meticulously researched *Military History of the First World War,* Gerard Lindsley McEntee wrote, "This placed the region of Verdun in a marked salient. From the French viewpoint the area was the pivot of the whole line. The defense could have been made from the west bank of the Meuse, but Verdun had such a great value from the point of view of the morale of the French people that that factor alone was sufficient to force the French Army to defend every foot of the salient."[61] The German general staff understood the psychological importance of Verdun, and realized what a devastating effect the capture of the city would have on French morale—they believed that the French would bleed themselves white to save the city. Additionally, the Verdun salient was a mere forty-five miles from Metz and the railway lines that formed the crux of the German supply lines for much of the western front; as one German described it, Verdun was a dagger in the side of the German army. In the region as a whole the Germans held the advantage of both elevation and a superb network of railways and roads, whereas the French were heavily dependent on a single road that extended from Bar-le-Duc to Verdun, a three-lane road that came to be known as *La Voie Sacrée,* or The Sacred Way.

This road was so critical to the effort to defend Verdun that nearly 10,000 men and 4,000 trucks were assigned to keep it clear.[62]

The artillery attack on Verdun was massive—it was reported that tremors from the barrage were felt as far as 150 kilometers away.[63] On February 22, the day after the Germans launched their assault on Verdun, General Joffre realized that he had badly underestimated the size of the German offensive and hastily began to shift more reserves to defend the city. Beston's ambulance unit was among those ordered to the front. They left at noon, and by midnight they arrived at a small village just south of Verdun. The night was bitter cold, but a steady stream of refugees were still plodding away from the besieged city, many using wheelbarrows and baby carriages to transport their possessions. As the troops and ambulance drivers slogged their way toward the front, the scene became increasingly chaotic, wrote Beston:

> The crossroad where the ambulances turned off was a maze of beams of light from the autos. There was a shouting of orders which nobody could carry out. Wounded, unable to walk, passed through the beams of the lamps, the red of their bloodstains, detached against the white of the bandages, presenting the sharpest of contrasts in the silvery glare. At the station, men who had died in the ambulances were dumped hurriedly in a plot by the side of the roadway and covered with a blanket. Never was there seen such a bedlam! But on the main road the convoys moved smoothly on as if held together by an invisible chain. A smouldering in the sky told of fires in Verdun.[64]

When the convoy approached Verdun, the roar of battle grew louder, and the night sky was filled with the glow of the burning city, punctuated by bright shooting stars of artillery fire. Every once in a while an enormous shell would strike, ripping "a great hole of white in the night, and so thundering was the crash of arrival that we almost expected to see the city sink into the earth."[65] Wounded men staggered or crawled through the narrow streets, clinging to each other like stricken shadows.

Throughout late February the German infantry made hard-fought gains on the French defenses, but were met with a constant series of desperate counterattacks. General Joffre sent an urgent wire to General Pétain, commanding officer at Verdun: "Any commander who, under the circumstances, gives orders to retreat will be brought before a court-martial."[66] To make things even more unbearable, the weather turned colder at the height of the fighting on February 24, with wind and intermittent heavy snow covering the roads with mud and a wet slush that would have made them impassable save for the feverish efforts of the work crews repairing the worst stretches with wagonloads of crushed rock and gravel. As Beston later recalled:

> The 24th was the most dreadful day . . . The cannonade was still so intense that, in intervals between the heavier snow-flurries, I could see the stabs of fire in the brownish sky . . . Exhaustion had begun to tell on the horses; many lay dead and snowy in the frozen fields. A detachment of khaki-clad, red-fezzed colonial troops passed by, bent to the storm. The news was of the most depressing sort. The wounded could give you only the story of their part of the line, and you heard over and over again, "Nous avons reculés" [We are pulling back].[67]

The following day, things seemed even more hopeless for the French. Fort Douaumont, one of the key fortresses defending the city, but one that had been virtually stripped of artillery and defenders, fell. Just before the fort was taken, Beston transported a French officer who had been bayoneted through the shoulder in the desperate fighting there. "They may take Douamont," the officer told him, "but that is about as far as they will get . . . If you could see our men at this minute, fighting like fiends, you would realize that this spirit is worth a thousand of Germany's giant mortars."[68]

The *poste de secours* to which Beston and the ambulance drivers in his sector ferried the wounded was an eighteenth-century château located a few miles outside Verdun that had been converted to a rough field hospital. The hospital reeked of ether and iodoform, mixed with what Beston called "the smell of war." A steady stream of ambulances churned through the muddy roads to the hospital, where exhausted hospital orderlies unloaded stretchers of wounded soldiers: "messy bundles of blue rags and bloody blankets turned into human beings."[69] The surgeon in charge of triage would quickly examine the diagnosis card attached to each stretcher and ask the fatal question: "Have you spit blood?"[70] After unloading the wounded, the ambulances would either be sent back to the front for another pick-up or take some men who had been successfully treated to a convalescent barracks behind the lines. On one such trip, Beston was ordered to transport three men to the barracks. The road had been churned into thick mire, and was crowded with troops headed to the front and horse-drawn supply wagons. Beston's ambulance was just behind a two-horse wagon carrying medical supplies and another wagon drawn by a single horse, when he heard the sound of anti-aircraft fire behind him, followed quickly by the sound of a German airplane:

> A few seconds later, there sounded the terrifying scream of an air-bomb, a roar, and I found myself in a bitter swirl of smoke. The shell had fallen right between the horses of the two-horse wagon, blowing the animals to pieces, splintering the wagon, and killing the driver. Something sailed swiftly over my head, and landed just behind the ambulance. It was a chunk of the skull of one of the horses. The horse attached to the wagon in front of me went into a frenzy of fear and backed his wagon into my ambulance, smashing the right lamp. In the twinkling of an eye, the soldiers dispersed. Some ran into the fields. Others crouched in the wayside ditch. A cart upset. Another bomb dropped screaming in a field and burst; a cloud of smoke rolled away down the meadow.[71]

After successfully delivering the convalescents, Beston was making the return trip to the field hospital, when he caught a glimpse of the French commanders Joffre, Castelnau, Poincaré, and Pétain, who were directing the battle from a field headquarters located in Souilly, a small village outside Verdun. He noted the look on Poincaré's face, at once worried and brave; within a few hours, the ambulance drivers were given the order to prepare to evacuate at once if the Germans continued to advance. That night Beston and the other drivers slept in their ambulances, waking occasionally to start the engines to keep them warmed up in case of a call to retreat. The retreat was never ordered. The French held the city, and the German offensive on Verdun ground to a halt on February 26. By July German troops had ceased offensive operations and fallen into a defensive posture. While the fighting at Verdun would continue until December 1916, the French defenses held, but at a staggering cost—the French lost approximately 377,000 men; the Germans lost almost the same number.[72] Verdun was not the bloodiest battle in the war, but as historian Marc Ferro asserts, "it was

Verdun that gripped the imagination and veterans specifically of Verdun who were lauded."[73]

Beston's six-month enlistment in the Field Service ended even before the assault directed at Verdun. He had remained with his unit, however, unwilling to leave France during its moment of greatest need: "It was my design to leave at the beginning of the year, but why should I go? I am very happy to be able to do something here, very proud to feel that I am doing something . . . To half jest, I am enduring war for peace of mind."[74] In March, a few weeks after the German attack at Verdun had been halted, Beston was making his plans—with the blessing of the Field Service's chief, A. Piatt Andrew—to return to the United States. Andrew had encouraged Beston, like some of the other volunteers with a literary bent, to return stateside and write about their experiences in France as part of the recruitment and fund-raising efforts of the AFS. Andrew wrote a letter to the French Commissioner of Passports on March 20, 1916, to try to expedite the passport approval Beston needed before he could leave, explaining that Beston had purchased a ticket without realizing that a new two-week waiting period had gone into effect, stating, "His object in returning home is to raise money for the American Sectiones Mobiles at the front."[75] Piatt's intervention was to no avail, however, and Beston had to exchange his ticket for a passage two weeks later; on April 4, 1916, he boarded a ship for the United States and home.

CHAPTER THREE

The Violence and Imbecilities of Men

1916–1919

> Never such innocence,
> Never before or since,
> As changed itself to past
> Without a word—the men
> Leaving the gardens tidy,
> The thousands of marriages
> Lasting a little while longer:
> Never such innocence again.
>
> PHILIP LARKIN
> "MCMXIV"

WHEN BESTON ARRIVED HOME in May 1916, he found that attitudes about the war were still in flux. While the United States had not yet entered the war and was officially neutral, public opinion (at least on the Atlantic seaboard) strongly favored the Entente. The German invasion of Belgium in the opening months of the war had appalled other neutral nations, and allegations of German barbarities—some of which were manufactured by Allied propaganda, but others of which were substantiated—in occupied Belgium inflamed anti-German attitudes in the United States. The sinking of the *Lusitania* the previous year also remained fresh in the national consciousness, and the heroic defense of Verdun had won a great deal of admiration for the valor of the French army. Perhaps most importantly, the predations of the German U-boat fleet on commercial shipping were viewed with anger and resentment on the part of many Americans, who tended to downplay the fact that the shiploads of supplies sent from the United States to Europe were seen by the Germans as critical to the French and British war effort. As Robert K. Massie writes in *Castles of Steel: Britain, Germany, and the Winning of the Great War at Sea*, "In theory, U.S. commercial loans and trade in food and munitions were equally available to the Central Powers, but theory and actual usefulness to the German cause ran up against the implacable barrier of Allied control of the oceans."[1] Commercial interests and "freedom of the seas" arguments resonated more strongly with American businesses and the general public than did any fine distinction between legal and actual neutrality that might be made by the Kaiser's government.

Beston's own views on war had begun to change, albeit slowly and incrementally. He still maintained few doubts that the war against the central powers was a just cause against militaristic aggressors who had attacked smaller, weaker nations such as Serbia and Belgium, and his political sympathies were unequivocally aligned with the democracies of France and Britain. Before his experiences on the western front, however, like many of the young volunteers Beston had a decidedly romantic view of the "adventure" upon which he was embarking. At Harvard, Beston had been Professor Charles Copeland's assistant in the development of a class on Sir Walter Scott, and it is striking how often references to notions such as chivalry, valor, and self-sacrifice appear in his wartime memoir, *A Volunteer Poilu*. This naïve, romantic sensibility toward war was continually confounded, however, by what Beston actually saw on the battlefield and in the trenches. Such passages point toward a dawning realization that the ideals of chivalry and valor derived from literary works like the novels of Sir Walter were absent, or at least, radically transformed, in modern warfare. Instead of the colorful and largely fictional notion of battle as a place where courage, chivalry, and honor reigned, modern industrialized warfare wrote Beston:

> [Has] robbed war of all its ancient panoply, its cavalry, its uniforms brilliant as the sun, and has turned it into the national business. I dislike to use the word 'business,' with its usual atmosphere of orderly bargaining; I intend rather to call up an idea more familiar to American minds—the idea of a

great intricate organization with a corporate volition. The war of to-day is a business, the people are the stockholders, and the object of the organization is the wisest application of violence to the enemy.[2]

Perhaps more than anything, this realization explains why Beston, despite his strong sympathies for the Entente, didn't come out publicly for American entry into the war. As was the case with many war correspondents, such as the famed English reporter Philip Gibbs, Beston's view of war was transformed by what he witnessed on the western front. The most striking images in *A Volunteer Poilu* and in Beston's war correspondence are not stirring set pieces of martial valor and glory, but horrifying descriptions of the impersonal slaughter that generally constitutes modern warfare.

There is little doubt, however, that during this period Beston leaned toward the position of former President Theodore Roosevelt, who was vociferously in favor of entering the war on the side of the Allies. Beston's friendship with his Harvard classmate Ted Roosevelt Jr. had deepened since their graduation in 1909, and he considered German submarine attacks on merchant ships flying the flag of neutral countries as a base violation of international law. Like many on the Eastern Seaboard, Beston hoped that Roosevelt would once again throw his hat into the ring, reunite the Progressive Party and the G.O.P., and sweep the coalition to victory in the elections of 1916. Roosevelt *was* sorely tempted to make another run at the White House, partly because of his strong views on the war in Europe, but due also to his personal animus toward Woodrow Wilson; as Roosevelt biographer Nathan Miller notes, Roosevelt felt that Wilson was a timid man, and often used words such as "unscrupulous," "shifty," "cold-blooded," and "hypocrite" in referring to him.[3] When the United States later entered the war, Roosevelt eagerly offered to raise and lead a division of volunteers, and was infuriated when Wilson spurned the suggestion.

The American presidential campaign of 1916 was dominated by the war in Europe. The Progressives were eager for Roosevelt to once again head their slate of candidates, but the Republicans were more ambivalent about selecting the man who had split the party in 1912. Roosevelt's reluctance to immediately declare his renewed presidential ambitions emboldened the party's "Old Guard" to seek an alternative to the charismatic but polarizing former president; in June 1916, the delegates to the Republican Convention selected Supreme Court Justice Charles Evans Hughes as their presidential nominee. Later that month, the Democrats nominated President Wilson as their candidate, emphasizing the theme of "He kept us out of war."[4] Many Americans, particularly in the West, believed that the war in Europe was largely an internecine struggle between the despotic, imperialist powers of the old European order, and that the United States was best off sitting this one out. In addition, ethnic ties—particularly in regions such as the Midwest—played a significant role in the debate over the war. Many members of the German-American, and to a lesser extent the Irish-American, community viewed the pro-Entente campaign for preparedness with distrust and bitterly resented any insinuation that "hyphenated" Americans had dubious loyalties to the nation. The economic advantages to neutrality were also readily apparent; American businesses were piling up huge profits selling food and supplies to the combatants, most of which went to the Allies. The results of the 1916 presidential election demonstrated how starkly divided the electorate was on the war issue. Hughes won most of the states in the Northeast (including Wilson's adopted home state of New Jersey) and the upper Midwest. Early returns from the East had Hughes leading Wilson in both the popular and electoral votes, and for a while it looked as though Hughes would be the winner. A jubilant Theodore Roosevelt declared "the election of Hughes is a vindication of our national honor."[5] When late returns came in from the western states, however, Republican elation morphed into despair as Wilson eked out a popular majority of some 600,000 votes and a slim 277–254 victory in the Electoral College.

Meanwhile, during the spring and summer of 1916, Beston had been hard at work writing a flurry of newspaper and magazine articles about the war. Almost immediately upon his return to Quincy in May, Beston was approached by the *Boston Post*, the most popular daily newspaper in New England, to write a series of articles about his experiences on the western front for its Sunday edition. The first installment of the series was published on May 7, 1916, and subsequent feature articles appeared in the newspaper for the next three weeks. In their rather breathless introduction to "Mr. Sheahan's thrilling story of his terrifying experiences," the editors of the newspaper stressed Beston's local connection to the great events going on in Europe, writing: "With the shrieking of the wounded and the screaming of the shells still echoing in his ears, Henry P. Sheahan, a Massachusetts boy, from Topsfield, graduate of Adams Academy and Master of Arts at Harvard University, late member of the American Ambulance Corps at the French front, has returned to Boston." Subsequent articles in the *Sunday Post* described such things as a struggle to control fire during an artillery bombardment, an aerial dogfight, and the war in the trenches.

Beston scored a more significant reportorial coup when *The Atlantic Monthly*, one of the country's preeminent magazines, accepted two of his articles on the western front for publication. The first of these, "Verdun," appeared in the July 1916 issue of *The Atlantic*, providing Beston's firsthand account of the initial days of the battle. The final paragraph of the article, which reads as though Beston had just returned from the front (he had actually left several months previously) in order to give the report a sense of currency, concludes: "The smoke of the artillery hangs low on the buff-brown moor. There are German assaults at Malancourt and toward the Hauts de Meuse. But the great attack is over. Both sides know it. Verdun is beyond all question out of danger."[6] A second piece, "The Vineyard of Red Wine," appeared in the August edition of *The Atlantic* and supplemented Beston's description of what he had seen during the battle of Verdun. The article included a chilling account, which he had also used in one of the articles published in the *Boston Sunday Post* a few months earlier, of a French lieutenant leading a group of men in search of a missing soldier at the battle for Fort Douamont and discovering several dying German soldiers in the bomb crater where they also found their wounded comrade. One of the Germans begged the officer to kill them and put them out of their agony. The horrified officer refused, but the German continued to plead until he relented. After taking their comrade back to the trenches, the officer returned with a dozen hand grenades and dropped them one by one into the crater until the moans of the wounded men ceased.[7]

The intense interest of the American public in what was going on in Europe led the distinguished Boston publishing house of Houghton Mifflin to offer Beston his first book contract for a memoir about his experiences on the western front. The catch was that, given the topicality of Beston's subject matter, he had to submit the manuscript in just a few months. Drawing from his wartime notes and reusing material that he had published previously in the *Boston Sunday Post* and *The Atlantic Monthly*, Beston managed to meet the abbreviated publishing deadline and his first book, *A Volunteer Poilu*, came out in October 1916. For the most part, Beston eschewed any sweeping statements on the war, its causes, or its conduct, focusing instead on what he had personally seen or had heard from other eyewitnesses. Despite his family ties to France and a strong sense of fraternity with the French soldiers with whom he had served, Beston maintained a semblance of journalistic neutrality; while he expressed outrage at atrocities perpetrated by the Germans in Belgium and occupied France, he was careful not to present the war as a false dichotomy between the forces of good and evil. He was also quick to acknowledge the resolute bravery of soldiers on both sides. The book reflects one of Beston's great strengths as a writer, his remarkable talent for description. In later years, Beston would shrug off his writing during this period as mere "journalism," and in comparison to his later, more literary efforts this self-assessment has some merit.[8] When writing what he considered to be literary work, Beston was careful and precise in his choice of language, and wrote painstakingly slowly. In contrast, he completed *A Volunteer Poilu* in less than six months, while simultaneously producing articles and lectures.

Beston realized that the conflict in Europe signaled a sea change in the manner in which warfare would be conducted in the twentieth century. The full mobilization of industrial states at war meant that civilian populations were now at risk, and on the battlefield itself trench warfare and the introduction of horrific new weapons produced mind-numbing casualty figures. "A future historian," he wrote in *A Volunteer Poilu*, "may find the war more interesting, when considered as the supreme achievement of the industrial civilization of the nineteenth and twentieth centuries, than as a mere vortex in the age-old ocean of European political strife."[9] While it might be argued from the perspective of the early twenty-first century that it was the Second World War, with its death camps and atomic bombs, that represented the "supreme achievement" of modern industrial civilization, Beston was correct in realizing that this was a new type of conflict. The industrial infrastructure of the combatants spewed forth a seemingly limitless series of innovations in weapons of destruction. Poison gas, machine guns, tanks, zeppelins, airplanes, flame-throwers, and numerous other weapons were put into mass production by the warring nations, and the Germans used their remarkable railway system to rapidly shift troops and supplies between two fronts. Beston was unstinting in his portrayal of the war's horrors. In his first article for the *Sunday Post* he described a new malady that had appeared among the frontline troops on both sides, a condition resulting from the pulverizing artillery barrages that had become a commonplace of trench warfare:

> More than once I had men without a scratch but suffering from the horrible shell-madness, brought on by the continuous bombardment. A struggling form would be lifted from the ground by three or four soldiers. Even as the stricken soldier battled with his comrades, there would issue from his lips a weird imitation of the swishing noise of a shell in its flight.
>
> Into the ambulance would tumble the struggling mass, and off I would dash, my little "flivver" rocking back and forth from the struggle inside as the accompanying soldiers endeavored to restrain the maddened man.[10]

The following week, in the second installment of the *Boston Sunday Post* series, Beston described another incident where he saw something odd hanging from a tree; upon closer inspection the object proved to be a human heart.[11]

Beston's primary focus in *A Volunteer Poilu* and his war correspondence was, of course, on the horrors of war; even the occasional humorous anecdote tends to be ironic or used as a reflection of the grim gallows humor of those on the front lines. One such incident occurred soon after he arrived in Pont-à-Mousson, when he was caught out in the street one day just as a German artillery attack commenced. He dove into a dark passageway, and when the next shell burst he was surprised to hear a voice behind him call out "Park Street." He turned around and found three other Bostonians taking cover from the attack. As each shell hit, one of the men would call out a stop on the Boston subway line. When the fifth shell whistled by, he sang out "Central Square, we're on the way back." A moment later, an enormous shell exploded near the passageway, and the men were knocked off their feet and showered with debris. As they got up and dusted themselves off, the station caller ruefully remarked, "I guess I was mistaken. That stop must have been pretty close to Mt. Auburn Cemetery."[12]

After the publication of *A Volunteer Poilu*, Beston took a break from writing for several months. He delivered a series of lectures to benefit the Ambulance Service and—probably due in part to the influence of his wartime *marraine*, Mabel Davison—a relief fund set up to aid soldiers who had been blinded, most of whom had been exposed to poison gas.[13] In the meantime, reviews had come in for *A Volunteer Poilu*, and Beston was gratified to see that they were overwhelmingly positive. The reviewer in *Catholic World*, for example, wrote that "[i]t is not only trench life that this little volume treats; many other phases are illuminatingly touched upon. It is all admirably written and holds the attention closely."[14] Another reviewer praised Beston's "[a]dmirably written sketches giving an excellent interpretation of the French private soldier in the trench and in action."[15] The reviewer in the popular magazine *The Outlook* said that the book was a "well-written, human account of the author's experiences as an ambulance driver, and is filled with the humor and pathos of life at the front," although he couched his praise somewhat by calling the work a "distinct though not considerable contribution to the war literature contributed by Americans who have taken part in the struggle."[16]

The number of significant literary figures who served as ambulance drivers during the Great War is impressive, and is a phenomenon that was largely unique to that conflict. The list of literary volunteers includes American writers such as Ernest Hemingway, E. E. Cummings, John Dos Passos, Malcolm Cowley, and numerous others. Critics have pointed out that the enthusiasm for the ambulance service shared by these writers was not indicative of a desire to avoid active service, since many of them volunteered before the United States entered the war. Some, like Hemingway—and this probably applies to the astigmatic Beston as well—were eager to serve, but would not have passed the physical test for entrance into the armed forces because of their weak eyesight. Others, like Dos Passos were willing to serve but were not willing to kill in order to do so. It has also been suggested by

The Violence and Imbecilities of Men

Arlen Hansen that the ambulance drivers, many of whom were products of an Ivy League education, were treated as "gentlemen volunteers" akin to officers; had they enlisted in the army as privates, they would have served under far different conditions.

Given the attention paid by critics to this group of volunteers, it is rather surprising to see that the name of Henry Beston is rarely included. This seems particularly odd since Beston was one of the earliest to volunteer and spent far more time at the front than many of his more celebrated literary contemporaries, including Hemingway. In Arlen J. Hansen's *Gentlemen Volunteers: The Story of the American Ambulance Drivers in the Great War, August 1914 September 1918*, Beston (or rather, Sheahan) is barely mentioned except for a fictionalized version of an incident described in *A Volunteer Poilu*.[17] In the introduction to *Gentlemen Volunteers*, George Plimpton names numerous literary figures linked to the ambulance service in the Great War, including some that were only fleetingly connected, but once again Henry Beston is overlooked. The same omission is made on websites dedicated to the literary volunteers and in most articles about them. It seems highly unlikely that the reason for this oversight is intentional depreciation of Beston's work with the American Field Service or as a slight to his literary reputation. In fact, it is probably indicative simply of a failure to realize that the "Henry Sheahan" who served in France and wrote *A Volunteer Poilu* did not simply disappear after writing his memoir of the western front, but gained literary fame under a different name.

After war was declared by the European powers in August 1914, the American public and their elected representatives closely followed developments in Europe, particularly the war on the western front. The aspect of the war that affected America most directly, however, was not the ground war in Europe, but the naval contest in the Atlantic. The British blockade of German ports was a source of irritation to the Americans, but it had not resulted in the destruction of any merchant ships from neutral countries. This was not the case with the German U-boats, and it was becoming more and more difficult for the German chancellor, Theobald von Bethmann-Hollweg, to fend off the growing chorus of influential voices in the Kaiser's government and military calling for the resumption of unrestricted

[65]

submarine warfare. By the fall of 1916, military setbacks for the Germans at Verdun and the Somme in France and a renewed Russian offensive on the eastern front, combined with growing food shortages and hardship at home led many Germans to question why they shouldn't avail themselves of their primary naval weapon, one that would cause the English and French to suffer the same deprivation that the British blockade had caused the German people. Bethmann-Hollweg, however, understood what many in the German military did not; freedom of the seas was the issue upon which Woodrow Wilson had tied his entire moral and political rationale for neutrality. American outrage over highly publicized submarine attacks on neutral shipping, such as the sinking of the *Lusitania*, had been ameliorated by the German pledge to halt unrestricted submarine warfare, and Wilson had—over and over again during the presidential campaign—reiterated his position that, while his strong preference was to keep the United States out of the war, the resumption of unrestricted submarine warfare would not be tolerated by the American people.

On December 22, 1916, Admiral von Holtzendorff, the German chief of the Naval Staff, who had previously sided with Bethmann-Hollweg on the issue of unrestricted submarine warfare, sent a memorandum to Field Marshall Paul von Hindenburg and the Supreme Command in which he reversed his position and called for an immediate resumption of unrestricted submarine warfare. He wrote that this step was necessary "if the war is not to end in the exhaustion of all parties and consequently disastrously for us. Of our enemies, Italy and France are economically so hard hit that it is only by the energy and force of England that they are still kept on their feet. If we can break England's back, the war will immediately be decided in our favor."[18] Holtzendorff claimed that a U-boat offensive that attacked, without warning, any ship found in the war zone, would sink 600,000 tons of shipping per month and, within a matter of months, force England and the Allies to their knees. Shortly thereafter, Kaiser Wilhelm issued an order to his Supreme Command to resume unrestricted submarine warfare which began on February 1, 1917. When an Associated Press bulletin announcing the German decision was handed to President Wilson by his secretary, the shaken Wilson murmured "This means war."[19]

The Violence and Imbecilities of Men

President Wilson broke off relations with Germany on February 3, but was still reluctant to take the next step and call for a declaration of war on Germany in the absence of any overt act of hostility on the part of the Germans. Two events later that month made it impossible for Wilson to continue his policy of neutrality. The first was the revelation that the Kaiser's foreign secretary, Arthur Zimmermann, had sent a telegram to the German minister in Mexico ordering him to secretly inform the Mexican president that Germany would soon resume unrestricted submarine warfare and offering an alliance with the Germans against the United States. In return, once the Allies were defeated, Germany would reward Mexico with territory in Texas, New Mexico, and Arizona. The telegram was intercepted and decoded by British Intelligence, who passed it along to the American government. When the State Department released the contents of the telegram to the press on March 1, 1917, public reaction was predictable. In March, the other shoe dropped when four American merchant ships were sunk by U-boats. With that, American entry into the conflict became a foregone conclusion; Theodore Roosevelt wrote to his friend and political ally Henry Cabot Lodge, "If he [Wilson] does not go to war, I shall skin him alive."[20] On April 6, 1917, the United States formally declared war on Germany.

Admiral William S. Sims, tall and white-haired, a career navy man who had been sent secretly to England shortly before the official declaration of war by the American government, was charged with the task of coordinating American naval operations with those of the British Navy. On April 10, 1917, Sims met with Admiral John Jellicoe, commander of the British fleet, who showed him the tally of British and neutral shipping losses since February. Sims was shocked by the figures. When he asked Jellicoe about them, the British commander confirmed that it would be impossible for Britain to go on with the war much longer if the U-boats were not speedily neutralized. Sims realized that if France and Britain surrendered, the United States would be left alone to fight a German Atlantic fleet that was superior to anything the United States could put to sea. He immediately cabled President Wilson with a request for thirty destroyers. On April 13 he was informed that six destroyers were on their way with more to follow. The destroyers were to serve as escorts for convoys of merchant ships crossing the dangerous seas of the Atlantic war zone, a tactic that had already achieved encouraging success on a limited scale. The convoy method not only improved the chances that the merchant ships would reach port, but they also lured U-boats in where Allied destroyers and other anti-submarine craft could attack and destroy them. The primary obstacle to employing this method in the great Atlantic shipping lanes had been a dearth of destroyers—and the American entrance into the war solved this difficulty. Beginning in May, American battleships began arriving in Queenstown, the Irish naval port that would serve as the primary terminus for joint British-American naval operations in the Atlantic. By the end of July 1917, thirty-seven American warships were based in Queenstown.[21]

Meanwhile, the response to Beston's first book and his articles had been so encouraging that he had spent much of early 1917 casting about for another major writing project. Understanding the crucial importance of the war at sea, sometime early in the autumn of 1917, Beston contacted Ellery Sedgwick, the editor of *The Atlantic Monthly*, inquiring whether the magazine might be interested in a series of articles on the United States Navy. Sedgwick expressed interest and wrote a letter of support for him that read in part, "Mr. Henry Sheahan, a valued contributor to *The Atlantic*, who has made excellent use of his opportunities for writing on the French front and elsewhere, now desires the privilege of gathering material for stories taken from the Naval Service of the United States . . . Mr. Sheahan has, in his relations with this magazine, always proved himself discreet and reliable, and we hope that his present efforts may meet with help and success."[22] Beston then wrote to the Secretary of the Navy, Josephus Daniels, asking the Secretary for permission to cover the operations of the Atlantic fleet in its efforts against the German U-boats. Secretary Daniels agreed and wrote a letter to Admiral Sims recommending that Beston be permitted to report on the Navy's operations for *The Atlantic*.

Beston's timing for a work about the U.S. Navy could not have been better; when America entered the conflict it was the war in the Atlantic that first drew everyone's attention. If the British and Americans failed to neutralize the U-boat threat, not only supply ships but troop carriers

Beston as a twenty-nine-year-old war correspondent for *The Atlantic Monthly* with Allied Fleet's "Grand Armada," based at Scapa Flow in Scotland, 1917.

ferrying American forces to the front would be endangered. By April 1918, Beston was with the American fleet commanded by Rear Admiral Hugh Rodman at the British naval base at Scapa Flow in the Orkney Islands. The flagship of the American contingent was the USS *New York,* a coal-burning dreadnought with fourteen-inch guns that had been commissioned in 1914 and sailed under the command of Captain Charles F. Hughes, a fifty-one-year-old native of Bath, Maine.[23] The *New York* and five other American ships formed the Sixth Battle Squadron of the British Grand Fleet, and had arrived in Britain early in December 1917. When Beston reached Scapa Flow in April 1918 he was assigned to the *New York*. The ship's chaplain, a Methodist minister named J. Luther Neff, who was to become a lifelong friend of Beston's, later recalled how they first met:

> In April Henry Beston Sheahan, a correspondent with the *Atlantic Monthly* press, joined our ship on his round of the Naval Bases in European waters. Admiral Rodman, who didn't particularly care for 'writer fellers,' asked me to be Sheahan's host while he was aboard. Fortunately, in this period, the Fleet put to sea—a most impressive sight and experience—and we steamed the old Viking route eastward to Norway and the mouth of the Baltic Sea. Henry and I became good friends during those days together in the North Sea, and the stimulating talk sessions in my cabin in the evenings.[24]

For the next four months Beston traveled with the fleet, writing articles for *The Atlantic* and for other periodicals such as the *North American Review* and *The Outlook*. Despite Admiral Rodman's suspicion of "writer fellers," Beston was received warmly by the crews he stayed with during his time with the fleet, and he struck up lasting friendships with a number of the men, including Reverend Neff and several of his comrades on board the USS *New York*. Much of Beston's time was spent with the American destroyers and sub chasers, but he also had an opportunity to visit the aviators at a naval air base in southern England, talk to men whose ships had been torpedoed, and interview an enormous variety of specialists within the fleet—marines, signalmen, and members of the merchant fleet and the armed guard. Beston was particularly fascinated by the American submarine fleet, and when he was invited to come along with one of the submarine crews on a training mission he was enthralled by the experience, writing "there is no more thrilling game in the world than the game of periscope *vs.* periscope."[25]

In the late summer of 1918, Beston returned once again to Massachusetts, splitting time between his rooms at the Parson Capen House in Topsfield and the family home in Quincy while he worked on turning the notes from his months with the Navy into magazine articles and his second book, *Full Speed Ahead: Tales from the Log of a Correspondent with Our Navy*. Not long after returning home, he received the news that his friend Major Ted Roosevelt Jr., who was leading a combat battalion in the U.S. Army on the western front, had been with his battalion when they were hit with a poison gas attack. Ted's wife Eleanor, who was working with the YMCA in Paris at the time, was shocked at her husband's appearance when he unexpectedly visited her in Paris: "His face was scorched and inflamed, the whites of his eyes an angry red. He was thickly covered in dust and had a wracking cough."[26] Ted's younger brother Archie, the third son of the former president and an officer in Ted's battalion, had also been severely wounded, and was still in a Paris hospital. After visiting his brother, Ted returned to the front, but was back in a Parisian hospital in July after suffering a gunshot wound at a battle near Soissons. The worst news was yet to come for the Roosevelt family; in late July the youngest of Theodore Roosevelt's four sons, Quentin, an aviator in the U.S. Army, was shot down behind the German lines. A true believer in the cause for which his son had died, the former President wrote in a letter to his daughter-in-law Belle Willard Roosevelt (the wife of his second son, Kermit), "I would not for all the world have had him fail fearlessly to do his duty, and to tread his allotted path, high of heart, even although it led to the gates of death. But it is useless for me to pretend that it is not very bitter to see that good, gallant, tenderhearted boy leave life at its crest."[27] Quentin Roosevelt was just twenty-one years old at the time of his death.

Amid the sorrows of wartime loss, there were moments of joy. Henry's brother George, a surgeon with the Harvard Surgical Unit attached to the British Expeditionary Force in 1916 (which served with distinction during the first battle of the Somme) had come back to Quincy to resume the medical practice established by his late father. He was soon recalled to active duty; on September 1, 1918, he was commissioned a captain in the medical corps of the United States Army and assigned to the base hospital at Camp Lee in Virginia, where he spent much of the next six months performing reconstructive surgery on soldiers who had been wounded overseas. Before he left for Virginia, however, he asked a local girl, Marie Magee, to marry him; on November 2, 1918, they were wed in Quincy, with Henry serving as best man. As a token of his fraternal affection, Beston dedicated *Full Speed Ahead* to his brother George.

As was the case with his first book, Beston worked quickly and efficiently on *Full Speed Ahead*, recasting most of the material published in the magazines as chapters in the new book. *Full Speed Ahead*, which was the first book he published under the surname "Beston," is not straight journalism in the usual sense, but is more of a collection of impressions and stories of the war at sea, particularly as it related to the efforts to neutralize the German U-boat fleet. Part of this is due to the fact that Beston was what would later be referred to as an "embedded reporter," and was therefore prohibited from providing too much specific information about what he saw. Indeed, it is evident that Beston often identifies more closely with the sailors on board the ships to which he was assigned than with the press. For example, on the night of April 22–23, 1918, Beston was on board one of the ships assigned to the Grand Fleet when news came of the British raid on the German submarine base at Zeebrugge. The men were ordered "to keep our knowledge to ourselves. As a result we spoke of it at breakfast with bated breath. I myself, a modest person, was stricken with a sudden access of importance at possessing a Grand Fleet secret."[28] Beston goes on to castigate those members of the press who were less discreet about keeping such secrets, writing, "The thing that *we* [the sailors] have most against *it* [the press], however, is *its* conduct during the great offensive in the spring of 1918" [emphasis added].[29] This is not to say that Beston accepted military censorship without question—he scoffed that at times the press was not permitted to mention that water was wet for fear of providing this information to the enemy.[30]

As was the case with *A Volunteer Poilu*, the descriptive talent that is one of the hallmarks of Beston's writing in later works such as *The Outermost House* is again evident in *Full Speed Ahead*. One such example is in the chapter entitled "The End of a Submarine," where he describes a submarine hunt that he witnessed while aboard an American destroyer. The destroyer was moving into position to escort a convoy when a U-boat's periscope was spotted about three hundred yards away. The general quarters alarm was sounded and the ship raced toward the submarine. The destroyer then "began a beautiful manœuvre," writes Beston, placing a buoy near the place where the submarine had last been spotted before submerging, then dropping a series of depth charges along the projected path of the U-boat. For several hours, nothing more was seen of the submarine, until a report came in from another destroyer that signs of oil coming to the surface had been spotted. When Beston's destroyer returned to the scene of the morning's battle, he saw:

> a great area defiled by the bodies of fish, purple T.N.T. dust and various bits of muddy wreckage which the explosions had shaken free from the ooze. Gulls, already attracted to the spot, were circling about uttering hoarse cries. In the heart of this disturbed area lay a great still pool of shining water and into this pool, from somewhere in the depths, huge bubbles of molasses-brown oil were rising. Reaching the surface, these bubbles spread into filmy pan cakes round whose edges little waves curled and broke.[31]

Vivid and straightforward, the understated description evokes an eerie, chilling sense of the terrible events that must have transpired under the waves.

A significant difference between *Full Speed Ahead* and Beston's earlier account of his experiences as an ambulance driver in *A Volunteer Poilu* arises from his reliance on interviews and other secondary sources in his work about the naval service. Much of the material in *Full Speed Ahead* was told to Beston by the men—officers and ordinary seamen—that he met. While the formal interviews that Beston conducted with commanders such as Sims and Rodman are somewhat stilted due to their reluctance to share information with a reporter, his conversations with junior officers and ordinary seamen yielded more interesting material. Although Beston was far better educated than most of the sailors, his friendly, open nature and obvious admiration for them and their mission gained their trust and cooperation.

There are numerous anecdotes in *Full Speed Ahead* that come directly from the sailors themselves but are related so well and clearly by Beston that it feels as though he actually witnessed the event rather than merely hearing about it. He is particularly skillful at removing himself from a setting such as when the sailors gather together in the mess hall or the wardroom and exchange stories. In one chapter a group of officers on board ship recalled a three-day storm that hit the American flotilla during their ocean crossing in December 1917, and Beston lets the story unfold through dialogue, straight from the officers themselves. The result is a fine description of a dangerous yet thrilling tempest at sea that makes the reader feel as though he too is sitting in that wardroom.

There is also a marked change in authorial tone between *A Volunteer Poilu* and *Full Speed Ahead*. Beston's partisanship, his identification with the Allied cause, is far more evident in *Full Speed Ahead* and at times he seems uncomfortably close to becoming a cheerleader for the Allies, something he was largely successful in avoiding in his first book. Adjectives such as "resolute" and "gallant" are often attached to his descriptions of the British and American sailors, while the disparaging "Hun" is frequently used in referring to the Germans. He pointedly mentions that newcomers to the Queenstown naval base are brought to see the nearby *Lusitania* cemetery, "a gruesome pilgrimage to which both British and American tars are horridly partial," and one that served as a stark reminder of German atrocities against civilian shipping.[32] The harsher tone was undoubtedly due partly to the fact that the United States was now an active combatant in the war, and partly to the German resumption of unrestricted submarine warfare, which Beston—like most Americans—saw as an act of barbarism, denouncing it as an "infamous policy."[33] In one chapter, Beston describes an incident where he was aboard a destroyer responding to a merchant ship's distress call. They arrive just in time to see the sailors rescued by another ship and the merchant ship itself slide under the waves. The attack was, Beston wrote, "an act more terrible than murder, more base than assassination."[34] Beston was also cognizant of the fact that he was essentially a guest of the navy, and the book contains numerous acknowledgments of the courtesies extended to him. As would be the case many years later with the "embedded reporters" covering the Iraq War, such a situation can lead to an identification with the military that compromises the impartiality of the reporter.

When it came to deciding which branch of military service he preferred, Beston made no pretensions to impartiality. In a conversation with Chaplain Neff included in the book, he frankly states that, "The very idea of being with the Grand Fleet is thrilling. It's the experience of a lifetime . . . no sight of the land war can match the impressiveness and grandeur of the first view of the fleet."[35] In the final chapter of *Full Speed Ahead*, "On Having Been both a Soldier and a Sailor," Beston compared the two and unequivocally declared his preference for the navy.[36] In later years, Beston was fond of wearing a sailor's tunic, finding them to be "the most comfortable thing in the world to write in."[37] His partiality for the navy, Beston confessed, was "coloured by a passion for the beauty and the mystery of the sea with which some good spirit endowed me in my cradle. I was born in one of the most historic of New England seacoast towns where brine was anciently said to flow through the veins of the inhabitants. . . . So I admit a bias for the service of the sea."[38] Technically speaking, it must be averred that he was neither a soldier nor a sailor, despite his identification with the latter class of servicemen.

The reviews for *Full Speed Ahead: Tales from the Log of a Correspondent with Our Navy* were once again strongly favorable. The response of the reviewer from the *American Library Association Booklist* was appreciative and accurate: "[t]he stories are often breathless with excitement, they are full of information and they pay the navy a fine tribute."[39] There were a few mixed reviews, such as that from Illinois's *Springfield Republican*, which concluded that the book was "full of spirit, but without distinction."[40] Oddly enough, the chief criticism—in fact, one of the few substantive criticisms—leveled against the book was that Beston was occasionally guilty of being too "literary." The reviewer from *The New York Times*, for example, wrote: "Except for the occasional intrusions of 'fine writing,' the log sets forth calmly a breathless succession of the perils which beset our boys in hunting down the Hun seawolf that keeps one reading hard to the very end. It is as exciting a tale of the sea as any fictionist has given us, and with the added strength that it is true."[41]

A few months before *Full Speed Ahead* came out in March 1919, the cataclysmic events in Europe were drawing a final curtain on the pre-war era. Nicholas II, the last czar of Russia, and his family were murdered, and in November 1917 the Bolsheviks swept to power. The czar's deposal was merely the forerunner to the epochal changes that took place the following year. As British, French, and American forces took the offensive, the exhausted Central Powers finally collapsed. In late October, the Ottoman Empire signed an armistice with the Allies, followed by Austria-Hungary on November 3. Less than a week later, Kaiser Wilhelm II abdicated the throne, and fled into exile in the Netherlands. On the morning of November 11, 1918, in a railroad car in the forest of Compiegne approximately fifty miles northeast of Paris, a German delegation met with the Allied Supreme Commander Ferdinand Foch. Later that morning—eleven o'clock on November 11, 1918—the guns finally fell silent in Europe and around the globe as an armistice ending the Great War was declared. Over nine million people had perished during the four years of war, and now the autocratic regimes that had initiated the war had perished as well, victims of what Beston castigated as "the violence and imbecilities of men."[42]

CHAPTER FOUR

Weary of Armageddon
1919–1923

O what fine thought we had because we thought
That the worst rogues and rascals had died out.
All teeth were drawn, all ancient tricks unlearned,
And a great army but a showy thing;
What matter that no cannon had been turned
Into a ploughshare?

WILLIAM BUTLER YEATS
"1919"

WHILE BESTON and most of the world rejoiced in the cessation of hostilities between the warring parties in Europe, the armistice did not end the political chaos and enormous suffering caused by the conflict and its aftermath. Europe was filled with soldiers who had been maimed, blinded, or mentally unbalanced by the terrible carnage of modern industrial warfare. New nations tentatively emerged from the rubble of old empires. In early 1919, the victorious Allies began negotiations for a formal peace treaty with the newly formed German government that had taken power after the abdication of the Kaiser. The Treaty of Versailles, which was so complex and contentious that it was not formally ratified until June 1919, was a far cry from the Fourteen Points proposed by President Wilson as the basis for a lasting peace.[1] Indeed, the terms of the treaty were so punitive that they inspired bitter resentment in Germany. Among other things, the treaty stipulated that the Germans reduce their army to 100,000 men and pay war reparations to the Allies in the amount of 269 billion marks. The reparation figure was later reduced to 132 billion marks, but the amount was so astronomical that it stunned the Germans, and would have taken over fifty years to repay. By 1921 the German economy and monetary system had collapsed, bringing on a period of hyperinflation in the early 1920s that doomed the post-war Weimar Republic and contributed to the rise of Adolf Hitler's National Socialists. The situation in Russia was also dire; after the overthrow of the czar in 1917, a provisional government headed by Alexander Kerensky was formed, but by November 1917 Lenin's Bolsheviks had ousted the Kerensky government. Concerned by Russia's withdrawal from the war and by the enormous amounts of munitions that had been shipped by the Allies to Russia (and were now in danger of being appropriated by the Bolsheviks) the Allies sent an armed force into Russia in the summer of 1918 to assist the pro-czarist White Army forces against the Bolsheviks. Allied soldiers remained in Russia until late 1920, when they were finally forced to withdraw in the face of a series of military successes by the Red Army.

As hard as it might be for a war-weary populace to comprehend, things were about to get even worse. In early 1918, a virulent strain of influenza appeared on the continent; in May of that year, it was reported that eight million people had died in Spain due to the virus. The "Spanish Flu," as it came to be known, raced through Europe and then the world. By the end of 1918, the second wave of the pandemic hit the United States, first appearing in Boston and then diffusing at a calamitous pace over the rest of the country. In its annual report the *Journal of the American Medical Association* averred that 1918 was notable: "a year momentous as the termination of the most cruel war in the annals of the human race; a year which marked the end, at least for a time, of man's destruction of man; [but] unfortunately a year in which developed a most fatal infectious disease causing the deaths of hundreds of thousands of human beings."[2] Influenza is generally most dangerous for the very young and the very old; the Spanish flu hit people aged 15–34 unusually hard, with one researcher estimating the mortality rate for people in this age group to be twenty times higher than in previous outbreaks of influenza.[3] Approximately 675,000 Americans died from the flu outbreak and worldwide fatalities are estimated at 20–40 million—more deaths than were suffered on wartime battlefields, and more than in what was previously considered to be the world's most virulent pandemic, the "Black Death" of the mid-fourteenth century.[4]

While the United States was geographically distant from the ongoing troubles in Europe, the war and the influenza epidemic had graphically demonstrated to the American people that they were not insulated from events in Europe and the rest of the world. Events in Russia led to increased fear of political radicalism spawned by foreigners living in the United States and a series of laws targeting aliens were enacted, culminating in the Sedition Act of 1918. In April 1919 a plot allegedly instigated by politically radical immigrants to send mail bombs to American business leaders and government officials, including Attorney General A. Mitchell Palmer and Supreme Court Justice Oliver Wendell Holmes, was uncovered. In *Political Hysteria in America: The Democratic Capacity for Repression*, historian Murray B. Levin describes the Red Scare of the post-war period as "a nationwide anti-radical hysteria provoked by a mounting fear and anxiety that a Bolshevik revolution in America was imminent—a revolution that would destroy property, church, home, marriage, civility, and the American way of life."[5] This period initiated the deeply ingrained anti-communist fervor that would become a part of American national character and policies for the remainder of the twentieth century.

Against this backdrop of a troubled post-war world, Henry Beston must have felt that he had been singularly blessed. Handsome, well-educated, and with two favorably received books to his credit, he was still just thirty-one years old. He had survived his service on the western front physically unscathed—something that should not be discounted thanks to a mistaken belief that ambulance drivers were somehow immune to harm due to their status as noncombatants. Beston's views on the war and its implications for the modern world were still coalescing, but in the meantime, his third article for *The Atlantic Monthly*, "With the American Submarine Fleet," came out in November 1918; it was the first of his articles to appear under the name Henry Beston. On January 3, 1919, he received notification that the French government had awarded him the American Field Service Medal in token of his service to France—an honor that meant a great deal to Beston.[6]

At this point in Beston's life his needs were few and his financial circumstances were fairly comfortable; he and his brother George shared the house at 12 School Street in Quincy that they had inherited from their father along with a modest cash estate. For a taste of city life, or when George and his wife Marie were away, Henry would often stay at the Hotel Touraine, a beautiful building in the French Renaissance style located at the corner of Tremont and Boylston Streets in Boston, conveniently close to the theater district. Once spring arrived, Beston returned to his rooms at the Parson Capen House in Topsfield, where he resided on the second floor, leaving the first floor of the historic home open for visitors. This would be his regular lodging pattern for the next several years.

Working on *Full Speed Ahead* helped keep the thought of his friends still serving in the United States Navy fresh in Beston's mind. He carried on a regular correspondence with some of them, including Chaplain Neff and signalman Cressy Phinney (referred to as "Idaho" in *Full Speed Ahead*) from the USS *New York*. As he wrote to Neff, "I can't be more of a Navy man if I'd been born in the boiler room, cradled in the galley, and come to maturity as a Bo'sun. When I see the great ships in the harbor, I feel that I am a secret sharer of their life, and look back to my service with the Navy of the United States as *the* episode of my life."[7] Beston regularly sent packages of "goodies" and books to his former hosts, who in return would send him news and greetings from old shipboard friends and occasionally procure for him the naval tunics to which he was so partial. Phinney, who had been transferred to the Bay Ridge Barracks in Brooklyn, wrote chatty letters to Beston with news of some of his former shipmates. "Pop" Mehrer, Phinney reported, was "still the same old "Pop": [he] is still firmly determined to go in the pig business as soon as he gets out of the Navy. Ha Ha! Wouldn't he look great in a grove of pig-trees?"[8] As soon as *Full Speed Ahead* was published, Beston hastened to send copies out to Neff, Phinney, and other shipboard friends, writing to Neff, "You'll find yourself in it. I did my friendly best for you, though I did not reveal your incognito."[9]

A few months later, Beston was pleased to hear that the book had been very well received by his naval buddies. Phinney wrote to Beston lavishly praising the book and stating, "All of my 'Gob' friends who have seen the book are trying to borrow it. It is very popular with them. Perhaps the publishers would do well to advertise in a Navy magazine." In thanking Beston for his portrayal in the book, Phinney self-deprecatingly wrote, "I fear anyone who knows me will never recognize me in the word-picture you have painted, for 'intelligence,' upon which you bear so strongly, is one of my minus qualities. Like the tin man in the Sunday cartoons, 'Brains I have nil.' But I hope to get them someday, if I keep pegging." Phinney's modesty notwithstanding, the nineteen-year-old mariner was a sharp enough reader to notice Beston's tendency to repeatedly use favorite words: "Whereas the descriptions are fine, I was several times somewhat startled by the sudden appearance of the adjective 'romantic' applied to objects which made it look a trifle incongruous in my eyes. I hope you'll forgive me mentioning it, but it made me feel as though my enthusiasm over the thing described was being forced, and I think it should be lead gently on instead."[10] Phinney would probably have been surprised to learn that a reviewer for *The Harvard Graduates' Magazine* had recently made the same point in an otherwise laudatory review of the book: "There are also moments when the 'pet word'—like 'thundering,' 'solemn,' or 'horribly'—seems a trifle overworked. Yet when a book has so distinctive a color and flavor as this one, it is a dangerous business to begin suggesting its improvement by the omission of individual strokes."[11]

Just weeks after receiving this letter from his young friend, Beston was stunned to receive word that Phinney had suddenly died of sepsis. He immediately wrote a letter of condolence to Cressy's mother in Caldwell, Idaho, praising his young friend's "high chivalry of ideals . . . [and] steadfast adherence to them." Beston also promised to send her a copy of *Full Speed Ahead* with its references to her son, "Idaho."[12] Mrs. Phinney's response was poignant in her heartfelt gratitude: "Your letter of Aug. 9th at hand and oh! I thank you for your kindness and thoughtfulness. I have read and re-read, drinking in the life of every word of it, for it is food for a mother's soul. No friend could pay a more beautiful tribute to another . . . Those letters are as healing balm to an aching heart; I thank you for your kindness and thoughtfulness. Testimonials of love, esteem and respect from those who recognized his clean, pure soul."[13] Cressy Phinney was buried at the Canyon

Hill Cemetery on the outskirts of his hometown of Caldwell, Idaho. For several years, Beston regularly corresponded with Phinney's heartbroken mother, who repeatedly expressed deep gratitude for Beston's friendship with her son: "I was much pleased [to receive your letter]—Because you had not forgotten me, I knew that the memory of Cressy was still in your heart."[14]

In the summer of 1919 Luther Neff and Helen Frisch, whose father was minister of the First Methodist Church in San Diego, were engaged to be married. After two and half years in the Navy, Neff had come to the conclusion that service as a navy chaplain was no longer the life for him—he longed to be with Helen and settled in a home and parish. He submitted his letter of resignation to the navy and prepared for his return to civilian life as a student at the Boston University School of Theology. Beston promptly wrote to congratulate him: "Lucky fellow, but then sailor folk are always well seen of the fairer sex; we poor literary rogues, whose lives smack of typewriters, proof sheets, shears and paste pots, never are so well regarded." The letter included an article that Beston had recently published about the Parson Capen House, along with an earnest entreaty for Neff to visit: "You must come and visit my old house at Topsfield. I am sending you herewith a copy of a magazine which has an article by H.B.B. on his own dwelling, It's really very odd, old, and pleasant, an excellent Jap. houseman looks after things and, I suppose, keeps an eye on me to see what I am printing. There are wide fields and roads everywhere about, BUT—I am lonely for the sea . . . [b]eing a New Englander, I have brine in my blood."[15]

On the professional front, Beston's work with *The Atlantic Monthly* had impressed its editor-in-chief Ellery Sedgwick sufficiently to offer him a full time job as editor of the *Living Age*, an *Atlantic* publication housed at 41 Mount Vernon Street in Boston. The *Living Age*, founded in 1844 (from 1844–1900 it was also known as *Littell's Living Age*), was an old and quite conservative weekly magazine that had been purchased by *The Atlantic Monthly* in early 1918.[16] The magazine was a mix of reprinted articles (many of which were originally published in British periodicals) and original work, and it was Beston's job to cull through the possibilities then select and edit his choices for publication. Beston's duties at the *Living Age* were not particularly demanding; as he disparagingly described it in a letter to Luther Neff, it consisted of "editing, reading, writing, bullying aspiring poets and budding authors, refusing "Beautiful Snow," "To a Daisy," et al. et al."[17]

The relatively easy work at the magazine did enable him, however, to maintain an ambitious writing schedule. Even before shipping the galleys for *Full Speed Ahead* off to Doubleday in early 1919, Beston had commenced another writing project, albeit one far removed from his war correspondence—indeed, one unlike anything else he had written before. As he wrote to Luther Neff, the new book was to be "a kind of wonder book a la Alice in Wonderland. Weary of Armageddon, I fled as far away from it as I could. You'll find the sea in it . . . romantic galleons, wild dark coasts, enchanted surges, palaces on the mountains on the ocean floor."[18] Some of the ideas for the fairy tales that Beston was working on for the new book had probably begun to take form in Beston's mind several months earlier, but it was not until early 1919 that he began to seriously consider the possibility of putting together a children's book. He astutely took advantage of his *Atlantic Monthly* connection and submitted a book proposal to The Atlantic Monthly Press, which was readily accepted.

The illustrator chosen by the publisher for the book was Maurice E. "Jake" Day, a twenty-six-year-old artist from Damariscotta, Maine. The choice was a fortuitous one; not only because Jake Day was an immensely talented artist and illustrator at the outset of a brilliant career, but because he and Beston immediately formed a productive literary and artistic partnership and a fast friendship that would become one of the most important of Beston's life and career. As Beston finished the revisions for each chapter he would immediately ship the story to Day for the accompanying illustration. In consultation with the editors, Beston would occasionally offer some suggestions to Day for specific revisions: "The Master Mariner illustration is a hummer! May I, however, suggest one change on which we all seem agreed, viz the complete blotting out of the eyes you have done on the bow of the vessel? They take one's attention immediately, and one misses the action—also, the ship is better as a real Elizabethan sort of ship. The eyes bring in an archaic Greek note."[19] Jake Day took the friendly suggestions in the spirit in which they were offered, and Beston soon became a regular visitor to the home of Jake Day, his wife Beatrice, or "Bee," and their infant son Maclure on Mason Street in Cambridge, Massachusetts. When the Days' second child, another son, was born on May 26, 1920, they named him Richard Beston Day, and asked Henry to serve as godfather.

In November 1919 Beston's first book of fairy tales appeared under the title of *The Firelight Fairy Book*. The collection consisted of thirteen original stories that have more in common with the beautiful, finely wrought fairy tales written by Hans Christian Andersen than they do with the bawdier, more gruesome tales of the Brothers Grimm. As Elizabeth Dalton writes in her introduction to a 2003 reprint of *Grimm's Fairy Tales*, their stories were originally intended for adults, and "have been criticized ever since they first appeared as inappropriate for children—too frank about sex, too violent, too dark. The Grimms themselves began censoring the sex as they brought out successive editions, and subsequent editors and translators have continued the process, modifying the violence as well. But the darkness remains."[20] The Grimms did not create the tales that appeared in their book either, but collected them from the oral traditions of the German country folk. In this, Beston again has more in common with Andersen, who created original tales of strange creatures, magical enchantment, and evil punished/virtue rewarded in the classic "happily ever after" formulation.

Some of Beston's fairy tales are reminiscent of classics such as Charles Perrault's *La Belle au Bois Dormant* ("The Beauty Asleep in the Wood," commonly known as "Sleeping Beauty"), narratives that would have been widely familiar to the children for whom his stories were intended. In "Prince Sneeze," for instance, when a son is born to the king and queen of Fairyland, "the royal parents took good care to invite every single fairy in Fairyland, for they knew very well the consequences of forgetting to invite fairies to christenings."[21] Unfortunately, Malvolia—an elderly and quite petulant fairy from the Kingdom of the Black Mountains—takes offense when she is served a chocolate éclair rather than a piece of the strawberry tart baked by the queen herself specially for the occasion. In retribution, the aggrieved fairy casts a spell that causes something to change drastically whenever the prince sneezes. An ill-timed gust of wind drowns out the last words of the enchantment; which, unfortunately, includes the part that provides a clue to what will end the spell. In desperation the king sends the young prince to an isolated tower on the Golden Mountain, where it is hoped the healthful air will prevent him from sneezing. Prince Rolandor is imprisoned in the tower for years with only his loyal French poodle, Poldo—"who spoke both French and English exceedingly well"—for companionship. During this period he sneezes only three times:

> At the first sneeze, all the dogs in the kingdom except Poldo changed into cats, and all the cats into dogs. . . . At the second sneeze, all the elderly gentlemen over seventy changed into elm trees, a proceeding that caused a lot of trouble. . . . [and] at the third sneeze, all the people in the pictures at the Art Museum became alive, and for a week the soldiers of the royal guard spent most of their time rescuing poor, bewildered fauns, satyrs, nymphs, Roman senators, and long dead celebrities and historical personages from the worst destitution. The King finally had to build a special castle for them.[22]

Poldo leaves on a quest to find the way to end the spell. He succeeds, discovering that the spell will end when the prince marries. He carries the joyful news back to the king and queen and they arrange for Prince Rolandor to wed the one princess who is not afraid of the spell, a princess who is herself under the spell of a jealous witch who "turned her golden hair bright blue, and [gave] her a nose a foot long."[23] Halfway through the ceremony, Rolandor sneezes; but because he was "half-married," the spell is ended and collapses in on itself—"The cats became dogs again, and the dogs became cats; the elm trees became cross, elderly gentlemen looking for their families; the poor, excited Roman senators, fauns, nymphs, satyrs, celebrities and historical personages, went back to their pictures; and to cap the climax, the ugly bride became once more her sweet and lovely self."[24]

Beston was careful to retain the archetypes of the classic fairy tale, realizing that familiarity contributes to making fairy tales accessible to a young audience. Brave princes and beautiful princesses abound, as do evil-doers who must be vanquished, enchantments, magical creatures, and talking animals. Happy endings are *de rigueur*, although only after quests are successfully concluded, dangers gallantly braved, and good deeds generously recompensed. In tales such as "The Adventures of Florian," "Mariana," "The Treasure Castle," "The Master Mariner," and "The City Under the

Sea," characters prevail who are brave, honorable, and generally follow the rules. In one of Beston's most charming stories, "The Lost Half-Hour," a princess chooses a young simpleton, Bobo, to be her page because "so silly a lad might amuse her."[25] Bobo's innocent gullibility becomes the butt of jokes as he is sent on numerous fool's errands: "Now he would be sent to find a white crow's feather or a spray of yellow bluebells; now he was ordered to look for a square wheel or a glass of dry water."[26] His one true friend is Tilda the kitchen maid, whose advice Bobo seeks to avoid being sent on wild goose chases. One morning the princess oversleeps; when she complains that she has lost a half-hour, Bobo offers to find it. The amused princess and her court send Bobo on a quest to find the lost half-hour. In his journeys he meets people who have lost other items—an old man who has lost his reputation; a fierce fellow who has lost his temper; and a king who has lost his daughter who "was stolen by the fairies on midsummer eve fifteen years ago."[27] The king promises Bobo that if he is able to find the lost princess that he will be richly rewarded. For three years, Bobo searches for the lost items, and grows to be a handsome—if still comically simple— young man. He finally reaches the island of Father Time, who agrees to give Bobo the lost half-hour in return for a year of service. Bobo agrees, and after a year of faithful service receives two gifts: the lost half-hour and a draught from a cup holding the water of wisdom. No longer a simpleton, Bobo finds the lost reputation and the lost temper, and discovers that the king's lost daughter is none other than Tilda, his friend the kitchen maid. Bobo returns to the kingdom with the lost half-hour just in time to rescue Tilda from a ferocious dragon. They are, of course, wed and live happily ever after.

While Beston's stories are usually structured in accordance with the familiar archetypal forms and characters of the traditional fairy tale, there are some intriguingly contemporary themes built into several of the tales. In "The Seller of Dreams," the aunt of the protagonist is a courageous and steadfast woman, who frequently reminds her nephew, "there's nothing that a woman of determination and energy can't accomplish."[28] In one of the most interesting stories in the collection, "The Adventures of Florian," a gender-swapping element is developed as the main character, Isabella, the young daughter of a poor widowed nobleman, is raised in an androgynous manner by her father: "Knowing that his death would leave Isabella quite alone in the world and practically penniless, her father brought her up more like a boy than a girl; she could ride a horse as gracefully as an Amazon, she could swim like a born mermaid, and even outdo her father in his favorite sport of fencing."[29] When Isabella's father dies, she leaves their ruinous home and assumes the identity of a boy, now calling herself Florian. The brave Florian becomes the page of a fearful Enchanter, who comes to admire the bravery and fidelity of Florian; upon the completion of Florian's term of service, the Enchanter rewards him with three magical gifts. Florian then becomes the squire of Prince Florizel, whom she saves from numerous dangers and finally weds after her true identity is revealed to the prince by the Enchanter.

In "The Enchanted Elm," Beston develops a proto-environmental theme that is of particular interest given the turn toward nature writing he would take just a few years later. After a wicked witch turns a young prince into a towering elm, an orphaned girl who dwells with a family of wood-cutters nearby develops a fondness for the magnificent tree. When the girl learns that the wood-cutters are planning to cut it down, she protests; when they ignore her pleas to spare the elm, she hides in the topmost branches and calls down to the woodsmen, pretending that the tree is speaking to them and warning that "He who strikes shall breathe his last,/Before Midsummer Eve hath passed."[30] The tree-sitter's deception is eventually discovered, and both the girl and the tree/prince are saved only by the last minute intervention of the King of the Trees and his friend Gorbodoc, a mighty enchanter. Gorbodoc restores the prince to his human form, and, true to type, the grateful prince marries the brave young maiden. The wood-cutter is far less gently dealt with by the tree-loving necromancer, who proclaims: "'As for you,' and here the enchanter turned fiercely upon the wood-cutter, 'you shall be a green monkey, until you have planted and brought to full growth as many trees as you have cut down.'"[31] It is tempting to surmise that the seed of this particular twist may have been sown at the Roosevelt family's home at Sagamore Hill when Beston had visited his Harvard classmate Ted Jr. years before, and was startled to have a monkey suddenly bound up onto his shoulder while he and the Roosevelts were sitting down to dinner.

In any event, the fate of the wood-cutter probably owes at least as much to the conservation ethos of Theodore Roosevelt as it does to the conventions of the classic fairy tale.

As soon as *The Firelight Fairy Book* was published in November Beston sent an inscribed copy to Ted Roosevelt Jr. and his wife Eleanor for their children. Ted promptly replied (he was the only one of Beston's friends to refer to him as "Harry"), writing: "Dear Harry: on behalf of the little Roosevelts I want to thank you for the book. I like fairy stories myself very much and read it myself last night. It was perfectly delightful. How did you happen to start writing fairy stories?"[32] The letter included an invitation to visit Ted and Eleanor, and "all of the rising generation" at Sagamore Hill, as well as a handwritten addendum: "Simile where you say the castle looked like an elephant upside down is very good. I also particularly liked the description of the lost reputation." For the 1922 edition of *The Firelight Fairy Book*, Ted Roosevelt (who was now Assistant Secretary of the Navy) contributed a foreword to the book, where he cited "Prince Sneeze" and "The Lost Half-Hour" as his particular favorites. He continued on to say that he was not alone in his high regard for the book: "I have given the book as a Christmas gift, not only to my own children, but to other people's children, and to one of the prominent Senators of the United States. They have universally acclaimed it, and who can question the judgment of such a jury?"[33] While Ted Roosevelt may not have been entirely impartial, his opinion of the book was consistent with those of the book reviewers, who showered Beston's stories and the illustrations by Maurice Day with praise.

For Beston, writing fairy tales was not only a way of coping with troubling wartime memories and disillusionment; it was also a way of dealing with a job that was becoming increasingly tedious. The editorial position at *The Living Age* provided Beston with a steady income, but little intellectual or literary satisfaction—and no excitement whatsoever. In his letters to Luther Neff, Beston exudes nostalgia for the exhilarating period he spent with the navy, often expressing a wistful desire to be back on board ship:

> What have you been doing, you far away tamer and civilizer of wild gob souls? . . . Friendly indeed are my memories of the *New York*. Please give my very best to the friends aboard. Is the Major still with you, or MacRae,

who saved my life and disposition with a gift of sugar and introduced me to a turret drill, Commander Woodward, Lt. Smith, and the others of Scapa Flow and Rosythe days? I wish to heaven I were back with you for a while. Editing, however, is a tread mill occupation, and chains one to one's desk. Especially in these days when the printing trade is so undependable.[34]

One benefit of working in Boston, however, was the proximity of the magazine's office on Mount Vernon Street to Boston's theaters and restaurants. Beston's love of the theater was a constant throughout his life, and on Fridays he would often go out for dinner and a play after work, then stay at the Hotel Touraine. On one such evening in the late spring of 1920, Beston was walking to dinner when he chanced to meet F. Morton Smith and his wife Margaret Coatsworth Smith. Morton Smith was a Boston attorney who had been a friend and classmate of Henry's at the Adams Academy in Quincy and at Harvard University, and was now living in a house on Beacon Street with his new bride. As Margaret's sister Elizabeth later told the story, Margaret was a stranger in the city, and Henry was one of the first of Morton's friends whom she met. "It was characteristic of Henry's outgoing quality," wrote Elizabeth, "that he at once invited them both to dinner and the theatre."[35] The three of them had a wonderful evening, and the Smiths invited Beston to come out to visit them for a weekend at a house they were renting that summer in Medford, a quiet country village northwest of Boston. A few weeks later, Beston took the Smiths up on their offer and called on them at Medford, where Margaret's mother and her sister Elizabeth were also staying. As Elizabeth later recalled, she found Beston to be "charming," and the feeling was apparently mutual as Henry made a point of including Elizabeth in an invitation to luncheon at the Parson Capen House that he extended to the Smiths.

Elizabeth Jane Coatsworth had just turned twenty-seven when she met Beston, but she was already a remarkably accomplished young woman. Born in Buffalo, New York on May 31, 1893, her father, Thomas Coatsworth, was a successful Buffalo businessman. He and his wife Ida Reid Coatsworth, a woman of Scottish ancestry with a serene, unflappable temperament, had four children of whom only two survived past infancy—Margaret and

Elizabeth (who they called Bessy or Betsey), who was four years younger than her sister. The family lived with Thomas's mother in a large, beautiful house designed by the world-renowned architect Henry Hobson Richardson. Their home was located on Soldier's Place in Buffalo, a circular drive lined with magnificent elm trees where three parkways met. Soldier's Place (now called Soldier's Circle) and its connecting parkways were part of a remarkable system of public parks and parkways designed by Frederick Law Olmsted, one of the foremost landscape architects of the nineteenth century.[36] Margaret and Elizabeth both attended the Buffalo Seminary on Park Street, a very strict, academically rigorous private school. After graduating from the Buffalo Seminary, Elizabeth went on to attend Vassar College, graduating with a B.A. in 1915, and Columbia University, where she earned her master's degree in 1916.

Wanderlust was a common characteristic of the Coatsworths—as Elizabeth recalled in her aptly named memoir *Personal Geography* (1976), "we always seem to have done a good deal of traveling."[37] Elizabeth's mother had relatives who lived in Pasadena, California, and her parents brought the children there for a lengthy wintertime visit before she was even one year old; on the return trip her father brought the family up the Pacific coast to Washington, then through the Olympic Mountains before driving out to see an encampment of Blackfoot Indians on the plains east of the mountains. While Elizabeth was still a young girl the family went on numerous excursions to exotic places; many years later, Elizabeth asked her mother how she and her father dared to take young children on such adventures, and she replied, "In those days people didn't consider the children first of all in doing anything. They made their own plans and the children went along."[38] In Elizabeth's teens she spent her freshman and sophomore years in a private high school in Pasadena, before the family returned to Buffalo. Summers were often spent in Canada, and when she was just five the family went abroad for a year-long sojourn through Europe and Egypt.

In 1912, just after Elizabeth had completed her first year at Vassar College, Thomas Coatsworth died under tragic circumstances. For an extended period of time he had suffered from a stomach ailment that had grown progressively more painful, to the point of being debilitating. The doctor attending Coatsworth recognized its severity, but the treatment he recommended proved disastrous. For three months Coatsworth was limited to a milk diet and secluded in a dark room; not only did the condition worsen, but by the time he emerged from his room he had plunged into a deep depression exacerbated by the prescribed treatment. Without divulging his intentions, he obtained a handgun then quietly made his final goodbyes to family and friends. Thomas Coatsworth's suicide was nothing if not carefully planned—he had deliberately chosen a small caliber pistol in an attempt to limit the horror of the scene that the shooting would inevitably cause. Still, the effect on his family was devastating; for the rest of her life Elizabeth remained bitter about the treatment the doctor had prescribed for her father and its likely role in his decision to kill himself.[39]

After Thomas Coatsworth's death the house at Soldiers Place was sold, and Ida Coatsworth decided to leave Buffalo, hoping to put some geographical distance between her daughters and the tragic circumstances of their beloved father's death. She and the girls alternated between apartment living and extensive traveling, although, as Elizabeth noted about this period, "I had a four-year harbor at college."[40] In the summer of 1914, the year before graduating from Vassar College, Elizabeth joined her mother and sister in London. Differences in age and temperament had long caused friction between Margaret and the tall (5'11"), introspective Elizabeth, but that summer of walking trips and travel served to tighten the bonds of affection between the two sisters. As Elizabeth recalled in her memoir:

> Three important things happened that summer: Margaret and I became life-long friends; I began writing poetry from an inner urge which never left me until . . . Henry's death; and less personally, the first World War began. We happened to be in Stratford the evening before war was declared. The company played *Henry V* and when the young prince says, "Let us make alliance with the King of France," the entire audience rose to its feet and shouted. Later we were to see the Scots Greys in their kilts marching down the streets of Edinburgh to the skirl of their pipes. People said that you could hear the guns across the Channel. I am not sure that I did but I thought so.[41]

Elizabeth returned to Vassar College that autumn to complete her senior year while her mother and sister continued their travels, with Elizabeth often joining them on school breaks. After Elizabeth earned her master's degree from Columbia University in the spring of 1916, the three Coatsworth women went on an extended trip through China and the Far East that entailed the better part of a year: "In 1916–1917 came our Wanderjahr, our miraculous adventure in the friendly Far East, a year of which I can only say that it has colored all my life. It had everything in it to excite a young heart."[42] The trip to Asia provided Coatsworth with an abundance of material that she worked into her poems. She soon began publishing her work in periodicals, including Amy Lowell's influential imagist magazine *The Dial*. In 1919 Margaret married Morton Smith and moved, first to Boston and then, a year or so later, to Hingham, a small town on the south shore. That year Elizabeth and her mother moved to Cambridge, where she attended Radcliffe; about two years later they also moved to Hingham, buying a lovely eighteenth-century sea captain's house they called "Shipcote."

Sometime in the mid-summer of 1920, Morton and Margaret Smith drove to Topsfield with Elizabeth Coatsworth to visit Beston at the Parson Capen House. Even many years later, Coatsworth's recollection of the visit and her second meeting with Henry was vivid:

> As our car drew up at the gate Henry came through the seventeenth century doorway of the manse and walked down a green field to meet us. He was wearing a white navy uniform which set off his height and broad shoulders, but above all, the tanned vitality of his face and fine hands. Henry has always had the magnetism that is an inborn gift, something over and above his voice, the clear cut of his mouth or the expression of his eyes. His father, a physician and surgeon, who died not long before Henry went to college, must have had this same power, for old patients of his have told me how the sun seemed to come out when he entered a sick room.[43]

The relationship between Henry and Elizabeth slowly bloomed, and seems at first more of a literary, intellectual friendship than a romance. Part of this was due to the unsettled nature of their respective lives. Looking back on this period, Elizabeth later recalled, "I think that during this first year the pattern of things to come was set, but Henry and my mother and I were seldom in or near Boston at the same time. When we were, Henry and I always had dinner and went to the theatre together, or he came out to the old house where my mother and I were living overlooking Hingham harbor."[44]

From late 1920 until their marriage in 1929, however, no matter where they found themselves, Henry and Elizabeth carried on a steady correspondence that overcame the barriers of distance. Shortly after the mid-summer visit to see Beston at the Parson Capen House, Elizabeth went on another extended trip with her mother and sister, touring through Normandy, Brittany, England, and Scotland. In a note dated November 30, 1920, Beston mentioned a letter that he had received from a mutual friend, the noted English poet Laurence Binyon, who was headed to Brittany with his family, and asked if Elizabeth had managed to meet up with Binyon while they were both in Brittany. He added a postscript to the letter urging her to publish a collection of her poetry: "You really must publish your collected verse. Is your heart still hardened against a London publisher? Have you seen the *Four Seas* people here in town?"[45] By December, Coatsworth was in Pasadena visiting family once again, having returned from her travels through England and France. Beston responded warmly to her description of southern France, and once again wrote to urge her to find a publisher for her poems:

> So you got to the Roman provinces of France,—my own, own land, the region I know best in all Europe. (When I was studying at Lyons in 1911–12, I was forever wandering off down the Rhone, and visiting the old Roman towns). I have a peculiar liking for any land on which the shadow of the great empire has lain. The Romans had a cruel streak in them, their civilization was founded on slave labor, and I suppose their fiscal system died down into nothing but a squeeze, yet their empire has always seemed to me to be on the whole the greatest achievement of mankind. There was something noble and mighty in the notion of a great empire of civilization constructing roads, draining marshes and building aqueducts every where from the pillars of Hercules to the Parthian marshes. The present European system is much inferior to the great organization of law, tolerance, and administrative unity which ruled the past. Of course the empire had faults, yet it never led Europe to such an incredible and fratricidal debacle as the Great War.
>
> I thought your Sun in China perfectly delightful. When are you going to give us something else? I snatch "Asia" from the Atlantic table every month.

And the book? Have you tried Knopf? Why don't you send me two or three of your favorites, and let me send them to Conrad Aiken, American editor of that English *dernier cri* called *Coterie*.[46]

As for himself, Beston wrote, "The fairy book continues to go so well that I am thinking seriously of leaving the port of the L.A. [the *Living Age*] and setting bravely out on the literary sea once more."[47]

Beston was writing some new fairy tales, although he was finding that his editorial duties at the *Living Age* were a hindrance to his creative energies. Early in 1921 Beston and Jake Day began tentatively planning another collection of fairy tales, but as Beston complained in a letter to Day written from the magazine's offices in Boston:

> The Room in which I now prepare the 'Living Age' was once a butler's pantry or a janitor's shower bath, a high narrow, one ugly window kind of den. It gives my artistic temp. an awful pain; in fact this steady downpour of newspapers, reviews, books and magazines is slowly crazing me. I am begining (sic) to think that I shall have to get out for my soul's sake. I don't know whether I'm lazy or just bored. Probably both. But I'm begining to crave a little time all to myself. Writing with me is a very subjective thing; I can't do it in the midst of a hullabaloo . . . Will you let me come up [to Maine] some time when there's a storm brewing, a great dark, enveloping storm, a tempest of howls, windy cries, shrill bleak whistles that make one shiver, and a mad fury of soft, wet flakes?[48]

Before closing up the Parson Capen House for the season—it was open from April 1 to November 1 each year—Beston had also come to realize that there was "a dash of the recluse" in him. Once the school year began, the Japanese housekeeper and cook at the Capen House returned to his studies, and Beston was forced to cook and keep house for himself. He was somewhat surprised to find that he enjoyed the solitude and was perfectly able to cook for himself. As he wrote to Luther Neff, "I've learned how to make a peach of a cake, and desire for my own corn bread would divide a loving family."[49]

Beston once again spent the winter at the School Street House in Quincy with his brother George and his family. Their daughter Marie Beston Sheahan, nicknamed "Mimi" by her Uncle Henry, was now just over a year old and was the household's bright new center of attention.[50] Beston spent much of that winter wrestling with the question of whether to finally make a clean break and resign from his position at the *Living Age*—and if so, what to do next. In addition to his plans for another collection of fairy tales, Beston and some friends, including Ted Roosevelt Jr. and Rupert Hughes, had kicked around the idea of forming an association of "soldier's authors," that might lead to some sort of collective work.[51] On January 21, 1921, Beston took the train from Boston to Oyster Bay, Long Island, to spend the weekend with the Roosevelts at Sagamore Hill. He described the experience in a letter to Elizabeth Coatsworth the following week:

I've just had a most interesting week end at the Roosevelts in Oyster Bay. Dear T.R. Jr. was a classmate of mine, and these last years have drawn us closer together. He is one of the best comrades in the world, no mere echo of his father, but his own good self. It was a family party, Archie and Mrs. Archie, Kermit and Mrs. Kermit, and Dr. and Mrs. Derby (Ethel Roosevelt). A big house full of books and friendly, energetic young people. I'm afraid we all talked at the same time, and *shouted* favorite poems at each other. Four blessed good kids Grace, T.R. Jr., Cornelius and Quentin, something going on, Roosevelt fashion, all the time. I have seldom seen a face so sweet and happy as Mrs. Theodore Roosevelt Sr. She still lives at Sagamore Hill; T.R. and his youngsters at "Council Rock." It was great fun wandering around Sagamore Hill, looking at Sultan's rugs, Mikado's swords, and so on. Some of the Japanese screens given by the Japanese government to T.R. were glorious. Then we had great fun chopping wood into fire wood, a bully walk, and home to a good *din din*. No airs, no lugs at all, every thing friendly, pleasant, and American. I'm to go again soon when G.K. Chesterton is also to be the house's guest. Won't it be fun? Mrs. T.R. Jr. is awfully nice; she was an Ohio girl; her name was Eleanor Alexander.[52]

In another indication that his heart was no longer in his work at the *Living Age* and city life generally, he added, "It was great fun, too, being out of doors. I love hiking, wandering, and vagabonding over hill, over dale. To paraphrase Wordsworth 'The world is too much *indoors*' etc."[53] He was eager to reopen the house at Topsfield again, which he said was "an escape into the out o'doors, into clean, sweet smelling air, into green, unsullied field."[54]

It was inevitable that spending any time with the Roosevelts would call one back to nature, as outdoor living—the "strenuous life" as the former President called it—was central to their family. Even before the forty-two-year-old Roosevelt succeeded the assassinated William McKinley into office as the 26th President of the United States, he had made a mark as an outdoorsman and conservationist—as an author, as a hunter and rancher, a founder of the Boone and Crockett club in 1885 (one of the nation's first conservation societies), and as the Governor of New York State, where he ushered a plethora of conservation measures into law. He was a skilled amateur naturalist with a particular talent for ornithology, which led him to write a letter of admiration to the nation's foremost nature writer and bird watcher, John Burroughs, a note that led to an enduring friendship between the President-to-be and the literary naturalist. In the early spring of 1903, President Roosevelt went on a tour of Yellowstone National Park with Burroughs, followed by a tour of Yosemite with John Muir. Later that summer, Roosevelt steamed the presidential yacht up the Hudson River to West Park, where he tramped up to "Slabsides," Burroughs's writing cabin in the woods for a luncheon of chicken, celery from Burroughs's own celery swamp, and potatoes roasted in the cabin's fireplace. When the President departed, he left behind his eldest son, fourteen-year-old Ted Jr., to "camp out" with Burroughs for a week or two. When Burroughs died on March 29, 1921, the death of the great naturalist and writer was front page news; like many Americans of the period, Beston had grown up on Burroughs's nature essays and was saddened to hear of his passing.

A few days later, Beston finally decided to make his "escape" from the *Living Age*, handing in a letter of resignation effective April 3, 1921. His high spirits about the decision are clearly evident in a letter dated February 1, where he exults, "I'm getting out of here.—My sentence has been commuted for good behaviour and they have discovered that it was really Gyp the Blood who pinched the sterling silver sphagetti (sic) winder."[55] Beston realized that if he wanted to make a go of it as a writer that he would have to take the plunge and leave the comfortable, albeit boring, job at the *Living Age*. "If you *can* write and *don't*," he declared, "something within you withers & dies, and with its death envenoms the soul."[56] Money was a concern; Beston calculated that if he worked until April 3rd he would have saved enough money to take him through another summer at the house in Topsfield without too much trouble. Before leaving the *Living Age*, Beston took the opportunity to once again urge Elizabeth Coatsworth to send him some poems to submit to *The Atlantic Monthly* while he was still working there and could exert some influence on her behalf: "What of the poems for the Atlantic, have you sent them directly to the Atlantic's urn or am I to expect them? I hope the latter, for I wanted to see them, and give them a word of blessing ere they went to the judgment seat."[57]

Now that he had taken the momentous step of quitting his job to write full-time, Beston found that it would not be as easy as that—first he had to decide what to write. He had plenty of ideas for a new book of fairy tales, but he wasn't entirely sure that fairy tales were what he ought to be writing. There was also the "soldier writers" project with Ted Roosevelt Jr. and Rupert Hughes (the uncle of industrialist Howard Hughes), and several other ideas he had for magazine articles. Unsure of what project to pursue he became dilatory, spending more time traveling and socializing than writing. In early May, Beston celebrated his escape from the *Living Age* with a trip to Damariscotta, Maine, to visit Jake and Bee Day, where they discussed some ideas for the new collection of fairy tales but did not establish any deadlines or specific details about the project. That visit was followed by a motor trip through New Hampshire with his brother's family, where they drove from Plymouth to the Franconia Notch in the White Mountains   a "superb" trip thought Beston, who was seeing that part of New England for the first time.[58] He returned to Topsfield in late May intending to settle down to write in earnest, but found instead that his pen had seemingly run dry, and he was only able to concentrate on his work in fits and starts. In late summer Beston's writing was detoured by a brief foray into politics, working as a volunteer for A. Piatt Andrew, his former chief in the American Field Service, who was running for Congress as a Republican in a special election to fill the seat vacated by Representative Willfred Lufkin.

Beston stayed at the Parson Capen house in Topsfield until November 5, 1921, then returned to Quincy to stay with his brother's family for the winter. Dissatisfied with the pace of his writing, he rented a small office in Quincy, telling Bee Day hopefully, "And now for real serious work; I've played just about long enough."[59] Beston's "office" was really just a small, gray room in an office building downtown, but it did give Beston a semblance of structure to his writing routine; he would leave home to go to the office and work in the mornings and stay there writing for several hours before returning to School Street in the late afternoon or early evening. A few days after Christmas, his routine was dramatically disrupted when a spectacular fire broke out in Quincy. The Quincy Fire Department notified residents of School Street to quickly pack their essential belongings and prepare for imminent flight as the fire spread rapidly through the closely packed neighborhoods of wood-frame houses. As Beston observed:

> [We] had our goods packed and were ready to beat it any time. Most spectacular fire I ever saw, very terrible and beautiful. The houses which caught fire seemed to bake first and then pop into flame just like a newspaper one tosses into a grate. The whole façade ignited, the flame showing curiously along the clapboards in flickering parallel rows. When they all were going together, it was certainly one wild night! But a magnificent, terrifying sight. The huge furniture store, a big wooden building (about the size of the auditorium of the Park St. Church) had a brick front to give it an air, and when that collapsed, the fire within the walls seemed to roll out on to the street as if it had weight and mass,—a great tumbling content of fire. Fallen wires and darkness made it all frightfully dangerous.[60]

After a heroic effort the Quincy Fire Department was finally able to control the fire. The Sheahan home at 12 School Street was spared, but the fire left a scorch mark on Quincy that was visible for several years.

Although the fire was only a temporary, if spectacular distraction, Beston continued to have trouble settling into a comfortable, productive writing routine—an issue that would plague him for much of his career. He was also starting to display some ambivalence about the fairy tale project, writing, "I ought to be doing something more serious, but I have just had an attack of fairy tales."[61] Just as quickly, however, the "attack of fairy tales" would dissipate, and the pace of his writing would once again slacken— the rigorous discipline that he had displayed with his war correspondence, when he was forced to write against challenging deadlines, was far more difficult for Beston to muster without a contractually set due date for a manuscript. Beston's correspondence during the period from early 1921 when he resigned from his position at the *Living Age* until 1923 suggests that there were numerous distractions that kept Beston from focusing on his writing. Handsome and charming, with three successful books to his credit, Beston received countless invitations to dinners, parties, and other social events that significantly broadened his circle of literary acquaintances but did little for his productivity. One of these literary contacts was the influential critic and poet Louis Untermeyer, whom Beston met at a party held by their mutual friend Gamaliel Bradford. "At first," Beston wrote to Elizabeth Coatsworth, "[Untermeyer] pontificated, but presently he saw that we were all sufficiently impressed, and climbed down from the high horse and became very agreeably human." For Coatsworth's sake, Beston assiduously cultivated Untermeyer, writing, "He said your *Orientales* (his word) were very lovely, and wanted to know how you came to write them. And he was very glad to hear that Knopf was bringing out a collection. Untermeyer and his anthologies have a very real critical influence, so I did my best to establish a friendly relationship."[62] Untermeyer's high regard for Coatsworth's poetry was genuine, and her work was always included in his immensely popular anthology *Modern American Poetry*, which appeared in six editions from 1919 to 1942.

At another party Beston met the poet Amy Lowell, who was closely associated with the Imagist movement in American poetry and who used her substantial family wealth to publish numerous American poets in a literary journal she edited. Lowell was heartily despised by Ezra Pound (widely considered to have founded the Imagist movement), who called Lowell's circle of poets the "Amygist" movement, and unfairly derided her as simply a rich patron of the arts with little talent of her own. In a letter to Elizabeth Coatsworth, Beston wrote:

> Had another long talk with Amy Lowell at a Christmas party. What a terrific person she is, that stout dominance of exuberant flesh, that trumpeters voice, with the clear intensity of one accustomed to life long obedience from others, that grey, feminine eye. Do you know her? And her companion, her duenna, a middle aged Miss Somebody or other, one of those spinsters who

look like married folk,—what a bewildered expression! Leaving Amy to her acolytes, Miss Somebody fled to the quietest corner of the room, and you could see that she was busy rebuilding her spiritual and intellectual walls while the redoubtable Amy was elsewhere occupied.[63]

Lowell's "duenna" was Ada Dwyer Russell, a divorcée and former actress with whom Lowell had entered into what was often called a "Boston marriage"—a common euphemism used during the early twentieth century to refer to a long-term lesbian relationship. Beston either didn't know or didn't care (the latter is more likely) about either Ezra Pound's opinion of Lowell or Lowell's sexuality, saying, "I liked them both, and we had a good talk."[64]

As Beston slowly succeeded in putting more of his fairy tales on paper, his enthusiasm for the book project returned, and by April 1923 he could report to Elizabeth Coatsworth that he was "busy as can be fixing up details of The Wonder Book. 'Jake' Day is coming to Boston tonight, and tomorrow we have a great Atlantic 'confab.' The Wonderful Tune is to be in the June number of *the Atlantic* as well as in the book, and the *Mentor* has asked me to write something about the Flying Dutchman for their July issue, a sea number."[65] On September 1, 1923, more than two years after Beston had resigned from his editorial position at the *Living* Age, The Atlantic Monthly Press published his new collection of fairy tales as *The Starlight Wonder Book* under the name "Henry B. Beston." The book contained twelve original fairy tales and included thirteen beautiful full-page illustrations by Jake Day and was dedicated to Mabel Davison, "My war-time godmother with the homage and grateful affection of H.B.B." While Davison was several years older than Beston, she was attracted to the handsome Beston and it is possible that their relationship may have been for a time more than platonic—he dedicated two books to her and even after he married Elizabeth Coatsworth he kept on his bureau a framed snapshot of Davison sitting sidesaddle on horseback.[66]

The Great War was still much on Beston's mind during this period. As was the case with *The Firelight Fairy Book*, a number of the stories in the new collection featured a character overcoming fear to perform a selfless deed, and receiving in turn a magical gift. For example, in the initial story of the book, "The Brave Grenadier," the title character rescues a wounded enemy soldier during a battle and is rewarded for his courage and compassion by the wounded soldier's father, who happens to be the Enchanter of the Green Glen. The enchanter gives the grenadier a green wand, and tells him, "Whatsoever you strike once with it will continue to grow until you cry 'stop'; whatever you strike twice with it will grow smaller till you bid the magic cease."[67] The grenadier travels to the distant land of the Golden Plain where the people are menaced by a terrible creature called a hippodrac, "a kind of fearsome winged horse . . . larger than any earthly animal, black as midnight in color, and armored over the chest and head with a sheath of dragon scales. Add to this a pair of giant wings . . . a wicked horse-like head with huge jaws, hoofs of blue steel, and an appetite like a devouring flame, and you will see that the people of the Golden Plain had true cause for alarm."[68] The grenadier shrinks the hippodrac with the magical green wand, but when he enters the royal city to claim his reward, the evil Lord Chancellor who not only refuses to reward the grenadier but steals his wand and sentences him to prison. While imprisoned, the grenadier befriends the now tiny hippodrac—in effect, not only controlling his fear, but making it an ally. He then instructs the hippodrac to retrieve the stolen wand, and uses it to return the creature to its original size. The reconstituted hippodrac seizes the Lord Chancellor and flies away, never to be seen again.

The need to conquer one's fear is once again developed in "The Adamant Door," but in this story there is a wartime setting that strengthens the thematic link to Beston's own experience. A young countryman named Hugh sees a company of soldiers and, seduced by their camaraderie and colorful uniforms, begs his mother for permission to enlist. He becomes best of friends with another young soldier, Jocelyn, and when the soldiers are called to war to defend their kingdom the two young soldiers "fought as in a dream, scarce knowing what they did."[69] The enemy captures Hugh, but Jocelyn bravely fights his way through their ranks and rescues his friend. The battle rages through the night, and in the fray Hugh becomes separated from his comrades. Although Hugh knows that he should return and help them he succumbs to his fears and flees. The runaway soldier watches in hiding as his company, including Jocelyn, are led away to captivity. Ashamed of his cowardice, Hugh does not return to his own land, but instead flees to a neighboring country where he takes work as a farmhand. Here he learns of a ruined castle where a knight who was also a mighty magician once lived. Local legend holds that there is a great treasure in the castle, but no one has ever obtained it because the riches are guarded by a ferocious beast. Hugh determines to confront the monster, retrieve the treasure, and ransom his friends from the enemy. He climbs up to the ruined castle where he sees a giant door of "blackest adamant." Carved over the archway of the door is a legend that reads: "He who would share the treasure must conquer a mighty foe within." Hugh summons all his courage and enters the dark castle and succeeds in finding the treasure, but is puzzled by the absence of a ferocious guardian, until he realizes "It was all a wise jest of the old knight. The foe to be conquered was fear, and 'the mighty foe within' meant the host of silly fears which run and hide in the house of one's heart. The treasure had been guarded against men by their own fears. Brave men, who sent fears hurrying and scurrying out of their hearts alone were worthy of the prize."[70]

Reviewers of *The Starlight Wonder Book* were lavish in their praise; the *Boston Transcript* proclaimed that the tales even surpassed those of Burton's translation of *Arabian Nights*, saying, "It is better than the enchanted carpet of the ancients."[71] Writing for the *International Book Review*, M.G. Bonner wrote, "It is just as alluring as its title indicates. Every story is a gleaming, merrily twinkling wonder tale."[72] Everett McNeil's review for *The New York Times* called particular attention to Beston's beautifully poetic style, writing:

> These are real stories and will delight those children who want their fairy tales filled with marvelous and daring adventures, with weird and mystical beings in the wonderful realms of fairyland. Henry B. Beston has an unusually poetic imagination, and these tales are rich in gorgeous and poetic descriptions that will delight the imaginative child. This is especially true of 'The Palace of the Night,' 'The City of the Winter Sleep,' 'The Wonderful Tune,' and 'The Adamant Door.' The illustrations by Maurice Day are particularly good.[73]

Beston had taken to writing children's stories as a way of dealing with his response to the war, but they were not his only means of coping with troubling memories. He also devoted a considerable amount of time to delivering readings and lectures on behalf of organizations performing charitable work for disabled veterans, and was active in the Quincy chapter of the American Legion, helping to organize a pageant in 1922 to raise money for veterans in need. In his contribution to the Harvard Class of 1909's 15th year report he wrote, "I am interested in the social, economic, and spiritual questions which beset the war generation (our own generation) and belong to a great many organizations whose purpose is to help the soldiers in misfortune and alleviate present misery."[74] While Beston was able to take temporary refuge in writing fairy tales, he was keenly aware that such relief was fleeting—innocence once lost can never be recovered—and that the ills of modern industrial society could not be rectified by escapism. The wrenching societal changes brought into the open by the Great War and its aftermath were *the* great intellectual issue of the 1920s and were vividly manifested in the literary and artistic movements of the era, and Beston's work reflects this development.

Beston was also becoming increasingly restless; his life seemed to be falling into a routine devoid of any great meaning. Winters were still spent with his brother's family in Quincy, but the house at 12 School Street seemed to become a little smaller every year. On October 15, 1922, George and Marie Sheahan had a second child, Joan. While Beston adored his newborn niece and her three-year-old sister Marie, it was difficult to find a quiet place to write in a house with two active young children. Every April Beston would return to the Parson Capen House, but Beston was forced to concede that even his beloved "Tops" was starting to lose its charm:

> The spring finds me here still at Quincy, meditating a swift return to Topsfield. I actually haven't been to old Tops since the day I left it November last. I suppose roofs have leaked and windows blown open. And that moths are as thick as snowflakes . . . I don't know how much longer I can stand that orustiferous, grambagerous, solitudous life at Tops. And I don't think it's a good thing for me to hunk away on my island. I like to have a finger in the world pie. I may go to the MacDowell Colony in Peterboro for June (I haven't heard from 'em yet however) and during part of the summer I may be at Mt. Desert . . . I suppose the truth is that Tops, dear lovely Tops which meant so much is begining (sic) to bore me.[75]

As for his writing, despite the success he was enjoying as a creator of fairy tales, Beston was convinced that he had more to offer as a writer than children's stories, no matter how well-received they might be. When he had resigned his position at *The Living Age* he had done so to embark upon a literary career, asking himself "Can I write? Then what the deuce am I doing here?" It was now two years later, he was thirty-five years old, and he was still asking himself the same question. Then, in early 1923, he took on a magazine project to write an article about the coastguardsmen of Cape Cod. That fortuitous assignment proved to be the turning point of his literary career.

CHAPTER FIVE

A Gallant Vagabond
1923–1926

Let the blow fall soon or late,
Let what will be o'er me;
Give the face of earth around,
And the road before me.
Wealth I ask not, hope nor love,
Nor a friend to know me;
All I ask, the heaven above
And the road below me.

ROBERT LOUIS STEVENSON
"The Vagabond"

B ESTON MADE A MID-WINTER VISIT to Cape Cod in early 1923 to spend some time with the coastguardsmen of the Cape, about whom he planned to write an article for the monthly magazine *The World's Work*. While this was not Beston's first trip to the Cape, the research that he did for the article exposed him to a different aspect of the great outer beach of Cape Cod that stretches from Provincetown south to Monomoy Point, approximately fifty in Beston's words, "wild, breaker-beaten miles."[1] In many ways, the coast guard's duties along the Cape's Atlantic coast harkened back to the pre-twentieth-century era of sailing ships; the sight of commercial and fishing vessels under sail had not vanished from the New England coast even as late as the 1920s. Coast guard stations were positioned about six miles apart along the length of the beach, with eight men based at each station. The coastguardsmen continuously patrolled the beach looking for any sign of a ship in danger of foundering on the treacherous sand bars hidden just offshore. The men were trained to warn vessels away from dangerous waters and, should the need arise, to use cannons fitted with "breeches buoys" or to launch surf boats into the crashing waves to rescue the crew and passengers of any ship in peril. Beston stayed at the Race Point Station near Provincetown for several days, talking with the men about the life of a "surfman" and accompanying them on their nightly patrols along the beach. This was an aspect of the Cape with which most people were unfamiliar, Beston wrote: "There are two Cape Cods in the world, one the picturesque and familiar land of toy windmills, picnickers and motorists, the other the Cape that the sailors see, the Cape of the wild, houseless outer shore, the countless tragic wrecks, the sand bars and the shoals."[2]

"The Wardens of Cape Cod," which came out several months later in the December 1923 issue of *The World's Work* is a paean to the courage and steadfastness of the Cape's coastguardsmen, who patrolled the great beach day and night throughout the year no matter what the weather might bring, frequently risking life and limb to rescue stranded sailors. One anecdote from the article detailed the rescue of survivors from a stranded Italian steel bark, the *Castagna*, which had struck a sandbar off Nauset during a terrible winter storm. Beston's narrative of the incident is so vividly portrayed that it almost seems as though we are right there with the rescuers, peering into the stormy darkness for a glimpse of the stricken ship. The coastguardsmen managed to fire a line for the breeches buoy onto the ship, but most of the *Castagna's* crew were so numbed by the cold and ice they were unable to secure the line, as "knots cannot be made with frozen fists big as boxing gloves."[3] The surfmen then launched a boat into the icy night sea in a last-ditch attempt to rescue the surviving sailors: "The task was one of cruelest difficulty, and it was only after several hard battles and a show of finest courage and boating skill that the coast guards' vessel was tugged to the *Castagna's* pouring side. Two of the crew of thirteen had perished overboard, two were dead in the rigging, their faces and bodies glassing over in strange mummy shrouds of ice, a third lay dying in the racing waters of the deck." Beston pointed out that the average salary for the coastguardsmen was between seventy and eighty dollars a month, which made it difficult to recruit and retain the type of men necessary for the service, and he concluded the article with an appeal for additional governmental support for the coast guard: "The service of patrol upon the Cape is genuinely heroic, and its fine traditions are rich in honor. Surely a great Nation will not allow a great national service to fall into the pit of evil days?"[4]

Although the coastguardsmen of Cape Cod were central to the piece Beston wrote for *The World's Work*, there was another aspect to the article that foreshadows the turn toward nature writing that he would soon take. On one windy night patrol along the beach, Beston and his coast guard companion found a loon crouched on the shoreline, its feathers matted together with sand and fuel oil; "The oil kills the wild fowl by thousands on the Cape," Beston wrote, "for it gums their feathers together when they have settled in a pool of it." The two men turned on their flashlight to get a better view, and the "motionless, calm ray of the electric lamp lent an ironic serenity to the vast, wild dark, and the dying creature lifted its eyes to the white ray, dark, uncomprehending eyes awaiting something incomprehensible and dread." Beston felt himself irresistibly drawn toward such awesome, sublime aspects of the great beach, a place where—not far from the great city of Boston—life could hinge on a whim of the weather and ocean, and where the beach portrayed "Nature in the elemental mood, thirty miles where night reveals no welcoming window light, and the world vanishes into a darkness full of unutterable mystery, keen, moist, ocean smells, and thundering sound."[5] This was a landscape where, as Henry Thoreau described Mount Katahdin in *The Maine Woods*, there is a sense that human beings are but spectral, transient presences in "vast and Titanic" nature: "Talk of mysteries! Think of our life in nature—daily to be shown matter, to come in contact with it,—rocks, trees, wind on our cheeks! The *solid* earth! The *actual* world! The *common sense! Contact! Contact! Who* are we? *Where* are we?"

Before returning to Quincy for the rest of the winter of 1923, Beston made arrangements to rent a summer cottage in Eastham from the Sullivans, a local family. The time on Cape Cod reinvigorated Beston, and through the rest of the winter and that spring he worked steadily on the new collection of fairy tales, corresponding regularly with Jake Day and lavishly praising Days' illustrations and exulting, "We've both grown up a bit, both advanced in our mastery of our styles."[6] He spent the winter writing in Quincy, and when he opened the Parson Capen House in April he continued working at a feverish pace. In early June he left Topsfield for the Cape, and in less than a month completed the final revisions for *The Starlight Wonder Book*. He was still so fired up about the book that rather than mail it to the Atlantic Monthly Press, he took the train down to their New York City office to hand deliver the manuscript.[7]

To celebrate the completion of the book, Beston went from New York City to Washington, D.C., to visit Ted Roosevelt Jr., who was now serving as Assistant Secretary of the Navy under President Warren G. Harding. Roosevelt casually asked if Beston might be interested in briefly reprising his role as naval correspondent once again, joining a submarine crew on maneuvers off the coast of Long Island. Beston eagerly accepted the invitation (as Roosevelt knew he would), and in early August he traveled to New York to join the crew of the S-19. On August 8 he sent a postcard from Long Island's Montauk Point to Elizabeth Coatsworth writing simply, "Anchored here for the night. On the S-19. Been having torpedo and target practice. Been diving a lot. Best of best, Henry."[8] Beston spent five days on the S-19, which was one of the Navy's new S-class submarines; while he thoroughly enjoyed the adventure, the fact that he did not write an article about it probably indicates that it did not quite capture his imagination the same way his stint with the grand fleet in Europe had. There may have been some gentlemanly discretion involved as well, a reluctance to say anything critical about the competence of the submarine's officers and crew. Several months later while Beston was again on Cape Cod he received word that a submarine had run aground off the shore of Nauset Beach near where he had rented his cottage. He dashed out to the beach and found that the sub was the S-19: "[It] hit the Atlantic bar just off my land; in fact, it lies just about in my backyard between the fourth row of clothesline and the incinerator . . . By curious coincidence I was attached to this same ship for 5 days. She was the hoodoo of the submarine Navy—now she's ashore I must say the navigation her officers must have employed would have caused the 'resignation under fire' of those picturesque roughnecks who skipper the swan boats."[9] The bad "hoodoo" of the S-19 continued even after the grounding, as the Nauset Coast Guard had difficulty in spotting the ship, hidden as it was by heavy surf crashing directly upon it. The S-19's misfortunes then spread to its rescuers; the coast guard launched a lifeboat from the shore, but they were capsized by a giant wave that spilled the crew into the icy waters of the Atlantic. Both crews were rescued without casualties, but the submarine remained stranded off Nauset Beach for three months until navy salvage vessels could work it loose and return it to port. The ill-fated S-19 was refurbished and returned to duty, although in a fitting conclusion, the navy deliberately scuttled the submarine off the coast of Hawaii in 1938.[10]

As was typical during this period of Beston's life, he spent most of the summer traveling. After the submarine voyage aboard the S-19, he joined Mary Cabot Wheelwright and some other friends in Northeast Harbor on Mount Desert, Maine for a trip aboard Wheelwright's yacht *Liria*.[11] Following the cruise Beston stopped in Damariscotta, Maine, to visit with Jake and Bee Day and celebrate the forthcoming publication of *The Starlight Wonder Book*, which came out in September 1923. After his summer travels, Beston returned to Topsfield, where a particularly beautiful autumn almost made him forget his boredom with "dear, lovely Tops." Still, memories of wartime France made even the spectacular beauty of the season feel bittersweet:

> [W]hat days, oh Olympian Gods, what days. Mild, blue, sunny-warm, mellow and clear. Is there any region of the world lovelier than New England in autumn? I love it though the melancholy of it now and then seizes upon me. And I went to the French front on October 8th, 1915, and whenever autumn comes, the doors of the caverns of memory are opened and I see again the silent, ruined towns in the autumnal landscape, the deserted fields, the shattered trees, and the grass dying away in the haunted and forsaken streets.[12]

More than anything else, Beston yearned to roam once again, but travel was expensive, and while he was not in dire financial straits his book royalties did not permit extravagances. The next best thing he reasoned, was to write about travelers, and so while he was in Quincy that winter he began to work on a series of biographical sketches about wanderers whom he called "gallant vagabonds."[13] Much of that winter was spent in the Boston Public Library and the Boston Athenaeum researching the lives of his vagabonds and daydreaming about travel to exotic places.

Orion on the Dunes

The solution to Beston's fiscal shortfall soon came in two forms; the first was robust sales of *The Starlight Wonder Book* which, bolstered by excellent reviews, surpassed all expectations. The second came from his brother. After the death of their father, Henry and George had received an interest in the family home on School Street in Quincy. In late 1923 or early 1924, George offered to buy out Henry's share of the house. While the division of the paternal estate took a while to settle, the outcome certainly made sense for both brothers: George's medical office was located at the School Street house, and was thriving. The part of the house used as living quarters for the family was also getting crowded, housing Joseph Sheahan's widow Mary, George, Marie, their two children, Marie and Joan, a housekeeper—and, often during the winter months, Henry. As fond as he was of his family, the busy household provided Henry with little of the quiet time needed for a writer to work. Feeling more financially secure than he had since resigning his position at *The Living Age*, and looking for a quiet place to write, Beston rented the Sullivan cottage in Eastham for the entire year and gave up his residence at the Parson Capen House, where he had lived on and off for several years.

Before settling down to write, however, Beston decided to do some of the adventuring for which he yearned. In May 1924 he left for Spain, spending the next five months traveling throughout the country. Beston hiked through the Pyrenees, the Basque country in northern Spain, and throughout the Spanish countryside. For at least part of the tour he was accompanied by his friend Joe Wood, who would later serve as a brigadier general in the Second World War. Beston and Wood visited the Alhambra, the great fourteenth-century castle built in Granada for the last emirs of Spain, where they posed for a photograph in the flowing Moorish robes of the era. While traveling Beston sent few letters back home, writing to Jake Day upon his return that autumn, "I haven't given any signs of life for a long while. I've been in Spain—blessed Spain—the most interesting and civilized country in the globe."[14] With his facility for languages, Beston was soon speaking fluent Spanish, and found the culture and history of Spain to be entrancing. Unlike Ernest Hemingway, another American aficionado of Spain, one Spanish tradition Beston did not find to be alluring was bullfighting. While in Madrid, Beston attended a bullfight, describing the experience in an article he wrote for *The Independent* a few months later: "Civilization has no tolerance of institutions which have lost their emotional significance. The 'beauty' of the Spanish bullfight is romantic nonsense long outworn. Some ages have called it wicked, others cruel; it has remained to our jazz age to call it ridiculous. *Ridiculous*, a new and deadly word. And that is why the bullfight is slowly corrupting to an end in Spain."[15]

After Beston returned from Spain in September, he went to Cape Cod where he lived at the Eastham cottage until November. "Eastham is a quiet place," Beston wrote to the Days, "The little children all swear like pirates, they only swear quite innocently, using G-d-d-n as an adjective. 'Have you been fishing, Ormand?' 'Yes and all I been catching is G-d-d-n sculpins. God, but you oughter seen the one father caught. It was the God-d-est biggest one I ever seen.' 'Thank you Ormand.' And to think the little dear is only in the 3rd grade! I love it here. Who wouldn't?"[16] The vagabond book was temporarily put on hold as Beston—full of enthusiasm for all things Spanish—was distracted by an idea (soon abandoned) to do a book about Spain. In the meantime he was "drudging out articles so as to be free to go ahead on my book."[17] The 1920s were a golden age for popular magazines, and Beston could count on a steady stream of income from his articles. Two months later he was still busy writing articles rather than working on his book, telling the Days, "I've got to do some articles on Spanish architecture for the "House Beautiful" and a paper for Ellery [Sedgwick, editor of *The Atlantic Monthly*]. I've had a lot of holum in the month's magazines, but I've had to spend it all on clothes, for I came back from Spain with only a few rummage-sale-looking duds . . . Got a new overcoat out of the Outlook, and a pair of shoes out of the N.Y. Tribune."[18]

For Beston, a snappy if sometimes idiosyncratic dresser, this state of affairs was simply unacceptable. In *Especially Maine* Elizabeth Coatsworth states that Beston:

> took a sporadic interest in his appearance and was very independent about how he dressed. His tweed jackets were made to order in London. Usually he wore a French dark blue beret. His shoes were casual and unconstrict-ing; he liked wool ties and viyella shirts, of a scarlet or glowing yellow with

bishop sleeves, often worn with an Indian vest instead of a jacket; he was one of the first to wear walking shorts. But Henry had a sense of occasion and could dress formally for formal appearances. Whether dressed in his best or in an old shirt and shorts with bare feet, he was equally at his ease.[19]

Beston's "sporadic interest" in his wardrobe sometimes manifested itself in rather odd ways. He had a fondness for bright colors and occasionally sported orange or canary yellow suit jackets—which certainly drew attention during his later years in rural Maine. During his time on Cape Cod he often wore Bermuda shorts, well before they came into fashion, which were apparently a source of some amusement to the local girls who were not used to grown men—particularly very large grown men—wearing shorts in public.[20]

During late 1924 Beston spent a significant amount of time in New York, renting a room at the Prince George Hotel, his favored lodging when visiting Manhattan. Beston had become a regular book reviewer and some-time columnist for the *New York Herald Tribune*, and in November gave a reading of his fairy tales at the New York Public Library. The reading was a great success, with a full house and a great deal of enthusiastic interest in Beston and his work: as Beston related it to Jake and Bee Day, the reading generated "buzz . . . that I trust will later turn into bizz."[21] Always a great socializer, the all-night charms of the jazz era "City of Towers" as Beston called it, were not lost on him: "This New York jazzing process positively works wonders. I have undergone a change that makes the 'before' and 'after' of an old fashioned patent medicine full of 99 44/100 triple distilled hooch. I go to the theater, stay up all night, have breakfast at Childs at 4 A.M., drink artificial gin which would burn a hole in armor plate, and live entirely by artificial light. It's great, but I'm wondering what price glory."[22]

Even during this high-flying time in New York, however, Beston's mind was still focused on Cape Cod. Not only was he looking forward to spending the summer in his rented cottage in Eastham, he had also signed a five-year renewable lease for a parcel of marsh and dune land owned by Mercy A. Mines in Eastham. As described in the lease, the land was situated:

Between the ocean and the salt channel south of the Coast Guard station in said Eastham, said leased land being bounded and described as follows;

starting at a point at edge of said channel three hundred feet north of the Lessor's southern bound and then running northerly two hundred and seventy feet along said channel then turning and running easterly to the Atlantic Ocean, then turning and running two hundred and seventy feet bounded on said Ocean and thence turning and running westerly to the point of beginning making a strip two hundred and seventy feet in width extending between said channel and said Ocean.[23]

Mines retained the right to cut salt hay on the property for the duration of the lease, and Beston was given the right to renew the lease after the expiration of the first five year term on December 31, 1929, and the right of first refusal were the land ever put up for sale. Beston's plans for building a small house on the dune land were already well along a few months later, as indicated by a March query to Jake Day as to what colors he should use for the interior.[24]

By the late spring of 1925 Beston was back at his rented cottage in Eastham, and within a few months he had finished the volume he now called *The Book of Gallant Vagabonds*, which he dedicated to his friends Colonel and Mrs. Theodore Roosevelt Jr., and sent it to the publisher, the George H. Doran Company. The dedication was in part, an expression of friendship and personal loyalty given what had happened to Ted that past autumn. In 1924 Roosevelt ran for governor of New York against the Democratic nominee, the incumbent Alfred E. Smith. Smith was a popular governor, but the Roosevelt name was still a powerful one in New York State politics— the former president had been elected governor of New York in 1898, just two years before being named William McKinley's running mate in the 1900 presidential election. The Smith campaign turned to Ted Roosevelt's cousin Franklin Roosevelt to link Ted, in his capacity as assistant secretary of the navy, to the Teapot Dome oil scandal of the Harding administration. When a reporter compared the charismatic FDR to the former President, Ted Jr. dismissed the comparison, declaring, "Franklin is a maverick. He doesn't wear the brand of our family."[25] The comment apparently irritated FDR's wife, Eleanor, to the point where she took an active role in defeating Ted Jr., showing up at several campaign rallies in a car that prominently featured a steaming teapot on its roof. The smear tactics worked, as Smith eked out a narrow victory over Ted Roosevelt, winning by just over 100,000 votes. The election widened the gap between FDR's Democratic wing of the family and TR's Republican wing, and neither Ted Jr. nor his friend Henry Beston would ever view FDR or his wife in a favorable light again. Indeed, Beston wrote an article that appeared in the May 1924 edition of *The Independent* arguing that not only was Ted Jr. completely blameless in the Teapot Dome scandal, but that he had done everything possible within the limited scope of his power to "safeguard the interests of the nation and the Navy." Beston's view of FDR was permanently colored by that gubernatorial campaign of 1924, and he forever after viewed FDR as a duplicitous and unprincipled political operator.

"There are times," Beston wrote in the foreword to *The Book of Gallant Vagabonds*, "when everyone wants to be a vagabond, and go down the road to adventure, strange peoples, the mountains, and the sea. The bonds of convention, however, are many and strong, and only a few ever break them and go. In this book I have gathered together the strange and romantic lives of actual wanderers who did what so many have wished to do; here are some who gave up all to go and see the world."[26] Beston differentiated his "gallant vagabonds" from both "professional travelers and the vagabond ne'er-do-wells," stating that the true gallant vagabond was neither an idler nor one whose journeys were based on a quest for riches or a purely geographical interest; theirs was a romantic fascination with "the whole fantastic mystery of life."[27] While this may arguably have been a point of view shared by his vagabonds, it certainly describes Beston's own romantic fascination with the "fantastic mystery of life" very well, making *The Book of Gallant Vagabonds* a revealing window into Beston's state of mind at this point in his life. Beston chose six wanderers to feature, all of whom shared an urge to travel, an insatiable curiosity about the world, and a spirit of adventure.

The first profile was of John Ledyard, who was, Beston wrote, "a man who was born with two great gifts, one the most precious in the world, the other the most perilous. The first was an abounding physical vitality which made the casual business of being alive a divine adventure, the second, an imagination of the sort which refuses discipline and runs away with the whole mind."[28] In 1773 young Ledyard left Dartmouth College, paddling a dugout canoe down the Connecticut River in search of adventure. His travels led him to England where he joined the crew of the *Discovery*, commanded by the famed navigator and explorer Captain James Cook. Ledyard sailed with Cook's expedition to Hawaii, and from there to the coast of Alaska, "whose memory was to shape the greater adventures of his life."[29] On the advice of Captain Cook, Ledyard went ashore unarmed on one of the islands to accompany native guides in search of white strangers said to be on the island. The white men proved to be Russian fur traders who spoke of the fabulous riches to be made in procuring furs for the Chinese market, and when Ledyard left Hawaii he took this idea with him. The Cook expedition spent over four years at sea, and when they returned, the American colonies were engaged in a war for independence from Great Britain. Unwilling to fight against his countrymen, Ledyard was confined to a British prison ship off the coast of Long Island. Conditions on board the ship were wretched, so he managed a daring escape and spent several months hiding out with relatives in Connecticut while he wrote an account of his voyages with the Cook expedition. After the war Ledyard tried to raise funds for an expedition to return to Alaska, but without success, so he embarked on an audacious journey on foot through Europe and across Russia in an attempt to reach Alaska. After thousands of miles, he had nearly reached the Pacific coast when he was arrested on trumped-up charges of being a spy. "I was banished from the empire, and conveyed to the frontiers of Poland," wrote Ledyard, "six thousand versts from where I was arrested. I know not how I passed through the kingdoms of Poland and Prussia or thence to London where I arrived in the beginning of May, disappointed, ragged, penniless."[30] The African Society in England asked Ledyard if he would accompany an expedition to explore the interior of the continent, but shortly after leaving Cairo he was struck by illness and died, having never returned to the Alaska of his wanderer's imagination.

The second adventurer profiled by Beston is Giovanni Belzoni, who was born in Padua in 1778, one of fourteen children. While in his early teens he was sent to a monastery in Rome in preparation for becoming a monk. When the French Revolution spilled over the border into Italy, the monastery was closed, the monks evicted, and Belzoni—who had become a young giant standing six feet seven inches tall—became a homeless wanderer at the age of twenty-two. Possessed of enormous strength, for a time he earned a living performing as a strongman at small village fairs. Working his way through Europe to England, he became renowned for his feats of strength, and, writes Beston, married an Englishwoman "with a stature almost as magnificent as her lord's."[31] After several years traveling throughout Europe and the Levant, the couple ended up in Egypt, where Belzoni became consumed by a plan to solve the riddle of the pyramids. When he returned to England in 1819 to display his findings, he and his work caused a sensation and he earned lasting fame as a one of the Western world's first great Egyptologists. Like John Ledyard, Belzoni could not rest on his laurels, however, so in 1823 he departed for a journey of exploration in West Africa where he contracted an illness and died thousands of miles from home.

James Bruce, the third of Beston's wanderers, differed from Ledyard and Belzoni in that he died at home at a good old age after completing his journeys, but there are numerous other similarities of character. Like Belzoni he was tall and powerful, and had a self-assuredness that drove him to take chances that others would have shied away from. After resigning his post as consul in Algiers in 1765, the thirty-five-year-old Bruce wandered throughout North Africa searching for Roman antiquities while posing as a physician. He shrugged off the moral implications of his charade, claiming: "I did not occasion a greater mortality among the Mohametans and Pagans abroad than may be attributed to some of my brother physicians among their fellow Christians."[32] When he returned to Scotland at long last, he discovered two things—first, that in his absence he had become a wealthy man because large deposits of coal had been found on his family's property; and second, that there were few who accepted the verity of his tales of adventure and discovery in Africa.

A common thread connecting Beston's gallant vagabonds, in addition to their wanderlust, is the writing they left behind. All of them wrote fascinating accounts of their adventures, but three in particular—Edward John Trelawny, Thomas Morton, and Arthur Rimbaud earned a reputation as men of letters in addition to that of adventurers. Trelawny was a man with a wild, almost barbaric temperament who enlisted in the British Navy then jumped ship in Bombay at the age of seventeen. He disappeared for seven or eight years, a period during which, it has been suggested, he became a pirate. He then reappeared in England in 1815 or 1816. He became close friends with Percy Shelley, his wife Mary, and Lord Byron, and accompanied the Shelleys to Italy. When Shelley and a friend who were sailing in the Gulf of Spezzia disappeared during a squall, it was Trelawny who searched for and recovered the body. When Lord Byron joined the cause of the Greeks who had rebelled against the rule of the Turks, Byron begged Trelawny to come along. Trelawny returned from Greece carrying with him a number of wounds and a young daughter, whom he took with him to Italy. Many years later, Trelawny returned to England and was greeted as a living legend: "English society welcomed him back; Shelley was coming into his own, the Byron legend had taken root . . . and all the English world was anxious to see the last of the great company."[33]

That Beston, a native of Quincy, would have selected Thomas Morton as one of his gallant vagabonds comes as no surprise. The plantation of Captain Wollaston co-opted by Morton and transformed into "Merry-Mount," the bane of the Puritans of Plymouth, was located just a few miles from Beston's boyhood home. Beston's sympathetic portrayal of Morton, however, probably came as a surprise to many of his contemporaries given the strong slant toward the Pilgrims still prevalent in America's reading of its history. Beston's depiction of Morton's book, *The New English Canaan*, emphasizes its reflection of the culture and mores of Elizabethan England and its rapturous depiction of the American landscape exulting in "its zest of life, its eagerness to find and make use of beauty, its adventurousness of the spirit and the flesh, its honest earthly good humor, its literary conventions, and even its delightful pedantry."[34] When Morton arrived in New England his whole-hearted embrace of the landscape and its native inhabitants alarmed the dour, unyielding Puritans of the Plymouth Colony who saw Morton as a threat to the very existence of their colony. Morton was clapped into irons by the Puritans and charged with selling firearms to the Indians, but when he was sent to England as a prisoner he was promptly freed by the authorities: "The arrest was illegal, the whole process and the imprisonment an outrageous injustice," writes Beston, "and there is not a scrap of real evidence to show that there was a word of truth in the specific charge."[35] There is an element of tragedy to the remainder of the tale, however, for although Morton returned to his beloved New England, he was once again arrested and deported by the Puritans after cruel treatment at their hands. He managed to sail to the colonies once more, but by then he was a broken old man, and he died shortly afterwards.

Beston saw Morton's story as a farce that became a tragedy orchestrated by the Puritans. He points out that prior to leaving the Netherlands for New England, the rigid orthodoxies of the Puritans had "severely tried the tempers of their exceedingly tolerant hosts at Leyden."[36] Once they had established their isolated colony in the New World, these "Cruell Schismaticks," as they were characterized by Morton, engaged in conduct that often made a mockery of their professed piety. Beston contrasts Morton's friendly open-handedness toward the native inhabitants with that of the Puritans, citing Cotton Mather, a Puritan two generations removed from the founding of Plymouth, who wrote, "the woods were almost cleared of these pernicious creatures to make room for a better growth."[37] Beston's main point, however, is not simply to bash the Pilgrims, but to highlight a perennial source of friction between worldviews:

> It has been wisely observed that Puritanism is not so much a form of religion as an attitude to life, and that there are Puritan sects in Islam as well as in eastern and western Christianity. A meeting of the mind which comes into the world already "Puritan," and the mind which is liberal by temperament has always meant a struggle, and the first named has never troubled to make a declaration of war, but has offered instant battle to his soul's antagonist. Once victorious, the repressive type has shown no mercy to victims of its aggression. The story of the merry man of the Merry-Mount is the tale of such a challenge and such a defeat.[38]

A variation on this theme is found in Beston's profile of Arthur Rimbaud, *l'enfant terrible* of late nineteenth-century French poetry. In 1870, at the age of fifteen, Rimbaud left home on his "first vagabondage." For the next few years he traveled through France, writing poetry, enduring hardship, and enjoying the "bohemian adventure." As Beston notes, he also "found a place in his mind for its sordid side."[39] Rimbaud lived briefly with the poet Paul Verlaine and his family, then he and Verlaine took to the road on a "vagabond tour" in 1872. They parted company in 1873 while traveling through Belgium, when "Verlaine, while in some kind of mental state best studied by psychopathologists, shot his fellow poet in the wrist with a pistol, and was promptly imprisoned by the Belgian authorities."[40] Modern critics are convinced that the relationship between Rimbaud and Verlaine was homosexual in nature, but Beston does not raise this issue at all in his biographical profile. Rimbaud was not seriously wounded but he ceased to write poetry, choosing instead to embark upon a series of journeys over the next several years that culminated in a stint as an arms merchant in Africa. Shortly before his premature death in 1891 from a mysterious infection, Rimbaud's poems were published in Paris and created a literary sensation— Rimbaud himself, however, had long since given up any interest in poetry, and greeted the news with complete indifference.

Rimbaud's was the most contemporary by far of any of the lives chosen by Beston to profile for *The Book of Gallant Vagabonds*, and Beston's biographical sketch of Rimbaud required more original research than for any of his other subjects. Furthermore, what little material existed was written in French, which may have been part of the allure of Rimbaud for Beston: "No account exists in English of the mysterious last years of Rimbaud turned vagabond and African trader; for the material is difficult to assemble, and the tale has to be pieced out from notes in stray letters, reports of the Colonial office, and even the proceedings of British learned societies. Moreover, there exists no study of the purely vagabond side of his unique career."[41] In contrast to the others, writes Beston:

> Rimbaud remains the most mysterious of all vagabonds. The ceaseless, embittered, eager search for something that was his life,—what shall be its last interpretation? Did he seek something which had fled him, or something to replace the thing which had fled? From the Latin quarter of the 80's, with its book shops, its old dank houses, and drizzling rain of the cloudy Parisian spring to the lifeless oven of Aden, his mind had known but one aim, and that an aim unlike any other sought by the great vagabonds. No answer may be found by scanning the poetry, for Rimbaud the poet and Rimbaud

the Somali trader were two men. Active, nervous, intellectual, difficult and often utterly unpleasant and unsympathetic, he wanders about his bales of goods in the warehouse shadows, a mysterious and intriguing figure. After all, though he did not find the answer he sought—who does?—he found activity, and for him activity was the soul's rest.[42]

Rimbaud's story also differed in an odd way from that of the other vagabonds selected by Beston in that, unlike the others, he began as a writer—but whereas the others left written records of their journeys, Rimbaud did not. Finally, the other vagabonds all had something of an element of the quest in their journeys—Bruce and Belzoni's archaeological studies, the Alaska of Ledyard's imagination, Morton's New England, Trelawny's vague but omnipresent thirst for adventure.

Despite the fact that his new book was a significant departure from Beston's previous work, the critical reception to *The Book of Gallant Vagabonds* bolstered his conviction that he had more to offer as a writer than simply journalism and children's stories. Writing for the *New York Tribune*, Harrison Smith wrote, "Whether these vagabonds were gallant or miserable, or both Mr. Beston has told their tales most entertainingly."[43] In the *Literary Review* of the *New York Evening Post*, A.H. Gibbs wrote, "Mr. Beston's fine enthusiasm adds color to every page. He has long since won his literary spurs, but in this most excellent volume he proves himself to be a worthy squire to his sextet of knights of the open road."[44] The reviewer for *The New York Times* also waxed enthusiastic, writing, "It is difficult to see how one could be other than captivated by the spirit which pervades 'Gallant Vagabonds' and the highly lifelike movement which the author imparts to his narratives."[45] One of the few modern (or relatively modern, at least) critics who has written at length about Beston's work, Winfield Townley Scott, accurately states that while one can see the style of Beston's mature prose coalescing in *The Book of Gallant Vagabonds*, "Beston was simply out to write with gusto about adventurers who lived with gusto . . . *The Book of Gallant Vagabonds* has verve and dash and especially in its chapter on Rimbaud, oversimplifications which are rather boyish." Scott, a friend of Beston and a great admirer of his later work also opines that, "[Beston] has always looked somewhat larger than any room he is in. It may not be persiflage to suggest that sometimes a man writes a book because of the way he looks."[46] Whether this latter speculation is accurate or not, it may well explain why several of the men Beston chose to portray in the book were, like himself, physically imposing.

It seems odd, however, that none of the reviews drew the connection between Beston's vagabonds and the modern temper that Beston saw as one of the primary differences between their approach to life and the post-war *zeitgeist*, at least as reflected in the writing of the period. Beston shared much in common with his "Lost Generation" contemporaries, including a deep mistrust of those who had led a generation of young men to the slaughter of war, but he resisted the trap of falling into nihilistic despair: "My new book is just out and has started well . . . Everyone says it's *exhilarating*. There's so much literature about that's pessimistic and disillusioned—indeed, the thing today is make up your mind that life is a bad banana, and then write about its little reticences with the grace and frankness of a first year student at a veterinary school. But my vagabonds loved life and hungered and thirsted to see it—bless 'em!"[47] While the Great Depression of the 1930s and the Second World War later stole much of Beston's *joie de vivre*, during the decade after the Great War he resolutely sought to find hope—through his fairy tales, his vagabonds, and later through the timeless cycles of nature and the earth.

During the summer of 1925, while he was finishing *The Book of Gallant Vagabonds*, Beston was also drawing up the plans for his new dune shack in Eastham and had engaged a local carpenter, Harvey Moore, to build it. In early September, Beston took a short trip to Maine to visit Mary Cabot Wheelwright in Castine and the Days in Damariscotta but he soon returned to the Cape, eager to see how construction on the new cottage, which he had dubbed "the Fo'castle," was progressing. Before the summer was over, construction of the dune shack was completed and Beston spent the next several weeks there, reveling in the beauty of the great beach. Perched atop the dunes, the small house was a trim twenty-by-sixteen-foot structure with a small "piazza," as Beston called it, facing east and overlooking the ocean. There was but one door, leading from the porch to the main room of the house. As he described the Fo'castle in *The Outermost House*:

It consisted of two rooms, a bedroom and a kitchen-living room . . . a brick
fireplace with its back to the wall between rooms heated the larger space and
took the chill off the bedroom, and I used a two-burner oil stove when cooking.

My neighbor built well. The house, even as I hoped, proved compact and
strong, and it was easy to run and easy to heat . . . In my larger room, I had
a chest of drawers painted an honest carriage blue, a table, a wall bookcase,
a couch, two chairs, and a rocker. My kitchen, built yacht fashion all in a
line, stood at my southern wall. First came a dish and crockery cupboard,
then a space for the oil stove—I kept this boxed in when not in use—then a
shelf, a porcelain sink, and the corner pump. Blessed pump! It never failed
me or indulged in nerves.[48]

The water quality on the beach varied greatly, so Beston was delighted to
chance upon a well of fresh water as good as he could possibly have hoped.
In what he called his "somewhat amateur enthusiasm for windows," Beston
installed ten of them, seven in the main room and three in the bedroom. He
soon found that the glare of sunlight, sand, and sea was often overpower-
ing and he was forced to close the shutters originally intended for winter
service.[49] While he never mentions the sanitary facilities of the Fo'castle,
that rustic staple, the outhouse, was located a short distance from the dune
shack.

The solidity of the house's construction was soon put to the test when
a powerful autumn gale hit the Cape. The afternoon before the night of
the gale, the winds and rain suddenly picked up as the storm hurtled out
of the northwest. "All the afternoon before the night of the gale," Beston
wrote, "a raw, rainy, wild afternoon, the fo'castle was the Hotel Astor of
the dunes for I had a succession of frozen gunners, clammers, Eastham
high school boys, eel-pot setters and quahaugers come in to get warm. It
was ever so interesting and picturesque. I gave 'em all a cup of hot tea and
milk and a blessing. Then came swift night and the rising hullaballo."[50]
The storm intensified that night, but the Fo'castle passed its first great
test with flying colors:

The little house stood solid as a rock, but it thrummed in the fearful wind just
the way a church window does when an organist steps on the gas. Outside,
in a dark of chaos, the whole beach was on the move; sand, pebbles, wave

spume, old wreckage, driftwood and seaweed all hurtling south through the pitch black night at 80 miles an hour. I went out to see if my house was still ashore and as I went around the corner, a skunk as large as an ant-eater went past me apparently a good three feet from the ground and dissappeared (sic) in the direction of Martha's Vineyard. I stood watch the whole night, wondering just when I would come to and say "Ain't Portugal Pretty?" but the blessed fo'castle stood like a tower and the exhausted dawn found us still anchored to the sands.[51]

Beston declared his first stay at the Fo'castle to be "about the best two months I've ever had."[52] Still, Beston had not yet determined that he would write a book about the Cape; indeed, he had not even decided for certain that he would spend the following summer at his new cottage, mulling

Beston at his dune shack in Eastham, Cape Cod, 1926. Built by local carpenter Harvey Moore in 1926 from plans drawn up by Beston, Beston called his dune shack "The Fo'c'stle" although it became better known as "The Outermost House."

over the possibility instead of renting a cottage near Jake and Bee Day in Damariscotta, Maine.[53]

One thing that Beston had decided for certain was that he needed a change of pace and that he would not be spending a great deal of time in Quincy or Boston during the winter of 1925–26. After a brief trip to New York City in November, where Beston learned that the early response to *The Book of Gallant Vagabonds* had been overwhelmingly positive, he traveled west to visit Mary Wheelwright, who had recently purchased a 174-acre ranch she named "Los Luceros" in Alcalde, New Mexico, near Taos. Wheelwright had raptly described the landscape and people of the region to Beston and invited him to make the journey out west to visit her. The centerpiece of the property was a 5,700 square foot house built in the 1800s, which Wheelwright renovated to create a magnificent hacienda. In 1921 Arthur and Frances Newcomb, who operated a trading post on the Navajo reservation, had introduced Mary Wheelwright to Hastiin Klah (1867–1937), a widely-respected Navajo singer and medicine man. Klah was greatly concerned that efforts by the federal government to "mainstream" American Indians would doom their language, culture, and religion; Wheelwright and Klah soon became close friends and joined together with Frances Newcomb to do what they could to preserve the spoken word rituals, songs, dances, and artworks that formed the focal point of Navajo religious practices. Their efforts resulted in the formation in 1937 of what came to be called the Wheelwright Museum of the American Indian in Sante Fe, New Mexico.

Ever since his trip to Spain in 1924, Beston had been fascinated by Spanish culture and architecture, and he had been interested in the American Indians since boyhood; the combination of both that he found in New Mexico was irresistible. As he wrote to Jake and Bee Day in a letter that reflects a hint of religious awe at the experience:

> This is a *great* place. The house I live in was once the estancia of the great Spanish land owner of the region, a noble house of thick adobe walls white washed within, old brown ceilings laid over *round* beams, corner fireplaces that seem like an adobe oven sliced in half, and the ancient Spanish furniture. And the country—the Indian dances—well I've just got to tell of em

viva voce. Imagine me up *all* night Christmas eve, tearing around the wild, moonlit country in a huge car . . . fording little streams and great ones, fringing roads clinging to fearful hillsides—on, on through the night from pueblo to pueblo. Dance in the churches, candles, drums, the gathered Indians, the ritual dancers—buffalo dancers, mountain sheep dancers, deer dancers—all with the mask-like heads of these animals on their fine bare brown shoulders—the church resonating to the drum and the hoarse, deep, magnificent chorus—who sing gathered in a stately group at the end of the nave by the entrance door. A thing to shake one as a tree is shaken by a mighty wind.[54]

A contemporaneous letter sent to J. Luther Neff reflected the same awe, but perhaps in deference to Neff's position as a minister there was less of a religious gloss: "After finishing and launching my new book, I felt as though I needed a change, so I accepted the invitation of some friends, old *amigos*, to come and spend a cowboy Christmas on their ranch. I must say it's been *great*! Indians, Indian dances, Mexicans, old Spanish church bells, pinto ponies, canyons, coyotes, and *caballeros*. It's like being in a movie!"[55] While in New Mexico Beston had an idea for a short book about an Indian folktale he'd been told during the visit, about two young Navaho boys, twin brothers, who had brought the "Healing Song" to the Navaho people. Over the next several months Beston worked on the story, which was published by the Macmillan Company the following November as *The Sons of Kai: The Story the Indian Told*. Beston dedicated the book to Mary Cabot Wheelwright, writing, "Because those who love the Southwest and its peoples owe to her courage, her discernment, and her venturing spirit more than they can repay." There was a rather unfortunate element of the book's cover design that would not become obvious for a few years. The publishing company chose a Navaho pictograph for the book spine, one that often appeared in Navaho designs for pottery, blankets, and the like. A version of the Navaho symbol was later appropriated by an obscure political party in Germany; within few years it had become notorious as the Nazi *Hakenkreutz*—the swastika.[56]

Beston spent about two weeks in New Mexico before heading back east, arriving in Massachusetts on January 12, 1926. The raw, winter weather he came back to was a drastic change from that in New Mexico. As he told Jake Day, "coming from New Mexico, where the air is dry and the sun the size of twenty cartwheels, I feel like a pet Persian kitten that's been forgotten in a snow storm."[57] He was also suffering some back pain that he attributed to carrying firewood while he had been at the Fo'castle the previous fall, but may just as likely have been caused by horseback riding in New Mexico—unfamiliar activity for the thirty-seven-year-old Beston. Whatever the cause, the condition was not helped by the damp, cold New England winter. He was also concerned about the effect that so much time sitting at a writing desk was having on him, telling Bee Day that when he came up to Maine for a visit that Jake must take him walking, for he was gaining weight from "the dratted sedentary writing desk life, and no chance to walk or exercise."[58]

Other than the trip to New Mexico, Beston's travels in early 1926 were primarily confined to stretches of time at the Hotel Hawthorne in Salem and The Prince George Hotel in New York City, as well as in Quincy with his brother's family. He no longer maintained a fixed address, using a post office box in Quincy to collect the mail that came in while he was out of town. While Beston was still enamored with the romantic notion of being a wandering vagabond, a plaintive tone often crops up in his letters to married friends. The footloose freedom of single life was losing some of its appeal to the thirty-seven-year-old bachelor, who now wondered if he was missing something by not having a home, a wife, and children. Beston continued to see Elizabeth Coatsworth whenever they were in Boston at the same time, but she was traveling so much that for the most part their relationship was maintained through letters. The vagabondage of the past few years was now starting to feel less romantic, less carefree, and more like an aimless, restless, and rootless casting about, like that of Whitman's spider:

> A noiseless, patient spider,
> I mark'd, where, on a little promontory, it stood, isolated;
> Mark'd how, to explore the vacant, vast surrounding,
> It launch'd forth filament, filament, filament, out of itself;
> Ever unreeling them—ever tirelessly speeding them.

A Gallant Vagabond

And you, O my Soul, where you stand,
Surrounded, surrounded, in measureless oceans of space,
Ceaselessly musing, venturing, throwing,—seeking the spheres,
    to connect them;
Till the bridge you will need, be form'd—till the ductile anchor hold;
Till the gossamer thread you fling, catch somewhere, O my Soul.

During the previous summer and early fall, Beston had spent a good deal of time at the Fo'castle while he finished *The Book of Gallant Vagabonds*, and now, with no writing projects or other commitments to occupy his time, he found himself thinking more and more about the Cape. Even while hard at work finishing up the book, Beston had kept a journal chronicling his observations of the beach and other items of interest like the stories told to him by the coastguardsmen and other local friends. Henry Beston probably had not formed a notion to write about the great beach of Cape Cod by the early summer of 1926, but like his favorite constellation, Orion the Hunter, he too was hunting for something—even if he didn't yet understand exactly what it was.

CHAPTER SIX

Orion Rises on the Dunes
1926–1928

Sky and sea, horizon-hinged
Tablets of blank blue, couldn't,
Clapped shut, flatten this man out.

The great gods, Stone-Head, Claw-Foot
Winded by much rock-bumping
And claw-threat, realized that.

For what, then, had they endured
Dourly the long hots and colds,
Those old despots, if he sat

Laugh-shaken on his doorsill,
Backbone unbendable as
Timbers of his upright hut?

SYLVIA PLATH
"The Hermit at Outermost House"

SINCE THE SEVENTEENTH CENTURY, the stretch of ocean off the eastern shore of Cape Cod has been notorious for its constantly shifting sandbars and treacherous shallows, which gave it a reputation as a graveyard for sailing ships. Until the mid-twentieth century one of the great, albeit rather grim, resources for residents of the Cape was the detritus left on the shore after shipwrecks. Henry Thoreau took four trips to the Cape between 1849 and 1857, and his posthumously published *Cape Cod* (1865) opens with an account of a shipwreck that occurred just before his October 1849 trip to the Cape. A passenger ship bound for Boston from Provincetown had foundered in a violent autumn storm, claiming the lives of 145 passengers.

On reaching Boston, Thoreau saw a handbill with the headline "Death! One hundred and forty-five lives lost at Cohasset." When Thoreau arrived a few days later at Cohasset, where many of the bodies had been cast ashore, he noted the casual attitude of a old Cape Codder he met on the beach: "It was the wrecked weed that concerned him most, rock-weed, kelp, and sea-weed, as he named them, which he carted to his barn-yard; and those bodies were to him but other weeds which the tide cast up, but which were of no use to him."[1] Salvaging items washed up by the sea was a necessary part of life on Cape Cod, where resources were scarce and mostly came from the sea, and Thoreau did not fault the residents of the Cape for their somewhat casual attitude toward the loss of life and property that was part of the equation. "Though there are wreck-masters appointed to look after valuable property which must be advertised," he wrote, "yet undoubtedly a great deal of value is secretly carried off. But are we not all wreckers contriving that some treasure may be washed up on our beach, that we may secure it, and do we not infer the habits of these Nauset and Barnegat wreckers from the common modes of getting a living?"[2]

While it might be shipwrecks and the attendant loss of life that drew the attention of most people, the changes wrought by the sea upon the land were just as fascinating to Thoreau. In contrast to his native Concord, this was a landscape that changed rapidly, not just from geological age to geological age, or from human generation to human generation, but often from day to day, even hour to hour. While he was in Cohasset he observed further evidence of the sea's power, one that impressed him even more than the wreck of the steamship had. Because the Cape is largely composed of sand, sudden and dramatic changes in the landscape wrought by large storms were fairly common. The previous spring a great storm had carved out a "handsome but shallow lake of some four hundred acres" separated from the sea by a narrow beach. Thoreau was told by some of the natives that during periods of heavy rain, the runoff sometimes created short-lived streams that bisected the Cape, temporarily isolating its northern reaches. The mutability of Cape Cod's landscape, particularly on the "lower" or "outer" Cape region north of Orleans, made road building difficult, and it was not until the early twentieth century that a paved road was built connecting the outer Cape towns. Indeed, despite its proximity to Boston, it was not until an improved rail line was constructed in the late 1800s that the Cape became easily accessible to travelers. Even into the early twentieth century, much of the outer Cape was still as isolated and wild as it had been a century earlier and was nothing like the tourist destination it would become just a few decades later.

Late in the afternoon of Saturday, September 18, 1926, Henry Beston boarded a train in Boston, heading to Cape Cod for what he later said was intended to be a two-week vacation at the Fo'castle. Walter Teller, who interviewed Beston for *The New York Times* many years later wrote that Beston said that at the time he went to live out on the Cape, "I was six feet, one and a half inches tall, weighed 190 and was strong as a bear."[3] He got off in Orleans after nightfall and went to the Southward Inn, where he had stayed several times during his previous visits to the Cape. After dinner at the Inn—"a good, hot chowder"—Mrs. Helen Clark, a friend of Beston's who operated a taxi service, drove him the five or six miles to Eastham, where he would walk the rest of the way to his cottage on the dunes. On the way to Eastham, Clark told Beston that she had been to the beach that morning and that there had been a high surf all day, one of the highest she could remember. Upon reaching Eastham, Beston bid farewell to Mrs. Clark and then shouldered the bag containing his clothing and provisions and trudged off toward the dunes.

The night was clear and cold with a sky full of stars, the constellation of Orion, the Hunter—Beston's favorite constellation—rising from the southern horizon. When Beston reached the beach he found a titanic surf crashing onto the beach all the way up to the dunes. The high tide and waves made a beach passage to the Fo'castle impossible, but Beston chanced to meet John Blood, one of the Nauset station coastguardsmen he'd befriended during his earlier visits to the Cape. The two men decided to take the inland route to the Fo'castle, slopping through two or three miles of flooded marshes and muddy tidal flats until they reached Beston's dune shack. Beston lighted a fire in the Fo'castle's cast-iron stove, and after a brief respite to warm himself, John Blood left to continue his patrol, promising Beston that he would send the next man on watch to wake him. At three A.M., coastguardsman

Everett Gross knocked on the door, and Beston dressed quickly to head down to the beach with him. It was now low tide and the beach was passable once again as Gross resumed his patrol. Beston wandered along the nighttime beach, finding it had been left "cleansed and clear" by the pounding surf, save for the ghostly skeleton of an ill-fated schooner, the *Lily*, which now poked up out of the sands, exhumed by the waves. Pausing for a moment to look up at the nighttime sky, he saw the aurora borealis, "an arc of northern lights and a fan of the zodiacal light" shimmering overhead, a sight that always filled him with wonder and awe.[4] The following morning Beston woke early to get a better look at the changes wreaked upon the beach by the high surf. The waves had reached half way up the height of the great dune, which towered some fifty feet over the white sand beach. At one spot the surf had washed over an opening in the dunes, flattening out the beach grass and spilling over into a tidal pool on the other side, "a feat," wrote Beston in his journal, "I don't quite like."[5]

The following day brought more high surf, once again cutting off the beach at high tide. Harvey Moore, the local carpenter who had built Beston's cottage, came down to the Fo'castle to do some work at 9 A.M. but soon left, realizing that he would be stuck there once the tide came in later that morning. Bob Whiting, one of the coastguardsmen stationed at the North Eastham station located several miles north of the Fo'castle stopped by, bringing some preserves made by his wife. Whiting and a local boy named Knowles stayed for supper and a walk up the beach before heading home. Despite the fact that he'd had very little sleep the night before, Beston stayed up long past dark, writing page after page of description in his journal by lantern light and wandering down to the beach from time to time to observe the surf and its impact on the beach:

> As I write this, I must note that I have *never* seen a more furious surf than tonight's—walls of water twelve feet high advancing out of the moonlight and breaking in Niagaras on the beach. They were breaking on outer bar. No sound of wind—all water. Sound a roar, a grind and a seething hiss all in one, continuous and terrible and undertone of blows and the dune trembling. Moonlight on the sea at foot of big dune, and the dune itself like the rampart silhouette of a world-mist ruling the marsh . . . so little margin

between myself & that elemental fury. Magnificent spray fountains in the moonlight, surely 25–30 feet high—on a level with the dune—seethe over a great heavy undertone of seething roar . . . Back of house towards marsh—croak questioning and monitory of heron. Piping of yellow-legs. My lantern making beads of brightness on the leaf-sword in the moon.[6]

The sublime power of the restless ocean and the stark beauty of the great beach enthralled Beston. In his journal he described the scene as if he were truly seeing the outer Cape for the first time, reveling in the "elemental"—a word that would become one of his favorite adjectives—character of untamed and unconquerable nature.

The people of the outer Cape who managed an accommodation with nature there, the coastguardsmen, fishermen, and others who had chosen to live in a world that seemed so distant in time and place from modern industrial civilization despite its relative proximity to the great cities of the northeast also intrigued Beston. These were people who still lived by the rhythms of the natural world, the sun, the tides, the seasons—and Beston detected in this life a "joy of Nature" that was not simply physical or aesthetic, but spiritual. This connection to nature added a dimension to their lives that seemed to have vanished from those who led their lives largely insulated from natural rhythms and Beston was anxious to understand this link more fully: "Living here," he wrote in his journal, "makes me curious in regard to wanderers on the dunes."[7] When Harvey Moore and Win Knowles came to the Fo'castle a few days later for some finishing work on the cottage walls, Beston listened raptly to Moore's stories of local life and the natural history of the beach. As Beston noted in his journal, "Harvey tells a story exceedingly well. Today he told of tame crows and of how one of 'em stood in a pan of dough, treaded it, and flew home with penants (sic) of dough clinging to his claws."[8] This was a landscape of primal beauty—"the moon revealing the black edge of the world—light on the sea below it. The swan, the quail, foxes, the crows"—but it was also a landscape with human inhabitants, living, working, and telling stories about the land. The usual Cape Cod response to stories that seemed to have an element of fiction to their depiction of the natural world and its creatures was the politely skeptical phrase, "guess I'll have to take your word for it," which seemed to Beston wholly appropriate for a world full of mysteries that often transcended human understanding.[9]

While Beston never descended into the nihilism and despair that afflicted many of his contemporaries in the "Lost Generation," in the years following the Great War he too found himself struggling to come to terms with a modern world that no longer seemed to make sense. The old institutions of community, government, and religion that had once grounded human existence now seemed less germane in the post-war world, leaving each individual alone to flounder about in search of meaning. On the Cape, living a life intimately connected with nature and the cycle of the sun and the seasons, Beston realized that the key ingredient missing from modern industrial civilization was this oldest of all human connections. In *The Outermost House* Beston describes why he went to the great beach in words that resonate as powerfully as Thoreau's pronouncement of why he went to the woods in *Walden*:

> I went there [the Cape] to spend a fortnight in September. The fortnight ending, I lingered on, and as the year lengthened into autumn, the beauty and mystery of this earth and outer sea so possessed me that I could not go. The world to-day is sick to its thin blood for lack of elemental things, for fire before the hands, for water welling from the earth, for air, for the dear earth itself underfoot. In my world of beach and dune these elemental presences lived and had their being, and under their arch there moved an incomparable pageant of nature and the year. The flux and reflux of ocean, the incomings of the waves, the gatherings of birds, the pilgrimages of the peoples of the sea, winter and storm, the splendour of autumn and the holiness of spring—all these were part of the great beach. The longer I stayed, the more eager was I to know this coast and to share the mysterious and elemental life; I found myself free to do so, I had no fear of being alone, I had something of a field naturalist's inclination; presently I made up my mind to remain and try living for a year on Eastham Beach.[10]

It is hard to say with absolute certainty that Beston had already decided to write a book about the great beach when he arrived for his planned fortnight in September 1926, but it certainly appears that was the case.

Orion Rises on the Dunes

He had spent several months on Cape Cod during the preceding year, and had begun to keep a journal again—something he had not done since his transformative experience as an ambulance driver on the western front in 1915–1916—which suggests that he apprehended that this was a place worth writing about. Further, it appears that Beston's epiphany about the power of humankind's connection to the natural world and the danger of losing that vital link must have come early in his stay at the Fo'castle in September 1926, for scattered among the descriptive passages of his early entries are notes regarding thematic emphases for a possible book about the beach.

One of the most important of these early thematic observations concerned how leading a life so close to nature's elemental forces affected the people who lived there: "The Cape being minus industrialism," Beston wrote in his journal, "has therefore a people with character, integrity, and vitality."[11] In a modern world that often operated as though the laws of nature had been repealed, the outer Cape was a world in which the sea could change one's life in an instant. The treacherous currents, storms, and sandbars just off the coast posed potentially disastrous challenges to shipping, and the great beach was littered with the detritus of ill-fated vessels that had met their end off the great beach of Cape Cod. There were local legends, some of which later proved true, of pirates and merchant ships that had sunk just offshore bearing a fortune in treasure. One of these was the pirate ship *Whydah*, captained by the notorious pirate Sam Bellamy, which was claimed by a storm off Eastham on April 26, 1717. The *Whydah* was rumored to be heavily laden with plunder from over fifty merchant ships, a legend that proved to have a basis in fact when the wreck was discovered in 1984. Most Cape wrecks, however, were of small fishing schooners and packet ships bearing more mundane goods. On September 22, 1926, Beston went down to the seashore to observe the demise of the *Katy V. Barrett*, a schooner that had struck one of the numerous sandbars off the coast. The ship had been transporting a load of ice when the heavy seas caused the men to panic and make a run for shore before night fell. The sailors lost control of the ship, which foundered; one man was badly hurt when the capstan bar whirled about wildly and struck him.

His mates wrapped him up in a sail and loaded him into a dory filled with seaweed to try to keep him comfortable, but he died from his injuries the following day.[12]

From the research he had done for his article on the coast guard two years earlier, Beston knew that life and death struggles between mariners and the sea were an aspect of the Cape largely unknown to all save a few year-round residents, but were stories well worth telling. Beston's admiration for the men of the coast guard was boundless, and he took every possible opportunity to call public attention to their courageous, unheralded work. The Fo'castle became something of an unofficial way station for the men of the Nauset Coast Guard station on their six-mile patrols of the great beach, particularly during the winter months, knowing they were welcome there whatever the hour to warm themselves at Beston's fire and enjoy a hot cup of coffee. Beston developed close friendships with several of the Coast Guard, including Yngve Rongner, who lived with his wife Selma and son George on Nauset Road, about four miles from the Fo'castle. The Rongners often invited Beston to their home for dinner (clam chowder and baked beans, two of Beston's favorites, were often on the menu) and conversation. Beston became something of a hero to young George Rongner, who later told Don Wilding, author of *Henry Beston's Cape Cod*, "After meeting Henry Beston my life changed; he was a magnificent person and he talked so glowingly about nature and about history that I too became interested in that sort of thing . . . I think probably Henry Beston had more influence on my life as a youngster than any other single person."[13]

As the year slowly turned to autumn, Beston marveled at the abundance of bird life on the beach, with flocks of semi-palmated sandpipers, sanderlings, terns, killdeer, plovers, gulls, and other shorebirds rising from the sands at his approach. "How singular it is that so little has been written about the birds of Cape Cod!" he wrote, "The peninsula, from an ornithologist's point of view, is one of the most interesting in the world . . . living here, one may see more kinds and varieties of birds than it would seem possible to discover in any one small region."[14] On Nauset Marsh, just west of his cottage, when the migratory geese, swans, and ducks arrived in great flocks the occasional popping of distant shotguns signalled the concurrent arrival of hunters. One day Beston thrilled to the magnificent sight of an eagle flying over the marsh behind the Fo'castle:

> The presence of the eagle disturbed the gulls . . . he was over the lagoon, flying high, and on his way down the marshes and over the south shoulder of the dune to the sea. As this magnificent solitary creature came down the sky, the coveys of gulls feeding by the muddy edges of the marsh islands and the sand bars of the channels rose in flurries and ushered like autumn leaves shaken from a tree into the current of a melancholy wind.[15]

Other bird visitors were initially unfamiliar to Beston. One morning he got up from his writing desk to get some driftwood for his stove, and while he was out on the little sea-facing "piazza" of his shack he spotted two large, dark birds standing at the edge of the breakers. Upon retrieving his spotting telescope he saw that they were skuas, large "piratical" birds that steal fish from other shorebirds such as gulls. "Formidable looking fellows!" wrote Beston, "I noticed that they didn't make much of a fuss about the wash of the breakers but stood in it and let it seethe past & about them. The ordinary gull doesn't like to get its feet too wet, and flutters up or walks out of the foam."[16] In his ornithological studies on the Cape, Beston made extensive use of E. H. Forbush's *Birds of Massachusetts and Surrounding States*, and when Beston wrote to Forbush to mention his sighting of the skuas, he was pleased to see his sighting get a mention in the bird-watching bulletin Forbush regularly published.[17]

Watching the great autumnal bird migration Beston saw a collective intelligence at work that was not yet fully understood by scientists and that would forever change the way he regarded animals. As he would later write in *The Outermost House*, "it is no confused and careless horde through which I go but an army. Some spirit of discipline and unity has passed over these countless little brains, waking in each flock a conscious sense of its collective self and giving each bird a sense of himself as a member of some migrant company."[18] All through September and October Beston observed the great multitudes of birds, fascinated by the mysterious force that seemed to be at work in their movements: "Standing on the beach, fresh claw marks at my feet, I watch the lovely sight of the group instantly turned into a constellation of birds, into a fugitive Pleiades whose living stars keep their chance positions; I watch the spiraling flight, the momentary tilts of the white bellies, the alternate shows of the clustered, grayish backs."[19] The more he observed the collective intelligence of birds in flight, the more he questioned Descartes's assertion that animals were merely *machina*, unthinking mechanisms of flesh and bone responding automatically to whatever stimuli came their way. In one of the most provocative and widely quoted passages of *The Outermost House*, Beston writes:

> We need another and a wiser and perhaps a more mystical concept of animals. Remote from universal nature, and living by complicated artifice, man in civilization surveys the creature through the glass of his knowledge and sees thereby a feather magnified and the whole image in distortion. We patronize them for their incompleteness, for their tragic fate of having taken form so far below ourselves. And therein we err, and greatly err. For the animal shall not be measured by man. In a world older and more complete than ours they move finished and complete, gifted with extensions of the senses we have lost or never attained, living by voices we shall never hear. They are not brethren, they are not underlings; they are other nations, caught with ourselves in the net of life and time, fellow prisoners of the splendor and travail of the earth.[20]

In an era where the anthropocentric view of nature still held sway despite the work of writers such as Charles Darwin, Henry Thoreau, John Burroughs, and John Muir, Beston's declaration is an eloquent reminder that man is—as his contemporary Aldo Leopold would write in *A Sand County Almanac* two decades later—a member of the biotic community, and not its master.

In a letter to Elizabeth Coatsworth sent during his year on the great beach, Beston jokingly refers to himself as the "Thoreauburrough," and there is no question that he is an intellectual descendant of the Emerson-inspired naturalists of the nineteenth century. John Burroughs wrote of Emerson that he went to the woods not as a scientist or as a naturalist, but to "bring the word of the wood god to men," and something similar might be said of Beston. As interested as he was in the bird life of Cape Cod, he did not go to the great beach as a scientist but as a writer-naturalist; indeed, there are some rather surprising omissions in his knowledge of natural history, such as his efforts to identify an orange and black butterfly that turned out to be the rather common Monarch Butterfly. Instead, he went primarily to see if he could gather some deeper truth about human existence, a truth that had a strong element of the spiritual, even the mystical, about it. In an interview, he acknowledged, "Living on the Cape brought out the mystic in me, showing me that the surprise of life was the biggest thing."[21] One October morning, he went down to the beach at sunrise to gather some pure white sand for Hastiin Klah, the Navajo medicine man he had befriended while visiting Mary Wheelwright the previous winter. Like Wheelwright, Beston sensed there was something profoundly spiritual about Klah: "he wanted sand taken from the shores of the Atlantic ocean with which to make medicine . . . No doubt it contained the magic that he was seeking. Later I received in return a beautiful, hand-woven rug, which I understand, is also full of magic."[22] Living alone on the great beach reinforced this side of Beston's personality. After acknowledging the importance of the companionship provided by his coastguard friends in *The Outermost House*, Beston goes on to say:

> It was not this touch with my fellows, however, which alone sustained me. Dwelling thus upon the dunes, I lived in the midst of an abundance of natural life which manifested itself every hour of the day, and from being thus surrounded, thus enclosed within the great whirl of what one may call the life force, I felt that I drew a secret and sustaining energy. There were times, on the threshold of spring, when the force seemed as real as heat from the sun. A sceptic may smile and ask me to come to his laboratory and demonstrate; he may talk as he will of the secret workings of my own isolated and uninfluenced flesh and blood, but I think that those who have lived in nature, and tried to open their doors rather than close them on her energies, will understand well enough what I mean. Life is as much a force in the universe as electricity or gravitational pull, and the presence of life sustains life.[23]

Immediately after this passage Beston abruptly shifts to a discussion of birds that winter on the coast, almost as though he were slightly embarrassed to have shifted in tone from the analytical observer to the mystic.

Beston's comments on "the life force" are reminiscent of the theories of some early twentieth-century scientific philosophers, most notably the

French intellectual Henri Bergson, with whose work Beston was certainly familiar. Bergson burst upon the scene in 1907 with *Creative Evolution* (the English translation was published by Henry Holt in 1911), and his theories soon became an international sensation. As Ian Alexander writes in *Bergson: Philosopher of Reflection*, "To his contemporaries, Bergson appeared as the 'liberator.' His historical role was, indeed, to free thought from the deceits of language and the illusions of conceptual thinking as well as from the mechanism and determinism of nineteenth-century 'scientisme.'"[24] Bergson's *Creative Evolution* swept through intellectual circles in the United States. William James, brother of novelist Henry James, became one of Bergson's influential early champions, describing *Creative Evolution* as "a real wonder in the history of philosophy." John Burroughs was also enthralled by Bergson's work; so much so, in fact, that when he met the French philosopher in 1913 he told Bergson that "Emerson was the inspiration of my youth, and you are the inspiration of my old age."[25] Burroughs's initial enthusiasm for Bergson's work was based on his fervent hope that in *Creative Evolution* Bergson had successfully bridged the gap between science and spirituality, satisfying the human longing for religion without ignoring what Burroughs called "the light of science, of emancipated human reason."[26] Perhaps the most influential concept in Bergson's work was that of "*élan vital*," which was his way of filling what he saw as a gap in the theory of evolution—the explanation of how organic life initially began on earth. This concept, which added a mystical or spiritual element to the scientific theory of evolution, was attractive to those—like Burroughs and Beston—who felt that modern scientific understanding could not account for everything in nature.

Like Henry Thoreau before him, Beston was fascinated with the people of the Cape and their lives in nature. He would often jot down short references to stories and observations that he might return to at a later time and flesh out in more detail. Many of the stories he gathered were told to him by coastguardsmen such as his friend Bill Eldredge, whom Beston would frequently accompany on his patrols down the beach. Friends from Eastham such as Mercy Mines, Prince and Edna Nickerson Hurd, and John Nickerson were also frequent visitors to the Fo'castle, and on one such visit in early October, they talked at some length about the *Portland* disaster of 1898 and other wrecks. "To understand this great outer beach," wrote Beston in *The Outermost House*, "to appreciate its atmosphere, its 'feel,' one must have a sense of it as the scene of wreck and elemental drama. Tales and legends of the great disasters fill no inconsiderable niche in the Cape mind."[27]

Eager to share his transformative experience with other people, Beston extended an invitation to many of his friends to come and visit him at the Fo'castle, and several of them did so. In early October, Arthur and Jeanette Gibbs came for a visit, where they spent a magnificent day on the beach and were treated to the sight of a flock of sandpipers who, Beston wrote, "look like they're dancing a Virginia Reel."[28] The person Beston was most anxious to have visit was Elizabeth Coatsworth, who was visiting relatives in Buffalo that autumn of 1926:

> Honoured Lady—
>
> I am arrived in a place where there is no more land, or only such land as the sea hath made from the flowing sands of her deeps; the sea girds me about. He to whom you sent me had great joy in my coming, gave me a friend; and a friend's friend and a dragon slayer's welcome, and hath appointed me the proudest place by his wall. Every night, when the earth is very still and the sea sings and thunders, I watch from my wall for the dragon of the great deeps to stir in the caves of the sea, and drag his scary terror fold by fold to the edge of the waves. I have not seen him yet, honoured lady, but I have seen the waves, plagued by an adverse wind, crumble together in convulsed and overlapping slides of foam, and I have watched the great Orion rise from the morning east, his quiver laden with winter and wild storm. Dragons of earth, dragons of the sea, dragons of the soul, I shall fight them all, and proffer thou my spear. And so, honoured lady, I bow again, and salute you in grave and grateful farewell.[29]

That same day he wrote Coatsworth another, less flowery, letter encouraging her to set a date for a visit to the Cape: "If Saturday's luncheon hour is free, do save it for me, for I have much to talk about, and I do so want to fix upon a date for a visit here. It is beautiful here; it is elemental beauty itself, great lonely earth, singing sea, and vast over-arching sky that is a footpath of gods."[30] Beston also invited Ted Roosevelt Jr. to come to the Cape for a visit, but Roosevelt wrote back telling his friend "Harry" that he was hopelessly entangled in political affairs and was unable to get away until after the November elections. In the Roosevelt family, politics often took precedence over the pleasures of time spent outdoors, and Ted responded to Beston's invitation with a melancholy resignation: "From now on my life is one gray horror, until after election in November. I suppose I shall be home some Sunday, but at this moment cannot tell which. When election has come and gone, and the dead and wounded carried from the field, can't you come down and stay with us? Then we can turn our minds to the really important things of life. 'For, oh! The song of a bird.'"[31]

Later that week, Beston got his initial experience of the elemental drama that makes up such an important part of the Cape's history. After spending two days traveling through Massachusetts with Arthur and Jeanette Gibbs, Beston returned to Cape Cod the morning of Friday October 15. After stopping at the Southward Inn for a bowl of chowder and dessert, Beston hiked back to the Fo'castle, where he spent the rest of the afternoon tidying things up. Just after sundown, he stepped out onto the porch of the cottage and looked out to sea, where he saw an enormous conflagration some ten or fifteen miles offshore. He rushed to get his binoculars and saw "a great mass of climbing fire with tall flames shooting out of it . . . that I felt were licking up masts and rigging. I couldn't make out the vessel itself at all, nothing but a mass of fire."[32] The ship proved to be a fishing trawler out of Gloucester, Massachusetts, the *Pioneer*, and Beston vividly described the incident in his journal:

> I looked up the beach to see what was being done at Nauset and through the deepening, clear, unspectacular twilight, I could see the Nauset crew dragging their boat to the surf, but whether they got off or not, I couldn't tell, because of the dark closing in. The distant group, the vague boat dissolved in darkness as I watched. I now wait to see if any seven o'clock patrol will pass, for if no one comes I shall know that the men are being held on boat duty or are out on that inky sea. Thinking that the men from the ship (whom I felt were somewhere out there on boats) might possibly land near the Fo'c'stle, I moved my table over to the front window, and put my big lamp on it.[33]

The fire from the ship blazed for several hours before dying down "to a red winking lamp which now and then glowed more brightly." Around eleven p.m. Beston dozed off, but coastguardsman John Blood soon knocked on the Fo'castle's door, telling Beston that the men from the ship were being landed just a short way down the beach. Beston hastily dressed and headed off down the beach toward the enormous hillock of sand he called "great dune." A half moon shone over the lagoon, providing some light for the rescue operation, and there was a spectacular display of the aurora borealis that Beston called "one of the most beautiful things I've ever seen in Nature," an ironic counterpoint to the human drama playing out just off shore.[34]

When Beston arrived at great dune, the men from the *Pioneer* were slashing through the surf and onto the beach in their fishing dories, a sight he labeled "one of the most thrilling things I've ever seen."[35] As he described the scene in a letter to Mabel Davison:

> The wrecked men, guided ashore by my Nauset C.G. friends (who had rowed out to do what they could, and had found the men at sea) came ashore between me & big dune, scarce a stone's throw away. Marraine, darling, it was once of the most dramatic and thrilling sights *I've ever seen*,—the C.G.s and their white boat on the beach, the roaring surf, the dark, and just seaward of the surf, the three dories working to try the dangerous landing. Just could barely, barely see 'em; they were presences rather than things. Much hallooing, (neither side could hear well) and then "Pull hard!" and three great black dories full of fishermen rushed through the surf full speed to the beach—exactly like sailors after a German submarine strafe. My big light, the electric flashlight you liked did great service (the C.G.s didn't land at the station because a strong N. wind was howling down the beach, and so they landed where they could, knowing that the other men would be too tired to row 2 miles more in the teeth of a strong head wind). While the C.G.s were securing the dories, I took the 15 fishermen to the Fo'castle, warmed 'em up, built up my fire, distributed a hot wine toddy & biscuit. Think of the old place, cram, cram jammed with Gloucester fishermen, all grateful and appreciative as could be, poor fellows! The told the C.G.s the little rest & wine & warmth had saved 'em just the second wind they needed. Two men, each with a whole arm with a bad surface burning—the engineers, father & son who had gone down into the flaming engine room to shut off the power so the others could launch the dories. These I dressed as I could.
>
> The C.G.s then came to take the men to the station, and looked after

'em in good style. My little help had given the C.G.s time to secure the boats and get a good hot supper ready. They were a bit tired, but carried on splendidly.[36]

Beston was particularly impressed by the stoic hardiness of the two burned men, James Morash and his son Chester, who, he wrote in his journal, were "[b]oth so patient, gratefully appreciative and uncomplaining."[37] The coastguardsmen then took the stricken men to Chelsea Naval Hospital for further medical treatment.

Despite the vivid description of the *Pioneer* incident in his journal and in his letter to Mabel Davison, the story was not included in *The Outermost House*, which recounted several other nautical disasters that happened during Beston's year on Cape Cod. This may have been due to modesty on Beston's part, omitting the story because he himself played a role in it. Despite the fact that he generally writes in the first person, Beston is habitually diffident when it comes to writing about himself—he generally positions himself as an observer, not a participant, in the scenes he describes. There may also have been a more practical motivation on his part to skip over this particular episode. Soon after moving into the Fo'castle, Beston had devised a signal system with his friends Tom and Mary Kelley, the proprietors of Eastham's Overlook Inn, located some two miles west of the Fo'castle. In those days much of Eastham was a treeless moor, and with a pair of binoculars the Kelleys could see Beston's cottage perched atop the dunes. During nights of particularly rough weather, Beston would place a lantern in his west-facing window to let the Kelleys know that he was safe and in no danger from the storm. Sometimes they would even use lanterns or flashlights to send messages in Morse code back and forth. Some casual passersby who saw the lantern signal came to an understandable if erroneous conclusion as to its meaning—they thought it was a signal to one of the many rum-running vessels that plied the coast. Beston's lonely dune shack appeared to some, not as an experiment in living close to nature, but as part of the enormous network of bootleggers that had sprung up since the beginning of Prohibition in 1919. Beston had undoubtedly heard some of the rumors passed on to him by friends and found them amusing, but since his story about aiding the survivors of the *Pioneer* included his admission that he had passed out hot rum toddies to the men, perhaps he realized that this was a story that called for a little more circumspection than usual.[38]

On Saturday, October 16, Elizabeth Coatsworth arrived at the Fo'castle with her sister Margaret and mother Ida. Beston took them to the beach where he regaled them with the story of the *Pioneer* and "[h]ad a peach of a picnic. Beautiful opalescent day."[39] That night Beston took the Coatsworths back to the Overlook Inn for dinner and lodging, but they returned again the next day for a long walk along the beach and lunch at the cottage before heading back to the mainland. After the Coatsworth visit, as the beautiful autumn turned to raw and blustery winter, there would be few visitors to the Fo'castle, save the coastguardsmen from the Nauset station and some of Beston's local friends from Eastham. Even the birds grew fewer, as he wrote in *The Outermost House*: "Mid-October and the land birds have gone. A few sparrows linger in the marshes. The [beach] plum bushes have lost their leaves. Walking the beach, I read winter in the new shapes of the clouds."[40] Much of October was spent gathering driftwood for winter fires and piles of seaweed to build an insulating wall around the outside of the cottage. "Now that I have settled down here for the winter," he wrote, "I find myself becoming something of a beach comber . . . All kinds of things 'come ashore' on these vast sands, and even the most valueless have an air of being treasure trove."[41]

As winter's cold, dark days settled in, Beston had a great deal of time for writing and reflection with little to interrupt his meditations. The driftwood fire burning steadily in his fireplace became his chief companion; "my fire was more than a source of heat—it was an elemental presence, a household god, and a friend."[42] By November, Beston seems to have ceased keeping a regular journal in favor of drafting notes for the manuscript that would become *The Outermost House*; if he did keep a regular journal after October 1926, it has apparently disappeared. The last few pages in his journal, written in late October, consist primarily of a list of brief references to topics of importance to him, starting with the notation "La priere sur les dunes—the joy & the distillation of joy out of this tragic world.—to awaken to its mystery and beauty, and to accept the honor of mortality—to be a sleep and a forgetting." Other topics Beston listed, not all of which would later appear in *The Outermost House* included things such as the sailor and the sea, the beach, great wrecks, protective coloration, instincts, death knowledge, an Indian clambake, clothes and nakedness, color and the joy of color, the use of the senses, and the static quality in societies.[43]

Other notations included topics such as "the results of living alone" and "being a solitary." While Beston spent a great deal of time alone during his year living on the great beach, he disavowed any intent of playing the hermit; he was a sociable person and recognized that man was a social animal. Beston felt that Henry Thoreau had made far too much of the hermit's life on Walden Pond, when in truth his cabin was located a scarce two miles from his native Concord. As Beston wrote in *The Outermost House*, "I lived as a solitary, yes, but I made no pretence in acting the conventional hermit of the pious tract and the Eighteenth Century romance. With my weekly trips to Orleans to buy fresh bread and butter, my frequent visits to the Overlook, and my conversations with the men on night patrol, a mediæval anchorite would probably have regarded me as a dweller in the market place."[44] For Beston, the elemental forces of nature took on added meaning in the context of a human presence, even though he was convinced that modern man desperately needed to change his relationship to nature. On October 1, 1926, he wrote in his journal: "A devastating civilization. At Orleans yesterday I was disgusted beyond words at the lazy piggishness of the people who have ruined the beauty by dumping their stuff over the cliff."[45] Yet later that same day, describing a solitary freighter heading south with the sun he concludes his description with the phrase "Must have people."[46] Thomas J. Lyon suggests that Beston's "positive, natural-seeming attitude toward mankind" in *The Outermost House* provides evidence for the healing effect of his year on the beach, pointing to his "interest and care" in depicting of the men of the nearby coast guard station.[47] Beston freely acknowledged the importance of his coast guard friends to his "experiment," and referred to many of them by name in his book, particularly friends such as Captain John Nickerson, Bill Eldredge, John Blood, and Yngve Rongner.[48] Still, particularly during the winter months, there could be little human contact for extended periods: "During the winter the world of the dunes and the great beach was entirely my own, and I lived at the Fo'castle as undisturbed as Crusoe on his island." [49]

The winter solstice in late December was marked by a snowstorm so heavy that Beston's view of the Nauset Light was completely obscured. "So began," he wrote, "the worst winter on the Cape for close upon fifty years, a winter marked by great storms and tides, six wrecks, and the loss of many lives." [50] Bill Eldredge visited Beston during his patrol one cold night to tell him of "a strange tragedy to the north, one of those dread elemental things that happen in an elemental world." [51] Two fishermen out of Provincetown had been seen offshore having trouble with their boat, a thirty-foot motor dory. The boat drifted into the surf and capsized, drowning the two men. A few nights later, Bill Eldredge stopped at the Fo'castle again to tell Beston that the bodies of the two men had been found: "You remember those two fishermen I was telling you about? They've found them both now. One of them had a son at Wood End Station, and when he was coming back from his patrol last night he saw his father's body on the beach." [52] On the night of Saturday January 1, 1927, the fishing schooner *A. Roger Hickey* ran aground approximately twelve miles north of Nauset. The coastguardsmen at the Cahoons Hollow station spotted the ship and rescued the crew before the ship broke up in the surf. The following day Beston was walking toward the wreck when he spotted three women from Wellfleet headed toward him, each carrying a large haddock wrapped in newspaper under her arm. The crew was giving away their catch, which would otherwise have gone to waste, to all comers. All this, Beston realized, was in keeping with the natural cycles of life—birth, death, decay, and rebirth—that were inescapable even in this new, synthetic age of human history.

Shortly after midnight on Friday, February 19, 1927, Bill Eldredge knocked on the Fo'castle's door. Beston had intended to walk the patrol with Eldredge, but he was so tired from gathering firewood all afternoon that he apologized for not having the energy to accompany Eldredge on his patrol. They chatted for a short time before the surfman left to resume his patrol, commenting before he left, "It's blowing up—I think we are going to have a northeaster." [53] At daybreak Beston was awakened by the rattle of wind-blown sleet against his windows, the opening salvo of what was said to be the worst winter storm on the Cape in thirty years. A few days later he wrote a letter to Mabel Davison that described the gale:

> The last three days have been terrors . . . on Saturday, a howling sleety, Nor'easter was on, the worst of the season, and by Saturday night I was caught in an elemental uproar worse than I ever could have imagined. The sleet was continuous and to step out into that multitudinous rush of crystals was like being whipped with a whip of tiny pins. Later on, sand began to fly, sand and sleet intermingled, a perfectly infernal combination. Stepping out into it, to hammer in my shutters, I had to crawl almost, shielding my face as I could, and when I entered again, there was sand and ice in the porches of my ears, sand in my hair and eyebrows and in my lip. I don't see how the Coast Guards do it! Bill Eldredge told me that he went north, going along the top of the great bank because the tide was sweeping the beach,—the crest along the top of the great bank being the worst place because of its exposure to the wind—and that after crawling and stumbling on through the ups and downs of the moors, through bushes and brambles and a rushing world of midnight and storm and sleet—he came to a place where he had to make it on his hands and knees. About 2 A.M. Saturday night, I got up and dressed, for the tumult of the gale was indescribable and I had neither the will nor the wit to sleep. (The blessed Fo'castle proved sound and snug and I had plenty of oil, food, and wood.) At about 3 A.M. it was beyond words, for the full moon had risen and was pouring her wan light through the clouds, pouring it on a sea of elemental wrath, weird breakers, great, spuming geysers, and seething rushes—all about *30* feet away, and the poor little Fo'castle clinging to the very brim of the land.[54]

By Sunday, the storm unabating, Beston decided to "make shore," so he slogged his way through the sleet with one of the coastguardsmen—who stoically continued to make their patrols throughout the gale—to wait out the storm at the Nauset Station. Arriving at the station he learned that a coast guard patrol boat was in danger off the Highland Light in Provincetown. Two crews stood watch on the beach hoping to spot the boat and launch a rescue attempt, and a pair of navy destroyers were sent from Boston, but to no avail: "The destroyers, in spite of a splendid battle, had been unable to reach the disabled patrol boat, and the luckless ship had gone to pieces . . . Nine men had perished. Two bodies came ashore next day; their watches had stopped at five o'clock, so we knew that the vessel had weathered the night and gone to pieces in the morning. What a night they must have had, poor souls!"[55] A fragment of the mast of the patrol boat later washed up on the beach just north of the Fo'castle. A great deal of wreckage from various shipwrecks was washed up on the beach during the storm—planks, boards, timber of all sorts—and salvagers immediately went to work, gathering what they could to be reused. As he walked the beach, Beston saw Bill Eldredge gathering together salvaged lumber that he intended to use for a henhouse. The Cape Codders were familiar enough with "elemental disaster and tragedy" to take it in stride. All the while, gulls flew overhead; as Beston noted, "[f]rom their point of view, perhaps nothing had happened."[56]

The fifth and worst wreck of the season occurred in mid-March when the three-masted schooner *Montclair*, transporting a cargo of wooden laths from Halifax to New York struck the shoals between Nauset and Orleans in a heavy sea. The rigging was iced up and strained by the extra weight and in the pounding of the waves, the masts broke and scissored across each other, ripping the ship in half. Seven crew members clung to the stern of the ship as it plunged madly in the icy, pounding seas: "Dragging over the shoal ground, the mass rocked on its keel, now rolling the men sickeningly high, now tumbling them down into the trampling rush of the seas . . . Bruised, wet through, and chilled to the bone, the unfortunate men dared not lash themselves down, for they had to be free to climb the tilted deck when the ship careened."[57] One great surge washed five of the men into the frigid sea where they soon perished, leaving only two men clinging to the stern-rail balustrade, "one a seventeen-year-old boy, the other a stocky, husky-built sailor," as Beston described them. The boy was momentarily washed from the balustrade, but the older sailor caught him and held on. The men from the Nauset Coast Guard Station rushed over to attempt a rescue, and managed to brave the treacherous seas and save the two men, but the younger of the two soon died of shock and exposure. The older man said that he would soon be returning to the sea: "He says it's all he knows," a coastguardsman told Beston.[58]

Shortly after the great storm, Beston left the Cape, traveling to Quincy to be with his brother George's family. The Sheahans had experienced a tragedy of their own that fall when their third child, a baby boy, had died shortly after being born. A short time later three-year-old Joanie fell gravely ill with diphtheria. "My poor family. They have had a cruel time," Beston wrote, "I'm going to Quincy to be near them for a few days. The little girl, little Joan, is very, very weak, but getting on as well as can be expected."[59] Joan proved to be a resilient little girl and within a few weeks she had recovered sufficiently to be out of danger. His experiences that year reinforced Beston's belief in the healing power of nature, as illustrated by an incident that he later related in *The Outermost House*. One day while Beston was walking along the beach in late October he chanced to find an old blue Navy jumper washed up on the sands. In true Cape Cod fashion, leaving nothing to waste, he was cutting the buttons off the disintegrating garment when he happened to look up and see a flight of swans far out to see and winging their way south: "Glorious white birds in the blue October heights over the solemn unrest of ocean—their passing was more than music, and from their wings descended the old loveliness of earth which both affirms and heals."[60]

One night in mid-April, Beston, who was a very light sleeper, woke up just after two o'clock. The main room of the Fo'castle was flooded with the light of the full moon and so—as was often his habit when he woke up in the middle of the night—he dressed and went out to the beach. The night air was cold and there was a light breeze coming in from the west as he walked south along the beach toward big dune. He had nearly reached the moon-thrown shadow of the dune when he heard a faint and distant sound coming from the skies behind the dune. He strained to hear it, and the sound now seemed to come from over the ocean, then disappeared. A few moments later he heard the sound once again: "the lovely, broken, chorusing, bell-like sound—the sound of a great flight of geese going north on a quiet night under the moon." Beston climbed to the top of big dune and lingered there for hours, simply listening to the wild music of the geese: "There were little flights and great flights, there were times when the sky seemed empty, there were times when it was filled with an immense clamour which died away slowly over ocean. Not unfrequently I heard the sound of wings, and once in a while I could see the birds—they were flying fast—but scarce had I marked them ere they dwindled into a dot of moonlit sky."[61] Spring, the season of birth and renewal, was returning to the great beach.

With the return of milder spring temperatures, Beston decided to undertake an adventure he had long contemplated, a walk across the Cape from the great beach inland to Cape Cod Bay similar to that described by Henry Thoreau in *Cape Cod*. The distance "as the crow flies" was only about 4½ miles, but the walking distance was nearer to 7½ miles each way. From the Fo'castle, Beston walked to the coast guard station at Nauset, where his friends there were taking advantage of the warm weather to do a bit of spring-cleaning. From the coast guard station he followed the Nauset Road to Eastham village through "a belt of wild, rolling, and treeless sand moorland which follows along the rim of the earth cliff for two thirds of its length and runs inland for something like a mile."[62] West of the grassy moorland, Beston walked up a long slope that led to the heart of the Cape and its inhabited regions. He observed that when Henry Thoreau walked through this area near Eastham in 1849 that he had described the region as virtually treeless, but that now, about seventy-five years later, it featured numerous pitch pines that had taken root and flourished in the thin, sandy soil of the inner Cape. In the village itself, the inhabitants had planted numerous species of shade trees, including a number of western cottonwoods reportedly brought back by Cape Codders who had temporarily emigrated to Kansas before getting homesick for the sea and returning. To the west of Eastham the elevation declined once again and the landscape returned to moorland, and Beston noted that large flocks of a recent European import, the English starling, had spread throughout the region disrupting the local ecological balance: "The presence of these rabble blackbirds disturbs the entire natural economy of the region, for they strip every autumnal bush and plant bare of its last seed and berry and leave nothing for our native birds to feed on when they return in the spring."[63]

After the moorland the road descended through a mile-wide area of sandy grassland and pitch pines dotted with ponds before reaching the western shore of the Cape. Walking along the bayside beach, Beston paused at a herring brook and observed a small school of herring schooling just offshore, whose passage up the brook to their spawning pond was blocked by debris:

As I stood looking off to the baffled creatures . . . I began to reflect on Nature's eagerness to sow life everywhere, to fill the planet with it, to crowd with it the earth, the air, and the seas. Into every empty corner, into all forgotten things and nooks, Nature struggles to pour life, pouring life into the dead, life into life itself. That immense, overwhelming, relentless, burning ardency of Nature for the stir of life! And all these her creatures, even as these thwarted lives, what travail, what hunger and cold, what bruising and slow-killing struggle will they not endure to accomplish the earth's purpose? and what conscious resolution of men can equal their impersonal, their congregate will to yield self life to the will of life universal?[64]

Nature's ardency to sow life came to "flood tide" with the return of summer, wrote Beston, "now do insects inherit the warm earth . . . the sand quivers with insect lives."[65] Beston was not always enthusiastic about this aspect of summer; he particularly loathed the swarms of biting flies, greenheads, that returned with the summer heat. More happily, the seasonal birds retuned as well, including a pair of song sparrows of which Beston became particularly fond. Each morning, he wrote, the first sound to reach his ears was the surf—"then do I hear a patter of tiny feet on the roof over my head and the cheerful notes of a song sparrow's homespun tune . . . My building of the Fo'castle has given them something to sit on, something they can see the world from, and on its ridgepole they perch, singing at life in general with a praiseworthy persistence."[66]

The Outermost House was, in a sense, Beston's way of "singing at life." In later years Beston would often summarize his philosophy as "being on the side of life." The phrase encompassed much of what Beston learned on the great beach about nature and its cycles, the importance of maintaining a sense of the poetic and spiritual mystery of nature in one's life, and regarding with distrust any of the new paradigms of the industrial age that failed to take into account the vital connection between man and nature. Beston was very much aware of his intellectual debt to writers such as the New England transcendentalists and others who had explored this theme, and considered his book to be "a new study of Nature in America and as a new link in the sequence of the English and American nature tradition of Thoreau and Jefferies and Hudson et al."[67] He felt, however, that the contrast he drew between a life spent in outer nature and this "fantastic civilization" of ours (a phrase not intended as a compliment) was a point particularly suited for a modern audience struggling with many of the post-war issues about modern industrial society that he himself had confronted after returning from the Great War. As critic Thomas J. Lyon observes "In the modern era, being alone in nature may still refresh the spirit, but the literary record observes there now may be, quite often, a certain shadowed quality to the experience. Henry Beston, for one, felt the historical moment keenly . . . He does not give his personal reasons for wanting to spend a year alone, facing out to the ocean not far from the pounding surf on the 'forearm' of the Cape but he does describe the insulation and malaise of modern man."[68]

Beston described his year on the beach as "the most important event of my life" and addressed the often-asked question of why he decided to leave "the excitement of city life" for a solitary existence on a secluded stretch of dunes:

> During the war, and afterwards, I saw many people writing in New York. I was hearing a different drummer, unlike that life of the hustle and bustle of a constantly moving and noisy city. I was anxious to see what a year, more or less alone, in the midst of great natural beauty would mean. Cape Cod had good people—hospitable to wild and unexpected things . . . I called my house "Fo'castle," which is the name of the crew's quarters on sailing vessels. When I moved in, I intended to stay a couple of weeks. I had no particular plans beyond this—everything just went ahead, developed in its own way. The weeks lingered on until I knew my stay would be a whole year. I found that I lived in the midst of an abundance of natural life, which manifested itself every hour of the day. I couldn't leave, for there was too much to discover in the natural, beautiful world that man too often forgets is there.
>
> Walter Teller later named me "a loner in residence," and maybe that's what I was. But it was the first home, and I was able to brood, uninterrupted as long as I wanted, watching the sea, the sky and the animal life around me. I possessed them and was possessed by them. The longer I stayed the more eager I was to know more. The sky in the afternoon was a harmony of universal blue. It knew no discord. How could I give this up [?] The life I lived there found its way into my writing, shaped by the changes of the weather and seasons and the events happening each day. I realized that

man is earth's child who must not, in the mechanized and intellectualized forces of our modern age, lose touch with the rhythms she provides. Man must touch the earth, love the earth, honor the earth, and rest his spirit in her solitary spaces. Nature provides man the peace he needs very badly. I could see that living in outer nature keeps the senses keen, and living alone stirs in them a certain watchfulness. I was a little deaf, and nearsighted, but nature manifested itself within me, and I was keenly aware of her presence. Living indoors is only a journey along a paper calendar; living in outer nature is sharing in the pilgrimages of the sun.[69]

It was at the Fo'castle that Beston truly "found himself" as a writer, realizing that he needed, as Elizabeth Coatsworth recalled, "to possess and be possessed by his surroundings. He needed to brood, uninterrupted, for as long as he wished. He needed to observe at leisure. Lastly, he needed to write when he was ready to write, mostly in the mornings, his best time, though he put down notes at any hour." While Beston's work often seems to have an "inevitable" quality to it, it was a hard-won inevitability: "He wrote with pencil or pen—on typewriter paper, except when taking notes—he never typed, for the sound of a machine would have interfered with the rhythm of his sentences, which meant so much to him. As he worked, the floor became littered with discarded paper. He sometimes spent an entire morning on a single sentence, unable to go on until he was completely satisfied with both words and cadence, which he considered equally important."[70]

By August of 1927, Beston's year on the beach had come full circle, although it should be noted that the experiences he describes in *The Outermost House* were not strictly limited by that year alone; as was the case with Henry Thoreau's *Walden*, which is also structured around one course of the seasons, each man spent more time than that living alone, and occasionally took excursions away from the site of their "experiments" in leading a life close to nature. Eager to record his experiences, Beston spent the next several months working diligently on the new book. Mabel Davison took the train up from New York in early June for a short stay at the Fo'castle, and Beston's friend Corey Ford, an editor at *Vanity Fair*, came for a brief visit on Independence Day, but for the most part he saw almost no one, save for a few local friends. Usually a reliable correspondent, he wrote few letters during this period, causing his friends to wonder what had become of him. Ted Roosevelt Jr. wrote to him in August, "It has been a long and dreary time since I heard anything from you. Where are you? What are you doing? Why are you imitating one of the clams that lives on your own beloved Cape Cod?"[71] Several months later, his previous letter to Beston having gone unanswered, Roosevelt queried, "Where are you and what are you doing? I have not heard from you for such a long time that I am worried. Are you all right, and is the book going well? It is high time you came down to see us."[72] Coincidentally, on the same day that Ted Roosevelt sent this letter, Beston sent a postcard to Mabel Davison in New York City stating simply: "Finished! April 2nd 1928 9:13 A.M. Henry's love ever to Marraine." Beston immediately sent the manuscript, which was dedicated to Davison and Mary Wheelwright, off to his publisher, Doubleday, Doran and Company in Garden City, Long Island, then joyfully let his friends know that he had finished the book and was no longer incommunicado.

Save for a few short articles and book reviews, Beston had published little since *The Sons of Kai* was published in 1926, devoting his complete attention to the Cape Cod manuscript. He was certain that the book was shaping up to be the finest thing he had ever written, but since it was far different than anything he had published previously, he decided to gauge the possible response to the book by sending a chapter from the manuscript to Ellery Sedgwick, editor of *The Atlantic Monthly*. Sedgwick immediately responded to the query in a letter dated October 10, 1927.

Dear Beston:—

You send me a paper that I don't want to take. I want discussions or at any rate discussable ideas—not descriptions, nor symphonies in blue and silver, nor arrangements in browns. But this thing is so damned well done that I have got to take it. It is a very brief piece of writing, not only felicitous in expression but with dignity of attitude.

You see I think it is quite a poem.

As ever,

Ellery Sedgwick.[73]

The essay, "Night on the Great Beach," was published in *The Atlantic* the following June, and the response was so overwhelmingly positive that

Sedgwick immediately wrote to Beston, "Our susceptible public is so in love with your beach that if I do not write you for a sequel, there is evidently trouble ahead. May I not hope for new dithyrambics? I love them myself, but to tell the truth, I had no idea that your piece would attract the attention of so many people."[74]

Sedgwick probably should not have been surprised by the reception to Beston's article. It had not been so very long since the high water mark of the conservation movement in the United States, when nature writers had played a key role in gathering together the popular support for the conservation reforms of the Progressive Era, particularly during the presidency of Theodore Roosevelt. The greatest of that generation of nature writers, John Burroughs and John Muir, had only recently passed from the scene, Muir in 1914 and Burroughs in 1921. While there had been a lull in the American interest in nature writing during the Great War and its immediate aftermath, it had not disappeared completely—and Beston's book played a significant role in reviving it. But while *The Outermost House* has its roots in the nineteenth-century tradition of American nature writing, it was not just a nostalgic return to that genre but it reflects instead a modern, post-war sensibility that—sometimes subtly and sometimes quite overtly—questions the fundamental assumptions upon which modern industrial civilization was built.

In an essay entitled "Three Decades of Environmental Politics: The Historical Context," Samuel Hays draws a useful distinction between *fin de siècle* and early twentieth-century conservation movement and the post-World War Two environmental movement. He points out that the conservation movement was generally anthropocentric, with a few notable exceptions such as Muir and Burroughs, and emphasized such issues as the preservation of scenic areas and the efficient use and development of natural resources. He refers to these issues as "first generation" environmental concerns. Following the Second World War, a "second generation" of environmental concerns rose to the fore, beginning with fears raised by the specter of atomic weapons and later including regional and global environmental dangers posed by air and water pollution, the misuse of dangerous chemicals (as chronicled in Rachel Carson's *Silent Spring*), and then on to global issues such as overpopulation, ozone depletion, and global climate change.[75] Modern environmentalists often reflect a biocentric or geocentric perspective that takes non-human interests into account when contemplating the effect of anthropogenic change on the natural world.

In the historical context of the transition from first generation conservation to second-generation environmentalism, *The Outermost House* stands out as one of the most important transitional texts of mid-twentieth-century nature writing. To be sure, much of its enduring appeal has been primarily a result of the flawless prose and remarkable descriptions of the great beach in all of its seasons and mutable glory, but there is far more contained in it than beautiful descriptions of an extraordinary landscape and its people. Beston wrote his book during an era where Thorsten Verblen's "efficiency experts," Henry Ford's assembly lines, and Thomas Edison's electric lights had profoundly altered the way that people experienced time. The natural cycles of the seasons, of night and day, even of when and where people worked, had been changed. From a business standpoint, perhaps this change was profitable, but from a human standpoint Beston believed that a divorce from cyclical natural, time was insidious, slowly leaching out our true humanity:

> A year indoors is a journey along a paper calendar; a year in outer nature is the accomplishment of a tremendous ritual. To share in it, one must have a knowledge of the pilgrimages of the sun . . . We lose a great deal, I think, when we lose this sense and feeling for the sun. When all has been said, the adventure of the sun is the great natural drama by which we live, and not to have joy in it and awe of it, not to share in it, is to close a dull door on nature's sustaining and poetic spirit.[76]

In "Night on the Great Beach," the chapter that was published in *The Atlantic*, Beston made an even more emphatic declaration of what was at stake:

> Our fantastic civilization has fallen out of touch with many aspects of nature, and none more completely than with night. Primitive folk, gathered at a cave mouth round a fire, do not fear night; they fear, rather, the energies and creatures to whom night gives power; we of the age of machines, having delivered ourselves of nocturnal enemies, now have a dislike of night itself. With lights and ever more lights, we drive the holiness and beauty of night

back to the forests and the sea; the little villages, the crossroads even, will have none of it. Are modern folk, perhaps, afraid of night? Do they fear that vast serenity, the mystery of infinite space, the austerity of stars? Having made themselves at home in a civilization obsessed with power, which explains its whole world in terms of energy, do they fear at night for their dull acquiescence and the pattern of their beliefs? Be the answer what it will, to-day's civilization is full of people who have not the slightest notion of the character or the poetry of night, who have never even seen night. Yet to lie thus, to know only artificial night, is as absurd and evil as to know only artificial day.[77]

In the following chapter, "The Year at High Tide," Beston builds upon this theme, suggesting that not only have we lost touch with the poetry and mystery of the earth and its rhythms, but we have begun to lose our own physical senses: "What a stench modern civilization breathes, and how have we ever learned to endure that foul blue air?" Had he room in the book, he asserts, he would have devoted an entire chapter to the sense of smell, for "It is a sense that every lover of the elemental world ought to use, and using, enjoy. We ought to keep all senses vibrant and alive. Had we done so, we should never have built a civilization which outrages them, which so outrages them, indeed, that a vicious circle has been established and the dull sense grown duller."[78]

For a writer who was so attuned to the sensory phenomena of the natural world, and wrote so beautifully about that world, it is a "curious fact," as Elizabeth Coatsworth points out that Beston "was to some degree handicapped. In the first place, he was nearsighted. His old-fashioned steel- or gold-rimmed glasses were usually in his left-hand breast pocket. 'They make the world look too much like a publicity photograph,' he would say, 'When I don't use them everything seems more beautiful, like a tapestry'." Furthermore, as Coatsworth notes, Beston was also growing a bit deaf: "The babble of a room filled with people confused him. In talking with one person he usually sat with his 'good ear' toward the speaker. Yet distant sounds, like an approaching train or car or far-off shot, he heard before anyone else. Perhaps, too, he could distinguish the component sounds of a breaking wave more clearly than others could."[79]

Orion Rises on the Dunes

As Beston witnessed during his time on the great beach, it was not just people that suffered from the filth excreted by industrial civilization. "A new danger," he wrote, "threatens the birds at sea." Refiners were taking the residue of crude oil remaining after the refining process, pumping it into tankers, and emptying the "slop," as it was called, out at sea. The waste oil residue spread over large areas, fatally coating the feathers of any seabird unfortunate enough to land in the mess. During his winter stay at the Fo'castle Beston found on the shore "three unhappy little auks, *Alle alle,* who had dipped themselves in oil somewhere on their way down from the arctic." After some difficulty Beston managed to capture them and bring them back to the Fo'castle, where he covered the floor with newspaper and tried to clean the oil from their feathers and induce them to eat, "but all in vain; they would not eat, and I let them go just as soon as I saw I could not possibly help them and that Nature had best deal with the problem in her own way."[80]

Modern critics who have examined *The Outermost House* from the perspective of the development of environmental thought in the first half of the twentieth century have acknowledged the role Beston's work played in making the transition from, as Donald Federman writes, viewing "the natural world as fuel for thought . . . to [viewing] it more as food for survival." Unlike Thoreau, writes Federman, Henry Beston "was not merely a tourist in nature. But neither did he side with nature against man. Rather, Beston tied his idea of man's humanity directly to an attitude towards 'outer nature' . . . Beston felt that human culture could find sustenance only in its ties to the cycles of nature."[81] Sherman Paul points out that "Before Leopold asked us to be ethical in regard to nature, Beston reminded us that "grim arrangements" notwithstanding, nature's economy (ecology) "has an ethic of its own" . . . he said that "the animal shall not be measured by man . . . [that] animals are not brethren . . . [but] other nations," meaning, I think, that we should keep the respectful distance he does in his participation in nature."[82]

During the winter of 1927–1928, while he was working to complete the manuscript, Beston was occasionally asked by friends and acquaintances what understanding of Nature he had gleaned from his year on the great beach. He considered the question carefully and included his eloquent response to this question in the concluding chapter of *The Outermost House*:

> I would answer that one's first appreciation is a sense that the creation is still going on, that the creative forces are as great and as active to-day as they have ever been, and that to-morrow's morning will be as heroic as any of the world. *Creation is here and now.* So near is man to the creative pageant, so much a part is he of the endless and incredible experiment, that any glimpse he may have will be but the revelation of a moment, a solitary note heard in a symphony thundering through debatable existences of time. Poetry is as necessary to comprehension as science. It is as impossible to live without reverence as it is without joy. . . . Whatever attitude to human existence you fashion for yourself, know that it is valid only if it be the shadow of an attitude to Nature. A human life, so often likened to a spectacle upon a stage, is more justly a ritual. The ancient values of dignity, beauty, and poetry which sustain it are of Nature's inspiration; they are born of the mystery and beauty of the world. Do no dishonor to the earth lest you dishonor the spirit of man.[83]

As he later wrote to Luther Neff, this passage was critical to understanding the divine mystery of life on earth: "we are not living on a mechanism running down like a clock but on an earth sustained by an ever-creating outpouring stream of the divine imagination."[84]

After finishing the book, Beston remained on Cape Cod for a few months, but much of this period was spent not at the Fo'castle but at Tom and Mary Kelley's Overlook Inn. He had intended to leave the Cape by late spring, but as he wrote to Elizabeth Coatsworth, "I couldn't break away for the book was in the air, and after the proofs came the pictures and captions, and after the pictures and captions came a shuttle of consultations."[85] Beston finally left the Cape and rented an office in Quincy near the railroad tracks that looked out onto a grove of poplars and a meadow that was fast turning into a parking lot for commuters taking the train to Boston. The office itself was quite a change after the Fo'castle: "four pinkish-yallery walls and a fire place! Queer old suburban N.E. office building, vintage of the [18]70's, looks like Shakespeare's birth place transmogrified & Yankeefied."[86] For a brief time the familiar bustle of Quincy was once again appealingly comfortable to Beston. After his year on the great beach, Beston felt like one of his sea birds separated from the flock and was eager to rejoin the rest of humanity. After finishing the pre-publication work for *The Outermost House* midway through 1928 Beston felt "written-out," telling Coatsworth that he hadn't written a word all summer or wanted to. This wasn't completely the case, since he spent part of the summer trying to catch up on his correspondence, although he complained that "whatever knack I had of writing a letter seems to have evaporated, and when I do take myself by the shoulders and force myself to a desk, what I write is like luke-warm ginger-ale which has been standing open on a table all a long summer afternoon."[87]

One of the people he did write to regularly was Truesdell Fife, a high school boy who summered in Eastham and made a little money on the side by printing stationery on a small printing press. In the late summer of 1927 Fife printed an order of stationery with the Fo'castle's "address" on it: "The Fo'castle: Lat. 41° 51' 39" N. Long. 69° 57' 08" W." Beston was very pleased both with the stationery and Fife's earnest, open intelligence. Fife loved books and the arts and was fascinated by Beston's work at the Fo'castle, and in turn Beston took a kindly mentor's interest in Fife and his education. For many years, long after both Beston and Fife moved away from the Cape they stayed in touch, corresponding about literature, politics, and what was happening in their lives. Years later, after Fife had grown to adulthood, married, and had a son, he asked Beston to serve as godfather.

Although he wrote little after finishing *The Outermost House*, Beston read voraciously, like a man hungering to partake of other people's words, other people's worlds. Among others, he read Edmund Wilson's *Discordant Encounter*, Louis Bromfield's *Early Autumn*, and Eugene O'Neil's *Strange Interlude*, and was far more impressed with the former than the latter, saying, "[O'Neil's] bookish ghosts [act] as no human beings ever did . . . is it all but brilliant technique and outraged feeling?"[88] He was even more contemptuous of Aldous Huxley's new book, writing to Elizabeth Coatsworth, "Somebody gave me Aldous Huxley's *Point Counter Point* to read. Of all the worlds in corruption! There are numberless things the matter with it, but its own peculiar devil is its term for the intellectualizing that means death."[89] He was far more enthusiastic about Virginia Woolf's *Orlando*, praising it with the Rooseveltian adjective "bully" and admiring the way in which Woolf's "interest in the time sequence and its part in human life is something all her own, too, something one likes to stop and think over."[90] His friends Ted Roosevelt Jr. and Arthur Gibbs had also just published new books he was eager to read. Gibbs's new book, *Harness*, a *roman à clef* about a wounded war veteran trying to come to terms with marriage and post-war life particularly interested Beston due to its theme of the war-time generation's attempt to "figure it all out."[91] In addition to catching up on his reading, Beston was anxious to do some traveling once again—New York City, the Berkshires, up to Boothbay Harbor, Maine for a boating trip with Mary Wheelwright and some friends aboard Wheelwright's boat *The Liria*. He and his friend Alva Morrison also discussed the possibility of taking a trip to Egypt the following spring to see the pyramids.

Advance sales for *The Outermost House* had been sluggish, and so Doubleday, Doran did little to push the book until late autumn, when laudatory reviews of the book started to come in. Beston had received so many letters from admirers after his article "Night on the Great Beach" had come out in the June 1928 issue of *The Atlantic Monthly* that he had high hopes for the prospects of the book and he was disappointed that Doubleday didn't promote the book more aggressively. The series of positive reviews finally spurred Doubleday to action, and sales figures slowly rose accordingly. The review that Beston enjoyed most was John Riddel's piece in *Vanity Fair*: "Every time anybody comes into the room with it, I rise and retire blushing, or pretending to, usually the last."[92] He was particularly pleased to hear from Truesdell Fife how positively the "younger generation" responded to his work, although he professed to some mixed feelings about the prospect of overly "literary" readings of the book and about the modern study of literature generally:

> A great book is a work of art and is to be enjoyed as art, and its just as much a vandalism to break it up into paragraphs and word sequences and all that Ph.D. fudge as it would be to break the Venus of Milo with a sledge hammer and study the fragments. Not that I condemn literary study! Far from it. I know that a great work of art can be *analyzed*. But that is not what they do in the modern school. In the modern school they *dissect* it, chopping text

and author into tiresome little bits, making literary hamburg out of honest beef. If they should ever (in umpteen hundred years) get busy on me, "now children today we will all read together the last paragraph of The Outermost House and write the vowel sequences on the blackboard" . . . Truesdell, I'd give an enraged berserk yell that would trouble heaven, crawl [up from] under the earth again, re-vivify my bones, push up the clods of my grave and appear at the Puddleby Central High and raise—oh well . . . you know. But I musn't discourage you from literary "study" a la high school; I know you've got to go through it, so go to it, and my blessin' be with you."[93]

We shouldn't take this expression of literary diffidence *too* seriously—in reality Beston was quietly pleased that he had finally gotten around to writing a book that was worth being studied. As Elizabeth Coatsworth recalled, "From the beginning, he was certain that *The Outermost House* was really good, as he felt that none of his earlier books had been."[94]

The Outermost House is qualitatively as well as thematically different from Beston's earlier writing. As Elizabeth Coatsworth wrote:

> It was on the dunes that he found himself as a writer. There he was alone most of the time with only the sea, the sky, the beach and the marshes for company. He watched the seasons come and go on this vast stage. For the first time, he had a house of his own. He needed to possess and be possessed by his surroundings. He needed to brood, uninterrupted, for as long as he wished. He needed to observe at leisure. Lastly, he needed to write when he was ready to write, mostly in the mornings, his best time, though he put down notes at any hour.
>
> At the Fo'castle he observed carefully, brooded long, and wrote slowly at the sturdy kitchen table overlooking the west and the great Eastham marshes.[95]

After his long period of solitude on Cape Cod and the successful completion of a book that Beston felt defined him as a writer, his thoughts tacked to a completely different heading. On a pleasant Sunday afternoon some two years earlier, in October 1926, early during his yearlong sojourn on the great beach, Beston had entertained some of his Cape Cod friends—Mercy Mines, Prince and Edna Hurd, and John Nickerson—at the Fo'castle. He prepared them a lunch of cocoa, bread and butter, and creamed chicken, which they ate while discussing the *Portland* disaster and other famous wrecks off the outer Cape. In his journal that night, Beston cryptically noted another topic they touched on during their luncheon conversation: "Three debts—write a book, beget a son, or build a house." The "three debts" he referred to may have been a jumbled version of the three debts of the householder as contained in the Hindu Vedas (debts owed to the gods, teachers, and ancestors), and a saying often attributed to the Cuban writer and national hero José Martí. When asked what things a man ought to do before he dies, Martí responded, "plant a tree, write a book, have a son." Now forty years old and having completed *The Outermost House*, Beston's thoughts turned more and more to having a family. Many of his friends, as well as his brother George, had long since settled down and had families of their own and now that Beston had reached middle age he increasingly longed for a wife, family, and home—which meant that the time had finally arrived to take a dramatic step in changing his long-term, often long-distance friendship with Elizabeth Coatsworth.

CHAPTER SEVEN

Henry and Elizabeth
1929–1932

Orion is your chosen constellation,
Orion striding through the pathless height,
With Betelgeuse and Bellatrix at his shoulders,
His sword suspended from a belt of light.
Your eyes seek out that proud and insolent figure,
Your head goes back to face into the skies,
And I who watch beside you, turn and dimly
See all the constellations in your eyes.[1]

ELIZABETH COATSWORTH BESTON
"Orion" (1931)

WHILE BESTON HAD BEEN ISOLATED at the Fo'castle, engrossed
in writing *The Outermost House*, Elizabeth Coatsworth was traveling
extensively—first to Taos, New Mexico, to see their mutual friend Mary
Wheelwright, then to visit with relatives in Pasadena, California—and
making her own literary mark as one of the most prolific and widely published poets of the 1920s. Although Coatsworth and her mother had their
home in Hingham, Massachusetts, they spent as much time, if not more,
traveling. After returning from California in the winter of 1927–28, they
spent the spring at Hingham and then left for a summer journey through
France and North Africa. There was something of a plaintive note in a
letter that Beston sent to her while she was abroad, as he commented on
the lack of a letter from her in response to a long letter he sent in June, and
wondered if "either you have erased [me] from the tablets of memory or
failed to receive [my] epistle."[2] As it happened, Coatsworth's travels were

simply keeping her too busy to write much, but it is evident from Beston's comment that as far as he was concerned their long distance romance was still very much alive—and was becoming more and more important to him.

As for Elizabeth, she had never been in any particular hurry to get married, although she apparently had some interesting suitors, including George Patton and the naturalist William Beebe. Between her frequent traveling and her ambitions as a poet, she may have felt that the time for marriage would come later—and while she was traveling in France in the summer of 1928, that time arrived. As she later told her daughter Kate, she was now 35 years old and "all of a sudden, the waiters everywhere addressed her as 'madame' instead of 'mademoiselle.' It gave her a shocking sense of time going by." A match between her and Beston certainly made sense— they had already established a lasting friendship and had an enormous amount in common. Further, writes Kate Beston Barnes, her father "always had a taste for distinction, and she had it. She was nice-looking, sensitive, honest, generous, and very intelligent (she was not a looker in the way that he was: waitresses used to take him for Errol Flynn when they went out to dinner, a fact which always amused & charmed her)."[3]

In January of 1929, Beston and Coatsworth were having lunch at the Ritz in Boston when he asked her—apparently not for the first time—if she would marry him. This time she said yes, although they did not immediately set a date for the wedding. Winfield Townley Scott, who later became a friend of the Bestons, claimed that the completion of *The Outermost House* was Elizabeth's *sine qua non* for their marriage, conveying to Henry a "no book, no marriage" message, but the truth remains unclear. According to their daughter, Kate Beston Barnes, her mother maintained that she had never issued such an ultimatum to Henry. But while there may have been no explicit stipulation by Coatsworth on this point, the fact remains that she did not accept his proposal until after he had completed the book—and when he received a very tempting invitation to tour the Greek islands in the winter of 1928–29 he opted instead to continue working until the book was finished and sent off to his publisher.

The engagement period was to be—as was probably fitting for two vagabonds—a long-distance relationship, since Henry was planning to embark upon a trip to Egypt with his friend Alva Morrison in early February and Elizabeth and her mother almost immediately left Hingham for an extended visit with relatives in Pasadena. They even delayed the purchase of an engagement ring, as Henry hoped to pick up something "ancient and interesting" in Egypt. Once they made the commitment to marriage, however, it was whole-hearted—for the next five months Henry wrote long, ardent love letters to Elizabeth on nearly a daily basis. The very day after she left for California he wrote:

> Elizabeth darling you are gone from me a while and the world that was once all yours and mine haunts me with an ever-remembering wanting and need and ever-remembering pain. There is no one in any room I enter; whatever house I visit there is no one there. The windy and rainy night is all one thought of you. The quiet room and the light, you are mine in the loveliness of all beautiful and beloved things. I love you darling beyond all depth of words to utter, and the thought of your love returning is my very flame of life, but rest is not mine for who shall rest whom the gods have taken by the hands?[4]

Elizabeth responded in kind, writing to Henry from California nearly every day, and echoing Henry's sense of moonstruck wonder about the sudden change in their condition: "My life that hung so quiet and unstirred is shakier now. My heart almost seems to stop when I open one of your letters. What has happened to us? It is *most* disturbing. But oh my dear, aren't we as alive as we have not been before? Where I had peace I have—well what I value more, oh Mr. Jack-Ashore!"[5] Elizabeth wanted to tell only a few close friends of the engagement, and so Beston eagerly wrote to tell such friends as Ted and Eleanor Roosevelt, Mabel Davison, Alva and Amy Morrison, Maurice and Bee Day, and Truesdell Fife of the engagement. "A few close friends," as he wrote to Elizabeth, "even as you say so it shall be. Somebody somehow or other might get wind of it and ask me flat, but we won't cross any bridges til we get to them. And if we do cross them, we'll cross them like Tudors,—Henry and Elizabeth."[6] In later years this statement would take on an ironic twist, for like the English monarch, Henry VIII who yearned for a son and heir, both Henrys would be disappointed in having only daughters.

Beston was most anxious to tell his family of the wedding plans, and a few days after Elizabeth left for California he went to visit his brother George in Quincy. Beston arrived at the house to find that George and the family had gone to Boston, so Henry—who was to be the guest author at a weekly radio broadcast that night—left a note for George telling him about the engagement. "On hearing the news of our engagement," he wrote to Elizabeth, "my two little nieces were most terrifishously (sic) thrilled, and going to their library—they remembered your name—reached out for The Cat and the Captain, and read it all over again with most supreme satisfaction."[7] Jake and Bee Day had not received a letter from Henry for over a year while he worked on *The Outermost House*, but shortly after the engagement he sent them a thick package containing a copy of his book and news of the engagement. The delighted Bee promptly wrote back: "All is forgiven! Come home to ma-ma. Fatted calf on way to butchers, special committee of Rotary Club meeting to prepare reception."[8]

As the New Year began, sales of *The Outermost House* remained steady and Beston did his part to promote the book appearing on radio show broadcasts and making personal appearances to talk about it. Doubleday, Doran sent Beston a copy of the jacket design for the new edition illustrated by Edward Wilson—"a distinguished and expensive gent"—but Beston was not happy with the result. Wilson's design featured a bleak, stormy landscape and a lone figure walking on the beach, and had what Beston felt was a "sinister quality of storm and human disaster." Although he described several shipwrecks in the book, Beston maintained that the book's theme of nature's cycles and humankind's place in nature was an affirmative, uplifting one and that to focus on natural disasters missed the point: "People who've read the book don't like it. I don't like it because it presents the book out-of-key . . . people who *haven't* read the book like it, and booksellers are divided."[9] Coatsworth sympathized with Beston and offered a few suggestions and a whimsical poem for the cover:

> Open, reader!
> Winds shall blow
> Stars shall rise
> And suns sink low

Henry and Elizabeth

Birds shall light
And tall waves bellow
Between this cover
And its fellow![10]

In the end, the book jacket didn't affect sales at all as *The Outermost House* continued to find an appreciative and growing audience.

As for the remarkably productive Elizabeth Coatsworth, in addition to publishing poetry in a wide variety of venues she had begun to write stories for a younger audience, including *The Cat and the Captain* (1927) and *Compass Rose*, published in 1929. She was particularly enthused with an idea she had recently begun work on: "[I] have been deep in the *Cat Who Went to Heaven*, a tail (sic) on which to hang the life of Buddha; the stories of the birth of the Enlightened One, and some Japanese legends."[11] Beston loved the idea, writing to tell Coatsworth, "I love the Bhudda (sic) book idea tremendously; the title is appealing. I like Gautama; he was a noble and great prince; his wisdom, born high, fell like rain; it descended while the Christ's wisdom, born low, rising, fought against a kind of law. That beautiful, wise, princely compassion! A great spirit surely."[12] When the page proofs for *Compass Rose* arrived, Elizabeth experienced a bout of pre-publication anxiety, telling Henry, "Perhaps you'd better change me and get another girl. I've just been seeing my proofs. And really I'm hardly worth keeping."[13] As a writer, Beston understood her jitters and immediately responded with encouragement and praise: "You are a great artist, dear, and no one in all the world knows it better or has a profounder sense of it than your own man." Beston also mentioned that David McCord—who was then the Boston representative for her publisher, Coward-McCann—was a friend of his, and while he did not want to "seem to come striding in, walking heavily and intrusively," that he was more than willing to help in any way he could.[14]

Although Beston himself had not yet regained an urge to write, he was starting to cast about for ideas. He and Elizabeth played with the romantic notion of going to France, where Elizabeth could write poetry and Henry a novel, but that idea never got much further than a pleasant daydream. Given the success of *The Outermost House* and the pleasure Beston took in writing the book, he was leaning toward writing another book about nature:

I want to do some more nature interpretation of the American scene, a field I have a real name in now, and one I have entirely to myself. But the new thing hasn't begun to come through yet. And I must see John Farrar, too, and get his notions and opinions. I shall probably see if there isn't a possibility of doing something which I can serialize first, for there's that side to be thought of,—the bread-and-butter, milk-and-morning-porridge side. John wants to have me meet the McCall people. What I have vaguely in mind is a series of some ten or fifteen essay-cum-nature-cumadventure things about American backgrounds, a southern plantation and its people and its trees and its birds for instance, the Banks of Carolina for another, spring and the desert in flower for a third, an Ohio valley farm for a fourth, the Mississippi for a fifth and so on. It's only a notion till I see Farrar. It's a book that would take a lot of time, but it would be an interesting one to live. America, of course, and the thing *lived* as well as seen . . . as far as possible. Nous verrons [we'll see].[15]

For now, however, coming up with another writing project was secondary to the wedding and planning for a trip to Egypt with his friend Alva Morrison, a Boston attorney and fellow bird watcher. In January Beston applied for his passport and made tentative arrangements to take the passenger ship *Roma* from the port of New York on February 2, 1929, sail to Madeira, then travel to Alexandria with brief stops in Gibraltar, Algiers, and Naples. After two weeks on the Nile, they would see the pyramids at Giza and then proceed home after stops in Athens, Rome, Florence, and Paris: "All a bit rushed save Egypt," wrote Beston, who planned to be back in the United States by late April or early May.[16] A complicating factor in the plans was whether Morrison would be free to go; two of his young children had recently fallen ill and Beston was unsure if he would himself follow through with the trip if Morrison was unable to leave his family. Alva's wife, Amy Gallagher Morrison, sent Beston regular updates on the children's health, holding out hope that they would recover in time for Alva and Henry's trip, but Beston realized that there was every chance that Morrison would not feel free to leave—and rightfully so—while his children were ill, and so he began to consider possible alternative plans in case they had to cancel the trip to Egypt.

Henry and Elizabeth

As another cold New England winter set in, Beston was increasingly eager to leave Massachusetts. Looking out upon Quincy after a snow storm one day in mid-January, the dreary winter bleakness of the scene quickened his desire to leave for adventure and warmer climes: "The wind having swung over to the southwest during the night, the snow of yesterday's overclouded harshness of cold is now dissolving into ice with a glaze of water; people walk timidly on the side streets, trucks go by with fans of slush accompanying them like the attendant waves of speed boats; there are dodgings leapings to safety and angry looks and damnings, and over all gathers a milkiness of cloud spread like thin breath on a mirror of milky blue."[17] There were, as always, cultural advantages to living near Boston, including the opportunity to enjoy plays, concerts, and parties, such as one hosted by Mary Wheelwright that featured a performance by the noted pianist George Copeland. Copeland was a native of Boston who had lived in Majorca and London for an extended period and had not performed in his home city for over ten years; at the Wheelwright home he played some of his signature pieces by Debussy, some pieces inspired by Mozart, and then about seven or eight of what Beston called "stunning Spanish things, a folk song or two, some Mallorcan dances, an Andalusian love song, and a fine, trampling, all-Spanish peasant dance to finish with."[18] Mary Wheelwright was ill, and therefore unable to attend her own musicale, but Beston left her a note telling her of his engagement to Elizabeth Coatsworth. The following day she sent Beston a lovely letter congratulating him: "I'm *so* glad you found your harbour, and I'm sure it's the right one. I knew you were great friends and that's a fine basis and I wish you every good thing so that your story may end like your fairy tales."[19]

As the winter progressed, the prospects for the trip to Egypt with Alva Morrison became increasingly tenuous as his daughter's illness took a turn for the worse. Beston continued to weigh contingency plans; one possibility was to go through with the Egypt trip, but on a much-reduced scale; another was to go to southern Spain; and a third was to go to the West Indies with his friend Corey Ford, who had recently written to Beston. After apologizing to Henry for the "triteness" of his words of congratulation on his planned nuptials ("If the Pope took off his sixteen lace skirts and did a clog dance on the roof of the Vatican, probably I should only be able to murmur: 'Well, well.'"), Ford wrote a beautiful letter congratulating him on the engagement:

> I know you for one of the greatest of living artists, one of the most beautiful stylists in American literature, whose genius is already a permanent contribution to the human thirst for beauty. And I know that you will write yet greater works. And I hope that this new spirit who comes to share the Outermost House with you, and share also for the first time that hidden room which you have kept inviolable, will maintain those dwellings in the peace and sympathy that will give your genius the continued inspiration to soar. She has a great duty to you, and to mankind.[20]

After postponing the departure day for the Egypt trip for a week in the hopes that Alva Morrison's daughter, Nicky, would recover sufficiently for Alva to go, Beston and Morrison finally acknowledged that given her condition they would have to scrap their travel plans. In a spur-of-the-moment decision, Beston opted to go to England to tour the countryside and visit with some friends, including Grace Corson and Norreys Jephson O'Conor, the poet and scholar of Celtic literature, both of whom were longtime friends of Beston from his days at Harvard. As was the case with the wedding proposal to Elizabeth, once Beston made his mind up, he moved quickly, and on Thursday, February 21, 1929, he boarded the *American Trader* in New York City and sailed for England just as Coatsworth was preparing for a journey of her own to Guatemala. They still had not set a firm date for the wedding, and were unsure about whether a June or September date would be best, considering their respective travel plans.

The *American Trader* was a freighter with derricks on the fore and aft decks and a set of passenger cabins jammed into a portion of the upper deck. A wet, heavy snow had fallen the night before the voyage, and narrow paths had been shoveled on the deck so that the boarding passengers could trudge their way to the cabins while freight continued to be loaded into the ship's hold. Beston was assigned a corner room with a narrow berth that ran from port to starboard, rather than the customary fore and aft. When the weather got rough a few days into the voyage, Beston wrote that he "felt like a performing horse on a see-saw."[21] He was finally compelled to make his bed on the window seat, which did run fore and aft, and after cramming his six-foot-two-inch frame into his makeshift bed he managed a fitful rest in the chilly, uncomfortable quarters. After several days of unsettled weather, the ship entered the mouth of the Thames, arriving in London on March 6. A bus took the ship's passengers from their dock at the Royal Albert basin to the heart of the city, and as they traveled Beston got a sobering sense of what the aftermath of the Great War had been like in England and much of the rest of Europe:

> [A]s our special bus approached the inner city though a grim and inhuman wilderness of mean streets, the tragic meaning of the phrase "unemployment in England" began to take shape in sauntering straggles of dirty and miserable human beings. They saunter alone, they stand in street corner groups, they form sordid and piteous lines outside government relief offices, and they have a lost dog horror about them; I say horror for it is something which has happened to man . . . adult unskilled labourers for the most part, men of the docks and roustabout types, a lot of them seemed men in the middle forties—family men—but there were a great many young men, too. An unutterably dreadful hopelessness on the face of the younger men, the most terrible look . . . I think I've ever seen on a human countenance in this civilization . . . No "air", no bravado, not a lingering sign of the old insolence of living which walked Piccadilly, nothing but the faces of people with an inward as well as an outward struggle, and shabby-ish clothes of two seasons before last season's style. At the big teas, shabbiness "carrying on", at the best hotels people in proper clothes with borne-down faces. Pretty terrible, all in all.[22]

At the London offices of Doubleday, Doran, where Beston went to see through the publication of the British edition of *The Outermost House*, he visited with some people he had known from the New York office, many of whom told him that the situation in England was so bad that at first they thought they wouldn't be able to stand it. Not long after arriving in London, Beston was saddened, but not entirely surprised to hear that little Nicky Morrison had died the week after he had set sail for England; a "cruel little bit of news" that cast a pall over his trip and reaffirmed Alva's decision not to go through with the planned excursion to Egypt.[23]

Shielded as they were from the worst of the post-war economic slump, many Americans, Beston included, really had little concept of what was going on in Europe during the 1920s. The post-war recovery had been slow and painful. Substantial parts of the war zone were still in ruins, new and inexperienced democratic governments had succeeded many of the old autocracies, and runaway inflation in Germany had crippled the Weimar Republic. High unemployment, an economic slowdown, fears of bolshevism, and bitter resentment over the harsh terms of the Versailles Treaty made the political situation in Germany particularly dangerous. In November of 1923, a little known political agitator in Bavaria, Adolf Hitler, instigated an uprising against the government that became known as the "Beer Hall Putsch" for its flashpoint in a Munich beer garden. The putsch was swiftly put down by police, but not until nearly two dozen police officers and Nazi sympathizers were killed. Hitler was convicted for his role in the riots, but spent just nine months in prison, during which time he wrote *Mein Kampf*—a chilling preview of what would play out in Europe over the next twenty years.

During the 1920s fascism was on the rise throughout Europe, often supported by wealthy industrialists who saw it as a counterweight to bolshevism, and who applauded fascist plans to reinvigorate faltering post-war economies. In 1925 Benito Mussolini brought the *Fascisti* to power in Italy, the first European government to elect a fascist regime. To the millions of people suffering through the economic disaster of the post-war period—and later the worldwide economic depression of the 1930s—the promises of the fascists were alluring, and the darker sides of their agenda, such as ultra-nationalism, military expansion, repression of civil rights, and a murderous xenophobia were just shadowy abstracts on the horizon. Even democracies such as Britain and France were not completely immune to the siren call of a political ideology that promised to harness the might of industrial capitalism while simultaneously uplifting living conditions of the working class. When Beston arrived in London that March he got a first-hand view of the new political climate. In Piccadilly Square he saw a two young British fascists standing near the entrance to Shaftsbury Avenue hawking copies of *The British Fascist*. Dressed in black and wearing what

Beston described as a "sort of Tam o' shanter *cum* beret," the young men were formidable looking fellows in their early twenties who looked as if they "could give a good account of themselves." Beston stopped to talk briefly with them and found them to be "frightfully earnest and polite."[24]

Despite this passing encounter with the political movement that would shape the fate of Europe over the next fifteen years, Beston's time in England in early 1929 was spent not in observation of the present-day condition of the country but in contemplation of "old" England—its literature, art, and culture. He visited numerous museums, including the United Services Museum, the British Museum, the National Gallery, and many other historic sites and art galleries. He wrote on a nearly daily basis to Elizabeth Coatsworth, and his letters are replete with references to references to English writers, particularly the Romantics. Evenings were often spent at the theatre, social events and authors' banquets, or with literary friends such as Phillip Gibbs and Norreys and Grace O'Conor. He also shopped for books, clothing, and a ring for Elizabeth, having decided that he wanted to bring her a London ring, "for I love this old city far better than any other European capital."[25] Beston was a cultural anglophile of the highest order, but held no truck with its imperial politics or colonialism generally, and in the years since the Great War he had gradually distanced himself from former President Theodore Roosevelt's vigorous pro-war stance. Beston now suspected that the United States had been duped by Britain into entering the war (he had grown particularly suspicious about the circumstances leading to the sinking of the *Lusitania*) and had drifted toward the large segment of the American public that desired to keep a healthy distance between the United States and the political affairs of Europe.

For much of the first part of his trip Beston stayed not in London but East Bergholt, a rustic town in Suffolk, an hour or so by train from London. English friends of Beston had arranged for him to stay with a couple, Mr. and Mrs. Tricker, who occasionally rented a room out to people who came well recommended. In addition to a bedroom, his lodgings included a small sitting room where he took his meals. Beston did a great deal of traveling, much on foot, through the surrounding English countryside, visiting Cornwall, Winchester, and various other historic towns. One of the great highlights of the trip came when Charles Stewart Davison, the elderly brother of Beston's wartime godmother, Mabel Davison, made special arrangements for Henry and Norreys O'Conor to visit Owen Morshead, the king's librarian, at Windsor Castle. The residence of the royal librarian was a red brick house with a garden that opened into a private park surrounding Windsor castle. As the court was not then in residence, Morshead treated Beston and O'Conor to a private viewing of the king's library, "the most rare of privileges," as Beston called it. The library held a number of magnificent paintings, a collection of Holbein miniatures, and relics from the royal family including an old lace collar from Charles I still spotted with an old bloodstain from his execution by Oliver Cromwell's Puritans. There was also a sketch of Christina, Duchess of Milan, made by Holbein for Henry VIII. The story, as told to Beston by Morshead, was that in response to the impetuous monarch's marriage proposal the Duchess responded, "Alas, I have but one neck, but had I been born with two I would have been only too delighted to have been of service to your majesty."[26]

In early May Beston received an invitation from his friend Conrad Ormond to spend a week at the Ormond residence on Cheyne Walk in the Chelsea section of London. Ormond drove out to Cornwall to pick up Beston for a motor trip through the English countryside before reaching London. They paused to eat a box lunch atop a hill affording them a splendid view of Dartmoor, a vast and scenic stretch of moorland in south Devon punctuated with numerous bedrock hills commonly called "tors"; they then proceeded on to Salisbury and Amesbury, where they spent the night. As soon as it was dark, Beston and Ormond left their lodgings and drove out to the Salisbury plain, some two miles distant, and like two adventuresome boys, scaled the wire fence at Stonehenge, where the enthralled Beston said, they "had Stonehenge and the vast night of broken cloud all to themselves."[27] The next day they drove to London, where Beston spent a few days suffering from a "cavernous cold" he had picked up in Cornwall. Staying at the Ormond house was as good as visiting an art gallery, however, as Ormond's mother was the sister of John Sargent and the house was filled with beautiful watercolors "It all goes to my heart like rest after a spacious day," Beston wrote to Coatsworth.[28]

Henry and Elizabeth

While in East Bergholt, a telegram arrived from Elizabeth, who had just returned from Guatemala, suggesting a date in June for the wedding. Beston immediately and enthusiastically agreed, writing, "June, yes, and may the days go speeding . . . June it shall be, and then the lovely summer to wander around and be explorers in, to make plans in too."[29] Beston was increasingly anxious to begin married life and had already begun to formulate plans for the honeymoon: to spend the first days of marriage with Elizabeth in two of the places he loved most—Cape Cod and the English countryside. To Beston's young Cape Cod friend Truesdell Fife he wrote, "yes, the rumor is true; I am going to get spliced; the embattled bachelor at last hauls down his flag, and only wishes he had done so long before."[30] On May 10, 1929, Beston boarded the *American Farmer* at the port in London and sailed for home.

On June 18, 1929, Beston and Coatsworth were married in Hingham; as Elizabeth later wrote, the ceremony took place "in the Smiths' living-room on one of the hottest days imaginable."[31] After the wedding Henry and Elizabeth drove out to Cape Cod in her Ford, which Henry had dubbed the "Fore and Aft," for a two-week stay prior to sailing for England, arriving on June 20. "We're down here at the Fo'castle," Elizabeth wrote to her mother, "with the sea pounding outside with the high tide, the rooms shining with our recent industry, and the happy game begun."[32] Fittingly enough, their first visitor at the Fo'castle was a young coastguardsman making his rounds who stayed to talk with the famous literary couple for over an hour before resuming his watch. For the most part the newlyweds spent their days writing or walking along the beach before heading to the coast guard station to get their car and drive to the Overlook for dinner and to visit with the Kelleys and other Eastham friends. "I pity all the rest of the world," Elizabeth wrote to sister Margaret and her husband Morton Smith:

> we have had such weather as you haven't dreamed of—and such seas, whales, porpoises, banks of stars, breakers, phosophorous, schooners, fogs, moors and happiness as—oh well. Everyone at Eastham eyes me carefully to make sure I'm a fitten wife for a Cape Codder, and weighs me with a jealous eye to make sure I'm not planning to wean their man from his dunes. Then they look downright relieved at my praise and on we go. It's such a friendly

jolly spirit of well-wishing that one enters into here—I hate going away—
potential green heads or no potential green heads—England waiting or
not waiting.[33]

Henry too was blissfully happy, writing to Ida Reid Coatsworth, Elizabeth's
mother, "Of all the lucky hombres, your Henry is certainly the first in place.
The blessed Fo'castle is certainly *the* honey moon house of all the world,
for we have the whole vast scene to ourselves, and house and dune and sky
and sea are each and every one doing their special and particular best to
please their lovely new lady."[34]

Two weeks later, Henry and Elizabeth embarked upon the second part of
their honeymoon, sailing to England on the White Star Line's *Albertic*. They
arrived in Liverpool on July 16, then traveled to London for a few days before
leaving for Cornwall, where they spent several days in Tavistock, a little
village on the edge of the Dartmoor. At another Cornish village, St. Maw-
gan's, they stayed at an inn just across the street from a thirteenth-century
church that had a plaque dedicated to "Henry Beeston," which, said Beston,
"deepened a sense that I've always had half-formed within me, a sense of
life as a mystical pattern," albeit one often formed "with lost threads and
unraveled edges."[35] From Cornwall the couple then traveled to East Anglia,
rooming in East Bergholt and exploring the surrounding countryside on
foot. As they wandered through the rural landscape, Henry observed that
"Elizabeth is getting to be a perfect stunnerino as a naturalist's wife; I
find myself armed now with another and far better pair of eyes."[36] While
in East Bergholt, a congratulatory letter from Ted and Eleanor Roosevelt,
who were traveling in the Far East, arrived, inviting Henry and Elizabeth
to stay with the Roosevelts in Puerto Rico that winter.

After a week in Cornwall the Bestons headed toward Northumberland,
staying at small hotels and rooms in old English public houses along the
way as they walked through the moor country toward the River Tyne and
Hadrian's Wall, the old fortification marking the dividing line between the
fierce tribes to the north and the furthest extent of the Roman empire. At
Humshaugh-on-Tyne Elizabeth wrote to her family:

We meant to stay here one night and have stayed three . . . half a mile up the
river is a great estate, and on it the remains of a great Roman camp, baths,

Elizabeth Coatsworth Beston's mother, Ida Reid Coatsworth, with her brother, Frank
Reid, and Mr. and Mrs. George Chester. Probably taken at their home in Pasadena,
California, in mid-1930s.

dormitories, heated officers house, chapel and treasure cellar . . . Yesterday
we drove eight or nine miles to another camp high on the hills and walked
a couple of miles along the top of the wall at the edge of cliffs overlooking
the moors—the wall is about five feet high and six or seven wide, boldly
following the heights, over moors where sheep bleated. We didn't lay eyes
on a human being until we rejoined our car near a black lake under a crag.
We were mad about it all. In the afternoon we walked to the village church
with an altar for a font and five Roman pillars in the nave—each evening
we've had a coal fire in the bedroom with its light flickering up on the ceiling,
and there was an old bound year of *The Strand* without covers in which we've
been reading Sherlock Holmes avidly.[37]

After an idyllic week in Northumberland the Bestons then turned toward
Liverpool and the voyage home, setting sail on September 21. Reluctant to
end the honeymoon period, however, they accepted Mary Wheelwright's
wedding invitation for a cruise onboard her ninety-four-foot yacht the *Liria*.
From the *Liria's* homeport of Northeast Harbor on Maine's Mount Desert
Island they sailed around the offshore islands of Maine to Boothbay Harbor;
then took an automobile trip to the White Mountains of New Hampshire.

After that they came full circle, returning to the Fo'castle in time for the
great fall migration of birds and the yellow-russet colors of the autumnal
Cape. As Coatsworth recalled many years later:

All that fall and winter the Cape was a continual lodestar. We were there
in autumn sunlight and winter storms . . . I learned what a good beach
walker Henry was, tireless in any sort of sand; how well he could cook an
Indian pudding, but above all how often some casual thing he might say
would open a whole vista of thoughts in a listener's mind. Again and again
he would take me out to look at the night sky trying in vain to teach me the
names of the constellations or he might show me a planet rising out of the
sea. That passion of his for the stars is, I think, the greatest of all the loves
that have bound Henry to nature. Often through the years he has wakened
me to see some midnight or pre-dawn wonder overhead. The night sky and
the first budding of the footlights of a theatre—these are the strong magics
which have held and charmed Henry from his earliest to his latest years.[38]

Happily absorbed as they were in their honeymoon and the early months of their long-delayed marriage, the troubling news of the stock market's abrupt plunge in late October of 1929 seemed just a passing concern in an otherwise joyous time. The full impact of the crash on Wall Street and its role in what would become the most disastrous economic depression of the twentieth century would not become clearly evident for another year or two, and the financial situation of the Bestons—due in part to their literary income and to the modest investment portfolio brought to the marriage by Elizabeth—seemed at the time to be fairly secure. After returning from the Cape, Henry and Elizabeth settled in at "Shipcote" in Hingham. For their first Christmas together as a married couple, Henry and Elizabeth printed up a stanza from her poem "The Barn" to send to family and friends:

> There was her baby born
> And laid to sleep in the hay
> While music flooded the rafters
> And the barn was as light as day,
> And angels and kings and shepherds
> Came to worship the Babe from afar,
> But we looked at Him first of all creatures
> By the bright strange light of a star!

Elizabeth's gift to Henry was a lovely hand-written manuscript of her poems and artwork on the night sky and their new life together. Many of the Bestons' acquaintances and even some of their friends did not realize that they had been married until they received the joint Christmas card. After the holidays Henry and Elizabeth once again drove down to Cape Cod, with Henry reserving rooms at the Overlook in Eastham rather than subjecting Elizabeth to the harsh January weather battering their little house on the dunes. During the off-season there were seldom more than just a couple of guests staying at the inn, and often it was only the Kelleys and Bestons.

During this early winter stay at the Cape in the first year of marriage, a writing pattern was established that would occasionally cause some concern for Elizabeth over the course of their marriage. One morning, for example, Elizabeth wrote to her mother that she was relaxing while at the Overlook—sleeping late, eating breakfast in bed, and writing a few letters. But during the course of that "relaxing" week or two at the Cape she also wrote about a third of one children's book and half of another, as well as completing three fairy tales and several poems. Henry, on the other hand, spent the week reading (mostly poetry) and musing about what subject to undertake for his next writing project—an issue he had already been considering for nearly a year. The great success of *The Outermost House* had established Beston as a nature writer of note, and he felt considerable—almost paralyzing—pressure to follow it up with a worthy successor. Beston was now being mentioned in virtually every new book or article that discussed modern nature writing, such as Henry Chester Tracy's survey of American nature writing, *American Naturists* (this was, of course, well before the use of the term "naturist" became a euphemism for nudist) which was published in early 1930 by E. P. Dutton & Company. Beston was mentioned approvingly, although as Ted Roosevelt Jr. complained, it failed to appreciate him enough. Like his father, Ted, Jr. had only disdain for nature writers who took liberties with the facts of natural history, such as endowing animals with human characteristics and emotions. He grumbled to Beston that Tracy's book included Ernest Thompson Seton, proclaiming, "No naturist can be a 'nature faker.'"[39]

In late March, Beston took a train down to New York City to meet with publishers and to visit friends such as Mabel Davison and Katherine Butler Hathaway. As usual, he stayed at the Prince George Hotel at Fifth Avenue and 28th Street in Manhattan, which was not only close to his publishers, but to the theaters and museums he often frequented while in the city. His first stop was to see John Farrar, who had been his editor at Doubleday, Doran and Company for *The Outermost House*. In 1929 Farrar left Doubleday to found Farrar and Rinehart in 1929, and he would later go on to form Farrar, Straus, and Company in 1945. Beston felt ethically obliged to offer Doubleday any "sequel" to *The Outermost House*, but John Farrar urged Beston to try his hand at fiction: "he is all for my doing a novel anywhere and anytime, will give me a contract anytime I ask for it, and will read the stories I submitted to him (Santo Thomas et l'autre) and do his level best to place them. I couldn't have been more friendlily received."[40] The following day Beston visited the editors at Doubleday, Doran, where he found that the success of *The Outermost House* had significantly elevated his status as an author. The idea that he had been musing about for almost a year—a book on the inner shore of Cape Cod, the bay side, that would complement his previous work about the great beach—was greeted with great enthusiasm and an on-the-spot acceptance. As he wrote to Elizabeth back in Hingham, "they are writing me a contract, one with rather better terms than the last, and in a few days it will arrive at Quincy and be sent on to the Cape to be signed. So begins a book, and a more industrious husband! They were all more than nice to me at Doubleday's, and I am relieved, ready, and happy about the whole beginning."[41]

Despite the success of the trip Beston was anxious to leave the city and return home. While he still enjoyed the theaters, museums, and other cultural attractions of New York, the hyperactive frenzy of the greatest of modern cities now hit a raw nerve with a man who was now more attuned to the rhythms and poetry of nature than to the cacophony of urban life. "I wouldn't stay one damned second longer in this demonia," he wrote:

> It's just an insanity of taxicabs crowded as closely together as teeth in a jaw, all rushing together in one infernal rhythm of attack, in a vibration which makes the human heartbeat drunken and overborne. The people look so wild and tired all at once, their eyes full of the moment's immediacy and nothing much else. Next to the Grand Central, the new Chrysler building, a hundred feet or more taller than the Eiffel Tower has reached the sky, an insanity of height and blue prints; New Yorkers being so tired of it all that hardly a one knows what or where the building is.[42]

Beston had another reason for being anxious to return home to Hingham and Elizabeth; she was pregnant with the couple's first child. Henry was so pleased by the prospect of becoming a father that—despite his desire for a son—he seems not to have really cared whether the baby would be a boy or a girl: "I bet the doctor said girl this time. John [Farrar] says his girl (number 2) was announced regularly as a boy. He also says girls, even baby girls, are nicer with their da's."[43]

The prospect of an addition to the family and the just-signed contract with Doubleday, Doran and Company for his new book on the Cape seemed to have briefly energized Beston into working more assiduously on his book manuscript. Soon after returning to Hingham in April, the Bestons closed up Shipcote and left for a month on Cape Cod, renting a cottage on Great Pond, the largest freshwater pond in Eastham. Situated just a mile or two from the western shore of Cape Cod, Great Pond was one of a large number of kettle ponds formed when the glaciers retreated thousands of years previously, leaving enormous chunks of ice broken off from the glacial sheets to form depressions in the freshly exposed land that gradually filled with melting ice water. As Beston wrote to his young Eastham friend Truesdell Fife, "I have signed a contract for a new Cape book, and am already laying the keel. Next time I get you by the coat tails, I am going to ask you for whatever data you can help me with concerning Eastham ponds, . . . birds, animals, adventures, unusual awareness, etc. It was to gather the 'feel' of the pond region that I hired the cottage."[44]

Beston stayed on in Eastham after Elizabeth returned to Hingham in mid-May, sending her regular updates as spring revivified the Cape. "Everywhere one goes the beach plum thickets are in a drift of bloom," he wrote, "the twigs each one a stick of flowers like Aaron's rod. Here and there, in the opening wild shrubbery by the ponds and salt swamps, the wild pear sways in the hurrying warm wind; only the great, dead 'silver oaks' preserve the rhythm of naked winter."[45] Just a few miles away from the beach on the Atlantic side where he had spent so much time observing nature, Beston was finding a whole new aspect of Cape Cod as he explored the pond and bay regions. He went digging for quahogs (hard shell clams) with his friends Kenneth and Ted Young, staying overnight on Kenneth's small boat:

We had so rough a night of rolling and tossing, and so windy and wave-buffeted a morning, that even so late as an hour ago, I felt the room move uneasily and the floor rise in a dream toss. How that curious sense lingers on! After a very good supper of quahaug chowder fresh from the sea and coffee and homemade cake, Kenneth and I had returned to our own boat "Gypsy," leaving Ted aboard the boat which had served supper, the "Gypsy" being secured astern the other, the "Seabuddy." About 1:30 or so it began to blow from then E., and we both woke up out of a heavy sleep,—I remember the spot of moonlight sliding up and down Kenneth's bunk as the boat rocked. We went on deck and by the obscured moon saw the ghost of Billingsgate behind us with its ruined, Poe-esque house, the lights of far away Wellfleet, and our own bow line hauling and tugging, and the dark shapes of two other boats far away. After giving ourselves more slack, and looking to the anchor, we turned in again and slept catnaps with talkative intervals between, the length of our catnaps seeming to harmonize. One of the other boats, by the way, was named the "Tradewind." The morning was much colder but no rougher—even a grain less rough perhaps—and we began dragging at 7, dragging for 10 minutes and then hauling. The old grain bags filled one by one with the clams, the cold spray sluiced our oil skins, a N.E. fog came across the Cape and hid the Wellfleet shore, the billows raced with tracers of wind, whitecaps gathered, and finally, the last bag filled, we put for home. It seemed warmish and hazy when we put into the home creek. Back at the Kelleys, I simply fell into a stupor of sleep and had to be called to supper. But every minute of the adventure was interesting![46]

Burton Kelley (the son of Tom and Mary Kelley) and Truesdell Fife were of great help in Beston's explorations of the inner Cape. Both boys were tremendously fond of Beston and did everything they could to aid in the research for his new book. Burt Kelley was a skillful young fisherman, catching large hornpout, pickerel, and bass in the ponds near the Overlook. Truesdell Fife eagerly helped Beston gather information about the ponds and bay, and was always ready to assist in whatever way possible. As spring progressed, however, Beston found himself more and more distracted from his literary work. Friends such as Corey Ford and Mabel Davison arrived at the Fo'castle for visits, and as the due date for the baby approached, Beston found himself unable to concentrate on any systematic study of the inner Cape; as he confessed to Truesdell Fife, he was "working towards my Cape book rather than at it."[47]

All literary work ceased at the end of June, with the birth of the Beston's first child, Margaret Coatsworth Beston, on July 2, 1930. The Bestons and their infant daughter spent much of that summer and fall at the Hemenway's lodge "Whalewalk," a hobby farm in Eastham, so that Henry could—at least ostensibly—continue his research for the new book, although baby Meg was generally more compelling than work. Once the cold weather arrived, Elizabeth and the baby returned home to Hingham while Henry remained on the Cape. Although he continued to work on the new book, writing long descriptions of what he saw on the bay side, there were already telling indications that the quiet, isolated life on the beach that had proved so conducive to writing *The Outermost House* had now lost some of its charm for Beston. He spent relatively little time at the Fo'castle, preferring instead to stay at the Overlook, where meals were provided and there were people with whom to socialize. "I'm afraid I'm pretty well exploded as a hermit, dear," he wrote despairingly to Elizabeth in early January. "In other days I would have pulled this isolation in around me like a spiritual cloak; now I wear it uncomfortably, wriggling my shoulders in it and fidgeting with the sleeves."[48]

While transition to married life for the Bestons may have been a "gay adventure" as Elizabeth put it, the arrival of a child dramatically changed the rhythm of their lives. Henry and Elizabeth adjusted as necessary to each of the charms and trials of parenthood, although Elizabeth adjusted more gracefully than did Henry. She proved to be capable of snatching time to write no matter what the circumstances, whereas Henry needed long, uninterrupted, quiet periods to get into a creative frame of mind. When they were in Hingham making time for writing was somewhat easier for Elizabeth, as she had the aid of a housekeeper and cook—something that was still common for upper middle class families during this period. Additionally, Elizabeth's mother, Ida Reid Coatsworth, who also lived at Shipcote, was a great help, although she generally over-wintered in warmer climes such as Pasadena, California, or Charleston, South Carolina. As for Henry, while he was in Hingham he generally wrote little; in part because of the distractions of family life, in part because he found little natural history to inspire him in Hingham, and in part because of the distractions of nearby Boston and frequent social calls.

In August 1930 Elizabeth Coatsworth's (she continued to write under her maiden name, which was well-known in literary circles) most successful children's book to date, *The Cat Who Went to Heaven,* was published by Macmillan. The story was set in ancient Japan, where a poor young artist struggles to make enough money to feed himself and his elderly housekeeper. One day he gives the housekeeper the last of their money to buy some food at the marketplace, but instead she returns with a kitten. Initially

Henry and Elizabeth

Beston and daughter Meg at Cape Cod with their dog Bo'sun, ca. 1929.

the artist is annoyed that the housekeeper has not only wasted the last of their money, but has spent it on a cat. In ancient Japan the cat was often associated with devil and mischief, since in the story of the Buddha the cat was the only creature that did not pay homage to the enlightened one. The artist's kind heart yields to his housekeeper's tears and the kitten, which they name Good Fortune, is permitted to stay, leading to a series of events that change the fortunes of the artist and his housekeeper. Coatsworth was honored with the prestigious Newbery Medal for Children's Literature for *The Cat Who Went to Heaven* in 1931, and the book became a perennial favorite that went through many printings.

During the winter of 1930–1931, Beston tried to gain traction by taking frequent short trips to Cape Cod, sometimes staying at the Fo'castle and sometimes opting for the comforts of the Overlook Inn. Still, work on the book progressed only in fits and starts—Cape Cod and the Fo'castle were simply not drawing forth the same wellspring of literary output that they had just a few short years ago—in fact they had seemingly become so mundane that they no longer seemed to possess the magic that had fired Beston's imagination during the writing of *The Outermost House*. In the hope that a complete change of pace would improve his mood, in early March of 1931 Beston boarded the train in Boston for a trip to visit Jake and Bee Day in Maine. The Days and their two little boys, Maclure (Mac) and Richard (Dickie) had moved back to Jake's hometown of Damariscotta, where they lived in a house on Route One that had been in the Day family for five generations. Beston was very fond of the Day children and stopped at a sporting goods shop in Boston to buy pedometers as presents for the boys before proceeding to Maine. Leaden skies and a heavy snow enveloped the train all the way along the route of the Maine Eastern Railroad route, and when Beston got off at the Newcastle-Damariscotta station he found that the relatively short walk to the Day home in Damariscotta was a slog: "getting to Jake's was a plunge through huge drifts new-whitened."[49] As always, Beston was greeted like family by the Days, who had prepared a spare bedroom for him with an enormous bed painted New England "wagon blue"—"such an enormous bed to miss one's gal out of!" he wrote to Elizabeth back in Hingham.[50]

Beston spent the next two weeks in Maine with the Days, and his letters home to Elizabeth have the same quality of ecstatic discovery that is evident in his earlier missives from Cape Cod. The morning after his arrival in Damariscotta, Beston described the scene to Elizabeth: "The snow is very deep here, real snow-shoe depth, and the evergreens are a show of close-packed pyramids with drooping branches. Today there is less sunlight than a sense of it as the great cloud mass grown vaporous and vague closes and opens, illuminating one's door yard now, now this far field. Jake's studio on the hill, a quarter to a half mile away, emerges like a fairy tale house from its pines."[51] Two years previously, Jake had gone through what Beston referred to as a "nervous upset"—he moved the family from Boston back to the comforting familiarity of Damariscotta and according to Beston, "pulled himself out of it largely by building himself a real workshop for wood working" in the barn near the house. There he designed and made beautiful, hand-crafted items including a present for Meg's nursery that he and Henry designed during the visit, although as Henry confessed, "my contribution [was] about 5% to Jake's 95." Beston delighted in the warm family atmosphere of the Day home, retelling numerous family anecdotes that he heard during his visit in letters to Elizabeth, and saying of the Day children, "Dickie is a darling . . . Mac, too, is a blessed kid. Mac, who looks like Jake, has much of Bee; Dickie, who is Bee all over, is Jake mentally through and through."[52]

Although he never said as much in his letters to Elizabeth, there is also a sense that Henry's visit to the Days was in part a crash course in how to raise a family. Beston was now past forty, and his sudden transition from footloose vagabond and literary man to husband and father was often over-whelming, despite the enthusiasm with which he had made the change to marriage and fatherhood. His own childhood, with the untimely death of his mother and the chronic irritability of his overworked father, had not provided him with a useful model for harmonious family life—although the home life of his brother George and his family probably would have done so. Perhaps the attraction of the Days was also attributable to the fact that like Beston, Jake Day was a creative artist, and managed to successfully balance his art with the pressures and challenges of raising a family.

Part of the secret of happiness for the Days was their shared love of the outdoors, camping, hiking, and swimming. During the warmer months, the family spent a good deal of time on a houseboat they had christened the "Dazark," and which they moored in Deep Cove (off East Neck) on Damariscotta Lake. Jake offered Henry and Elizabeth the use of the house-boat for a vacation that summer, and Henry was eager to do so, writing Elizabeth, *"We are to have it anytime in May or early June* we might like. Wouldn't that be gorgeous, dear? Jake says May is great, also September. We could have it for a while in September as well. He also says it is thrilling when the alewives are running. He says he loves the bird life and the beast life . . . says you get only bird life on the shore."[53] The Dazark had been drawn onto shore for the winter, but on March 12, Jake and Henry packed some food and snowshoes and slogged to Damariscotta Lake's East Neck, a trip that Henry described to Elizabeth in rapturous tones:

> I've seen the "Dazark," and had an afternoon of outdoor adventure which missed perfection only in that you were not there to share its joy. First we got into Jake's car with our lunch kits and snowshoes, motored some five miles due N. along the state road, and left her at a corner grocery. We then faced a five mile walk over a side road scarcely broken out, a road climbing and descending two great hills from whose summits one could look over a great Maine wilderness wood to the Camden mountains blue and white in the far air. Deep snow everywhere, five feet of it on the fields, and roadside drifts as high as my head, heavy, water cemented snow . . . snow and space and woods. At the end of it a farm, an old, old couple with cheery blue eyes, a deep well in living rock, a grandfather clock and a library of paper novels of the 1880–90 "can you forget her?" kind. Then across a most beautiful pine and beech and hemlock pasture to a slope in deep pines and hemlocks, then a cove, a dream of a cove, woods all around, no cottages. Nothing but superb trees—"old growth" as they say here, an ampitheatre of snow and towering green, the bush beneath buried deep save for some out-struggled twig here and there; the floor of the cove, an untrodden, stainless carpet of level snow. (I had been fitted to borrowed snowshoes at the farm and was carrying on perfectly easily and liking every step. My very worldly Piccadilly blue overcoat plus snowshoes was voted a great success). Across the cove sky, a passing-very high, of menad clouds. And on the unvisited shore, a houseboat, princess, queen of houseboats, the Dazark . . . much larger than the Fo'c'stle and higher, . . . much the same idea—kitchen-living room and two superb bunk rooms, also a very good yacht bath room. In the living room, a wood burning range. There did we sit down and cook potatoes and steak, eaten with lettuce sandwiches.[54]

Beston was thrilled by the prospect of staying in a place that combined the elemental simplicity of his time on Cape Cod's great beach with the type of potential for an experience close to nature, hoping it might result in the same sort of fresh new insights that had inspired him to write *The Outermost*

House. A few months later the Bestons took Jake Day up on his offer and spent several weeks living on the Days' houseboat, which was essentially a floating cottage with stove, kitchen, bedrooms, and other amenities. Jake kept a couple of canoes tied to the Dazark, and the Bestons spent many hours paddling around the lake watching for loons, eagles, moose and other wildlife. They also explored the woods and fields of the shoreline enclosing Deep Cove, and spent many hours hiking, swimming, and enjoying picnics on the lake. Coatsworth would later draw on the experience for her young adult novel *Houseboat Summer* (1942), which includes illustrations of the Dazark and a map of the Deep Cove area.

Beston made a late winter visit to Cape Cod and the Fo'castle in early 1931 to survey what damage the winter storms may have wreaked and to try to get back to work on his book. His trip to Maine had renewed the interest in nature that two years in Hingham seemed to have dampened, so he was once again writing, drafting a chapter describing winter on the inner Cape. After arriving at his dune shack on March 24, and building a fire in the fireplace to warm the house, Beston immediately set off to explore the beach. A "dry" nor'easter had summoned forth a thunderous surf, and the air was filled with ocean mist. "The day," wrote Beston, was "so wild and beautiful that moments and glimpses of it were scarce to be borne; it was like seeing Angus Og in the grave dawn of the high places."[55] Beston roamed the beach gathering driftwood for the Fo'castle's fireplace, an easy task given the havoc that the winter had wrought along the great beach: "There is wood everywhere, especially on the marsh side where a wide belt of debris runs through the dead grasses, making surprising detours and wedge-like advances into the very heart of the dune country. Because of the rain, I've relaxed the strict proprieties of magic, and have burnt good and easily obtainable parts of the wrecked houses."[56] The Fo'castle, however, had weathered another Atlantic winter without incident.

After a week on the Cape, Beston—after a brief stop home in Hingham—returned once more to Maine, staying with the Days while he wrote in Jake's studio. His letters to Elizabeth during this period are heartfelt and affectionate, but it is clear that he was relieved to once again feel inspired to write:

Things take shape. Words are beginning to come to finer ends, like blood to a nipped hand. It is certainly blessedly still and withdrawn here; I simply could not ask or find anything more what I want. And the rooming arrangements are excellent, too, so "en avant, Henri!" When I return, dear, you shall read me your newest Chinese tales, and I shall read you the chapter. (I have put aside flowers for the moment and am doing "winter on the Cape".)[57]

Unfortunately, this burst of productivity would not last long, and Beston's enthusiasm for the new book on Cape Cod soon waned once again. In April Beston returned to Hingham to care for daughter Margaret while Elizabeth was in New York meeting with publishers. When Elizabeth returned from New York, Henry took the opportunity to head out to the Fo'castle to work on the book, but once again found that Cape Cod was no longer working its expected literary magic for him, writing to Elizabeth: "Miss you like everything, dear. As a hermit, I'm a washout,.... *totalamente*. Lots of love, honey, and a good hug, and a huglet for Meggles."[58]

Beston returned to Maine again that spring and while there an opportunity arose that he impetuously seized, barely considering the implications. While visiting the Days in Damariscotta Beston learned that a nearby farm had come up for sale. The farm was owned by Allen Bennett and was located on East Neck, right near Deep Cove where Jake Day moored the Dazark on Damariscotta Lake, and it had first been seen by Beston during his snowshoeing trip with Jake the previous March. When Henry returned home, he took Elizabeth out to lunch and sprang the news on her that would soon change their lives:

> Jake told him that the farm's woodlot partly enclosed Deep Cove. This was enough for Henry. Without more than a passing glimpse of the house, he decided to buy the place. He who might hesitate for hours on the choice of a few words, could make up his mind on the future course of his life in an instant.
>
> Once back in Hingham Henry took me out for lunch in Quincy. I remember that we ordered fish sticks (for Henry haddock was the only fish that existed).
>
> "How would you like to have us buy a Maine farm?" he asked at the end of the meal, and I said, also in a split second, "It sounds fine."
>
> A few weeks later we bought the farm.[59]

Henry and Elizabeth

A local attorney, Robert K. Tukey, handled the negotiations for the farm on behalf of the Bestons, and on April 25, 1931, he sent them a Western Union telegram reading simply "We have met the Bennets and they are ours vane map and manure."[60]

That September, Elizabeth stayed in Hingham with Meg while Henry remained in Nobleboro jotting down plans and making arrangements for some much needed updates and repairs on the farmhouse. The property—eighty-eight acres of fields and woods—was beautiful, and Beston reveled in his new surroundings, writing, "The view from the study is beyond telling of, the lake is so big and blue, and the pasture is glorious."[61] The house itself, however, was built in 1835 and needed a significant amount of work. It had no indoor plumbing except for a pump in the kitchen, so Beston had indoor plumbing and a bathroom installed. New windows were set in place, the inside walls were papered and painted, and a porch put in. The faded yellow exterior of the house was repainted a bright farmhouse red. While work proceeded on the house, Beston stayed on the houseboat in Deep Cove with Jake Day, who was working on a series of sketches. Beston reveled in the work of preparing the house: "I like working with these people; they are honest, friendly-minded, and know their job," he wrote to Elizabeth, "It's a nice feeling, dear, preparing a house for you, which you in your turn are to prepare for your *hombre* and your own. I want to fill your hands with so many things, darling, and all of them things you will like. I'm keeping a lot of surprises for you."[62] Elizabeth also had a surprise; in late September she wrote Henry to say that she was pregnant again.

The news from home was not all good, however; as the worldwide economic downturn deepened, the family's financial situation also became more clouded. The modest investment portfolio that Thomas Coatsworth had passed on to his wife and two daughters had been wisely invested, much of it in oil companies and similar blue chip stocks, but the economic depression had battered even these solid, conservative investments. Morton Smith, Henry and Elizabeth's brother-in-law and an astute financial advisor did a fine job of managing the family's assets, but as companies reduced or eliminated dividends, investment yields plunged. In late September of 1931, Elizabeth wrote Henry to tell him that they were no longer drawing from investment profits generated from Elizabeth's account in Buffalo but were eating into the capital. Other investments were also looking precarious, and for the first time since the Great Depression began two years earlier, a note of uneasiness began to affect the Bestons' discussions about finances: "It may be, too," wrote Henry, "that certain investments, due for September payments, have suddenly gone sour. I hope not. We shall just have to see. Don't worry, dear. If we are going to have to pare cheese, live by budget, and take a reef, we can do it . . . As for Union oil, if that goes sour, it will undeniably be thin butter for awhile, but I have not heard of any such little horror yet, and, moreover, I think the dividend would be reduced rather than cut."[63]

Although Elizabeth would never have said so to Henry, the purchase of the farm and expense of repairing it were also a drain on the family finances during this period of economic uncertainty. Furthermore, Prince Hurd in Eastham presented Beston with the opportunity to buy the property on which the Fo'castle had been built (until now, he had been leasing the property). Beston was eager to finally own the dune property outright: "Glory hallelujah! I haven't the slightest idea where I shall find the money, but we'll work it somehow."[64] Henry's proposed solution—which Elizabeth was reluctant to do—was to sell "Shipcote," the Hingham house, and escape entirely "from that thrice accursed boulevard without too much financial wrenching!" Enamored with the thought of moving to rural Maine, Henry endeavored to sound a note that would persuade Elizabeth to sell the house. When Elizabeth mentioned that little Meg was having trouble sleeping, Henry expressed concern and placed the blame on the constant traffic passing by close to the house:

> That front hall is very noisy and the noises are sudden and abrupt in their coming and then of a fairly long duration. I had a very broken sleep there the night I went there for to sleep off my day of packing for the farm, and moreover, Truesdell said he was waked up again and again. Might it be that which is making her fidgety? She wakes easily, anyhow, and those hellish motor noises simply crash through the ears and down into the brain of anyone in those front rooms. Didn't I mention this before? Is there any other place to put her? The back entry? Now, honey, I want you to get some

Henry Beston at Parson Capen House in Topsfield, Massachusetts, 1926.

sleep, and if necessary I will drop everything here and come right home. Hingham doesn't over well agree with our little lady anyhow; she always begins to perk up when we get her away from it . . . Thank God we have this place, dear, and not a day passes which does not enlarge its loveliness, and reveal its spaciousness; it is beautiful, liveable, and *wide*, and our purchase of it was one of the wisest things we've ever done. I am happy, dear, to feel earth, air, water, and fire around me,—the "old stabilities of life" to know that sweet spring in the meadow is ours, and that perhaps—heaven being kind—our children's children will drink from that clean stream. I have been wandering all over the hayfield slope, every foot of it a gracious joy. The young alewives, in procession formation by the thousands, a stream of lives like the milky way, goes round the brim of the lake; there is already a loon in deep cove, and another at the hayfield landing. . . . As for next summer and Mr. Hemenway's—I really don't see how we could do it for a month—it could be done, but at what a lot of bother and fussing back and forth. We'll talk it over, dear. I am trying to leave this place in A1 condition, everything in order and good and sound and workable. My girl will have to make it sweet and liveable. There will be a good kitchen easy to run and handle—with a possibility of piping water down from the spring, plenty of wood, etc, an oil stove and so on. I think it could be done, dear, provided one were willing to try it comfortable farm style. We've a world to talk over, dear. Meanwhile, I wish you and Meg some sleep in that motor nightmare, daddy's view being that perhaps you aren't getting sleep because you can't *stay* asleep. And I want both my gals to have everything they want.[65]

Beston spent much of the fall working on the house, lovingly detailing each improvement to Elizabeth and extolling the potential benefits to the children of growing up in the country rather than what he saw as the suburban dullness of Hingham.

Beston returned to Hingham shortly before the end of October 1931, with the repairs at the farm well under way. Since purchasing the farm, however, the Cape Cod book had not progressed nearly as well as had the renovations at the farm: "I'm supposed to be doing a book on the Cape," he wrote to Luther Neff, "but I haven't got very deeply into it . . . more shame for me."[66] When Beston did think of the Cape, it was primarily out of concern for the Fo'castle, as winter storms battered the ocean-facing bluffs on Nauset beach. After one particularly bad storm in January 1932, Beston got in touch with Harvey Moore, who had built the cottage, and asked him to check to see how close it was to the edge of the eroding bluff. Moore reported that there was still some thirty feet between the house and the edge, but with two more months of winter storms ahead, it now began to look inevitable that sometime soon the Fo'castle would have to be moved back from the edge of the dune or be lost to the sea. Early in March, Henry and Elizabeth (now eight months pregnant) drove to Eastham to check on the house and to close the sale for the land with Prince and Edna Hurd. Despite his struggles in making headway on the new Cape Cod book, the stretch of dune and marshland on which the Fo'castle stood had such an emotional and spiritual hold on Beston that owning the property where he had built the dune shack was cause for celebration.

A few weeks later there was another cause for celebration with the arrival of the Beston's second child, Catherine, on April 9, 1932. "We have had our little 'party'," he wrote to Truesdell Fife, "and 'tis another lass, a strong, lively pretty child who is the real Cape Codder of the family. Her name is Catherine after her grandmother Beston. Elizabeth is now home with me here in Hingham, resting easily & well. As for me, I'm bound for the Maine farm, thinking it wiser to go there and get things finished up while this house is full of people."[67] There were certainly enough willing helpers to assist Elizabeth with the baby and little Meg—in addition to Ida Reid Coatsworth, Elizabeth's sister Margaret and brother-in-law Morton (who had no children of their own) were eager to help out with their nieces. So while Beston was not leaving his wife completely in the lurch when it came to childcare, it is evident that he was somewhat reluctant to take a particularly active role in the day-to-day affair of caring for two young children, preferring instead to leave that task to Elizabeth, her family, and a hired nurse. As for himself, he would go to Maine and Chimney Farm.

Henry and Elizabeth Beston's beloved Chimney Farm in Nobleboro, Maine. Beston bought the farm from the Bennet family on April 25, 1931. When the sale went through, the Bestons' attorney, Robert Tukey, sent them a telegram reading, "We have met the Bennets and they are ours, vane, map, and manure."

Beston daughters Kate and Meg enjoying haying time at Chimney Farm, mid-1930s.

CHAPTER EIGHT
The Revelation of the Earth
1932–1935

This is the hay that no man planted,
This is the ground that was never plowed,
Watered by tides, cold and brackish,
Shadowed by fog and the sea-born cloud.
Here comes no sound of bobolink's singing,
Only the wail of the gull's long cry,
Where men now reap as they reap their meadows
Heaping the great gold stacks to dry.

ELIZABETH COATSWORTH
"This Is the Hay That No Man Planted" (1936)

I	T WAS A RELIEF for Beston to get to Maine where he could temporarily
escape from the responsibilities of family life without worrying about
whether Elizabeth had enough help with the children. He was anxious to
get busy and complete the repairs on the farmhouse, but this responsibility
was far less taxing on him than was a "house full of people" or fussing over
a writing project that seemed hopelessly stalled. His first experience with
the early spring "mud-season" in Maine was, however, an eye-opener; as
he wrote to Elizabeth shortly after his arrival in Maine on April 24, 1932:

Cold again, and praise God for that for the road was, as the fat boy who
brought the hay said, "a caution." It was April all over, but a sudden and
not-quite-ready-for-it April; and the road, or rather the geographical delimi-
tations of a road, was a long course of appalling muck in whose deeper gulfs
I distinctly saw the roofs of China. In one place, for all my snail-like creeping, I fell into a mud hole under the muck, going over the chasmed edge of

a submerged stone, and 'pon my word, dear, the jar made me queasy for a few minutes. The road via Vannahs was usable till you came to the top of the Vannah Hill, and that level fifth of a mile was almost worse than the long slough of the Palmer Road. You must imagine a slough no less, of mud just soft and plasticine-ish enough to keep its shape, all ridged, rutted, gullied, and masticated by such desperate motorists as ventured its despond. I just about got home, having gone to Damariscotta to get some quite necessary oil. Yes, said the fat boy—"she's a caution!"[1]

As a naturalist Beston was particularly fascinated by the daily wonders brought to his new surroundings by the incrementally arriving spring. The annual run of alewives upriver to the lake had begun, accompanied by a myriad of eagles, ospreys, and seals—spiritual balm and literary inspiration for a frustrated nature writer at a creative impasse in suburban Hingham.

Beston's plan to escape to Maine ran into an unexpected complication when Mabel Davison, "Marraine," decided that she would take the opportunity to spend some time in Damariscotta while Henry was there apart from his family. Elizabeth had always been gracious about Henry's pre-marriage friendships with other women, but she had not failed to notice that with Marraine there was something different.[2] Bee Day had apparently noticed the same thing, as Henry wrote to Elizabeth once he learned of Marraine's plans to come to Maine: "Bee says exactly what you have always said that Marraine is possessed to get me when I am away from my family."[3] After carefully considering the matter, Beston wrote Marraine a frank letter telling her that should she come to Maine he would be forced to "close the house instantly, cancel this little rest which means so much to me, and return to Hingham."[4] Beston's note had the desired effect—to forestall the intended visit without wounding Marraine—and he passed a quiet period working on the farmhouse and writing while he stayed with the Days in Damariscotta or on the Days' houseboat in Deep Cove.[1]

Beston's usual routine while alone in Maine was to rise early, generally by six A.M., then compose a letter to Elizabeth before writing or working on some part of the farm that needed improvement. Each new experience at the farm elicited a delighted reaction that merited a note—the local custom of gathering tender spring dandelion greens from the fields, sighting a moose while driving with Jake Day, planting new apple trees (Baldwins, MacIntoshes, Red Delicious, and Astrachans) in Chimney Farm's small orchard. The lifestyle agreed with Beston spiritually and physically, and he was pleased to see that all the hard outdoor work he was doing had him feeling fit once again and his weight had dropped below two hundred pounds, closer to what he saw as his ideal weight of 190. He was anxious for Elizabeth to love the farm as much as he did, since it was she who would be making the greatest change in moving away from Hingham. Beston had convinced himself rather easily that it would be far better for the children to live on a Maine farm rather than in Hingham, which had little to offer in the way of the elemental presences that were so important to him:

> It's immensely quiet and somewhat retired, but not, I think, in any way darkly lonely . . . What we have wanted for children is here, and is here in beauty and plenty, earth, air, fire, and water. I do so want our household to know the realities of earthly living,—the earth under the plough, the stir and rustle of corn in the wind, the sound and the taste of purely running water, and the hunger of fire for the stored-away branch. All these are here.[2]

When the man hired to dig the spring-well told Henry that he had "never seen a more pure and beautiful flow of water," he relayed this news to Elizabeth with enthusiasm. He also triumphantly announced the hiring of a local woman to come in to do some cleaning—clear evidence of "a milestone on the road to completion."[3]

By early May of 1932, almost one year after buying the farm, Henry could report that the farmhouse was ready for the family to move in that summer. His time there alone had made him particularly eager for Elizabeth and the children to come join him in Maine: "it is good being domestic, and family-ish; it's a bully feeling, and I don't do a single thing here without a sense of it. I really felt happy today about what I've been doing here . . . and I keep thinking 'what a superb place for children.' Land, beauty, wildness, old realities, friends . . . Anyway, I think you'll like it, dear."[4] While Henry was separated from his family, thoughts of them were always foremost in his mind, and the longtime bachelor was seemingly surprised by the hold that his young family had on him: "I have to pinch myself a bit, dear, when

I think of those two young ladies, though their presence in the world touches the shape of everything I plan."[5]

After renting Shipcote out for the summer, the family packed things up for their first summer at the farm. Early on the morning of Wednesday, June 15, 1932, the Beston family, including Ida (or mother Coatsworth, as Henry called her), their housekeeper Olga, and their dog Bo'sun, who was relegated to the baggage car, boarded a train in Boston for the journey to Maine. Even with two young children and a large dog in tow, the journey went smoothly, and Henry was gratified—and understandably relieved—by Elizabeth's response to the house and their new surroundings. As Elizabeth wrote to Margaret and Morton, "The place is more beautiful even than I remembered and Henry has made the house *adorable*. I'm crazy to have you both see it."[6] Although the Bestons tended only a small garden and orchard that first summer, the place still had the feel of a working farm, as their neighbors, the Olivers, rented out much of the pasture for hay and there were often horses kept in the barn. The Days were regular visitors and as the Bestons got to know their new neighbors, such as the Howard and Agnes Rollins, Irving and Barbara Oliver, Carroll Winchenbaugh, Hudson Vannah, and their families better, the farm soon came to feel like home. In late July, Margaret Smith came for a visit, and Elizabeth and her sister explored the new surroundings, driving out to Boothbay Harbor and Ocean Point and made plans to spend a night on Monhegan Island. A constant stream of family and friends came that summer to see the new house that summer and to explore the Maine coastline with Henry and Elizabeth.

The Bestons' first autumn in Maine was by turns inspirationally beautiful and—for Henry—full of bittersweet memories. He wrote to Truesdell Fife:

> Now that autumn is here and the green foliage begins to rustle drily, and bro-ken branches wither in an hour, and the first maples give over random twigs and branches to the pageant of colour, my wayward thoughts turn as ever to two paths, to memories of the French front (which I first saw in a golden, melancholy mid-September, loneliness, old ruin under a mild French sky) and to our own great beach and my resolve to winter there if I could,—the beach in September with the people gone, the nights growing cool, and the winter stars rising above the leagues of ocean and the midnight roar at my feet.[7]

The Revelation of the Earth

Memories of Cape Cod were also sparked by the great flocks of waterfowl that stopped at Damariscotta Lake on their southern sojourn and by the brisk sales of the new edition of *The Outermost House*: "The Doubleday Doran crowd very pleased at the way the O.H. has dug itself in, and a nice letter comes from the *Old Corner* [a Boston bookstore], saying that they are going to do their best for the new edition."[8] While Beston's editors at Doubleday, Doran were certainly happy with the sales of the new edition of *The Outermost House*, they were just as interested in Beston's progress on the new book about the inner Cape—and as to this he remained circumspect, not yet willing to tell them that his work on the project was at a complete standstill.

After the family left Maine for Hingham in November, Beston stayed on a few weeks to close up the house in preparation for winter. He then traveled to Cape Cod to close up the Fo'castle during a warm stretch of weather in early December. Beston was warmly greeted by his old Cape Cod friends, lunching at the Nauset Coast Guard Station with Kenneth Young, Yngve Rongner, and Herbert Eddy (who often looked after the Fo'castle during Henry's absence), and several other "amigos of the dunes." After closing up the Fo'castle, Beston stayed with the Kelleys at the Overlook Inn and visited other Cape friends before leaving for Hingham and the holidays, which included Kate's first Christmas. Meg, who was now two years old, was already talking, and Elizabeth wrote to Margaret and Morton Smith, "She asks every night to look at the stars . . . We're seeing much more of her than usual & it seems to work well—as long as you don't do anything else!"[9] Henry proudly noted how well Meg enunciated her words and that her vocabulary seemed to be growing on an hourly basis. As for little Kate, he said, "[she] grows to an almost grown-up size, and is daily put down to rug-wriggle on a rug in spite of her protests. She doesn't crawl yet but turns round in one spot in some special manner, spinning on her little sit-down."[10]

The Bestons had not been in Hingham long before Henry had to hurry to Cape Cod to once again check on the condition of the Fo'castle. A fierce winter storm had struck the outer beach and when he called the Kelleys at the Overlook Inn on the night of January 27, 1933, they told him that the shoreline near the Fo'castle was taking a savage pounding from the breakers. Worried about the fate of his dune shack, he rushed out to the Cape the following day, finding that the Fo'castle was now perched only a few feet from the sheered-off wall of the great dune. The front door and "piazza" of the house were so perilously close to the drop-off that Beston had to enter through a rear window. The dunes protecting the Nauset coast guard station had also been hammered by the winter sea, and the station wall was less than thirty feet from the precipice. The storm winds hadn't been particularly bad, varying between forty and sixty knots, but it blew for three days running, combined with a series of unusually high tides. As Beston described the situation to Truesdell Fife, "so much water was pushed up against the coast, that the water over the 'long-shore' bars at Eastham and on the great beach itself was abnormally deep . . . the incoming waves were not breakers at high tide but *billows*, regular mid-ocean mountains."[11] Beston received so many inquiries from fans of his book regarding the fate of the Outermost House that he wrote an open letter to the *Quincy Patriot-Ledger*, where he reported on its condition:

> Readers of "The Outermost House" and friends of its author will be glad to hear that the Outermost House itself is still standing unhurt upon its sand dune, having had an almost miraculous escape from destruction. At eight o'clock on Friday night coast guards at Nauset reported a scant 20 feet standing between the house and the rising sea, on Saturday morning there were but five feet remaining, with another great tide due at noon and the gale still blowing. This same next tide, one of the most formidable ever seen in Massachusetts, took but a foot or so from the "Fo'castle's" defences, and hope began to rise that the house would last through the night. Many doubted if it would. Late that evening, however, the wind began to back into the northwest, and on Sunday morning the Outermost House was seen again through the snow flurries, the only survivor for miles north and south along the outer beaches of the Cape. At the close of the storm there was still a secure three feet between its door step and the breakers, the house being every where on solid ground and nowhere overhanging. Since the gale a very large number of enquiries have been received from all over the country as to its fate.
>
> As three feet of sand does not offer enough leeway or protection, I am now having the house moved back. Work has already begun.[12]

The Revelation of the Earth

The storm had opened four "cuts" through the dunes to the marshland behind them, and had washed out most of the high dune land. Concerned that one more winter storm would demolish the house, Beston contacted the Fo'castle's builder, Harvey Moore, and arranged for Moore to move the house back as far as he could without losing sight of the ocean.

As 1933 began, the nation was in the darkest days of the Great Depression, and voters turned to Franklin Delano Roosevelt in the 1932 Presidential election in the hope that he could chart a new economic course for the country. Enduringly loyal to the Theodore Roosevelt branch of the family, Beston was not enamored with FDR, but he conceded that the nation was ready for a change after three years of economic depression. When the new administration moved quickly to end prohibition in a bid to undermine organized crime and improve the nation's morale, Beston approved: "The declaration of independence of Beer seems to have cheered every body up, and people are beginning to smile again. Nothing right can be born of a mood of despair, no matter how bad things are. So here's to Beer, and decent beer gardens, and decent music, and well behaved people in 'em with human hearts under their ribs."[13] It would not take long for Beston's distrust of FDR to return, but for now he tried to stay optimistic, noting that people now seemed to be questioning the runaway consumerism of the "Roaring Twenties" and that was a positive development in itself.

Beston's "philosophy of these drear times," however, was becoming more and more dreary itself, and he continually railed that modern industrialism was "not a way of life but a way of death."[14] As the nation grew more urbanized, a widening divide between rural and urban values took place; as historian Ronald Allen Goldberg writes, "American Life was still largely dominated by small towns and frontier values. While new values emerged in the urban areas, the groundwork was laid for a historic rural-urban cultural conflict."[15] Beston was already convinced that a sea change in human attitudes, "coming first in the spirit of man" was necessary, and as the ranks of the unemployed and desperate swelled and hundreds of thousands of farmers were driven from their land by foreclosures and dust storms, the tone of his comments on the situation became increasingly bitter. When

Truesdell Fife wrote to him, depressed about his lack of success in finding employment, Beston commiserated with him, responding:

> Truesdell, old timer, these are difficult and evil days, I know it only too well, and let it be chiseled on my tomb stone that I was one of the few, the very few, who questioned this civilization and its values from the first. If it put money in my pocket, I took it, but I made no offerings on the altar. Its one great virtue, largely a negative one but a virtue nevertheless, is the freedom it allows the speculative mind. One can do and think almost anything one can "get away with." Its faults are legion and they are bad, bad faults, there is a venomous snake under the pillars of this order. The really terrible tragedy today is not so much the material debacle under which we are crushed and ground, but the emptiness of life which people must face when material benefits fail. They have no living popular art, no religion to give them human dignity or help make poetry out of life, they have no music, no creative belief of any kind. Man is a troubled creature, Truesdell, he has just enough god in him to die when he lives by the necessities. Take away the unnecessary things, as the philistines would call them, and he withers. So many things to live with, so few to live by. Material goods today are difficult to capture, and melt like snow from one's hand. Fill your heart & your pockets then with every kind of richness *which cannot be taken from you*, experience of life, mystery, beauty, courage, don't miss *a thing of the spirit or mind you can seize*. There's nothing else to do. Get as much fine adventure in as you can, and earth, air, fire & water, the four pillars of this earth be your friends!"[16]

Events overseas seemed to confirm Beston's worst fears about the modern world. In the Soviet Union, Stalin's drive toward industrialism and a forced collectivization of the land that returned the peasantry back to the status of serfs contributed to the great Soviet famine of 1932–33 that caused untold suffering. The one true test of a civilization is *life*, Beston maintained:

> Will a civilization increase and widen life, keeping near the blessed earth while looking skyward? That Russian business is nothing but a horrible Fordism of tractors, engines, regiments of slaves called something else, with humanity delivered over to machinery with its hands tied behind its back. It is the negation of life. Exploitative capitalism is foul enough, its values are clear poison, but a Ford-Detroit-Russia civilization is not even life with a bad twist, it is pure death, with gasoline fumes oozing from the rotten bones of a skull.[17]

The Revelation of the Earth

As the Roosevelt administration churned out a flood of job creation programs and economic stimuli, Beston gloomily predicted "an ugly moment of realization" when people realized that the only thing that had really been accomplished was to sink the nation deeper into debt and that it would be the young people, like his friend Truesdell Fife, who would ultimately foot the bill.[18]

By the mid-1930s, one European economy that seemed to be pulling out of the depression more rapidly than the Western democracies was that of Germany. The hyperinflation and joblessness that had dogged the Weimar Republic was giving way to much ballyhooed rebuilding projects, and under the auspices of the new National Socialist government a quieter—since it was in direct contravention of the Versailles Treaty—expansion of the military. Few Americans (or Europeans, for that matter) had read the new German chancellor's *Mein Kampf,* which outlined in chilling detail what horrors he planned; at this point, Hitler struck many as an anti-communist bulwark who was returning Germany to its rightful place among the nations of Europe. It is somewhat surprising, perhaps, that Beston was among these, writing to his friend David McCord, "I don't of course hold with Hitler's 'biological romanticism' . . . wish I'd thought of that phrase . . . but I can not but welcome the way in which he has given the disinherited young a new courage and belief."[19]

After a vacation trip to Cuttituck Island on North Carolina's Outer Banks (leaving the children with the Smiths), the Bestons returned to Hingham to pick up the girls en route to Maine. When they arrived it was late spring, and the farm was beautiful, with the lilacs in bloom and the last of the apple blossoms from the orchard slowly dropping down like spring snow. Henry was pleased to see that Maine was already beginning to feel as much like home as Hingham was for Elizabeth and the children. The Beston's cook and housekeeper Olga was temporarily detained from making the trip north to Maine with them, but their dog Bo'sun did, and they were able to hire a young woman to serve as a nursemaid for the children, which, it was hoped, would give Henry and Elizabeth time to write. According to Henry, Miss Flack made an immediate and positive contribution on the children, particularly Meg:

For the first two weeks here she wrung our withers with hour after hour of morose tears, and then turning the night into a fairy tale with sudden eldritch screams circa 2 a.m. This is now all part of a horrid little past. There is no more nightly leaking, the easy tears have practically stopped, the wearing fight against the obvious which was her "specialite de la maison" is turning upside down into an adjustment to things as God made them . . . She says her prayers every night, our own edition of "Now I lay me down to sleep," and ends with a grand blessing for everybody "n Olga n' Miss Flack", and then in a final burst *fortissimo* "n' Bosun!" The Puss-cats remains just what she always was, the best and most genial of babies. Her protests (and they are vigorous) seem to be almost entirely confined to occasions when somebody is being fed and she hasn't yet had her share.[20]

A short time later, the Bestons hired Miss Flack's sister to assist with the children, and they were henceforward referred to as "the two Miss Flacks." There were also plenty of children nearby to play with; a genial young family, the Grants, were renting the nearby Clive Hall house for the summer, and they had young children who were attending the Derby Academy in Hingham (which Meg and Kate would both later attend). After school was let out in mid-June, the Days spent a good deal of time on their houseboat on nearby Deep Cove. There were also numerous friends visiting throughout the summer, including Peg Pulitzer, Alva Morrison, Marraine, and Truesdell Fife, whom Henry took out to Monhegan Island.

Despite the uncertain economy and his inability thus far to follow up the literary success of *The Outermost House*, for the most part Beston had never been happier. Life on the farm was as satisfying, as close to the elemental influences as he'd hoped it would be. When the cold, rainy autumn weather arrived, he fed billets of wood to the farmhouse's iron stoves "which consume them like dragons," creating the pleasant incense of wood fires in the house. By day he often worked in the orchard sorting out apples—"wormy ones to one heap, 'seconds' to the cider heap, and the best ones to the kitchen basket." It was a "living task," Beston said, one that reaffirmed both the physical and spiritual nature of human existence, and complemented "the warmth of the kitchen, the quiet simmer of something cooking, and the busy peace of the house."[21] The house was filled with books, and Beston often played on an

Grandmother Ida Reid Coatsworth and Kate Beston under an ancient apple tree
at Chimney Farm, early 1930s

old upright piano. As his daughter Kate recalled, "He was fond of Granville Bantock's 'A Hundred Songs of England,' especially the Elizabethan love songs ('there is a garden in her face . . .' etc.). He had French and German children's song books and Walter Crane's "Panpipes" and "Baby's Bouquet." He had a book of sea chanties that was a favorite. He often amused himself by playing well-known bits of opera by ear."[22] On St. Patrick's Day he would often play "The Wearing of the Green," singing at the top of his voice while accompanying himself on piano. As pleased as Beston was with the quiet joys of family life and country living, there still seemed to him as though there was something missing. Luther and Helen Neff had recently had two children of their own, both boys, and when Beston wrote to congratulate Luther he added, "I envy you a bit for we should both like a pair of boys to go with the pair of daughters."[23] This yearning for a son would only grow as time went by and it remained unfulfilled, lending an unintended and somewhat bitter irony to his pre-nuptial remark that he and Elizabeth would cross the bridges of matrimony "like Tudors—Henry and Elizabeth."

Given the depths of the economic downturn, it was fortunate that Elizabeth was writing and publishing poems and stories regularly since it was primarily her income that permitted the Bestons to "squeeze through."[24] Her publisher, Macmillan, was in negotiations for a German translation of *The Cat Who Went to Heaven*. While much of the anticipated profits would go to the publishers, as Henry said, "It's a swell feather in a writer's cap," and whatever money they received would be "pure star-money."[25] The same could not be said of Henry's literary output, however; while he gave regular talks for which he often received a small speaker's fee, his writing had ground to a virtual standstill. They were able to supplement their income by selling hay and firewood from the farm, although a severe drought in 1933 and another downward slide in the already depressed economy limited this income source as well.

The Outermost House was about to be issued in a new edition, which would ease the family's financial strain somewhat, but Beston was becoming increasingly uneasy about his inability to once again buckle down to serious and sustained writing. Sometime during this period he finally abandoned his plan to write a book about the inner Cape, and destroyed much of what he had already written. As Elizabeth later wrote in *Especially Maine: The Natural World of Henry Beston From Cape Cod to the St. Lawrence*, "He finished a fine chapter on eeling at Eastham Salt Pond and part of another chapter on the marshes, but he was ruthless with his own work. He refused to write a minor book about the country of which he had written what he was sure from the first was a classic, and so tore up all he had begun."[26] While he had no qualms whatsoever about leaving Hingham for Maine ("miles, Heaven be praised, from the motor car rushes and noises which I hate so in Hingham"), Beston did confess to a "heresy of the loyalties" when it came to abandoning Cape Cod: "always there is a door in my inner spirit from behind whose panels rises a great sound, a sound which is part of life for me, the great roar of the October ocean beyond the dunes. No high wild cry of evergreens shall ever drown it, no sound of other waters confuse it, that vast and memorable cry."[27] In an effort to recapture the literary inspiration, the elemental magic, that Cape Cod and the Fo'castle had supplied, Beston decided to build a tiny shack overlooking Damariscotta Lake where he could write in peace and semi-isolation. He outfitted the studio with a small writing desk, an army cot, and some bookshelves: "I have built myself a studio out of left-over wood and begun to use it. The light is fine and I am far enough away from the house to be completely by myself, yet near enough to be got at in case of serious trouble."[28]

By early November Elizabeth and the children had left the farm for Hingham; reluctant to leave, Henry stayed behind to see to some minor work on the farm. One morning while on the way to the field he had named "Meg's Meadow," he observed a moose's hoof print in the mud, and later heard that "a neighbor's sheep has been eaten by something which ate it bones and all, right down to its head. A bob-cat, some say, others, a bear."[29] The onset of winter he greeted with the same delight that he had experienced during his first winter at the Fo'castle: "It's winter here now, real winter, with the ground frozen, and every night the cold striking deeper down, with snow thin strewn on the pale stubble, and the silence of the cold poised between land and sky. The clear days are beautiful; the nights magnificent with northern lights and burning stars."[30] Just before Thanksgiving Beston finally closed the house and returned to Hingham.

For the better part of two years, Beston's creative enthusiasm had primarily been manifested in his renovations of the farm, and relatively little had been transferred to paper; so the past summer, when he quietly began to work on a writing project, Elizabeth wrote to her sister Margaret, "Henry's deep in something of his own that I'm crazy to see."[31] Perhaps afraid that this project would prove, like that on the inner Cape, to be a literary dry well, Beston spoke little about it, not even to Elizabeth, until it was well underway. In a Christmas letter to Luther Neff, Henry finally felt confident enough about the project to refer to it, albeit in a somewhat oblique way:

> We are back in Hingham, Henry and Elizabeth and the little gals, Margaret and fat, genial obstinate Catherine. I am beginning another long piece of work, and feel more full of literary ginger than I have for years. *The Outermost House* comes out this winter in a completely new edition; pretty good for full depression times. The general impression roundabouts is that things are somewhat better. But I see no future for this form of civilization with its brutal egotism, its absence of a poetic relation to the earth, and its failure to give the meagrest life religious significance.[32]

In a letter to Morton Smith, Beston sounded a similar note, writing,

> Life will go on . . . The human spirit is inconquerable, I trust, but historic destiny drags man through some pretty dark woods . . . more people perhaps, will come to believe in the first article of my teaching, that the first peace is peace with the earth. And I should like to send a messenger, winged and bright yet cloaked about, a messenger dream such as Jove sends to the warring heroes of the Illiad, a messenger to cry aloud into many ears what I should call my second teaching. When something is [the] matter with man's world, something is the matter with man.[33]

In the late spring of 1934 Beston took a step toward putting his two teachings into practice and simultaneously furthering his writing project by pouring all of his creative energies into an herb garden on the east side of the farmhouse, sloping down toward the lake, that he had begun the previous year. "Two sides of the retreat," Beston wrote, "are formed by the house itself with its windows and green blinds, a third is provided by an adjoined shed and lengthened by a copse of cherries, the fourth is open to the sunrise and the lake. It is a pleasant and Virgilian place, much loved of birds." The "rustic guardian" of the garden was a great old apple tree.[34] All summer long Beston was fixated with the garden, and in August Elizabeth wrote to her sister, "Henry is starting his book—absorbed with that & his garden."[35] Beston approached the herb garden project deliberately, spending long hours poring through seed catalogues and at local greenhouses choosing the herbs for the garden. As his wife described the planting process,

> Henry dressed in his oldest working clothes, would go out to sit beside the border staring down at it. At long intervals he might crumble a piece of earth between his fingers, or pull up a weed. But mostly he was just staring and staring. When he came in, he would say, 'I've been working in the herb garden all morning.' It might indeed be the man-of-all-work who had spaded and planted and weeded, but in a truer sense Henry would have been working even harder in the herb garden, pondering the meaning of the earth between his fingers and the fragrant leaves about him. In fact Lawrence [Simmons] or Ellis [Simmons] or whoever was with us, had become a part of Henry. He himself would have found it hard to say which man had done what in the garden or on the place. Out of these hours *Herbs and the Earth* was born.[36]

Knowing how important it was for her husband to be writing once again, and how painstakingly he worked to get the sound and sense of his prose just right, Elizabeth did what she could to give Henry the time to work uninterruptedly. He was his own harshest critic, and Elizabeth could tell how difficult a particular passage was proving to come together by simply glancing at the number of crumpled wads of paper scattered around his writing desk. It was also a challenge to find a place to write, so he alternated between his shack by the lake, the farmhouse study or kitchen, or in the herb attic upstairs, where the fragrance of drying herbs helped to stimulate his literary production. In her poem "At Home," Kate Beston Barnes describes her father's never-ending struggle to find the perfect word, the perfect phrase: "I also remember my father / alone at the dining-room table, the ink bottle safe / in a bowl, his orange-red fountain pen in his big / hand. The hand moved slowly back and forth / and the floor below was white with sheets of paper / each carrying a rejected phrase or two / as he struggled all morning to finish just one sentence— / like a smith hammering thick and glowing iron, / like Jacob wrestling with the astonishing angel."[37]

After nearly six years of floundering about in search of a book project, in the autumn of 1934 Beston finally sent the manuscript of *Herbs and the Earth* to his publisher. Although this follow-up to *The Outermost House* was long in coming, Beston was pleased with the result, seeing it as "a book of the earth, a very small, unpretentious book, even as the O.H. was a book of the sea."[38] *Herbs and the Earth* was released by Doubleday, Doran & Company on March 12, 1935, and was dedicated to his daughters, "two young persons who never pull up or step on father's herbs." The book received positive reviews and notices, but while it was popular among herbalists and gardeners, the subject was not one likely to appeal to a larger audience as had *The Outermost House*. Still, Beston always maintained that there was a strong philosophical link between the two books: "[*Herbs and the Earth* is] only a small affair, but it continues the philosophy of the Outermost House, save this time it faces the relation of man to the earth instead of the relation of man to elemental nature and the rhythms of the world."[39]

In *The Outermost House* Beston had stated that "A year indoors is a journey along a paper calendar; a year in outer nature is the accomplishment of a tremendous ritual." Whether one tilled a farm or a small garden plot, working the soil permitted one to have a direct and, as Beston put it, a "poetic" connection to the earth:

> It is only when we are aware of the earth and the earth as poetry that we truly live. Ages and people which sever the earth from the poetic spirit, or do not care, or stop their ears with knowledge as with dust, find their veins grown hollow and their hearts an emptiness echoing to questioning . . . It is this earth which is the true inheritance of man, his link with his human past, the source of his religion ritual and song, the kingdom without whose splendor he lapses from his mysterious state of man to a baser world which is without the other virtue and the other integrity of the animal. True humanity is no inherent right but an achievement; and only through the earth may we be as one with all who have been and all who are yet to be, sharers and partakers of the mystery of living, reaching to the full of human peace and the full of human joy.[40]

Beston's herb garden was a modest one, not much more than 15 × 20 feet, the better to spend more time in poetic contemplation and careful observation

Kate and Meg Beston posing in their new kimonos, early 1930s.

of the herbs as they grew. "The emphasis," he wrote, "should always rest on the beauty and character of the plants and never for a moment on the size and variety of the collections."[41] There were two beds of plants surrounded by a New England-style dry stonewall that Beston had built as a border for the garden. The number of herbs that Beston tended reached as many as fifty, but he chose ten to write about: Basil, Marjoram, Balm, Bergamot Mint, Sage, Hyssop, Rue, Spike Vervain, Lovage, and Lavender.

As befits its topic, *Herbs and the Earth* is a book that is beautifully evocative of sensory impressions, calling forth the sights, smells, sounds, and tactile quality of the garden. In one passage Beston describes the transition from day to dusk:

> When the heat of some long summer day has followed the sun behind the pasture hill, when the glare has gone and the hour of the garden hose and the watering pot approaches with the dusk, when the whole of nature surrounding the gardener as he works is vibrating with a heavy-laden summer immediacy and profusion of life and there is a moment's flutter of birds in the apple tree, when the lake, the garden, and the hill are each released from the weight and splendor of day, how pleasant it is to be busy with the earth in this place of green![42]

Not only does the description beautifully portray the garden at dusk, but comprising just one lengthy sentence divided into a series of relative clauses all beginning with "when," it mirrors in the sentence's very structure the span of that "long summer day." When the reviews for *Herbs and the Earth* began to appear in the spring of 1935, the graceful power of Beston's prose was noted in nearly all of them. As the reviewer for the *Christian Science Monitor* wrote, "Beston's beautiful prose unconsciously approaches poetry and one finds one's self reading its cadences as though it were free verse . . . This book is thoroughly practical as well as poetic."[43] Writing for *The Atlantic Monthly*, Beston's friend David McCord noted the same attribute of Beston's writing: "his chapters are full of the right seeds, the right smells, the right words of 'honorable inheritance,' with the rhythm of the seasons in the prose."[44]

In *Literature of Place: Dwelling on the Land before Earth Day 1970*, Melanie L. Simo's cogent analysis of Beston's work asserts that "What distinguishes *Herbs and the Earth* from many other herbals is the intricate weaving of [the]

Kate Beston examining her father's herb garden at Chimney Farm, ca. 1935. Beston dedicated *Herbs and the Earth* (1935) to his daughters: "To Two Young Persons Who Never Pull up or Step on Father's Herbs."

human past with a human present and prospects for the future."[45] Simo perceptively suggests, "Beneath the quiet beauty and civility of *Herbs and the Earth* lay traces of sadness. Quite apart of the strains of the Great Depression, the age was a troubled one . . . Working with the earth, patiently, knowing and caring for plants as individual living things of great beauty and use, perhaps people would in time reconnect with the earth, make peace with it instead of abusing it, poisoning it. 'Peace with the earth is the first peace,' wrote Beston, words that may yet prove to be prophetic."[46] The somber tone that Simo detects in some of the passages of *Herbs and the Earth* is certainly in part a reflection of the *zeitgeist* of a troubled age as she suggests, but also, perhaps, the opening notes of what would later become a recurring sense of despair that would plague Beston for the next twenty-five years of his life.

To celebrate the completion of *Herbs and the Earth*—and to escape another dreary winter in Hingham—Henry and Elizabeth went to Mexico in January 1935, where they visited the Mayan ruins in Chichen Itza. The trip was idyllic; the couple stayed at a small bungalow designed to look like a Mayan hut albeit far more elegantly appointed. The windows of the bungalow looked over a stand of banana trees to a beautiful garden, with the ruins all about them "more superb & romantic than anything you can imagine—with the parakeets flying across in flocks—there are great cleared temples, pyramids and ball courts."[47] Elizabeth was amazed by how quickly Henry remembered his Spanish and was able to amiably chat with the locals. After Chichen Itza, the Bestons traveled to Mexico City for an extended stay and met Rosa King, an English expatriate who was the owner of the Hotel Bella Vista in Cuernavaca when the Mexican Revolution broke out in 1910. King's memoir, *Tempest Over Mexico*, came out in 1935, and the Bestons were captivated by her stories about the revolution:

> for three days with the garrison they fought their way over the mountains towards Mexico City shot down at the fords, decimated in the passes, the soldiers' women snatching up the guns and ammunition as one man fell to put in the hands of another; the civilians pressing on in ever lessening numbers—no real defense was possible for the Zapatistas chose their own ground behind rocks & merely shot them down. I think only a seventh

of the original group ever reached the federals and safety—among them Dona Rosa. And here she is talking of her cousin Mrs. Patrick Campbell, discussing love, as calm as you please.[48]

Rather than return to Hingham after the trip to Mexico, the Bestons went to Maine for a fortnight. Elizabeth was now nearly as enamored of Maine as Henry was, writing to Margaret and Morton Smith, "It really is heaven itself: glorious day after glorious day and long walks that bring us back rosy and tired to the shelter of our kitchen . . . Last night a mink walked all about our house—such small feet and such an ominous long stride! In the oak parlor were the tracks of the partridges, of rabbits, of squirrels, a fox and the same mink."[49] Henry was still eager to sell Shipcote in Hingham and move to Maine permanently, and although Elizabeth was willing for her own part, she was reluctant to take the children out of their schools in Hingham. When it came to living a life close to nature, however, Maine had it all over Hingham. When Elizabeth and the girls joined Henry at the farm in June of 1935 they visited Jake and Bee Day and the boys, Mac and Dick, who were staying at their houseboat, the Dazark, in Deep Cove. As was often the case, the Days were caring for a wide variety of animal life on board the Dazark—two young crows, two rabbits, a small dog, two tiny fox cubs, and a kitten. They had also adopted—or rather, perhaps, been adopted by—a silver baby harbor seal. As the delighted Elizabeth wrote to Morton, "it drinks milk from a bottle, bathes in the cove, loves people, follows Bee all about the kitchen. This morning she found it coming along the sidewalk up from the cove all by itself."[50] For Henry, life in rural Maine was far more in keeping with his conviction that living a life in harmony with nature's cycles was better for the human spirit, and the herb garden, orchards, and fields of Chimney Farm restored his desire to write once again. He'd had to drop his writing for several weeks early that summer due to an abscessed eye, but by August—"thanks to the doctor, a sharp knife, and heroism on my part"—he was back at work again.[51] The new book project was a collection of historical accounts that would tell the story of America and its people through their own words. The project was tentatively titled *American Memory*, which Beston said was "moving to write . . . every word must come out of the blood stream."[52]

ON WEDNESDAY MORNING, November 20, Elizabeth sent a note to Morton to confirm their arrangements for the trip to Hingham for Thanksgiving, which was the next Thursday. The following morning, a warm and sunny day for late November in Maine, Elizabeth and Henry then left for Augusta to return some books to the state library. Their car, a used Buick they had recently purchased from the Smiths, seemed a bit sluggish climbing hills, and at one point Henry noted this, telling Elizabeth that it might be due to the anti-freeze keeping the engine too hot for such a warm day. When they reached Gardiner, about ten miles from Augusta, Elizabeth told Henry that she was feeling a bit carsick, and asked to drive for a while. They continued on to the state library and were walking to a nearby hotel for lunch when Henry said that he felt very dizzy. Assuming that it was just from being overly hungry, Elizabeth encouraged him to "eat a good lunch, and you'll be over it."[53] After lunch Beston said that he was feeling better, but on the walk back to their car, which was parked a few blocks away, he began to stagger and reel; Elizabeth managed to get him to the car, where she made him comfortable then ran off to get directions to a nearby doctor's office. After a brief examination, the doctor realized that, whatever the cause, Beston was dangerously ill and immediately sent him to the hospital. For two days he was unable to keep anything down ("not even a swallow of red brandy," wrote Elizabeth to Morton Smith) and underwent numerous tests to discover the origin of his sudden affliction.

The doctors eventually concluded that Beston's illness was brought about by wood alcohol poisoning, although a mechanic who examined the car believed that it was more likely that it was exhaust fumes from a faulty muffler than the radiator's wood alcohol anti-freeze that had caused the problem. Elizabeth noted that she had seen exhaust fumes rising up from the front wheel well, but Henry's symptoms did appear to be consistent with wood alcohol poisoning, so repairs were made to the car that dealt with both possibilities. Not sure how long Henry would be in the hospital in Augusta, Elizabeth arranged for the children to go down to Hingham with their nurse, Barbara, and she stayed with him until his release from the hospital just before Thanksgiving Day. It was a week before Beston was able to walk a short distance, and even longer before he felt like himself again. As he wrote to Morton,

> I stood the journey from the hospital well, but for two days after my arrival home a gruesome sort of "morning after" wooziness complicated by a stunned feeling in the head—a feeling as if someone had neatly removed the small core of the brain and inserted in its place an irresponsive hard-boiled egg—that delightful feeling never quite left me. On he third day it began to go. I began to feel stronger, and the cerebral hard-boiled egg started to hook-up with the rest of the so-called gray matter. Today, (day after Thanksgiving) I'm feeling much better, and am venturing to use my eyes. The poison is famous for its effect on the eyes, and mine just got a share of it, there being an ache and tension in the ocular muscles and a blurring disarrangement of the power which the oculists call "accommodation." Outside of a lingering trace of that, an afternoon ringing in the ears, and some weakness, I'm quite o.k. Betsey has made the best, most loving, and wisest of nurses, and we have got on famously in this strangely quiet house . . . It was an ugly experience, and I'm still far from over with it though coming along fine. Wood alcohol is a notoriously slow poison to take its leave, and getting it by inhalation leads it through the blood stream right into the tissues. I've lost about ten or 15 pounds—the best part of the story![54]

Henry and Elizabeth remained at the farm until mid-December while Henry regained his strength and underwent some medical tests to make sure that the wood alcohol poisoning had not permanently harmed any of his internal organs, as Dr. Campbell, the attending physician at the hospital in Augusta, had initially feared. On December 7, 1935, Elizabeth wrote to her sister Margaret, "Henry is now up all day—still pale, & staggering a little when he walks, but off the sick list. I am fired as nurse—and he has been such a good patient and convalescent I feel almost out of a job. It will perhaps be another week before he is really strong and you will be thrilled at his waist-line."[55] Relieved of her nursing duties, Elizabeth busied herself closing the farmhouse up for the winter, and a week before Christmas she and Henry left Maine and returned to Hingham to be reunited with their family for a quiet but particularly joyous holiday.

CHAPTER NINE

The Divine Consciousness and the Soul of Man

1936–1940

Turning and turning in the widening gyre
The falcon cannot hear the falconer;
Things fall apart; the centre cannot hold;
Mere anarchy is loosed upon the world,
The blood-dimmed tide is loosed, and everywhere
The ceremony of innocence is drowned;
The best lack all conviction, while the worst
Are full of passionate intensity.

WILLIAM BUTLER YEATS
"The Second Coming" (1919)

As 1936 BEGAN, the Bestons were enjoying continued literary success with a second printing of *Herbs and the Earth* out in November and Elizabeth's new children's book, *The Golden Horseshoe*, selling briskly. Still, Beston found little reason for optimism regarding conditions in the United States or in the world generally. Despite a flurry of legislative activity initiated by the Roosevelt administration, the economic depression continued to deepen, the ecological destruction of the "Dust Bowl" that had begun in 1934 had intensified, and the spiritual malaise that Beston associated with modern industrial society had him on the brink of despair:

What is going to take place here? What is going to happen in this culture with its faith in the mechanics of civilization, with its childish reliance on laws and laws and more laws, and so little appreciation of the fact that only an indwelling spirit can make the mechanics of any civilization have a meaning or a working sanction? What are we going to do with an educational system in which study must first be made an agreeable play before the young will bother to notice it? Who could possibly blame Lindberg in his position? I don't see much to come that's really worth while unless some leader can shake the deeply-troubled young out of their "oh yeah" attitude of cynicism, and give them something to believe in. The country's too big, anyhow. Sooner or later, it will split up into departments. State despotisms have already arrived, vide Long and Mr. Curley.[1]

If anything, conditions were even worse in Europe, where the choice seemed to be one between despotism of the far left or one of the far right. If there was a way out of the abyss, Beston believed it would come not from government programs but from a reawakening of the spirit, what he called "the divine consciousness and the soul of man"; but from where such a widespread reawakening of the human spirit might come remained a mystery.[2] In Germany the pseudo-religious pageantry of political rallies staged by the National Socialists attracted massive crowds and the spectacle drew the notice of many people throughout the world, some of whom—like Charles Lindbergh in the United States—watched in hope. Others recoiled in horror, particularly as news of rampant anti-Semitism and brutality in a newly resurgent Germany gradually leaked out. While Beston seemed to believe the ultra-nationalism of Germany and Italy was preferable to the spread of communism or outright anarchy, Elizabeth saw the situation differently: "the dreadful news of Europe has been going on at a perfectly breath-taking pace and God knows what the end of it all will be. The swarming nations—Japan, Italy and Germany are all at it at once, and the devil is to pay."[3]

On January 13, 1936, Henry and Elizabeth left the children with Margaret and Morton Smith and departed Boston by train en route to another visit to Mexico to tour the great Mayan pyramids at Chichen Itza. During the stopover in New York City they saw the Broadway hit *Victoria Regina*, but were disappointed in the play, with Elizabeth telling her family that she and Henry "didn't think very much of Helen Hayes but it was fine Victorian furniture anyhow."[4] The trip south lasted three days, and was delayed briefly in Virginia when the tracks were closed due to a train wreck; but by January 16 they were happily exploring the French quarter in New Orleans prior to sailing to the Yucatán late the following afternoon. For most of the next ten days Henry and Elizabeth explored the Mayan ruins and the surrounding countryside, completely taken by the romantic beauty of the ancient land, which Henry said was like "Atlantis risen from the waters and become part of the Yucatan jungle."[5]

After Chichen Itza the Bestons boarded the SS *Orizaba* of the New York and Cuba Steamship Company and began the trip up the east coast of Mexico to Vera Cruz before taking the train to Mexico City. As they rolled through the countryside, Beston mused about the effect that the recent revolution had on the country. His comments on the revolutionaries' redistribution of land back to the *campesinos* reflects his doubts about the goals of the revolution and its relation to his core belief about the need for humankind to reconnect with the land:

> Intellectually and economically, the Mexican ship of state shows the many effects of the long storm of the violent and disorderly revolution. The great 'haciendas,' those Mexican plantations which so resembled our ante-bellum southern ones, have been broken up and despoiled by the agrarian laws, a percentage of the land of each distributed among the peons, and here at Cuernavaca, the greater number of the haciendas themselves were ruthlessly sacked and burnt by Zapata, the agrarian bandit so that you pass the ruins of many a great house as you wander about, old ruins in which Indians live in a sort of revived barbarism. The people themselves, the owners or "haciendados" throats cut or shot or fled away. Unfortunately, sugar raising, to be profitable, requires capital, capital to pay for sugar machinery, boilers, steam kettles and the like, and now that all these 'mills' are in ruin, the peon here can't seem to do much with the land that's given him and has taken to raising rice, a crop which has a diversity of agricultural and economic cussedness which cause much dissatisfaction and grumbling. There is no doubt that the average Mexican had become a landless man. He lost the land just as the English peasant lost it, by enclosure of the 'commons', by the encroachments of powerful persons. But why destroy everything in returning it to him?[6]

Part of the reason for his ambivalence was undoubtedly linked to his abhorrence for violence and destruction, and the tactics of revolutionaries such as "Zapata, the agrarian bandit." It is just as clear, however, that Beston's turn-of-the-century Roosevelt progressivism was now becoming more conservative with the passing years. He fails to comment on the economic injustices that led to the revolution in the first place, perhaps believing that the "cure" of revolutionary chaos and upheaval was worse than the "disease" of an exploitative economic oligarchy.

After returning to Massachusetts in late February, the remainder of the winter was spent in Hingham with the children. When Kate came down with a minor illness, Elizabeth noted that her young daughter had become a stickler for language: "When I said to her 'I hear Pussy that you're well now' she said 'I'm *getting* well.'"[7] Elizabeth was soon back to writing poetry again,'but Henry wrote very little. He took an occasional trip to the Cape to check in on the Fo'castle, but for the most part he impatiently waited for spring and the opportunity to return to Maine, formulating plans to clear some land near the barn for a kitchen and flower garden and to rebuild the stonewall of the herb garden behind the house. In late April he fled Hingham for Chimney Farm, leaving Elizabeth and the children to follow several weeks later.

Chimney Farm was becoming as integral to the lives of Elizabeth and the children as Beston had hoped. When the Bestons' neighbors, the Olivers, came by with two oxen to deliver some loam for the garden and to do some plowing, the girls were fascinated by the great beasts, spending hours watching them work and then following them to the barn to watch them rest and eat. Between Henry and Elizabeth, there were always stories to be told, and the girls' imaginations were vivid. When Henry gave Meg and Kate some leaves from his herb garden, Meg woke the next morning and announced that she'd had "green dreams from Daddy's herbs."[8] The summer included the usual string of visitors, the poet David McCord, the Neffs, and Marraine among them. They also visited numerous Maine friends, including the Days, Mary Wheelwright, and the Richards family of Gardiner, Maine. In July, Beston was invited to be one of the speakers at a religious conference held at the Isle of Shoals, jesting to Luther Neff, "If you were [there] I fear you'd hear from the south sudden cries of 'Throw out the Pagan!' 'Down with the Pantheist!' . . . 'Tithing man, tithing man, quick, . . . the gyves!' . . . [while] all the while I am dodging hymnbooks."[9] Despite Beston's joking, his talk on "The Spirit of Place in American Thought and

Style," was well-received, and as he wrote to Elizabeth, "People are being enormously friendly & kind: many of 'em know me; several herbalists have descended and various naturalistos."[10]

As the presidential election of 1936 approached, the country was still mired in the Great Depression. Franklin Roosevelt continued to push his New Deal agenda through Congress, although some of its major provisions, such as Social Security and bank reform, had already been enacted. The Republicans chose a Kansas moderate, Alf Landon, as their nominee, and many political observers anticipated a close election; instead, Roosevelt swept to the greatest landslide in presidential history, winning over 60% of the popular vote and taking all but eight electoral votes. Both Henry and Elizabeth voted for Alf Landon; a few days after Roosevelt's landslide Elizabeth wrote to Morton Smith, who had supported Roosevelt, "Wall Street's reaction surprised me—stocks rising I mean. In fact the whole affair surprised me. Only poor little Maine & Vermont really suspicious and frugal."[11]

A few weeks after the election the Bestons returned to Massachusetts for the winter. While Henry was thoroughly tired of Hingham, he took advantage of his usual solace; Hingham's proximity to Boston and its theater district. He went to a new play nearly every weekend, judging *Jane Eyre* to be good theatre ("though a bogus book can only father a bogus play"), as was *Pride and Prejudice* with Katherine Hepburn ("she had a good role and made the best of it, however, barring the really vital lack of psychic transference. Interesting looking gal: looks hard as nails").[12] He was impressed with Lunt and Fontaine—"real people of the theatre"—who were starring in *Idiot's Delight*, and appreciated John Gielgud's portrayal of the Danish prince in *Hamlet*: "No sensitive poet he faced with a repugnant task whose ghostly sanction he distrusts, but more your frustrated modern intellectual, intelligent, cruel, and damn dangerous to have round. Not much poetry, not much emotion born of the sense of beauty, but plenty of swift action, and wild nervous raging, an appalling and quite interesting young man just over thirty."[13]

There was another, more important advantage to being close to Boston that winter. In early January of 1937 Beston wrote to Truesdell Fife,

"I am deep in the arrangement of a new book, & just as soon as I can fight my way out, let's have a grandissimo party."[14] The new book, *American Memory*, was something completely different for Beston, a compendium of firsthand accounts of the "stirring and picturesque past of Americans and the American nation," and therefore involved a great deal of research in various archives and libraries in Boston, such as the Boston Public Library, Boston Athenaeum, and the Massachusetts Historical Society. Beginning with accounts of the early exploration and settlement of North America and concluding with the Progressive Era of Theodore Roosevelt, the anthology contains excerpts from many canonical sources—John Smith, William Bradford, John Winthrop et al.—but also includes an impressive selection of historical accounts from other, less familiar writers. In the foreword to the book, Beston explains that his intent was to combine both the "official and literary" current of American prose with the "unstudied, unpretentious, direct, and personal" accounts included in letters, diaries, and other obscure sources. Beston was convinced, and justifiably so, that he had succeeding in providing a fresh spin on a familiar topic: "I think, with pardonable pride of editorship, that it has tried and succeeded in the doing of something completely new,—a picture of the Union made out of the old, great records on the one hand and on the other out of the mass of private documentation, anyhow here you have it, Pilgrims and Mormons, Redskins and the Union Pacific, the Yankee trading captain and the Ohio boatman, the whole amusing gallery."[15]

One of the primary themes of the book concerns the connection between the land and its inhabitants, and here Beston's interest in the American Indians is reflected both by the number of accounts that deal with interactions between the Europeans and the Indians, and in his editorial comments on the long history of conflict between the two peoples: "bullied and dispossessed, weakened by new plagues, and his game driven off, the Indian had but two choices if he were not to starve—either to fight or retreat."[16] As he later noted with considerable pride, *American Memory* was "the first study of our history to give a proper perspective to the role of the American Indian."[17] The newcomers would in turn not become truly American until the land itself had shaped them "with its tensions of heat and cold, its tropical violences of summer storm, its incomparable and elegiac autumn, its cloudless winter nights of stars over the wilderness and the snow."[18] As in *The Outermost House*, where Beston states that "*Creation is here and now,*" a continuing process, so too does he remind us that the adventure of the American republic is still ongoing. However, whereas in the final chapter of *The Outermost House,* Beston confidently proclaimed that "to-morrow's morning will be as heroic as any of the world," the final selection in *American Memory,* from Henry Adams's chapter on "The Virgin and the Dynamo" in *The Education of Henry Adams*, betrays a deep anxiety about the forces shaping the modern world.[19]

Returning to Maine in the spring of 1937 Beston was anxiously looking forward to the quiet and rural beauty that was so beneficial to his work. He and the hired hand, Lawrence Simmons, had numerous plans for improvements to the farm, and he was finishing up the final revisions to *American Memory*. A disturbing element had invaded the quiet of East Neck, however; the prior year a new neighbor—Henry Norris, a retired surgeon from Philadelphia—had bought property nearby and had promptly built a skeet shooting range, sending the thunder of shotguns reverberating regularly across the lake. The Bestons sent him a polite note requesting that he move the shooting range to an area that would not resound so loudly at Chimney Farm, but after initially agreeing to do so Norris refused. "A great pity after saying that he would," Elizabeth wrote to the Smiths, but for Beston, Norris's noisy hobby was more than simply a nuisance; it was an existential affront to the senses.[20]

For now, however, the summer began pleasantly enough. Elizabeth was fond of hosting the occasional afternoon tea for friends and neighbors and at one such tea Felix Frankfurter (who two years later would be selected to serve on the United States Supreme Court) and his wife were guests; they also met Frances Sortwell, who would become a close friend. They also had fairly frequent visits with Henry Richards, a retired sea captain, and his daughter Rosalind, both of whom lived in nearby Gardiner. Captain Richards was nearly 100 years old, and his wife, now dead, was Laura E. Richards, the writer and daughter of Julia Ward Howe, who had written the classic song from the Civil War, "The Battle Hymn of the Republic." The

Beston girls hosted a birthday party attended by all the local children—the Vannahs, the Kennedys, and the Rickers—and Meg prepared for a stint at a nearby summer camp. As a consolation for not being old enough to join Meg at camp, her parents surprised Kate with a little white lamb with black ears: "Pussy is excited as she has never been before: probably the happiest child in America. She christened the creature 'Blanche' on sight and woke up at 2 A.M. to tell Barbara about it. 'I shall keep Blanche for ever and ever. She's mine and she's alive!' It's really touching to see her happiness."[21] In mid-July Elizabeth and Kate visited Meg at her summer camp, catching her just after a horseback ride: "[she] looked pretty as a picture; in a week she is already swimming."[22] The children's longtime nurse, Barbara, was engaged to be married in late September, and Elizabeth was already worried about finding a new nurse as capable and fond of the children, although as she wrote to her sister, "At least the problem doesn't seem as drastic as it did when they were little."[23]

While the Bestons continued to weather the lingering depression better than most, fiscal anxiety was a continuing spur to write. As was generally the case, Elizabeth was at work on several projects, finishing them quickly in turn. By the time they returned to Maine in the late spring, her winter work of children's stories was nearly completed: *Alice-all-by-Herself* was in proofs, *There's Margaret* had been typed and was ready for her corrections, and *Five Bushel Farm* had been sent to her typist. Macmillan had agreed to publish another set of stories about the title character from *Away Goes Alice* and Elizabeth soon wrote ten more of the stories of a small modern child set in the Days' house in Damariscotta.[24] For his part, Henry submitted a proposal to Farrar & Rinehart for a book in their "Rivers of America" series. Conceived by the Canadian novelist and historian Constance Lindsay Skinner, the series was initially planned as a set of twenty-four books on the great rivers of North America, all to be written and illustrated by prominent writers and artists who had a personal connection to those watersheds. The series eventually grew to sixty-five books written over a span of nearly forty years. Skinner's vision for the project was one that greatly appealed to Beston—the rivers were to be portrayed as living entities shaping the landscape and cultures to which they were connected. The

Elizabeth Coatsworth and Kate Beston with Kate's new pet, Blanche the lamb, Summer 1937. The lamb was a consolation gift for not being old enough to go to summer camp with Kate's sister Meg, and made her, as Elizabeth wrote, "the happiest child in America."

first volume in the series, *The Kennebec* (1937), was written by Maine poet Robert Tristram Coffin; Beston chose to write about the St. Lawrence, the great waterway separating the United States from Canada. Beston's proposal was readily accepted and he eagerly began research on the project, traveling with Elizabeth to Canada in mid-July and then proceeding by steamship from Montreal down to the mouth of the St. Lawrence, past the pulp towns of Quebec and Newfoundland and the fishing villages of Labrador.

By early August they were back in Maine, with Elizabeth correcting proofs for *Five Bushel Farm* and Henry writing down his observations from the Canadian trip and planning another excursion to the St. Lawrence in October. Luther Neff and his family arrived in mid-August for their annual stay in Maine at a cabin not far from Chimney Farm. As always, Henry was anxious to see his old friend: "We are crazy to see you all and celebrate. What about a meeting on Saturday next for a general luncheon party on the front lawn, the Neffs to come circa 12 o'clock, or Monday for a good, old-fashioned fish chowder supper, the Neffs arriving circa 4 so we can have a grand talk and fiesta?"[25] After several days of swimming at the lake (Henry was unable to join in due to a bad case of poison ivy—the first he had ever suffered despite numerous previous exposures to the plant), Henry went with Luther and his son John on a trip to Katahdin where they climbed Maine's most famous mountain. By the time they returned to Chimney Farm the galleys of *American Memory* were ready for his review, so Beston went down to New York City to work on them at Farrar, taking a weekend break to visit with Ted Roosevelt Jr. at Sagamore Hill in Oyster Bay, Long Island.

After completing the galleys for *American Memory*, Henry returned to Nobleboro to take Elizabeth to Katahdin, where they stayed at a small inn on nearby Moosehead Lake. They walked eight or nine miles through the autumn-tinted Katahdin wilderness each day, returning to the inn in the late afternoon. The window in their room opened on the mountain; at night the view was spectacular, "the northern lights blazing up, among stars, on Katahdin's head."[26] They returned to Chimney Farm briefly prior to another trip to Canada, while the children stayed with the Smiths in

Hingham. While this was a common arrangement with them, and was conducive to their writing, Elizabeth, at least, felt a pang about it, writing to Morton, "I miss the children more than ever before & feel that you and Margaret have done more than an uncle and aunt should be expected to do in fostering those lively brats."[27] Meg had recently returned home from summer camp, and Elizabeth was struck by the change that camp seemed to have made in her sometimes-combative daughter, who seemed to be more self-possessed and relaxed. "She may lose some of it," Elizabeth wrote to the Smiths, "but if some remains it will be a good thing."[28] The Beston's younger daughter Kate, who was just five years old, was showing a facility with words that thrilled her mother: "The other evening I had been reading poetry to Pussy. When she went to bed she said a poem for me—it rhymed, and its meaning was charming. I went downstairs and wrote it as well as I could remember it. The words were not exactly hers, but there had been no change whatever in the sense.

> And when I go to bed at night
> The candles shine about me bright.
>
> My little image jumps to bed
> And lays his head beside my head,
>
> And all the pictures round me say
> "Sleep, shadow, and let her sleep till day."[29]

For a change, Henry was anxious to leave Maine for the winter. In part this was due to his excitement about returning to Canada to work on the St. Lawrence book, but it was also in large part owing to his continued exasperation about his trap-shooting neighbor. Since August, shotgun fire had resounded regularly from the shooting range, and Henry's anger—more or less pent up—had resulted in chronic indigestion and a diastolic blood pressure reading that hovered around 190. His physician in Damariscotta, Dr. Belknap, concurred with Henry that the cause was his frayed nerves, and both he and Elizabeth felt that the trip to Canada would be a tonic. After nearly three weeks of travel throughout Quebec, including Quebec City, Île d'Orléans, and Trois-Rivières, Henry was feeling better, writing to Truesdell Fife, "I seem to be getting somewhat the best of a long siege of nervous indigestion which has deposited me, large, apprehensive, and tense into the hands of doctors. Something bothered me at the farm, a neighborhood row over the introduction of a skeet-shooting field just across our wood cove from us; I let it 'get' me, with worry and fury, et voila le resultat. Mais assez."[30]

Hoping that he was rid of the stomach pain that had plagued him since late August, Henry and Elizabeth traveled west to Arizona in February 1938, once again leaving the children in Hingham with the Smiths and their new nurse, Elva Knight. At least initially, the trip seemed to do Henry a world of good; they stayed at two ranches, went horseback riding daily, and explored the Sinagua cliff dwellings. Despite some trepidation, Beston climbed up the precipitous ladders of the cliff dwellings and took horseback rides along steep canyon trails, thoroughly enjoying the adventure. In early March they left for California to visit Elizabeth's uncles Frank Reid and George Chester in Pasadena, with a side trip to see Jake and Bee Day in Los Angeles. Jake was now working at the Disney studio in Hollywood, having been hired in 1933 to work on a new animated feature, an adaptation of Felix Salten's novel *Bambi*. It was at Jake's suggestion that Bambi should be portrayed as a white-tailed deer (rather than a western mule deer, as was originally planned) and it was Jake's sketches and photographs of the Maine woods and its creatures that were depicted in the film.

After California the Bestons traveled to Mary Wheelwright's estate in New Mexico where they stayed for a "marvelous" week before beginning the journey back east in early April.[31] Even before heading east, however, Henry's stomach problems had returned, and for the first time since buying the farm he was not looking forward to the return to Maine. Indeed, he had already determined that 1938 was their sabbatical year in Maine, and as such he intended to spend most of it in Canada working on *The St. Lawrence*. Beston was clearly thinking of his skeet-shooting neighbor in Maine when he wrote to the Smiths, "Schopenhauer says that the intellectual power of a mind is in parallel relation to its hatred of noise—a thing I've always found to be true. A noisy man is simply a noisy child & a noisy civilization is a child's civilization."[32]

The Divine Consciousness and the Soul of Man

Before leaving for Canada, Beston delivered lectures at Boston, Worcester, and Dartmouth College in Hanover, New Hampshire. His visit to Dartmouth on April 30, 1938, included a lecture in Professor Herbert Faulkner West's course on nature writing, which prominently included *The Outermost House* in the syllabus. The students were enthusiastic and receptive, and many of them attended a reception in Beston's honor held at the home of longtime friend Ray Nash (he and his wife Hope were Kate's godparents, and the Bestons were godparents for two of the Nash children) following the class. One of the students, Charles Bolte wrote to Beston shortly after the visit, still full of enthusiasm:

> I thought I should write you and express my gratitude for talking to me and opening my eyes on something really big . . . I have always loved nature and long suspected that man's salvation lay in something of a return to the earth, but your talk, your ideals and ideas, gave me new insight into the largeness of nature and the possible largeness of the human soul. Your talk to Prof. Nash's class, and more particularly your talk to me afterwards in Mr. Nash's home, gave me more ideas than I've received all year, and set me an ideal to shoot at in the way of personal grace and bearing and achievement that is as high and remote and worthy as Arcturus. I am tremendously impressed by your writing, restrained and beautiful and honest as the sun, and unlike most writers you have those same qualities in your conversation and personal contact.[33]

Over the next two decades, Beston became a frequent visitor to Dartmouth and Professor West's classroom, forming a close friendship with West and several other members of the Dartmouth faculty.

Beston headed north to Canada in late May and rented rooms at a farmhouse in Cap-à-l'Aigle, near La Malbaie, leaving the care of the farm to Lawrence Simmons. Elizabeth and the children soon joined him there. The differences between farming and attitudes toward the land between the French *habitants* and the Americans made an immediate impression on Beston: "Perhaps the single most interesting thing about this country is that the people do real *farming*, raising their own wheat, oats, barley, and buckwheat for their animals, and maintaining their own beautiful old mills . . . The people are grand,—old fashioned, entirely honest, and at peace with life and their own hearts. And the landscape is simply magnificent."[34] Elizabeth and the children were also delighted with their temporary home as the children picked up French quickly and enjoyed playing with the farm animals and the French children who lived nearby.

After a month at the farmhouse in Cap-à-l'Aigle, Henry, Elizabeth, and Kate drove to Maine to bring Meg to her summer camp at Camp Wabunaki in Hillside, Maine. Elizabeth was relieved that Elva Knight, who had worked as the children's nurse the previous winter, had been hired as a camp counselor; she was concerned that Meg, who was quietly strong-willed, might have trouble adjusting to her new tent mates. She wrote to Miss Knight and after some delay (Knight had been hospitalized with a streptococcal infection), received an honest and mostly reassuring letter: "Of course you know that Meg is an individualist—that in many ways she is superior to the average child—that her choice vocabulary surpasses that of the normal eight, nine or even ten year old—and that she possesses a quaint charm . . . she is too clever to be trusted passively, and she is a constant challenge to those about her."[35]

After the brief trip to Maine, the three of them returned to Quebec and rented a small cabin on the St. Lawrence near St. Joseph de la Rive. The cabin was tiny, but "fine as a teacup," Elizabeth wrote to Morton Smith, and was perched on a hill with a beautiful view of the mountains to the north, the St. Lawrence River, and the nearby village of Les Eboulements.[36] They stayed there for two weeks while traveling around the countryside and up the river valley as Beston conducted research for his book. Beston was delighted to be writing again—as he had hoped when he had first expressed interest to John Farrar about taking on the St. Lawrence project the previous summer, leaving Maine and the stress of "that accursed skeet-shooting nuisance" had invigorated him.[37] Unfortunately, abandoning Maine for the summer meant that he would, among other things, miss the now annual visit of his friend Luther Neff and Reverend Neff's family. In July Beston wrote to Neff to explain the circumstances that had driven him from Chimney Farm:

> The clouds have pretty much rolled away, but it was a horrid little year. No writer can possibly sit down to thoughts and his pencils when a sudden and

hostile crash is likely to shatter all his peace together with surrounding space and time; it just can't be done. Being a courteous person, I went over to see that grotesque vulgarian (one Henry Norris, a retired Philadelphia surgeon) and he assured Elizabeth and me that he would attend to the matter. Then I suppose, someone got hold of him, or his own natural vindictiveness bubbled in sewer foam to the top, and he wrote us a letter, breaking all his promises, and celebrated the next Sunday with a racket like hell's 4th of July . . . all summer long it went on, hateful, foolish, and noisy. I just couldn't concentrate, just couldn't lead myself into that never never land where you can hear the rumble of the waters of creation. The consequence was that worried, frustrate, sick with the corpse reek of personal hostility which had risen up about me, I came down with a bad nervous and physical condition, really something rather nasty, involving x-rays, and all that terrifying sort of ogling at one's innards . . . I just couldn't face another summer. If that vulgarian has nothing better to do than to drive two people of the spirit & the mind out of the region, I have. I'm hitting the middle years now, (Heaven only knows how many I have left) and what gift I have to make of interpretation, of the shaping of beauty, of the qualities of intelligence and joy, I must make, that is what I am here for. So I made a decision and a wise one (if somewhat of defeat) and closing the beloved farm, turned and left behind me a nightmare. I am now, God be praised, finding peace again in the beautiful country of the shores of the St. Lawrence, with the waterfalls of the country tumbling down the sides of the Laurentians and through my heart, and the great stream with its tides moving daily through my veins.[38]

The Bestons did not return to Chimney Farm until late August when they had to pick up Meg from her summer camp; even then, Henry dashed back to Canada in mid-September, intending to further explore the Laurentian mountain region. He traveled east on the south shore of the St. Lawrence, which he didn't find particularly interesting—"like a summer resort two hundred miles long, which has just been closed for the year."[39] Although it was still September, the weather was cold and gray, and there was talk of snow on board a ship he boarded in Matane, which was full of lumberjacks and wood cutters headed north to cut wood for the great pulpwood companies. After returning to Matane he drove eastward toward the tip of the Gaspé Peninsula, driving along the coast road up and down rolling hills. The roller coaster-like drive was "magnificent," although a stretch through a burned out forest along the cliffs gave him an anxiety attack he referred to as the "jim jams."[40]

During the autumn of 1938 the news from Europe was also anxiety-inducing; after annexing Austria in March, Hitler now had his sights on the German-speaking Sudeten region of Czechoslovakia. As Europe teetered precariously on the precipice of war, Elizabeth wrote to Morton Smith: "The shadow of war hangs heavily. I feel as though Hitler were mad, the leader of the mad. I dread to see the paper each morning."[41] Financial exchanges fell worldwide under the uncertainty of the international situation, and while Beston also saw the danger of the situation, he blamed much of it on France and England's weakness and ties to the Soviet Union, saying that he would "welcome from the heart's core anything which will kick Russia out of European politics!"[42] He also believed that turmoil in Europe had its roots in the post-war peace imposed on Germany that had created so much resentment, and (like British Prime Minister Neville Chamberlain) he took Hitler at his word when he claimed that Germany's territorial designs were simply aimed at unifying regions primarily comprised of ethnic Germans. Like many in America at the time, Beston had no insight into Hitler's true nature, viewing him as a strong national leader who was firmly anti-communist and formed a bulwark against the Russians, and whose primary goals were to right the wrongs of the post-war peace terms imposed on Germany by the Allies. Interestingly, Elizabeth—who was not as familiar with the politics and history of the Great War and its aftermath in Europe—saw the situation more clearly. After hearing a radio broadcast of Hitler's speech at Nuremberg in late September (translated into English), she was convinced that Hitler was mad and war was imminent. She wrote to Morton Smith (who also deeply mistrusted Hitler's intentions) that she had heard the speech while she and Henry were at an ice cream shop in Bath: "I walked back to the car feeling perfectly calm and repeating hysterically on a rising note: 'Well *I* hate him, *I* hate him, *I* hate him. I open the paper each morning in dread."[43] Henry's brother-in-law Morton Smith and his brother George Sheahan also despised Hitler; Dr. Sheahan referred to the Nazis as barbarians and told his brother he despised all their works.[44]

The Divine Consciousness and the Soul of Man

While a figurative storm was gathering in Europe, a literal one hit the East Coast—the great hurricane of September 21, 1938, while Beston was traveling in Canada. New York's Long Island and southern New England were hit particularly hard with sustained winds of over one hundred miles per hour recorded throughout much of the region. Torrential rainfall and a storm surge that reached twenty-five feet in some parts of Connecticut, Rhode Island, and Massachusetts produced severe coastal flooding and more than five hundred deaths. The worst of the storm had dissipated before reaching Maine but Cape Cod was hit particularly hard. The Bestons were relieved when the telegraph service was finally restored and the Kelleys in Eastham were able to report that the Fo'castle had survived the ravages of the hurricane, although someone had broken into the dune shack and stolen some furnishings. In Hingham, Shipcote and the Smith home had escaped any significant damage, although numerous trees throughout the town, including an ancient and majestic elm tree at the Smiths', were toppled by the high winds.

There was something about the fall that often triggered melancholy thoughts for Beston, and with each passing year his bout of autumnal nostalgia became more pronounced. Two weeks before the great hurricane hit New England, Beston wrote to his old Cape Cod friend Truesdell Fife:

[N]ow that the autumn is here all kinds of old memories, nostalgias and melancholies stir in my blood, sounding in the dark of the veins like old, sad music, summoning up again "the front" as I saw it in the golden autumn of France, and the old Topsfield house with the jade-green cabbages beyond, very beautiful under an October sky, and ever and always the vast autumnal beach, and the goldenrod heavily swaying in the sea winds on the dunes, and Capella, herald of winter, star of the charioteer of our northern snows, rising early in the night a little east of the pole, over "the long murmur and crying of the seas." What a superb adventure it was, Truesdell, something one man might have once in a hundred years! Now that I have a perspective on it, I know more than ever that what I stood in the presence of was 'the power and the glory' of the great elements and forces sustaining and fashioning the earth, for the beach is never the same but is forever remade. And these and this I saw in a setting as magnificent as may be found on earth. The beach, with the whole firmament for its pavilion and with constellations for its fires.[45]

Now that Beston was fifty years old, his mood was markedly grimmer—in part, no doubt, to the constant barrage of troubling news, or perhaps because he was starting to worry that his most productive years as a writer might well be behind him. In any event, in an ironic return to his own childhood relation with his father, he was becoming increasingly irritable at home, particularly with the headstrong Meg. After Elizabeth and the children returned to Hingham for the new school year, Henry brooded about the need for a firm hand in directing Meg's conduct. "It's so important for us and the peace of the spirit and the happiness of our house," he wrote to Elizabeth, "If I have to be the one to make her go when called, to put on the disciplinary screws, she will fight me all her life, facing me more and more as she grows older. And I'm too old for it, dear. The tension in the house, the constant sense of combat the child introduced, was destructive to me as a person; it doesn't go with the religious and poetic approach to life which is all I have or did have."[46] Beston missed his family terribly when he was separated from them; when Kate came down with some mysterious ailment he fretted that it might be because she missed him. At other times, however, he worried that he was such a peripheral figure in their lives that perhaps the children didn't miss him *enough* when he was gone.

It did not help matters that Beston was at the stage in life where the passing of family and friends becomes a regular and sobering occurrence; within the year two more people very close to him died. On April 1, 1939, his stepmother Mary Conway Sheahan—whom he always called "Muz"—died after a lingering illness. "She was my second mother," Beston wrote, "my own mother having died when I was a little boy of eight or nine, and this closing of the door brings to end a loving companionship of forty years. She was a lovely person, beautiful in mind and outwardness, and her spirit was always on the side of life. I shall miss her all whatever days remain."[47] Ted Roosevelt wrote him a heartfelt note that seems almost prescient in regards to his own death several years later:

> Dear Harry: I am greatly distressed at the news, for I know that your affection puts out deep roots. You do not change your friends like a garment, as many others do today. I know also what distress is brought by hours waiting for an inevitable end. Harry, I know this is easy to say and hard to do, but

The Divine Consciousness and the Soul of Man

> I think people should continually look forward, at least to strive to do so. There is a sort of grand culmination when death closes the chapter on many worth while years. That life is not finished any more than a chapter in a book is finished when the author has written the last words. That life, like a well-written book, remains a part of the wealth of the people, from which profit and pleasure are derived in years to come.[48]

Just a few months later on August 22, 1939, Mabel Davison, Henry's wartime *marraine* in France, died at the home of her sister in Ashfield, Massachusetts. She was seventy-seven years old at the time of her passing. After the services at All Soul's Unitarian Church in Manhattan, Beston wrote to Elizabeth, "Well honey it's over, and a rending of the heart it was. I didn't go to the cemetery, just said my own farewell. The herbs I put on the coffin, and they went with her. Now its early afternoon, and I am writing from the Prince George, the traffic noises coming in through the window, and a new emptiness facing us both."[49] To Truesdell Fife he wrote, "Light after light has gone out, quenched on the great altar of life . . . After the late 40s, the tree of mortality drops its apples faster; down they fall by ones and twos and threes, leaving bare and lonely boughs."[50]

As soon as the children were finished with school in the spring of 1939 the family returned to Chimney Farm where Henry worked steadily on *The St. Lawrence* while Betty worked on revising a reader, *The Long Adventure*, for school children. Meg spent most of the summer at camp while Kate split the summer between Chimney Farm and a small summer camp run by one of their neighbors, Estelle Hall. The continuing stress of the skeet shooting had abated, and as Henry wrote to Luther Neff, "I haven't made any inquiries about the skeet-stand situation or the aged pithecoid its promoter."[51] Shortly after Independence Day, the Bestons traveled once again to Canada, briefly visiting Toronto, Montreal, and Quebec City before staying for several days at Les Éboulements so that Henry could write up his notes for the book. Even with all the traveling, Elizabeth remained remarkably productive; after she finished revising the reader, she wrote another book, *The Fair American*, the third in the *Away Goes Sally* series, and a series of poems for a planned collection—all in less than six weeks.

Despite the usual rush of summertime activity at Chimney Farm, the predominant mood for everyone in August 1939 was one of anxious waiting. Hitler had demanded that Poland cede the Baltic port of Gdansk (Danzig to the Germans) to Germany and had given the Polish government a deadline of September 1 to comply with his terms. As Beston saw it, Great Britain was responsible for Poland's "foolishly belligerent" defiance of Hitler, as a result of their pledge to stand by the Poles in the event of German aggression.[52] As was often the case, Elizabeth saw the political situation in Europe far differently, writing to Morton Smith, "I hope Herr Hitler has died in his bed."[53] On September 1, 1939, Germany invaded Poland and the Second World War began. Beston was firmly on the side of non-intervention, writing to Luther Neff:

> I shall fight, as I can, to keep America *honestly* neutral. To my mind, her meddling in Old World affairs, her arrival from *outside* in 1917 to influence the European equilibrium is historically the cause of all this as well as anything else. She made possible an artificial victory & an artificially-balanced, artificially over-weighted peace. As a result we have Europe for 20 years trying to regain its old world normality. I hope Germany holds her own, that the war is short, and that there is no particular victim or victory. Western civilization is at stake and not the character of Hitler.[54]

While history has clearly demonstrated that "the character of Hitler" was indeed at stake, Beston was hardly alone in his isolationism. His friend Ted Roosevelt Jr. was also committed to keeping the United States out of the war, and like Beston believed that the Allies were trying to manipulate the United States into entering the war on their side.[55] Beston traveled down to New York to visit with Roosevelt in early October, and sent Elizabeth a copy of an article from the *New York Herald Tribune* about a speech by Roosevelt broadcast over WOR and the Mutual Broadcasting system where Roosevelt warned that "our representative democracy was shaken by the last war" and that it might not survive another.[1]

To Beston the outbreak of yet another war in Europe was a horrific confirmation of all his worst predictions regarding the fate of modern industrial civilization. Elizabeth was so worried about her husband's increasing moroseness that she supported his decision to spend most of the winter of

1939–40 in Maine, using the farm as a refuge where he could find "beauty and silence, and the eternal world."[2] While he missed Elizabeth and children, the time alone (or nearly so—he was often joined there by Lawrence Simmons, who came by regularly to cut firewood) seemed to raise his spirits. As he wrote to Elizabeth and the children in early March, "Can't tell you honeys, what joy it is to the Outermost Householder to be a part and participant in Nature. The sky is burning blue the vast snow a burning white, the sun a radiance of immortality."[3] But while war news reached the farm more sporadically than was the case in Hingham (the Bestons eschewed newspaper delivery or having a radio while in Maine), there was no real escape from it, so Beston continued to fume about the international situation and what he felt was the stupidity of the political leadership in the West. The fall of France in the summer of 1940 was predictable, but hit him particularly hard: "The destruction of France, of course, was simply the second death of a corpse. That's what made it all so horrible . . . horrible with a darkening of baseness, the officers leaving their men in the lurch, the looting and scavengering, the staff cars with their personal household goods, and everywhere, the broken, runaway, leaderless men. France died in the last war."[4] The war seemed to get a bit closer every day, with periodic shortages announced and the daily newspapers crammed with dark, foreboding tidings. Then in late September, Lawrence Simmons told Henry that he was planning to enlist. Despite his own feelings about the war, Henry gave him "the friendliest and most avuncular counsel & encouragement."[5]

In August the family's beloved dog, Bo'sun, who had been part of their lives for about fourteen years, died. Elizabeth wrote to her sister Margaret, "Henry was as unhappy as I, perhaps almost more. We wept steadily for twenty-four hours I think. Henry said he would give anything to bring him back but I wouldn't have him back for a minute—he was so stiff and lay in such strange unhappy positions; his goiter was choking him [. . .] it would have been cruel to have kept him for weeks in discomfort, healing him only to have to kill him when healed." It was truly fortunate, she said, that the Neffs soon arrived for their summer visit to Maine, which would help "take up the slack off our minds."[6] Once the girls began their school year in Hingham, there was another thing for Beston to fuss and fret about; while Kate was doing well in her classes, Meg was another story. Morton Smith wrote a long letter to Elizabeth about Meg's lackluster report card, to which she responded, "I think your idea of looking over her homework is good, & I shall have a talk with her teacher, perhaps this afternoon when I'm over at the book sale. But it doesn't worry me. Henry takes it harder. He takes everything hard, poor boy."[7]

In the months leading up to the June 1940 Republican convention held in Philadelphia, the three leading candidates competing for the right to face Franklin Roosevelt in November were Robert Taft (Ohio), Thomas E. Dewey (New York), and Arthur Vandenberg (Michigan). All three were outspoken isolationists. Theodore Roosevelt Jr. was a leading supporter of his fellow New Yorker, Dewey, who initially led in the balloting for the nomination, but found his support collapsing as a well-orchestrated campaign on behalf of Wendell Willkie, a dark horse candidate who had been a registered Democrat until 1939, gained strength at the convention. On the sixth ballot Willkie prevailed over Taft, who picked up votes from the fading Dewey to finish second. After the convention, Roosevelt—who was a delegate for Dewey—wrote to Beston that the convention was one of the most extraordinary he had ever seen, and that he had been flooded with telegrams supporting Willkie. Following the convention Roosevelt agreed to do everything he could to support Willkie although he had serious reservations about his foreign policy positions. Once again Beston voted against Franklin Roosevelt in the general election that November and once again was disappointed, as FDR swept into office for an unprecedented third term as president.

CHAPTER TEN

A Naturalist Looks at War
1941–1945

We thought we were done with these things but we were wrong
We thought, because we had power, we had wisdom.
We thought the long train would run to the end of Time.
We thought the light would increase.
Now the long train stands derailed and the bandits loot it.
Now the boar and the asp have power in our time.
Now the night rolls back on the West and the night is solid.
Our fathers and ourselves sowed dragon's teeth.
Our children know and suffer the armed men.

HART CRANE
"Litany for Dictatorships" (1935)

LIFE IN SUBURBAN HINGHAM had become a constant reminder to Beston of what he believed was missing in modern life—nature and a sense of the poetic, the spiritual—and just a month after leaving the farm in the winter of 1940 he was already pining to return, saying "my heart . . . has long ago returned to Maine."[1] As Beston would later state in his 1954 address to the American Academy of Arts and Letters, "I didn't really care for the grinding noise of city life, and we often visited the Cape. In Hingham there was no nature for a naturalist to see. It just wasn't a pleasant place for us. I noticed that as civilization became more populated and more urbanized, crime and war increased. In agriculture, the art of peace, there is no violence or aggression. The pace is slow and there is more responsibility and loyalty to the earth."[2]

By early April of 1941 Henry was back at the farm and was overjoyed to once again be immersed in the elemental presences of nature. He wrote to Elizabeth, who was still in Hingham with the children,

> Whatever the days may be in their contrast of sun and springlike air above the cold, reluctant earth, the nights are pure poetry. The western woods gather the twilight into their still, immemorial dark—they are not vocal woods in mood—and over the silence and the darkness, over the half-seen ledges and junipers the two great planets burn golden in a northern and luminous sky. Everywhere, now, before the earth dries out, they are burning brush, and last night again, somewhere on our own East Neck road, there was a pool of bonfire flame colouring the beautiful, still air.[3]

He decided not to return to Hingham for Easter as he'd planned, but opted to stay at the farm to continue working on *The St. Lawrence* and to revel in the Maine spring. He even felt moved to write a "thought for a poem":

> We the conquerors, we who came in ships.
> To this ancient and terrible land, the forest and the stone,
> To this earth which shakes off the plough as a horse,
> Shakes off a fly.
> Preferring the small paths of the red man, the savages.
> What has the earth to do with us? Nothing.
> Only the sky is here to tie us to our past.
> The moon is the moon of Stonehenge, and the stars,
> Are the stars of Delphi, and the valleys of Olympus.
> Orion is here, the hunter, and the dragon and the timeless Scorpion.
> Bidding us remember our ancient heritage
> While the earth battles our alien will and our feet.[4]

He was delighted to relay the news to his family that a large moose had been seen near the farm on East Neck, and was in turn relieved to hear that Meg's second report card showed great improvement.

In early May Beston traveled to Fort Bragg in North Carolina to visit with his old friend Joe Wood, with whom he had traipsed across the Pyrenees and through Spain nearly twenty years previously. John Elliott "Smokey Joe" Wood was now a brigadier general in command of the Army's 41st Combat Engineers. The unit, which later became famous as the "Singing Engineers" was comprised of African-American soldiers stationed at

Bragg, and Beston was tremendously impressed by what his old fellow vagabond had accomplished: "The venture—coloured engineers—pontoon builders, makers of bridges and roads—automobile mechanics, etc.—had never been tried before, and there were plenty who said it would be an impossible adventure. Well, he's done it."[5] Woods took a few days leave from training his troops to go on a short road trip with Beston through the Smoky Mountains. They stopped at the 56,000-acre Cherokee reservation in North Carolina, where they "had a simply gorgeous time with the blessed Cherokees. They are the most out-going Indians I've ever met, genial, un-complexed, ready to give grin for grin, and ready to talk. (I'm practically a chief now.) We talked of Indian things, of the war, of everything in sight."[6] He was less sanguine about the southern climate ("I can stand cold quite well, but heat bewilders me and "fogs" my mind") and southern cooking: "Tourist food in the South is just awful. Fried chicken like a tough lump of some old shoe, and bread which they call "toast" but which is just *fried* in butter, fried in a pan. *Terrible* stuff."[7] After visiting Wood, Beston stopped in Chevy Chase, Maryland, to spend a few days with the Neffs before meeting Elizabeth in Philadelphia and then traveling with her to New York and then back to Hingham.

Beston stayed only a few days at Shipcote before returning to Chimney Farm, accompanied only by the family's new dog, a terrier they named "Pug." He was troubled to see how much the war had changed things even in rural Maine: "Maine is in a queer state. All this "defense" indus-trialism has silenced and emptied the fields. Nobody seems to be able to get anybody to do anything."[8] The seemingly far-fetched notion of the United States entering the war became more likely every day, as friends like Truesdell Fife, Dick and Mac Day, and Lawrence Simmons entered military training programs. The job of hired hand at the farm was now filled by Lawrence's brother Ellis, who Henry told Elizabeth was "stepping nicely into Lawrence's shoes."[9] By June Elizabeth and the children joined Henry at Chimney Farm, in time to see one of the Oliver boys, Steve, arrive with his two oxen, Star and Lion, to plow the hayfields. Meg and Kate were fascinated by the powerful but gentle beasts and the children spent hours outdoors watching them patiently work. In an effort to impose order, Beston imposed a new regimen of behavioral rules on the children—neatness, courtesy, and no quarrelling. "The first two are easy," said little Kate, but the third will be very hard," to which Meg retorted "Nonsense, I'm going to stop quarrelling. It's easy."[10] When the illustrator Peg Davis arrived to do some sketches of Deep Cove and the Dazark for Elizabeth's new book *Houseboat Summer*, the girls enthusiastically joined in, wandering about East Neck with Davis and "drawing like two little whirlwinds."[11] On June 30, both girls left for their summer camps, with Elizabeth and her friend Frances Sortwell driving Meg to her camp and Henry driving Kate to hers, where the prospect of horseback riding kept her in good spirits. A few days later, Elizabeth wistfully commented, "The house seems very quiet. I miss their voices."[12]

The summer included the usual social rounds and visitors, but the great local excitement on East Neck that summer was when the elderly Howard Rollins set off in search of his wife, who had gone to bring the cows in from pasture. He got lost in the woods, and the whole neighborhood of nine or ten families was mustered to search for him. He was eventually found on the Oliver farm exhaustedly crawling homeward on his hands and knees. Ellis Simmons and another man found him and carried him home; as he saw each group of searchers he would bemusedly ask, "Well, what in the *hell* are you doing here?" Later that night as he sat resting by the fire, he gratefully remarked, "Man and boy, they were all with me."[13] In early September Elizabeth and the children returned to Hingham for the new school year while Henry remained at the farm to continue work on *The St. Lawrence*. He remained at the farm nearly until Thanksgiving before rejoining the family in Hingham.

On the morning of Sunday, December 7, 1941, Japanese armed forces attacked Pearl Harbor, destroying a significant portion of the United States Pacific Fleet. Unshakably convinced that this was all part of a plot by Roosevelt and the British to draw America into the war, Beston ascribed the blame for the attack squarely with Roosevelt, writing to Luther Neff:

> Well, he's got what he wanted. Apparently there has been a first and very serious defeat. No phrase of rhetoric, no artifice of speech can express what I feel at the circumstances connected with the battle. We seize the Japanese,

"pushing them about" politically and diplomatically exactly as some police ruffian shakes a criminal by the front of the coat—you know that gesture— and while we are thus engaged, in *the very height of our scolding and shoving*, we are so criminally remiss that our fleet is not manned, our men not at their stations, our fields quite unguarded . . . We are off to an American ice cream soda war, and our people will presently have to leave their chocolate sundaes and be men . . . But oh the humiliation of what has taken place: it is perhaps the most shocking incident in all modern military history.[14]

The only real question left, as Beston saw it, was "who would inherit the ruins of western culture."[15] He was grimly amused to receive a questionnaire from Selective Services that required him to answer questions regarding potential military service. The now fifty-four-year-old author was required to inform them what military work he "could do best." He told Morton Smith that he had listed three jobs he felt most capable of performing: "1. Dictator of the U.S.A., 2. Pope of Rome, 3. Indian Snake-charmer & Fortune teller."[16] He was considerably less amused to learn that Ellis Simmons was conscripted by the military, and was required to report to Mississippi for boot camp. "We shall miss him like fury if he has to go," wrote Elizabeth, "but thank heavens for these critical weeks of garden planting & settling he has done."[17] In mid-July a trial blackout was ordered in Nobleboro, a further indication that the war was creeping closer to home, as was the news that a contingent of troops was to be stationed in Damariscotta.

In the summer of 1942 an invasion of a different sort was underway at the farm; the apple orchard had an infestation of browntail caterpillars, and Beston spent several days trying to clear the trees of the voracious pests to save the orchard from defoliation. The job was a difficult one, made even more so by the severe skin rash caused by contact with them. Beston came down with a severe case of browntail rash over his neck, shoulders, and torso, which had him in terrible discomfort that kept him from sleeping. Fortunately, Jake and Bee Day stopped by for a visit and supplied him with a homeopathic remedy, using vinegar to soothe the rash, which worked quite well. Jake also brought a telescope to show Henry and Elizabeth a nesting loon on a small island in Deep Cove. The big news from the Days was that *Bambi*, the animated Disney film that Jake had worked on for the past few years, was now completed. When *Bambi* was released in the summer of 1942, it was originally intended that the film would make its world debut in the capital of Maine, Augusta, since the background illustrations in the film were based on Jake's photographs and sketches from Maine. The plan for the debut in Maine was apparently scuttled when state politicians realized that the anti-hunting message implicit in *Bambi* would not go over well with the state's large number of sportsmen. There was less ambivalence in the Days' hometown of Damariscotta about the film and the artistic contribution of their neighbor. Elizabeth took the eager Kate to see it in Damariscotta, writing to the Smiths, "Jake furnished all the photographs from which the background was created, so the town feels very personally about it."[18]

After many years of returning to Hingham each fall once the school term began, the Bestons were finally ready to try living in Maine full time. Henry had long disdained Hingham's suburban noise and disconnection from nature, and issues such as the rapidly escalating cost of maintaining two homes (three if one includes the Fo'castle) and the enthusiasm the children evinced when they learned there was a chance of staying on in Maine for school convinced Elizabeth that it was an experiment worth trying. "Our present decision is only for the first term," she wrote to the Smiths, "We'll see how it goes. There are many factors . . . It may not work out at all, but at least we will have given it a try. And this seems to me the year *to* give it a try—though we shall miss Hingham and you."[19] The early results were immensely encouraging, as Kate was elected president of the student council, and Meg told her mother that she loved the school in Damariscotta. But by November Meg was "restless" and Elizabeth checked with Morton Smith to see if Meg could return to the Derby school if it became necessary. Elizabeth was soon convinced it was, writing Morton, "Meg seems so restless that we've decided Hingham and Derby may be best—Heaven knows! But this isn't good. She's restless, and mischievous and Kitty is badgered half out of her wits, and Henry is enraged. And all that is good for nobody."[20] To make matters worse, in mid-November—shortly after Elizabeth had to send Meg to Derby School in Hingham—Henry was helping to push his car up the muddy slope to the barn when a spinning tire dislodged a baseball-sized stone that hit his foot, breaking a bone. He was in a cast for three weeks and unable to do much more than limp around the house using a pair of crutches.

The stress of Beston's forced convalescence was ameliorated by the release of *The St. Lawrence* on November 12, 1942, and the excellent reviews it received. In many ways, *The St. Lawrence* was one of Beston's most ambitious, multifaceted works; as literary critic Sherman Paul asserts, "it is at once a guide book, a children's book (when historical events, Indian captivities, and legends are recounted), and a nature book."[21] Beston realized his goal of writing an ecological reflection on the river and its people, as he had stated in the preface to the book: "I have tried first and foremost to keep my eyes on the river itself. It is not a chronological or anecdotal history of Laurentian Canada; where men and events appear in these pages they have seemed to me to have a living relation to the river."[22] As Beston emphasizes in the book, the different peoples that populated the Laurentian watershed differed markedly in the ways in which they interacted with the river and its landscape. For example, he draws a clear distinction between the ways in which the indigenous people of the St. Lawrence region perceived nature and the ways in which the European settlers who supplanted them in the region saw the land. Beston does not, however, make the mistake of assuming that all of the cultural mores about nature originating from the European experience were identical. Instead he draws a clear distinction between the French Canadians and the English settlers, arguing that "for all his redoubtable prowess with the ax [the French-Canadian] was at peace with his earth and his fields" in a way that Anglo-Americans were not.[23] He was forced, however, to concede that there were some regrettable similarities, such as in "the savage business" of pulpwood logging, "a commerce of pure destruction thoroughly bad in the long run for the psyche of any people. So far there seems little relation between the cutting and any rhythm of forest growth. Nature is there to be sacked and the fierce attack goes on."[24] Still, there were hopeful signs, Beston suggests, places where the inhabitants had partially resisted the siren song of modern industrialism, "adjusting itself to the chaos as best it can. Here it has succumbed or retreated, here it has made its compromise, here it has accepted the change as one might take a recommended but unpalatable dose."[25]

Reviews of *The St. Lawrence* were among the best that any of Beston's works had yet elicited, with one reviewer praising the book as "a welcome and appropriate contribution" to the *Rivers of America* series, citing Beston's "lyric treatment of Canadian nature."[26] Thanks in part to the illustrations by artist A.Y. Jackson, one of the founding members of the "Group of Seven," Canada's premier landscape painters, the book drew special attention in Canada. A Canadian reviewer declared, "Henry Beston . . . describes French Canada with succinct accuracy."[27] The strong reviews bolstered sales, and Beston happily reported to Morton Smith, "The *St. Lawrence* first edition is entirely used up, & the Farrars are rushing the second printing like mad to be out by the 17th, two days more. The order for a second printing has been in sometime, but as the managing editor says, 'it is taking longer and longer to get books printed.' So cheerio the good news."[28] Elizabeth echoed the sentiment, writing "It *would* be *so* fine for H. if he could *really* make some money from it, and have it that kind of a success as well as being such a knock-out with the critics!"[29]

Despite the success of *The St. Lawrence*, Beston entered 1943 feeling "low spirited." His broken foot was on the mend, but he was still limping, and wartime measures on the home front such as rationing and blackouts were daily reminders of the war and of his bleak view of the fate of modern civilization. In early January he took the train to New York City to meet with his publisher, and glumly reported what he saw there to Elizabeth:

> The gas-ban has emptied the streets and made life more complicated. Here it is Westchester County which is without oil, houses closed, etc. and all sorts of goings on . . . The town dim-out is "formidable," and you have to cross those terrifying streets in a thick gloom. The effect has beauty, but its an ebbing of life . . . As for our situation, I am convinced that a bad, even a *minor-famine* food shortage is on the way, and we will need all our "intestinal fortitude" to face it.[30]

One of the friends Beston visited while in New York was Margaret Hensey, Ted Roosevelt's secretary at Doubleday Books, who was filling in for him at Doubleday while Ted was on active duty in North Africa. Although Roosevelt was now in his early fifties and suffered from arthritis and a heart condition, he was leading the 26th Infantry Regiment, 1st Infantry

Division. When Hensey showed Beston a recent photo of Roosevelt in North Africa, Henry was relieved to report to Elizabeth that his old friend looked "particularly well."[31] The same could not be said for himself, he complained to Luther Neff: "I feel superlatively rotten. I haven't been warm one minor instant since my return [from Maine]: moreover, we have to underheat our palazzo in order to conserve oil. My temper is giving out, my naturally angelic good nature is going pop; in a short while I shall kick the cat & bust into tears."[32]

In late January, Beston received a letter from Charles Bolte, the young Dartmouth student who had been so inspired by meeting Beston in New Hampshire several years earlier. Bolte was now a lieutenant with an infantry regiment that had been fighting in North Africa and said that he had been reading Thoreau's *Walden* while in the desert and that it made him think of Beston. Then, he said, his unit went into battle where he had been wounded in the leg; it was subsequently amputated, and now he was in Cairo waiting for a flight to South Africa where he was to receive an artificial limb. "I'm not at all bitter about it," wrote Bolte, "sorry, of course: but they tell me the artificial limb will restore my mobility nearly completely. And I'm still glad I came early to the war, still have high hopes that some useful peace will come from it. Have you changed your mind at all? I remember you were terribly set against it, and I was sorry we differed. Yet I have had a tremendous experience, and feel older, even a shade wiser perhaps, for having had it."[33] In fact, Beston's dour view of the war and those—such as Franklin Roosevelt and Winston Churchill—that he blamed for dragging the United States into the conflict had not changed at all, and the resilient optimism of his youth had all but vanished: "I do not feel entangled in anything so clean as a net . . . I feel rather caught and en-twisted (in terms of the historical time) in some huge, foul mass of cordage old and new, some chaos of disorder which has closed about my feet as I advance into the deeper waters of middle age. Nothing to do, I suppose, except kick as vigorous a weary kick as one can, and swim to the dark water."[34]

When Beston returned to the farm in March 1943 he noted that five or six more of the young men from families near the lake had gone to war, writing to Luther Neff, "five or six less families, five or six more farms for the wilderness to re-occupy. The devil has taken over the nations, and only the last ramparts of the divine awareness stand between him and the conquest of the human spirit itself."[35] He then referred to a passage from *The St. Lawrence*, where he had written:

> There is one destruction that is of God, and that is the destruction inherent in the renewal of life; the dead leaf must wither and crumble in the cold, the flower give way to the relentless pressure of the seed below. Opposed to this is another destruction which is of the Devil; a destruction without necessity and without creative future, a destruction only conceivable in [an] age of the emptiness of the human spirit, and working itself out in brutality and the ruin of the heritage of men. Of this the earth is full, the smoke of the torment ascending, and it will need all the trumpets of Revelation to restore to us the earth which men have loved.[36]

For much of the spring of 1943, Henry was alone at the farm, "living hermit-wise" while Elizabeth and the children were in Hingham, where the girls had returned for school after the autumn experiment of attending school in Maine.[37] A heavy spring rain had washed away part of the road about a half mile away from the house, so East Neck was even quieter than usual, with plenty of time for Beston to observe the animal life returning to the lake: a large marsh hawk at the lake, an enormous porcupine waddling around the west pasture, and the returning tree and barn swallows. When Mac and Dick Day returned home on leave from the war, Henry reported to Elizabeth, "both [are] dandy young officers with shoulder bars and leggings. Dick has to do a lot of riding: sometimes he's eight and nine hours in the saddle at a daily stretch. He looks very well, but much too thin. We had a party at the ark."[38] Spring was the season for sprucing up the farmhouse and fields—cleaning, clearing brush, tending to the orchard and gardens—no easy task for a literary man now in his mid-fifties but a necessary one since many of the young men were now serving in the military. For the first time in several years there was no book project to keep Beston busy at his writing, although he did accept an offer from John H. Baker, executive director of the National Audubon Society, to serve as a contributing editor for *Audubon Magazine*, in which capacity he would write occasional articles for the publication—at least two annually due at his pleasure, at the rate of fifty dollars per article.

After the academic year at the Derby School ended in mid-June, Elizabeth and the children joined Henry at the farm for a few weeks before heading off to their respective summer camps, Meg at Camp Ridgeway on Clary Lake in Coopers Mills and Kate at Camp Adeawonda on Spring Lake in Flagstaff, Maine. While the girls were away, Henry and Elizabeth planned to take a trip to Montreal. When they drove to Damariscotta to take the train to Montreal, however, they discovered that everyone had mobilized to fight an enormous fire in the downtown area. They observed in alarm that the steeple of a church near the Days' home was going up in flames, as was a small house directly across the street. Henry dashed off to help the Days, who were working desperately to keep windblown sparks from setting their house alight. By mid-afternoon most of the blaze had been successfully extinguished thanks to the fortuitously timed high tide that aided the efforts of the townspeople in fighting the fire.[39] The Bestons took the train to Montreal the following day, and while in Quebec visited Abbé Tessier, the monk to whom Beston had dedicated *The St. Lawrence*, in Trois-Rivières. They only stayed in Canada for a week or so and then returned to the farm for the usual August round of social calls, including visits by Mary Cabot Wheelwright and the Neff family.

The local schooling of the past year having yielded mixed results, once autumn arrived Meg was enrolled in the High Mowing School in Wilton, New Hampshire. High Mowing was a Waldorf school emphasizing literature and the arts, which her parents hoped would motivate Meg to approach her studies with more enthusiasm. Kate returned to the Derby School in Hingham once again and stayed with the Smiths while Henry and Elizabeth stayed in Maine a few more weeks to take in the autumn colors and to write. Beston went to Vermont for a weekend in October, spending an evening chatting with Robert Frost about literature, their farms, and their mutual loathing of Franklin Roosevelt.[40] The following week, Mary Cabot Wheelwright came for a visit, and after dinner in town they called on the Days to see Jake's watercolors, which so entranced Mary Wheelwright she said they should be called "Maine woods magic."[41]

By the fall of 1943, the fortunes of war in Europe began to tilt decisively toward the Allies. On the eastern front the Russians went on the offensive and pushed the Wehrmacht back into Poland; British and American forces fought their way steadily up the Italian peninsula and Germany itself was subjected to massive aerial bombing day and night by British and American bombers. The Allied air raids not only targeted military sites in Germany but also struck civilian centers in an effort to break the will of the German people to continue on with the war, the same strategy that the Luftwaffe had unsuccessfully used against England three years earlier. A bombing raid in Hamburg that July touched off a horrific firestorm, and in November a massive air raid on the German capital, Berlin, resulted in tens of thousands of civilian casualties. Beston was utterly appalled by attacks on civilian targets, calling the attack on Berlin "the single most appallingly wicked act in all our savage human history."[42] After Pearl Harbor, much of the domestic opposition to the war quickly melted away, but Beston remained intractably opposed to the war. He was convinced that the United States had been duped into entering the war, and believed in the face of all the evidence that other intellectuals were slowly coming to the realization that the war had been a tragic mistake: "I am very much struck by the fact that the besotted liberal-intellectuals are waking up to the fact that this war—as I have maintained—is a fraud, morally, socially, and politically . . . a disgrace beyond rhetoric to our nation."[43]

In the years prior to the war, many had shared this opinion, but after Pearl Harbor and as more and more evidence was uncovered regarding the war crimes perpetrated by the Axis powers, the conflict came to be seen by most as a just one. Few people agreed with Beston's tendency to blame Churchill and Roosevelt for the war, and even his closest family—wife Elizabeth and in-laws Morton and Margaret Smith—parted ways with him on this issue. Ted Roosevelt, strongly in favor of American neutrality at the onset of war was now fighting in Europe, as were many of Beston's friends and neighbors. In January of 1944 (a full year after their last exchange of letters) Beston received a letter from Charles Bolte, that probably epitomized what many of Beston's friends must have thought about his unyielding stance toward the war:

A Naturalist Looks at War

The reasons for the long silence from [my] end are many, and not worth going into . . . There is, of course, another reason, which you must have sensed: my complete disagreement with you as to the nature of this war. Your letters of last winter left me with a hopeless feeling that on this great central subject of our time we were so far apart in our orientation that it was senseless trying to communicate; we would only wound one another, and perhaps it was best to wait for the bloody thing to end when we could again exchange thoughts and affections with that barrier down. I don't want to discuss it much now, but I must confess that as a "military expert" (I make most of my living now writing military affairs for *The Nation* and for the OWI, one article a week for each) I get a certain satisfaction out of reading those year-old letters of yours and seeing that you were wrong about the "bloody massacre" of the Second Front . . . Still, it was good to hear you say that you had "one more good book in you," and that our visit had warmed the fires. I hope you go on with it, for your essential position "on the side of life" is most important to be revealed and spread about between covers. I think it's foolish of you to say only "one" more good book; you may be on the edge of the twilit time of life, but it's a long way yet before sundown.[44]

Beston was not entirely alone in his staunch opposition to the war, and his anti-war convictions led to a connection with the outspoken pacifist, journalist Oswald Garrison Villard. In late 1943 Beston wrote to Villard, who had written a number of anti-war articles for *The Christian Century*, to praise Villard's opposition to the second front and to bombing raids on civilian targets in Germany, which they both believed only helped the Soviet Union's plans to dominate Europe. Villard wrote back, saying: "we are using means of destruction the Germans never employed . . . How could anything be worse than our liquid fire? All of this rests on my soul so much that I find sleeping difficult." Villard urged Beston to make his stance public and promised to send Beston's letter—which he called "splendid"—on to the editor of the *Progressive*.[45]

Other than a brief visit to Cape Cod in mid-March to check on the condition of the Fo'castle Beston spent most of the winter with his family in Hingham. He returned to Chimney Farm in April, where he was forced to deal with an infestation of rats that had moved into the farmhouse over the winter. With no writing project to keep him occupied and distracted from the war and family worries, Beston was feeling depressed and on edge, and wrote to Elizabeth on several occasions about the difficulty he was having in getting to sleep: "Slept just awfully. Couldn't manage a wink till after 2 A.M. in spite of aspirin and counting all Hudson's [neighbor Hudson Vannah's] sheep."[46] A particular source of irritation was a steady stream of low-flying warplanes from the airbase in Brunswick, Maine, some twenty miles to the south. On one occasion he was walking back to the farmhouse from the mailbox when a very low-flying plane "rushed like a thousand devils right over the chimneys, and cleared the barn ridge by a seeming half-inch. It was quite startling, a heart-gives-a-jump sort of experience."[47] It was not just the noise of the planes that irritated Beston, it was the constant reminder of war that they brought to the farm: "Another broken night . . . It may be all the hideous 'second front' tension and the sort of broken horror which haunts me of the diabolical murder of the cities."[48] What seemed to trouble Beston most about the widespread bombing of civilian populations during the war was the disconnection between the airmen perpetrating the violence and the human consequences: "The thing that I so object to in this world massacre by bombing is that the attack by plane destroys the relation between the human beings on each side—the plane is a thing of evil in itself: for once I shall be a Manichee!—and once that relation is destroyed, there is no compassion or possibility of compassion, and men are turned into creatures right out of a particularly ruthless hell."[49] It appears that for once Beston underestimated the savagery men were capable of perpetrating even while looking directly at their victims; had he known what was going on throughout Nazi Germany—or, for that matter, throughout Stalin's Soviet Union or areas occupied by the Imperial Japanese Army in the Far East—he would, no doubt, have been utterly stupefied by the magnitude of the evil at loose in the world.

On June 5, 1944, Beston noticed an enormous increase in traffic from the airbase in Brunswick: "The planes from the Brunswick field are out in force, by singles and squadrons thunder-pounding the higher and lower air, and as I have one of my blood-pressure headaches I can feel the damned things roaring in the hollow of my skull."[50] The following day Beston was alone at the farm and heard no war news, but on June 7 he received a letter from Elizabeth that quietly stated, "it has begun": the D-day invasion of Normandy. He immediately wrote back:

> I'm writing this little postscript to say how glad I am to hear the news from you and from no other. I hadn't heard a word, and went nowhere yesterday. There will be gains, there will be losses; there will be a killing beyond anything in human history. I don't think I shall make any effort to follow the massacre. This morning I wrote as I could. My work has been a recognition of what to the spirit of man passes for eternals; I shall try to hold on to sun and moon.[51]

One of the officers leading the attack on the beaches of Normandy was a fifty-six-year-old brigadier general with a heart condition and crippling arthritis that forced him to use a cane while leading his troops into battle. Despite his age and physical limitations, Theodore Roosevelt Jr. accompanied the first wave of troops to storm ashore at Utah beach and his calm, steady demeanor and quick thinking (the assault wave landed about a mile off course) in directing the men to their attack objectives won him the Medal of Honor for bravery. Roosevelt survived D-day, but a month later he suffered a fatal heart attack on the same day Commanding General Omar Bradley readied orders promoting him to major general and assigning him the command of the 90th Infantry Division.[52] The news of Ted Roosevelt's death in Europe was, of course, widely reported, and when it reached Beston he was devastated. He wrote to Luther Neff, "Last night's radio so the neighbors say, announced the death of Ted Roosevelt, one of the oldest and closest and dearly loved friends a man was ever privileged to have, and with this news closes part of my life, and I close off one of the great rooms of my house of life."[53] As soon as he heard the news, Morton Smith wrote a letter of consolation to Henry, praising Roosevelt as "a good and true friend," to which Beston responded, "It has hit me pretty hard, and no matter what happens, life just will never be the same again. In my lonely and musing youth, the years before the Outermost House, he gave me just the spiritual and intellectual encouragement I so needed, and warmed up my whole way of life with that friendliness and kindness which was so particularly his . . . I shall miss him all that remains to me of life."[54]

After Ted Roosevelt's death Beston heeded his own counsel about the healing power of nature, and took even more of an active hand in tending to the farm than he previously did. As Elizabeth wrote to Morton Smith, "Henry has been out pitching hay and two loads have gone—the cattle are staying in the barn. Such big patient beasts and Henry feeds them & waters them. He says he likes taking care of their front ends."[55] As with many of the neighbors, such as the Halls, the Rollins, and the Olivers, the Bestons kept most of their acreage as open pasture, selling the hay as feed for livestock and using a portion of the rest for the apple orchard and vegetable garden. Working outdoors had become Beston's primary corrective for the gloom of war and personal loss. He still gloried in coaxing plants to grow, although he said that he had proclaimed "a Corsican vendetta" against the weeds that were attempting to make inroads on his lettuce beds, which he said had become the "spécialité de la maison."[56] One day he came home after working in the hayfields with Hudson and Kenneth Vannah, still laughing at a joke one of the men had told: "Did you know a baby had been born in Damariscotta that was marked by two animals?" "No, you don't say!" "Yes it had a bear ass and a deer face."[57]

When the Beston girls returned home from camp at summer's end, they were tanned and fit-looking, and Elizabeth noted how tall they seemed to have grown over the summer; Meg had reached her full height of 5′ 7″ and Kate, who had not yet finished growing, was only a few inches shorter than her 5′ 11″ mother.[58] While taking pleasure in the growth of his daughters, Henry's post-summer camp comments reflect his wistfulness about not having a son: "Both kids look well, and Pussa [Kate] is as husky as a future Knight-Commander of the Amazons. She's the lass who'll help me move the stove and dig up these State of Maine rocks! She's more Latin than Meg, and looks Latin, I think; Michaelangelo would have had her for a model any day. Alas, that she was not a fine husky boy!"[59] In the fall, Meg would enter her second year at High Mowing School, and Kate would return for her final year at Derby.

In early September a hurricane (often referred to as the Great Hurricane of 1944) swept up the East Coast, leaving in its wake an enormous swath of damage stretching from North Carolina to New England. Nearly four hundred people lost their lives in the storm, which also caused approximately 100 million dollars in property damage. The destruction in Maine was fairly minimal, but Cape Cod was hard hit; the Smiths' summer cottage, "Plum Daffy," in Chatham was nearly ruined, and Henry waited anxiously for news of the Fo'castle, which had been moved inland after the hurricane of 1938 nearly swept it—and the great dune on which it was located—out to sea. The Kelleys, Beston's friends from the Overlook in Eastham soon wrote to assure him that the Fo'castle had weathered the storm, but Beston realized that it was once again time to relocate the house. This time, it was moved off the top of the dune to the landward side facing Nauset March. While the move was a prudent one, Elizabeth Coatsworth later told Nan Turner Waldron that it had diminished the Fo'castle considerably in her eyes: "What had been the cock-of-the-dunes became a pathetic little heath hen."[60]

As best he could during the autumn of 1944, Beston tried to keep himself from thinking too much about the war, concentrating instead on the farm and literature. While Elizabeth was in Hingham and Henry at the farm in late September, she sensed a depressed note in his letters and wrote to ask if he had been thinking of the Allied drive toward Germany. "No dear," he responded, "I'm not following it, and the last news I had of it was your comment that 'it seems to have slowed down.' Just exactly the tit bit of news one ought to have to keep one going. No, the melodramatic tension is over, & now the operation—so hideously full of military and political possibilities though they be..are just 'the war.' But this is a fateful summer for the republic."[61] With the Soviets employing a punitive scorched earth policy in their drive toward Berlin, Beston believed the fate of Western civilization was at stake, and felt that the aid provided to the Russians by the Western democracies was too bitterly ironic to contemplate. When Morton Smith was forced to the hospital for a second time by a painful nasal infection, Henry wrote to his brother-in-law to express his concern and sympathy, and saw a link between his own depression and Morton's illness, advocating a news blackout as part of the regimen for Morton's recovery:

> The hideous state of the world in which we live, this daily fare of murdering, burning, butchering, and killing, this daily breakfast of the diabolical massacre of the young is a *psychic poison*, and from our sick and assaulted

souls has moved on to attack our living flesh. Who could be well in such a psychic midnight of terror and negation, and who can escape from a poison as widespread in the air? Well, that's my belief, and I suppose it will be considered pure fudge by the world. Anyhow, do give yourself everything of the positive world. If you have to, seal off the radio and can the morning paper.[62]

For Beston the "positive world" was based in nature; he took Elizabeth on a five-hour-long canoe trip around the lake on one bright autumn day; as she wrote Morton, "I can't begin to describe it—all lighted along the shores by the maples with their colors burning in the water."[63]

Beston's publishers, Farrar & Rinehart, had long wanted to sign him to a contract for another book project, so when he raised the possibility of authoring a book about farm life in Maine they treated the idea as a proposal. Stanley M. Rinehart Jr. sent Beston a letter in October, hoping to pin him down to a delivery date for the manuscript, which he hoped to publish in June 1945. "I hate to be so damned persistent," Rinehart wrote, "but we are forced to make up our spring list sometime this month both because of the long delays in manufacturing and because of the necessity for allocating our paper . . . Perhaps you could send me some of the first pages, or a little outline with your comments thereon, so we can give the boys some of the flavor of it and possibly do something about the design. Four-engine bombers can be made faster than books these days."[64] Beston was apparently surprised how quickly his rather vague statement of a possible new book project to Rinehart had produced a contract. It may have been a subconscious slip that when he returned the contract to Farrar & Rinehart he forgot to sign it. In a note accompanying the unsigned contract Beston casually mentioned another project, one with a religious slant to it, that he was thinking about writing to be entitled "Night at Elensis." Rinehart urged him to submit that manuscript too, and said they could later decide whether to publish it separately or to include it in the farm book.[65] Realizing that he had vastly over-implied how much of the manuscript of either work had been completed, Beston hastily wrote back to Rinehart to clarify that his next work would indeed be the farm book. In fact, however, almost nothing of either work had been drafted by this time, and was little more than a concept, albeit one for which Beston now had a contract and a due date.

A Naturalist Looks at War

Beston was so adamantly opposed to the war that he could not refrain from publicly offering his opinion about world affairs, and published a piece entitled "Confusion in France" in the September 27, 1944, edition of *Human Events*. In the article he assessed the reception of the French people in occupied France and Vichy to the installation of General Charles de Gaulle's provisional government. Beston downplayed the welcome that de Gaulle had received, calling it a "provisional acquiescence" and forecast a wave of arrests and trials of "Vichyites and collaborationists all over France." He noted the trials and executions of those he referred to as "political adversaries" after the retaking of French North Africa and drew a parallel to the attacks on Bonapartists after the return of the monarchy in France: "So far as this quasi-terror represents the historic right of a regime to protect itself, the activity has some justification. To the extent that it represents an appetite for vengeance it is as foolish as it is evil." A significant portion of the essay was devoted to the possible emergence of the communists as the real *de facto* power in France, either in concert with the Gaullists or on their own—or rather, under the aegis of Moscow.[66] In another piece, a scathing letter to the *Christian Century* published on March 21, 1945, Beston vented his continuing frustration over the Allied bombing of civilian targets:

If the Christian Church can make no protest against the present bombings of Berlin, it had better cease its last uneasy hypocrisies and close its final door. That ruined city is full of wretched people fleeing before the Russian advance. They have nowhere to go in their confusion and despair, and on this mass of misery, on the shelterless women and little half-starved, half-frozen children, America is now pouring a sea of fire. Thermite and phosphorous bombs are splashing their hideous goblets of unquenchable flame on human beings. So helpless is the refugee population in its ignorance of the city, in its hunger and fatigue, that neutral observers describe the killing as the most terrible of massacres, the smoldering streets being everywhere strewn with dead. And day by day our press exults, and the fact that the city is packed with refugees has become a special point of gloating.

I have never been able to see a moral order in the universe related to our human values, but some instinct or intuition makes me certain that the killing of the innocent brings with it some destiny of retribution. It is the thing against which the Greeks warned us, the evil done "outside of life." If "a robin redbreast in a cage puts all heaven in a rage," the sight of "the body of a burnt child tossed into the branches of a burnt tree" should shake the *flamantia moenia mundi* of the cosmic frame.

There is no apology possible for cruelty. Its use and the justification of its use are diabolism. Nothing in the world is more to be held to, more cherished and honored than the natural compassion of man for man. The world is losing it, and if it slips from our grasp and reach we shall lose our humanity, and however bright the future we promise the young, it will be but the future of the pit.[67]

His loathing of the war was exacerbated when he received word that Lawrence Simmons had been wounded in Europe, although he said the message was "qualified by some such word as 'slightly' or 'lightly.'"[68]

Given his unyielding opinion about the war, Beston took something of a subversive's delight in the news that *The Outermost House* was soon to join *The St. Lawrence* as an armed services paperback edition printed for distribution to the troops. "Few things have pleased me more than this action," he wrote to Luther Neff, undoubtedly hoping that his cautionary words about the direction of industrial civilization would reach a receptive audience among the servicemen.[69] Only five hundred titles had been selected by a committee of publishers and critics to be published as an armed services edition, and the small, easily carried books were distributed free of charge to the servicemen; most of the authors, including Beston, waived their royalties. Beston was justifiably proud of the honor: as the *Lincoln County News* in Maine reported, "Henry Beston's *St. Lawrence* has been out about six months and *The Outermost House* is now being distributed. To have one book on the list is considered a high literary honor; to have two an unusual tribute."[70]

Just after noon on May 7, 1945, Beston walked out to meet the mail carrier to sign for a package when he overheard on her car radio that the war in Europe was over. A few moments later an enormous thunderstorm hit, accompanied by a torrent of hail. Beston wrote to Elizabeth, "No rainbow followed the clearing. Was it a kind of omen of storm to come and no new sky?" He quoted with approval an article in *The Catholic Worker* that said there were no winners in the war and only those who kept their hands free of blood, who refused to participate in the fratricide, deserved to be congratulated for their clarity of vision and for their courage and perseverance. "I feel free and clean from any smallest reddening of that hideous stain!" he declared, "Later on, I shall try to help the starving German children in any way that I can."[71] Beston was particularly eager for the annual summer visit to Maine by the Neffs and for the chance to talk with Luther and his sons: "I certainly have been one of the small band on 'the side of life' in all this hellish business of War II. The English destroyed beautiful Dresden at the very last of the war, bombing it for 18 consecutive hours with phosphorous bombs . . . *245,000 dead in the same 18 hours*. It is a world of Devils. Come, dear Luther, and help me stay a human spirit."[72]

The "hellish business" of the war was not yet over; in August 1945 American bombers dropped atomic bombs on the Japanese cities of Hiroshima and Nagasaki. Over 200,000 people were killed, most of them civilians. Elizabeth often disagreed with Henry on matters of politics, but regarding the war's concluding strikes they were in complete agreement; as Elizabeth wrote to Morton Smith, "Now that we have this peace, won in the most cowardly fashion by bombarding civilian populations, at least we can be glad that wholesale killing is over."[73] Beston got a note from Harold E. Fey from *The Christian Century* thanking him for a letter on the atomic bomb that Beston wrote, and telling him that it would be published in the August 23rd issue: "In this night of the spirit of man, it is with reassurance that I note on my personal chart that a light still shines out from Chimney Farm on East Neck at Nobleboro, Maine."[74] It was not light, however, but darkness that Beston felt was closing in all around, telling Luther Neff, "When sixty thousand people can be killed in one hideous instant by an annihilationist machine, the show is over. I irritated a group of the scientifically minded the other day with a Bestonian fang. I said yes, that I had seen photographs of the leading designers and scientificos of the Atomic bomb, and was always a little troubled not to see included the most distinguished scientist of all those connected with the exploit. *Chorus*: Who? *Henry*: the Devil." He went on to say, "When archbishops go about wetting down bombers with holy water and the Church as a whole acquiesced in the Atomic Bomb and the instant electrical disintegration of some 70,000 innocent people, I feel that the adversary is riding the wind. To use my most personal phrase, it is 'outside of life.' More than ever, now, must we talk when we can, act when we can, and beat our gongs like medieval friars."[75]

For the most part it was not Henry but Elizabeth who kept the light shining at Chimney Farm, particularly when he was in his bleak moods. The yearly stay in Hingham tended to stoke some of the recurring exasperations with family life that the late-marrying Beston felt. At the end of August Meg returned from camp, and Elizabeth wrote to her sister, "After two weeks of Henry & Meg at the farm together, & one week of Henry in bed with a fever (which he's over now tho' still weak) I take each day as it comes. We Coatsworths were not made to go day after day after day along the same track. Perhaps we have paddling blood."[76] In September Meg returned to the High Mowing School and Kate began classes at the Emma Willard School in Troy, New York. Kate's progress pleased her father; she was doing well in her classes, writing poems and hoping to get on the board of the literary magazine at the school. Meg had been having some trouble at school since the previous year and so counselors at High Mowing had referred her to an "anthroposophic doctor." Meg talked about leaving school, and as soon as the girls arrived back in Hingham for Thanksgiving holiday, the old tensions flared up; Henry fumed, "Meg came back at thanksgiving, just the same as ever, full of intense egotistic concern with herself, and no scholarly progress or progress in character whatever. That I could see. A completely destructive personality in this stage, and oh Great Snakes! That continuous idiot fooling."[77]

Responsibility for the tension between father and daughters, however, was certainly not all on one side. As Beston grew older, his desire for a son had turned into an unrequited yearning that undermined his relationship with the girls. "A psychologist ought to do a study of what happens to a man without sons," he wrote to Luther Neff, "down the slope he goes, fighting the incline, towards knitting and tasting, and frustration at the bottom."[78] He was a large man, so when Beston flew into a rage his daughters found it to be terrifying. The willful Meg often served as the lightning rod for her father's frustration, with Beston claiming that she was consciously "doing everything hateful possible to destroy all attempts of the family to have a family life."[79] But while Meg may have played the part of the rebellious teen in the family drama, Beston filled the role of the stern and distant father all too often, and did not always avail himself of opportunities to find common ground with his daughters.[80] Instead he was left to mournfully complain, "If my young ladies will only realize that some doors have to be opened through which their Da can pass, they will find him worth a word or two. But enough of the past, I have rolled it into a bundle, and dropped it off a cliff side so high and over-hanging sheer that no eye could follow anything fallen into its abyss."[81]

Formal portrait of Beston wearing his favorite orange jacket, early 1950s.

CHAPTER ELEVEN

The Cosmic Chill
1945–1952

> What can I give you worth your loneliness?
> What can I say that silence has not said?
> The solitary wanderer hears a music
> Vast as the wind, deep as the ocean's tread.
> The solitary wanderer walks through dewfall,
> For him each star shines like a crystal dove—
> What have I to exchange for your aloneness
> Except my love?

> ELIZABETH COATSWORTH
> "Except my Love" (1942)

As 1946 BEGAN there were still constant reminders of the recently concluded war all through Maine, where periodic shortages of staples like meat and sugar would continue for another year or two. Beston was deeply troubled by the graphic accounts of the terrible postwar suffering of civilians in the war zone. Although Allied propaganda had soft-pedaled the targeting of civilians in Germany and Japan, arguing that such tactics would bring the war to a speedier conclusion, Beston believed that this type of savagery—no matter which side was responsible—was simply another manifestation of the growing violence and inhumanity of a modern industrial civilization that was "without a truly human past and may be without a human future."[1] Beston was particularly irate about how British and American bombers had leveled most of Germany's great cities, killing enormous numbers of civilians and destroying much of the cultural heritage of Europe in the process, and he noted with considerable satisfaction any indication that there were others who shared his misgivings. He undoubtedly overestimated their numbers, however, commenting: "[t]he community as a whole, I think, has now an uneasy fear that I may have been right. I certainly did not acquiesce in any of the national skullduggery or pretend to believe one phrase of the official rubbish. It's only a wonder that I did not languish for years and months in the dungeons of the F.B.I."[2] The devastation of Europe seemed a bit closer when he got a letter from Eugene Schmitz, who had been one of his students at Harvard thirty years previously. Schmitz had lost his home in an air raid and was now living in Viersen, in the British zone in occupied Germany. He wrote to tell Henry that he had recently been reading *The St. Lawrence* in a British garrison library open to English-reading German civilians.

Beston's mood was so bleak during this period that Elizabeth fretted constantly about his state of mind. Since completing *The St. Lawrence* in 1942 Beston had written little, at least little about nature; what he did write tended to be diatribes against the war. Then in mid-1945, at the very nadir of Beston's continuing despair about the fate of the modern world, he was thrown a lifeline in the form of a letter from Morris Rubin, the editor of the populist magazine *The Progressive* founded by Robert M. LaFollette. Beston had written a few book reviews and short political pieces for the magazine, and Rubin inquired about whether Beston might be interested in contributing a regular column about nature to *The Progressive*. Over the next few months Rubin and Beston discussed the potential for a series of essays based on life in rural Maine. Strongly encouraged by Elizabeth and intrigued by the idea of having a regular forum to air his views, Beston agreed to the undertaking, and in late November of 1945 sent off his first "Country Chronicle" to *The Progressive*. The article described the coming of winter to the farm, as well as offering Beston's opinions on the dangers of man becoming alienated from nature. Rubin was so pleased by his readers' responses that he immediately sent Beston a check for the next five columns.[3] Beston was also delighted with his successful return to journalism, writing to Luther Neff: "How are you liking the Progressive chronicles as salvos 'on the side of life'? I keep my values & my humanist point of view always in clear sight."[4] Indeed, Beston was so gratified by his new writing gig that he sent out a number of complimentary subscriptions to friends and family including his brother George, Morton Smith, Alva Morrison, the Neffs, Eleanor Roosevelt (Ted's widow), Jake and Bee Day, Rosalind Richards, and his daughter Kate at the Emma Willard School in Troy, New York.

Beston spent most of the winter of 1945–1946 ensconced at Chimney Farm working on "Country Chronicle" articles for *The Progressive*. Beston's renewed concentration on nature and writing raised his spirits, and served as a convenient justification for spending as little time as possible in Hingham. Still, even Beston's relatively short visits, primarily limited to the holiday season, were increasingly distasteful:

> We came down the day before Thanksgiving, and ever since, I've led the existence here of an exiled bear. More and more every year, this still well-to-do, tidy (but-beginning-to-be-vaguely apprehensive) suburb drives me nuts. There is no nature for a naturalist to see, there are no birds save "the spotted Chevrolet and the Greater and Lesser Buick"—that's one of my best and grimest [sic] jokes! And the touch of Boston Harbor which lies in front of the house and beyond the cars has absolutely *no* meaning to me in terms of beauty and the spirit; it is nothing but a glacial spillover surrounding a tub de mud. If I am to be found here next year, I will have had to bow to the absolutely insurmountable or be in a box with the daisies![5]

Elizabeth's family connection to Hingham was stronger than Henry's but she too was weary of the expense of maintaining three homes. Not only was the cost of upkeep for Shipcote a drain on the family finances, but also, because they were considered residents of Massachusetts for tax purposes, they had to pay the state's rather hefty income tax—Maine did not enact a personal income tax until 1969.

After the end of the war, the pace of modernization in the United States, even in rural areas, accelerated rapidly. Beston's response to these manifestations of modern civilization was mixed; he was not interested in having a radio, or later, a television at the farm, but when a petition circulated among the residents of East Neck in September to bring in an electric line, sharing the cost among them, Beston was among the signatories. He remained ambivalent about the benefits of having electricity at Chimney Farm and may have signed the petition just to be neighborly. "An electric ice box would free us of this [ice delivery] nonsense—free us of its waywardness," he reasoned, but on the other hand, "it would "rob us of a human contact.""[6] In June 1946 Beston sent a tongue-in-cheek "birth announcement" to Morton and Margaret Smith: "Mr. and Mrs. Henry Beston announce the arrival of a dear little telephone Damariscotta 239–4, to be reached 8–9 A.M. & P.M.: other hours closed off."[7] The following year Chimney Farm was wired for electricity and indoor plumbing, and Henry reported to Elizabeth in Hingham, "The electric pump is installed and working. I had it connected up so you could use the *upstairs* 'terlet' . . . it is automatic, and one doesn't have to fuss about the gas engine in the shed. I really miss using the icy, the arctic, the meditative 'terlet' in the strawberry box. But this will be more civilized and certainly more accessible."[8]

There *was* one modern technology that Beston thoroughly enjoyed; as a corollary to his lifelong love of the theatre he had developed a fondness for the cinema and regularly frequented the movie theatre in nearby Damariscotta to see the latest Hollywood releases. After working on *Bambi*, Jake Day often got complimentary tickets to Disney releases that he shared with the Bestons. They saw the animated Disney feature "Song of the South," which Beston praised, but when he went with Bee Day to see *Lady in the Lake*, a film noir murder mystery starring Robert Montgomery and Audrey Trotter, he absolutely loathed it: "[I] came back spiritually sick with that vision of modernity, ruthlessness, and non-human hard boiledness; a *horrible* story. Human life lived as by dogfish or preying and murderous worms. Can that continue? What happens when man ceases to be man? Well . . . the answer, I suppose, is look at the world."[9]

For Beston, the question of what happens when man ceases to be man was an omnipresent question once scientists split the atom and created the atomic bomb. As J. Robert Oppenheimer, one of the men chiefly responsible for creating the bomb, later recalled, after the Trinity test detonation in the New Mexico desert in 1945, the thought that flashed through his mind was a quotation from the Bhagavad Gita: "Now I am become death, the destroyer of worlds. I suppose we all thought that, one way or another." In the foreword to the 1949 edition of *The Outermost House*, Beston restated his core philosophy, updated for the nuclear age:

The Cosmic Chill

Once again, I set down the core of what I continue to believe. Nature is a part of our humanity, and without some awareness and experience of that divine mystery man ceases to be man. When the Pleiades and the wind in the grass are no longer a part of the human spirit, a part of very flesh and bone, man becomes, as it were, a kind of cosmic outlaw, having neither the completeness and integrity of the animal nor the birthright of a true humanity. As I once said elsewhere, "Man can either be less than man or more than man, and both are monsters, the last more dread."[10]

The darkening of Beston's mood as he approached late middle age was not simply due to pessimism about the future of the modern world, but also tied to a growing preoccupation with mortality and what John Burroughs aptly called "the cosmic chill." In November of 1946 the Beston's longtime friend and neighbor, Agnes Rollins, died after a short illness. Elizabeth had tended to her for several hours before she died, and she wrote to the Smiths that during her final hours she kept saying at intervals "Oh dear me. Oh dear me why? It seemed like the voice of all mortality."[11]

The following April the Bestons were shaken to learn that Morton Smith—the children's beloved "Uncle Morton"—had suffered a serious stroke while he was in California. Henry was alone at Chimney Farm when the news about Morton's illness reached him, and he immediately wrote back to Elizabeth:

That is, indeed, deeply troubling news. I shall wait anxiously to hear your report of what Henry Robinson says for in such cases it is the medico *who knows the patient* who must be heeded. All is not completely black: people do rally: blood clots do move on, and leaks adjust or do something to bring about a control. But that's, of course, a fairy tale chance. The kind of stroke which has hit our Uncle M., is only too well known a variety known as a hemiflagia (or one-half stroke): it was what hit President Woodrow Wilson at about the same age . . . what was Morton doing at Santa Barbara? Touring? Visiting. Is he in the hospital now at Santa B.? I know that they will wish to move the poor old boy as little as possible. Poor Muz [Beston's stepmother] went through something of this sort with father, for he collapsed in Europe, at 50 and barely managed the steamer trip home. The doctors were far from sure they could get him to N.Y.[12]

When Morton was well enough to return home a week or so later, Beston traveled down to Hingham to rejoin Elizabeth and to help Elizabeth's sister Margaret look after him. During the summer of 1947 the entire family was encouraged by Morton's slow, seemingly steady recovery, but on September 9, 1947, he suffered another stroke and died. His passing left an enormous void—in many ways, it was Morton who served as the genial center of the family. When he married Margaret Coatsworth, he truly became a son to Ida Reid Coatsworth and a brother to Elizabeth. The energetic, intelligent, and perennially good-humored Smith had also long been the practical genius of the management of the extended Smith-Coatsworth-Beston family's financial affairs and had adroitly steered them through the Great Depression of the 1930s. His help and expertise extended far beyond the realm of finance, however; while they were themselves childless, Morton and Margaret Smith served as surrogate parents for the Beston girls on countless occasions while Henry and Elizabeth were away and were far more than simply uncle and aunt to Meg and Kate Beston—they were mentors, close friends, and trusted confidantes who could always be relied upon for emotional or financial support.

For Henry personally, Morton's death was yet another loss in a world that seemed as though it was growing a little colder and a little darker every year. Morton Smith had been one of the constant presences in Beston's life since they were boys. They had been classmates at Quincy's Adams Academy, had attended Harvard University together, and it was Morton who had introduced Henry to his wife-to-be Elizabeth Coatsworth some twenty-five years previously. While they did not always agree on political issues—Beston remained a Theodore Roosevelt Republican at heart his entire life, while Morton became a Franklin Roosevelt Democrat after Republican economic policy had helped turn the Wall Street crash of 1929 into a full-blown depression—Beston always respected Smith's point of view and his ability to support his arguments with fact rather than simply opinion. Just three months after Morton's death, Elizabeth's mother, Ida Reid Coatsworth also passed away after several years of declining health. Then in February of 1948 George Chester, the husband of Ida's late sister and the elder of their two uncles living in California (whom they frequently

visited) died at his home in Pasadena. As next of kin, Elizabeth and Margaret spent the rest of that winter in California attending to their uncle's affairs
and caring for their surviving uncle, Frank Reid.[13] Later that winter Tom
Kelley, Beston's old Cape Cod friend and the proprietor of the Overlook
Hotel where he had so often stayed, also died; "so grows the poor world
of ours ever smaller,"[14] Beston glumly commented. Elizabeth sadly noted
the ever-tightening circle of friends and family as well, writing to Margaret
on her birthday, "We shall be thinking of you on your birthday with all
manner of loving thoughts, and a present will be arriving from Newbury
Street which carries with it our love. As the circle narrows each person is
more and more important and necessary to the others—which just means
that I don't know what I'd do if you weren't somewhere in the world."[15]

For a time Beston's "Country Chronicle" column forced him to focus
on nature and to keep writing, thereby keeping him from obsessing about
aging and loss. But in early October of 1947 Morris Rubin informed Henry
that financial difficulties would force *The Progressive* to cease publication.
Beston would no longer have a regular outlet for his observations and ideas
and the loss of the "stimulus & interesting contacts & outlet" worried
Elizabeth, who remembered well her husband's blue moods before the
column's steady work had helped revive his spirits.[16] Elizabeth was afraid
that this most recent "death" in the family would hit Henry particularly
hard. It was fortunate, she wrote to Margaret, that he had just started work
on a new article for *Human Events* for which he was now a semi-regular
contributor: "Henry is hard at work on his new Human Events paper—
I am glad that he had started it before word came of the Progressive's folding
up. Whenever anything happens I think of how Morton would feel about it,
and he would surely have said 'That's too bad, Maggie. That's been good
for Henry.' And it *has*, but perhaps this will now make him start putting
the material into a book."[17]

For a writer who saw life in terms of the seasons, the unremitting losses
of this period must have felt to Beston like a winter of the soul. But like
spring with its promise of rebirth and renewal, the following year brought
forth a series of literary opportunities the likes of which Beston had not
experienced for many years. In January he received a letter from John

Farrar following up on a conversation they recently had in New York City, where the publisher had pitched to Beston the idea of doing an anthology of Maine writing as a part of a series of readers for Farrar, Straus and Company. Farrar immediately followed up on their talk, sending Beston a letter later the same day: "Dear Henry: It was so fine to see you this morning. I can't tell you how! I am hoping that you will want to do the Maine Coast anthology. It would be exciting to have you in camp again and I think it would be a book which would be pleasurable and profitable for us all."[18] Beston agreed to do the book, which would be titled *White Pine and Blue Water: A State of Maine Reader*, for which Farrar sent him a $500 advance on royalties in February 1948.

More good literary news soon followed when Rinehart & Company accepted Beston's proposal for a collection of essays culled from his columns for *The Progressive*. As happy as Beston was with the Maine anthology, he was even more pleased with the prospect of giving his rural essays a second, more lasting life, in book form. As he wrote to Luther Neff, "I think I ought to begin this letter with the word 'Hooray!' Rinehart & Co. (my regular publishers) have taken a book I made out of my Chronicles and called 'Northern Farm.' They hope to have it out late this fall or early next winter. Thoreau MacDonald, the Canadian artist who did the plough and the birdie-wirdie which used to head the column will probably illustrate it."[19] Elizabeth was just as pleased with the project as her husband, particularly since she believed that the "Country Chronicle" series had "saved" Henry during a rugged period of his life and was convinced that revisiting them and shaping them into a book would be therapeutic. Beston spent much of the first half of 1948 at Chimney Farm selecting and revising his "Country Chronicle" articles into chapters for the new book.

In February of 1948 the Communist Party of Czechoslovakia, with backing from the Soviet Union, staged a coup d'état that toppled the democratic Czech government and lead to forty years of Communist rule. The coup shocked the Western powers and helped to hasten the Cold War, but Beston scoffed that since Roosevelt, Stalin, and Churchill had already agreed to the partition of Europe at Yalta, "what are these nitwits hollering about?"[20] Beston's misgivings about current events were so dire that he probably shocked (and perhaps even worried) Elizabeth when he wrote to her while she was in Pasadena tending to her uncle George's estate: "N.B. *If Uncle George has a good pistol,* seize it: I am getting increasingly aware that one ought to have some sort of weapon here. I have never really wanted one in the house, but times are queer and people queerer."[21]

On a more positive side, both of the Beston girls were now preparing for college. Kate had skipped two grades and was now, although she was just sixteen, a senior at the Emma Willard School in Troy, New York. Kate chose to attend Scripps College in Claremont, California, and when she matriculated in the fall of 1948 she immediately turned her writing talent to good use by volunteering to work on the student newspaper. Even better from Kate's point of view was that near the Scripps campus was a stable that rented horses. Henry and Elizabeth regularly sent their daughter thirty dollars a month for clothing and sundries, but rather than spend the money on those things Kate rented a horse from the stables and spent every free moment she had riding and exploring the surrounding countryside: "I would get up in the morning and [ride through] the most beautiful range of hills . . . it was a drunkenness of joy such as I had never known . . . I just ate that landscape up. I couldn't get enough."[22] Meg had been accepted at Wilson College in Chambersburg and despite some reservations on Henry's part about the religious emphasis at Wilson, Meg enrolled there for the fall 1948 semester. A few months later the relieved Beston reported to Luther Neff, "Meg is back from Wilson, much improved and seemingly on her way to growing up. She has (just as I prophesied) fallen for Wilson's Presbyterianism like a ton of brick, and wants to be baptized and confirmed and be a member of the Presbyterian communion. I am really quite glad: anything . . . anything . . . to give her some sense of the religious nature of life."[23]

After Morton Smith's death Beston's longing for a son and male companionship within in the family unit resurfaced even more acutely than before. When Meg and Kate came home for the holidays after their first semesters at college, Beston wrote, "Kate flies back [to college] soon, and Meg is presently going to leave us for a week in N.Y. We are up from the farm, only a scant fortnight. Had a nice, gluttonish Christmas, rather a solitary one for me psychically, as I am the last male left in the two families."[24] Henry was not, however, the lone surviving male in his family; on the contrary, he still had two close male relatives in his brother George and his son George Jr. Beston had always been very fond of his nephew George and nieces Marie and Joanie, but as George Jr. grew to manhood, Henry took more and more pleasure in George's visits to Maine: "Georgie has just gone,—an incomparable guest, quiet, scholarly, undemanding, and *very thoughtful*. He had to go in order to register at his Quincy draft-board."[25]

On November 4, 1948, Beston received a congratulatory Western Union telegram from John Selby at Rinehart and Company announcing the publication of *Northern Farm*. Thematically and structurally, the book has much in common with earlier books such as *The Outermost House* and *Herbs and the Earth*; like them it is structured around the passage of the seasons and touches on many of Beston's familiar themes regarding man and his disconnection from the rhythms of the earth and the loss of a poetic, spiritual sense of nature. Beston sometimes referred to himself as a Virgilian in his essential outlook, and there is a touch of the Virgilian in *Northern Farm* that combines both a nostalgic, pastoral sensibility with a hard-edged appraisal of humankind's alienation from nature. In the opening chapter Beston describes the train ride back to Maine from Boston, several times returning to a refrain of "Home. Going home." Each succeeding chapter opens with a section that describes some aspect of life on the farm. Then follows a brief passage from Beston's "Farm Diary" before closing with a philosophical critique of the modern world that often deals with the general question of "What [has] gone out of American life as one sees it in the city and the suburb?"[26] After reaching the farm Beston includes a passage that could easily have come from *The Outermost House*:

> As I settle down in this familiar house, with the lamplight glowing from its windows and the great planets crossing the sky above the chimney tops, I find I am shaking off the strange oppression which came over me when I lived by an urban sense and understanding of time. In a world so convenient and artificial that there is scarcely day or night, and one is bulwarked against the seasons and the year, time, so to speak, having no natural landmarks, tends to stand still. The consequence is that life and time and history become unnaturally a part of some endless and unnatural present, and violence

becomes for some the only remedy. Here in the country, it all moves ahead again. Spring is not only a landmark, but it looks ahead to autumn, and winter forever looks forward to the spring.[27]

Winfield Townley Scott called *Northern Farm* a companion piece to *The Outermost House*, asserting, "It is a domestic orchestration of *The Outermost House* themes."[28] Like his earlier books on nature, the imagery in *Northern Farm* is often stunningly beautiful, such as in a passage where Beston describes the sounds made by winter ice on the lake, or describes the night sky, pointing out that people who were more closely tied to the land than we are now once called the Big Dipper the Plough. It is crucial to point out, however, that Beston's is not simply a nostalgic look back at a pastoral idyll, but is a reminder and a warning: "However various may be the tasks which man is given to attend upon this earth, his major occupation is a concern with life. To accomplish this duty, he must honor life, even if he honors it but blindly, knowing that life has a sacredness and mystery which no destruction of the poetic spirit can diminish. The curtain has just rung down on a great show and carnival of death and the air is still poisoned and we are poisoned. Our strength and intelligence have been used to counter the very will and purpose of the earth. We had better begin considering not what our governments want but what the earth imposes."[29]

Given how often and how consistently Beston returns to his assertion about the importance of *not* divorcing man from nature, it is mystifying to read the following passage from Dana Phillips's 2003 study on nature writing:

> The bad faith of American nature writing is most evident in its treatment of its own subject matter, the natural world, which it represents as alien, and therefore as something impossible to address, much less capture, in words—even when the words it uses to describe the natural world are in fact wonderfully eloquent and evocative. Consider just one example of eloquent and evocative words of the kind I have in mind. Henry Beston's attempt to describe the sound of snow falling against the windows of his farmhouse in Maine: 'Every now and then I could hear, even through the wind, the sound which snow makes against glass—that curious, fleecy pat and delicate whisper of touch which language cannot convey or scarce suggest." This self-admonishing passage is from Beston's classic *Northern Farm*, first

published fifty years ago. It shows how ingrained the contrary tendencies of nature writing are.[30]

While it must be conceded that putting nature into words can be difficult work—as is clearly evident from Beston's own struggles—time and again he stresses that nature is not alien, and that man not only should, but *must* be a part of the natural world. In just one of hundreds of such examples, he writes:

> In our good, native fashion (do they do so in other states?) all Maine is working in the hay fields without a shirt, making a sort of Yankee cum Abenaki golden age. I have always liked physical man *held up against nature*, and busy at the work of man and Nature. All our various Christian religions are altogether too much out of relation to the living year . . . they inhabit a sort of ethical vacuum removed from the norm of natural experience. I'm all for Harvest festivals and things of that kind. They are both emotionally and religiously right.[31]

In the final analysis, it seems that the passage cited by Phillips is less an example of the "bad faith" of American nature writing than of the captiousness of some contemporary literary theorists.

Among the literary acquaintances to whom Beston sent an advance copy of *Northern Farm* was the iconoclastic Henry Louis (H. L.) Mencken. A longtime columnist for *The Baltimore Sun,* Mencken gained national attention for his searing coverage of what he dubbed the John Scopes "Monkey Trial" in 1925. John Scopes was a high school science teacher who was brought to trial for violating a Tennessee statute that made teaching evolution unlawful in public schools. The trial became a national sensation, portrayed by Mencken as a contest between science and religious fundamentalism. Mencken's articles on the trial for the *Sun* relentlessly lampooned the prosecution, particularly former presidential candidate William Jennings Bryan, who was invited by the local prosecutors to join their team. Scopes was found guilty of violating the statute, but the press's coverage of the case, led by Mencken, succeeded in portraying Scopes as an honest, scientific seeker of truth and a dedicated teacher, while the Tennessee lawmakers who had passed the statute and the local school board who enforced it were depicted as narrow-minded, intolerant buffoons. Mencken's reputation as a writer was also advanced by his work as founder and editor of *The American Mercury*, a popular monthly, and as the author of *The American Language*, a multi-volume work on the American idiom.

Despite Mencken's reputation as a champion of science and reason over religious superstition and Beston's deep mistrust of a science that left no room for a sense of wonder about the divine mysteries of the world, they shared many political views and a love of literature and language. Like Beston, Mencken was a critic of Franklin Roosevelt who believed that Roosevelt and Churchill had conspired to manipulate the entry of the United States into the war. Shortly after the conclusion of the war Beston and Mencken began to correspond occasionally about books and politics. "I am delighted to discover a fellow-Aristotelian with a hearty dislike for Plato," Mencken wrote to Beston in early November of 1948.[32] A week later Beston sent Mencken a copy of *Northern Farm*, which Mencken apparently read upon receipt, replying "I have read 'Northern Farm' with the greatest pleasure. It is done beautifully, and it was worth doing. I should add, however, that its fundamental doctrine lies a bit outside my ordinary range of excitements. I am a cockney of the cockneys, and never feel really comfortable unless there is hard paving-stone under my feet. I like to go into the country now and then, but I also like to come back."[33]

Another friend to whom Beston sent a copy of *Northern Farm* was David McCord, a fellow Harvard alumnus (1921) and a prolific poet. Over the course of his long literary career McCord wrote or edited more than forty books in addition to editing the *Harvard Alumni Bulletin* for many years. McCord and the Bestons long maintained a regular correspondence and they frequently exchanged books. When McCord published *About Boston*, one of his most highly regarded collections of poetry in 1948, Elizabeth sent him a letter full of praise for the new book. In response McCord wrote, "Next year if my health holds out, I do hope to see you both at Nobleboro. It has been such a long time since my one and only visit. Let me close by telling you how much I admire your integrity as a craftsman and your persistence in the world of letters. Robert Frost has spoken to me more than once of his pleasure in your poems. That ought to please you!"[34] Sometime in early 1949 David McCord nominated Beston for honorary membership in the

Harvard chapter of Phi Beta Kappa, the nation's oldest academic honor society. When the delighted (and very much surprised) Beston received word that the honor would be conferred at Harvard's graduation ceremony in May 1949, he immediately contacted McCord to thank him and to make arrangements to visit with him in Cambridge. George Sheahan was particularly proud to learn of his brother's latest accomplishment, writing "Heartiest congratulations on your new honor! When you come down can't you stay with us at the shore? Phi Beta Kappa from Harvard, Henry, that's something like it!"[35] At the ceremony Beston was feted as one of Harvard's literary lions, and over the next two decades, and as long as his health permitted, he would travel down to Cambridge each June for the Phi Beta Kappa ceremony and reunion.

The summer of 1949 passed quietly at Chimney Farm; the big news was that in June the farm was wired for electricity for the very first time. Now in his early sixties, Beston left most of the farm work to farmhand Ellis Simmons. The fields were let out for hay, and his neighbors, the Olivers, would bring their oxen or team of draught horses, Major and Prince, down East Neck Road for the cutting. In September both Beston daughters left for their second year at college, leaving the farm just a bit lonelier than before. Relations between Henry and his eldest daughter Meg were still occasionally tense, but they seemed to have reached an uneasy understanding that they would never see things completely eye-to-eye. Although Beston was often overly critical of both daughters, he did have a better relationship with the good-humored Kate, who tried her best to take her father's criticism in stride. A few weeks after Kate left for California, Beston wrote to tell her that while driving along a back country road near Windsor he and Elizabeth had seen, hanging from a tree, a huge black bear that had recently been killed by trappers: "Poor, hairy man of the woods, I felt sorry for him, and wished he were back alive in the forest, happy with his stolen honey, his roots and berries."[36]

Even during the periods when he was not publishing much, Beston was perennially in demand as a speaker, and he was regularly invited to deliver lectures at colleges, seminars, and numerous other venues. As soon as he sent *White Pine and Blue Water* off to Farrar, Straus, Beston set to work on a series of four lectures he had been invited to give at the Bangor Theological Convocation in late January of 1950. The topic for his lectures was the relation of nature to the spirit of man, and while this was a subject central to his work, he confessed to Luther Neff that the presentations were something of a tall order for him, as he had never before given four consecutive philosophical discourses at a single event.[37] His lectures were very well received, however, and inspired a good deal of discussion and debate about his primary theme, an affirmation of the naturalists' faith in the earth and the necessity of taking a stance on the side of life. An "odious" press photograph of the convocation speakers appeared in the local newspaper, and Beston noted with resignation that he looked old and tired. He sent a letter to Kate in California that included a reporter's précis of the lectures with his own gloss on the topic, saying the lectures were "on the need of having again some 'concept of man,' i.e. some honorable notion of man about himself. Today a mood of dialectical materialism—a grim and negative mood based on a perception of first appearances—has made man nothing, no, not even an animal. Just something to 'liquidate' as one would a vial of bacteria. The point has not been raised by any other philosophical thinker, and it has created a great interest."[38]

Farrar, Straus set the official publication date for *White Pine and Blue Water: A State of Maine Reader* for June 23, 1950 (John Farrar pronounced the book to be "magnificent"), and worked assiduously to promote the book in advance of publication, scheduling Beston for a number of bookstore visits and radio interviews in June. Dedicated to Maurice and Beatrice Day (Jake and Bee), *White Pine and Blue Water* contains sixty-two selections, including poems, short fiction, and non-fiction, spanning from early accounts written by European explorers to modern writers including Sarah Orne Jewett, Celia Thaxter, E. B. White, Ruth Moore, and many others including Beston himself and Elizabeth Coatsworth. As Beston saw it, as reflected in the title, the two central facts of Maine were the wilderness and the sea. The continued existence of a wilderness frontier unique to the Eastern states, wrote Beston, "means the presence of the genuine North America and the earth influences rising from its green and archaic mystery. It means that the state of Maine still has room to breathe physically and metaphorically.

A moose may take it into its head to cross Route 1, but there is no pressure of the tragic, crowded, and inescapable mass to confuse and smother one about; one does not have to elbow or gasp to remain an individual and a human being." Most importantly, from Beston's perspective, "the people [in Maine] remain in relation to Nature, for there is no 'conquest of Nature' here—evil phrase!—and never will be. The people hold on to the sense of reality which springs from a relation to Nature, and to that other wisdom called common sense."[39]

As Beston himself knew, even in Maine there was no real refuge from the modern world; five years after the end of the war, periodic shortages of oil and coal persisted. He observed that many people in rural Maine had difficulty procuring enough coal to warm their homes over the course of the long, cold northern winter, writing to Kate that some people in Maine were "half freezing [during] their days to be able to carry their water-pipes through the night . . . [t]he world darkens, and we sit in the farm kitchen, grateful that we have plenty of winter wood."[40] While the world may have seemed like it was darkening to Henry, it was just opening up for his two daughters, both of whom had grand plans to travel to Europe. Meg had received some money from her aunt Margaret to put toward her trip, and Kate had applied to take summer classes in Paris.[41] Getting passports for Meg and Kate proved to be a bit more complicated than anticipated, as Henry's dilatory approach to legally changing his—and his daughters'—name to Beston often caused trouble when dealing with governmental bureaucracy. As Elizabeth noted, "Henry will see what he can do about getting a record of Meg's birth as Margaret Beston which he had registered here in Nobleboro. Otherwise she will have to be M.B.S., always confusing tho' Kate doesn't seem to have minded in the least."[42]

In early September Henry, Elizabeth, and Kate accompanied George Sheahan to Boston, where he was to sail for France. The following day they bade farewell to Kate, who was headed to New York City for her trip to France on board the SS *Ile de France*. "Kate was as good as gold," Henry noted with approval, "helpful, cheerful, and intelligent."[43] He was not nearly so sanguine about Meg, who was already in France but wrote only occasionally to her parents. The cold war with her father continued, with Henry acidly commenting that no one knew where she was but "She must live for she just sent a request for more money . . . I hope she does something and gets something out of her year." About a week after Kate arrived in Paris, she left her sister a note and her contact information at the American Express office: "The next day as I came in at dusk I saw a little figure in a plum-red coat enter the apartment building ahead of me. Curious, I quickened my step—there was Meg. We hugged rather shyly—then I took her up to my room and we . . . sat and talked of old days. The next day I went to call on her. She was living in a quiet little hotel in the Latin Quarter, right back of the faculty of medicine. She imparted her address as a great secret."[44] In a poignant letter to her parents several months later, it is evident that Meg was rather homesick and hoping to reconcile with her parents, particularly with her father: "I may be wrong but maybe you will be happier to have me home, anyway I shall be glad to be back with you. Certainly I am no daughter anyone would wish and please understand that I realize it, anyone as confused and horrible inside as me should be and is in hell."[45]

Beston's disposition was not helped when war broke out in Korea early in the summer of 1950. Although he was staunchly anti-communist, he feared that once again the American government was blundering into a conflict that it did not understand. "One of the most difficult things to do," he railed, "is to drive into the heads of Americans that there is *no such thing as a double standard of ethics*, one of which morally justifies every horror we care to use and inflict whilst the other forbids the enemy practically any weapon of self-defense."[46] In late July the Neffs arrived in Maine for their annual visit, and Henry and Luther talked much about the war, which was all the more troubling because by now two of the Neff boys, Robert and Paul, were eligible for the draft, with John just a short time away.

Convinced that to stay silent about the war was to acquiesce, Beston sought ways to share his anti-war views either in print or in other public forums. On October 3, 1950, at the Congregational Church in Rockland, Maine, he gave a lecture he entitled "A Naturalist Looks at War." While only fragmentary notes of the presentation survive, they give an illuminating glimpse into Beston's somewhat iconoclastic brand of pacifism. Beston structured his lecture around three primary ideas: 1) We must honestly face the reality that the world contains both good and evil, and if there is a light there is also a shadow; 2) We must retain the sense of compassion for man which is the essence of Christian teaching; and 3) We must have a sense of the divine nature of the world and the mystery of human life. Beston began with his observations on a "naturalist's inquiry" on war in nature, concluding that with the exception of highly organized communities, such as ants, "war [is] rare in nature. It is a peculiarly human activity." Beston then briefly outlined the manner in which war has been conducted throughout human history and contrasted armed conflict as the ancients knew it and modern warfare: in the pre-modern era, the outcome of warfare "[rested] on someone's strong body and right hand and willingness to risk death." He concluded that modern technology had made it too dangerous to wage war and therefore it should be limited by all possible means: "It must be fought *within the human limitations*. We are now out of these limitations as if we were devils. THE ATOMIC BOMB. Never lose sight that man is a creature of the divine mystery and the spirit of compassion."[47]

Since publishing *Five Bears and Miranda* (1939) and *The Tree That Ran Away* (1941) Beston had written few children's stories, ceding that literary genre to his wife while he concentrated on projects such as *Northern Farm* and *White Pine and Blue Water*. The steady sales of the 1950 Cadmus reprint of *The Firelight Fairy Book*—probably combined with the war in Korea and the somewhat sobering realization that his two daughters were no longer children but college women traveling in Europe—had Henry once again thinking about childhood innocence and fairy tales. So, in late 1950 when Lillian J. Bragdon, an editor at Aladdin Books in New York City wrote to inquire whether Beston would be interested in putting together a collection of his best fairy tales, he plunged into the project on faith, without waiting for a contract. Much of the winter of 1950–1951 was spent going through his old fairy tales and writing a few new ones. As he did so, he mused:

> I am gathering my old fairy tales together, the stories of about 40 years ago. Can it be possible that they have endured for over a generation? It seems that they have, and I imagine that the original collection represents the unique group of modern wonder tales thus to stay alive. As I read them, I find some

of 'em just so-so, and others merry and delightful with most ingenious plots. Anyhow, they've stayed alive 40 years, and there's hardly a week when the Seller of Dreams is not told over the bedside radio.[48]

A few months later Beston wrote to Bragdon to let her know that the rewriting of the fairy tales, which he characterized as hard work though "rather fun," was completed and that he could get the manuscript to her in a week if she was still interested in publishing it. Beston was very pleased with the result and indulged in a little bit of promotion, telling Bragdon, "If you'll forgive my putting a few feathers into my own hat, I can say that I think they are dandy stories with that appeal to beauty, the imagination and the great human values which, to my mind, is the true justification of writing for children." Beston's one condition was predicated upon Aladdin Books finding a "first rate illustrator with something of the romantic mind" to provide the artwork for the collection—but, he said, it was quality rather than his potential royalties that he was chiefly concerned with: "I would be glad to help rather generously in making such a thing financially possible."[49]

Many of the selections that Beston included in the collection received only minor changes in style and narrative detail, although he felt that some of the stories from *The Starlight Wonder Book* needed more extensive editing as they were too literary in style for children's tales. The general principles guiding his revisions were: "1. [T]o 'point up' and strengthen the interest of the story and the prose style, 2. to avoid any suggestion of what I call 'grue', i.e. literary terror and horror. Children can stand realities, but bogus horror should be avoided; all the modern psychologists are united on this point, 3. to keep the ethic always 'on the side of life'."[50] He was particularly horrified when he discovered that the original plates for *The Starlight Wonder Book* had been melted down during the war: "it [troubles] me to think of some wretched Japanese or blond Bavarian student being hit and doubled up by a fragment of 'once upon a time.'"[51] The book project moved along quickly; by July Bragdon had found a German artist, Fritz Kreidel, to do the illustrations, and the following month she sent Beston the contract for *Henry Beston's Fairy Tales*, which she said were "fully worthy of being classed with Andersen's, Grimm's, etc."[52]

While Beston was at the farm in August of 1951 working on some new stories for *Henry Beston's Fairy Tales*—"Diggory" and "The King of the Wood"—Elizabeth wrote from Hingham to tell Henry that his brother George had been rushed to the hospital. Doctor Sheahan had been suffering from a heart condition for several months, but he assured the family that he simply had a case of the flu and would soon recover. Two months later he was still in the hospital, and as George Jr. wrote to tell Beston, the stress of the situation had begun to affect his mother's health as well. The three Sheahan children—Marie, Joan, and George Jr.—were at the hospital constantly, and Elizabeth and Meg had also stopped by to see George several times. As hospital expenses mounted, Henry and Elizabeth contributed financial support, and in early December George Jr. wrote again to his uncle to give him an update on his father's condition and to express his thanks:

> Just a brief note from all here to thank you and Aunt Betty for your kind help. Mother is truly grateful (as are we all), for the expense is truly hideous. What the future will be I don't know; sometimes we are led to believe he might be able to come home, sometimes they say he will have to go to a VA hospital. In any event, we are gathering the necessary documents for the latter. Joan (especially) and Mimi (and, of course, all of us) do not much like the idea; but when one gets at the end of the rope, there does not seem to me to be much of an alternative. Certainly unless there is quite a good improvement we cannot care for him at home; there just isn't the money available. And at the current rate of expense, the Beth Israel (and all associated expenses) would cost us about $12,000 a year—money which just is not available, not a quarter of it. However, we shall do our best; and, as you say, there are special officers' quarters.[53]

On the letter Dr. Sheahan wrote an addendum in a shaky hand, "A thousand thanks for your kind contribution. Will repay you both as soon as we sell this house. Lots of love and again say I am very grateful. George [Jr.] isn't doing too well."

Less than a week later, on December 15, 1951, George Sheahan died. The emotional blow to his family was exacerbated by the cost of his hospitalization, an expense that nearly bankrupted the Sheahans. As was often the case in times of sorrow and loss, Beston's sought solace in the natural world. One morning in January, while Beston sat at the kitchen table writing with a fire blazing in the cast-iron stove, he looked out the window, where a number of chickadees and sparrows were pecking at the birdseed that Elizabeth had earlier spread on the frozen ground. In a flash, the flock scattered as a young Cooper's Hawk flashed in and seized one of the chickadees in its talons. "It was very troubling to see that tiny feathered lump of living substance being borne away, held visibly in those fierce claws," Beston wrote, but "so turns the wheel of earthly being, and unless the spirit of man can behold it poetically, it is a mistake to be anything but a good, robust animal. The poetic sense is man's justification of his humanity."[54]

After the death of his brother, Beston's relationship with his nephew George Jr. became increasingly close. George was helping his mother and sisters prepare the family's house at School Street and a small beach house owned by their father to put on the market even while he maintained his graduate studies in anthropology at Harvard, applying for a Fulbright grant so that he could return to the Pacific Islands to complete his research. Unfortunately, as he told his uncle, because his father had paid for him to go to Samoa for his initial field research, now he was apparently ineligible to receive a Fulbright and would need political help to obtain grant funding. Despite George's financial straits, when he went up to Chimney Farm that summer he declined Henry's preferred "honorarium" for all the farm work he did, telling his uncle in a post-visit letter that he loved the work and was sending along his "very best to Aunt Betsey and a big hug for the farm bear."[55]

As *Henry Beston's Fairy Tales* moved steadily through the publishing pipeline at Aladdin Books during the winter months of early 1952, Henry and Elizabeth enjoyed what proved to be a particularly snowy winter in Maine. They were both fond of snowshoeing and often set off for long treks around the fields and woods of East Neck before returning to the farm and a roaring fire in the cast-iron stove in their large country kitchen to write. Lillian Bragdon sent regular reports to Beston regarding the progress with the book through the publication process and raving about Fritz Kreidel's artwork: "Mr. Kreidel has brought in his jacket drawing which is out of this world. It is almost like a Medieval tapestry; the colors are magnificent.

I hope you will like it as much as we do."[56] When the book was released on August 18, 1952, the reviews were glowing. Beston was particularly flattered by a review by Robert P. Tristram Coffin that appeared in the September 28, 1952, edition of the Portland [Maine] *Press-Herald*: "such a review as a juvenile gets once in a thousand years."[57] Just as gratifying was the response of old friends such as Truesdell and Caroline Fife, who wrote Henry to tell him what a hit the book was with their son:

> Reuben simply loves the *Fairy Tales*. It is much more than mere "likes." When we say, "Well, Reuben, which one do you like best of all?" he always answers with the name of the story we just finished. The other night I remarked on this peculiarity, and he said craftily, "Why don't you read me some more tonight? Perhaps I'll not like the next one so well." He calls to Tru from his bed, "Trues, will you read Henry Beston?" and Tru goes up as I come down. They are delightful to read, beauty-full and full of pictures, wonderful things. We thank you from the bottom of our hearts for giving Reuben, and other children, these gems.[58]

Even before the book was published, William Jackson from the Houghton Library at Harvard contacted Beston to inquire whether he might be willing to donate the manuscript to the library. In a letter from Elizabeth Coatsworth to her sister Margaret, Elizabeth noted that her often-irritable husband was "very, very pleased" by this.[59]

In May, Henry and Elizabeth went to California for a month for Kate's graduation from Scripps College and to escape mud-time in Maine. Unknown to Henry and Elizabeth there was more drama lurking behind the scenes of Kate's graduation than they realized. As Kate confided to her aunt Margaret, "Tia," her prospect for graduating on time remained uncertain almost up to the last minute: "I didn't tell my parents but right up to the last minute I didn't know if I would graduate. It depended on the mercy of a certain professor who is, thank heaven, very merciful. I was completely exhausted and so glad to clutch that diploma to my bosom and have done with it. I feel completely and utterly disinclined ever to write a paper or take an exam again."[60] At Kate's graduation ceremony the Bestons met Richard "Dick" Barnes, a young man from Running Springs, California, a small mountain town near San Bernadino. With a thick shock of dark hair,

Barnes was slim, athletic, and perpetually tanned, and just slightly shorter than Kate. He was also a promising scholar and writer who had recently placed fourth in a writing contest sponsored by the *Atlantic Monthly*. Over the past several months Kate and Dick had become very close. Kate told her aunt (who had discerningly inferred from Kate's letters that this was far more than a passing friendship), "I was so over-joyed when you called and amazed that you should be psychic. I told Dick about it and he was amazed. I am filled with the most complete joy and confusion . . . I've visited his family many times and love them: they are warm and loving with one another."[61]

Kate and Dick planned to spend the summer after her graduation in Claremont, California, with Kate keeping house for a local professor and his family and Dick sharing part of a nearby house with two other graduate students. Henry's response to the news was noncommittal; as he wrote to Luther Neff, "Kate is staying over in California, nursing a college love-affair with what seems a steady whelp. Need your counsel. I am keeping out of this feminine adventure."[62] In private, Henry groused to Elizabeth about "this feminine adventure," complaining that "young people are selfish, no one listens to him, that she shouldn't hang around Dick's neck, that when they're married he'll burn one candle for her & two for him etc. etc. None of it warm or loving talk," Elizabeth told her sister about Henry's response to the big news, "just a general grumble."[63] In late October of 1952 Kate and Dick Barnes announced their engagement to be married the following summer.

Beston's response to the rest of the trip through California was, however, decidedly more enthusiastic—a "gorgeous adventure," he called it. Henry and Elizabeth stayed in San Francisco for a few days before borrowing a friend's little Studebaker and heading out for an extended road trip, starting with Yosemite National Park. "Because of the heavy winter snows," he observed, "the great Yosemite cataracts were more full of water than they had been for thirty years. A noble spectacle."[64] They then took the Pacific Coast Highway south where they visited the Palomar Observatory, and Henry indulged his lifelong fascination with the night sky, taking a telescopic tour of the heavens guided by the observatory's expert astronomers.

Following the stop at Palomar, Henry and Elizabeth turned inland, driving across the great central valley toward the Sierra Nevada Mountains. After the baking heat of the valley, the coolness of the high Sierras, still covered with snow, came as a great relief for the "two half-cooked State of Mainers."[65] Henry and Elizabeth stayed in a small cabin at Sequoia National Park for a week, reveling in the cool mountain air and awed by the great trees, the largest living things on earth. As he wrote to Luther Neff, "Perhaps what I shall most cherish is the week at Sequoia Ntl. Park, 7000 feet up in the Sierras, and our cabin under the giants. That was a week to remember! How beautiful it was to see the titans emerge from the moonlit night into the first coolness and glow of the mountain dawn."[66] Henry and Elizabeth returned to the farm on June 30, 1952, with visions of the High Sierras still looming large in Henry's imagination: "[it was] an adventure into a world of nature on another scale, and my ears are still haunted by the sound of great waterfalls, by the sight of snowcapped mountains, and by that western, inland light which is so unlike our own."[67]

As the summer of 1952 gave way to a brilliant New England autumn, Beston busied himself preparing the farm for winter. He had several ideas for book projects, including one on the elements and one on night that had drawn interest from his publishers. The one on night seemed particularly appealing given the perennial popularity of "Night on the Great Beach," Beston's oft-anthologized chapter from *The Outermost House*. In January 1953 Frederick "Ted" Rinehart at Rinehart & Company in New York wrote Beston to inquire about whether he had any additional thoughts on the topic:

> I haven't heard from you about any night thoughts you might have had about the Book on Night. But I have just been talking to Stan about it, and he conjured up an amusing, if slightly harrowing, picture of you crashing through the woods in the dark, falling over logs and otherwise imperiling the life and limbs of one of our most distinguished authors. This was such a horrible thought that I felt I had to drop you a note of warning. Please do be careful and always carry a flashlight or wear shinguards. It *is* a hell of an idea, this projected book of yours, and also I wish I knew more about the one on the Elements.[68]

Kate Beston, aged twenty, posing with guitar at Chimney Farm, December 1952.

Henry, Elizabeth, and Kate Beston at Chimney Farm, November 1952.

Beston never did follow through with either of these book projects, although he did receive some very gratifying news a few months later when *The Outermost House* was published in France as *Une Maison au bout du monde* ("A House at the End of the World"). When Beston received his copy of the French translation of his book he was elated, saying that, "it could not have been made with a more sensitive feeling for the poetry of the original," and proclaiming that the book was "even better in French!"[69]

CHAPTER TWELVE

The Minotaur Downstairs
1953–1958

I can hear my dead father
Still grieving and raging downstairs like the Minotaur
In the depths of the palace cellar; like water,
My mother's voice goes on soothingly.
Sleep now.

KATE BESTON BARNES
"Coming Back" (1994)

I T MAY HAVE BEEN the pleasure of having some of his works published in Europe, or simply the realization that in his mid-sixties the opportunity for travel was growing shorter, but on July 22, Beston boarded a plane in Boston for a flight to Bremen, Germany, his first trip to Europe in nearly thirty years. He had been invited to speak to the "Young Farmers of Germany," and planned to travel throughout the German countryside staying with friends such as his old student, Eugene Schmitz, and Erica d'Alquen and her husband, who had named one of their sons Tye Henry d'Alquen in Beston's honor. He stayed in Germany for a month, he wrote to David McCord, "not going from hotel to hotel or from bahnhof to bahnhof, but from friend to friend, chiefly those of the agricultural variety. One of my German agricultural students took me to his family farm in the lovely, peaceful 'Odenwald' and I felt like Prince Henry in Longfellow's 'Golden Legend.' A romantic experience."[1] The trip also gave Beston an opportunity to see the scarred ruins still evident from the bombing campaigns that he had decried nearly ten years previously: "The Germans are industriously repairing the repairable, a lot of the ruffian smashing is beyond only one generation, and one mourns at the beautiful old churches burned to terrible gothic shells. Even my favorite academic Münster (of the Anabaptists) got a fearful banging up."[2]

Elizabeth had also been traveling that summer, traveling through Scandinavia with Meg. The European journeys were cut short, however, by a pressing engagement in Hingham, Massachusetts: the wedding of Kate Beston to Richard Barnes on August 17, 1953. The ceremony took place at the Church of St. John the Evangelist and the wedding reception was held at the home of Kate's aunt, Margaret Smith, in Hingham. Shortly after Kate's wedding, Beston returned to Europe. His first stop was France where he visited several friends, including his former student and comrade-in-arms during the Great War, Pierre Gouvy. In contrast to his earlier stay in Germany, Beston was rather unenthusiastic about France, confessing, "I have never liked Paris though it is my mother's city. It has a curious heartlessness which chills me whenever I go there. Yet I confess that I write ungratefully for the dear French friends were ever so thoughtful and kind. But I just don't like that vast parade of rhetoric (c'est bien le mot) of rhetorical statues, rhetorical buildings, and rhetorical speech."[3]

After leaving France, Beston crossed the channel to England, and spent a few weeks in London. He was relieved to see that London's recovery from the war was better than he had expected and that "the cruel wind of recent years has swung to quite another quarter of social history, and that the town looks well and is well, and that the people have *entirely* lost that terrible starved look they had in the earlier photographs. Blessed old London has long been my beloved favorite of the world's great cities, and I rejoice to see her herself again." Beston took the opportunity to go to a few plays in London's theatre district, and wrote to friends in Maine, "Met some ever so pleasant people connected with Drury Lane, and was again reminded that the Beeston-Bestons were a famous theatrical family (XVIIth and XVIIIth centuries) related to the Shakespeares. The English strain in me, complicated with what the Irish call 'the old English' is Warwickshire, too, and I wonder if some connection explains the passion for 'the theatre' or 'the play' which is so marked in the family. Wouldn't it be fun?"[4] Beston was considerably less enamored with his flight home in early October, referring to it as a "shattering experience in modernity."[5]

The Minotaur Downstairs

The trip to Europe provided Beston with some fodder for his writing, and by November he was writing a paper for *Human Events* on "The Mood of Europe" while he recovered from a painful case of gout. While in Germany that summer Beston had met with a university professor in Stuttgart, Dr. Hans Ehlers and his wife, Dr. Ilse Ehlers, who had offered to make some inquiries about publishing *Henry Beston's Fairy Tales* in Germany. Erica d'Alquen was already working on a translation of the stories and Beston made clear that he was not particularly interested in how much money a German edition would make, and was in fact willing to subsidize the publisher's expenses:

> I thirst for no larger income from this book. What I want to do is to offer the book as sort of personal contribution to the world of children and to the civilized spirit everywhere. If certain moneys should ever chance to be due me, I should want 3/4th of such a sum to be paid to my beloved German friends, the parents of my little "pattenkind," Tye Henry D'Alquen, now aged 4, and put aside by them to help with his university education, and the other one fourth to be put in some German bank to be spent by me in Germany for some thing of benefit to German children or some like cause.[6]

Over the next two years Beston devoted much time and effort to trying to secure German and French publishers for his fairy tales, and while he found some who expressed interest it never came to fruition. Beston was more than willing to forego profit for the sake of a new audience of young readers and feared that Lillian Bragdon, his editor for *Henry Beston's Fairy Tales* at Aladdin Books, was trying to get too much money for the book from potential French and German publishers. When Dutton Books acquired Aladdin in 1955 and *Henry Beston's Fairy Tales* was assigned to a new editor, Sharon Bannigan, he renewed his efforts, writing her, "I would gladly forego my customary half of the payment for foreign rights. What I am immensely anxious to have is a French edition . . . Do for Heaven's sake, ask next to nothing for the rights or be ready to accept a proper token sum; as I say the French have no real money, and moreover, I feel that the prestige of a Parisian edition would be valuable for both author and publisher."[7] Dutton seems to have reluctantly assented, but left it to Beston to find a willing publisher. He pursued several promising leads but after several months he was forced to concede that "[a]pparently in such a world as the 'politicos' have made for us, even fairy tales have somewhat lost their universal appeal."[8]

Now that Beston and his nephew George Sheahan Jr. were the last surviving males in the Sheahan line, Henry paid close attention and took particular pride in his nephew's academic achievements, calling him "the one real scholar of the family." Since 1950 George had been a research student at Cambridge University and they corresponded frequently. Knowing how difficult the financial situation was for the Sheahans since the death of George Sr., Henry often included a small "honorarium" for his nephew with his letters. In the autumn of 1954, George wrote to tell his uncle that his doctoral thesis in anthropology was nearly completed. He had been a member of the Peabody Museum of Salem expedition to Polynesia in 1953 and his thesis was on Polynesian culture. Sheahan was anxious to find a position as soon as possible after completing his doctorate so as to relieve some of the financial burden on his family but despite sending out numerous applications for teaching positions, months passed with little encouraging news on the job front. He told Beston, probably only partly in jest, that he was thinking about applying for a position with the Central Intelligence Agency: "they sometimes hire anthropologists and I rather fancy myself as a spy."[9]

In early 1955 George Jr. returned to the family home in Quincy, but he didn't intend to stay long—in March he announced his engagement to Margaret Anne Searle, a beautiful young Englishwoman and graduate of Perse College, Cambridge University who was now employed at Cambridge. The engagement lifted his spirits, indeed those of the entire family, and he was eager to return to England to rejoin his fiancée. On May 9, George wrote to tell his uncle Henry that "things [were] beginning to look up a bit." His thesis had been approved pending a few chapter revisions, and he had a number of job interviews lined up. Combined with the joyful anticipation of his marriage to Anne Searle, he said, "I feel more hopeful . . . indeed, everything goes swimmingly."[10] Most of his job prospects were outside academia, but there was a teaching post at Purdue University that looked promising. To celebrate his improving fortunes, George wrote, he and a close friend from Quincy who was attending Trinty College in Dublin,

Joseph Lacroix, had planned to drive out to Cape Cod, but put it off for a day due to rain. He concluded the letter by urging his uncle to "watch out for your health."

The following day, May 10, 1955, George Sheahan Jr. and Joseph Lacroix left Quincy that morning for their trip to Cape Cod. They stopped in Chatham, where they planned to stay for a few days at a house that Lacroix's brother Harold had recently purchased. Late that night the two men apparently decided to drive to Provincetown for a late dinner. George was driving when the left rear tire blew out as they passed through Truro on Route 6 at approximately 11:30 P.M. As the Quincy newspaper reported the following day, "[their] car went careening across the street, ran over a traffic island and hit an embankment of the left hand side of the road . . . The car ended up on its roof and was described as being 'demolished.'" Sheahan was pinned in the wreckage and Lacroix was hurled through the front windshield, landing fifteen feet away. Items from the car, including a medical book were found as far as forty-five feet away, and the medical examiner determined that both men had been killed instantly by the force of the crash.[11] George Sheahan Jr. was just 27 years old at the time of his death; Joseph Lacroix was 28.

The untimely death of George Jr. devastated his family; as his sister Joan wrote to her Uncle Henry, "What complete & utter devastation I feel; what a void that cannot be filled. We are shattered, broken humans."[12] Beston felt the same way, writing to his son-in-law Dick Barnes, "I am really down to a rather lonely old age, for the young scholar who "got me" and so well understood what I was trying to be and trying to say is gone forever . . . it is a bit hard for me to see the ending of the old line with its intellectual strain clearly visible through a hundred years."[13] There is a certain sad irony to Beston's intense grief over the passing of the Sheahan line, as he had long since ceased to use his patronymic surname for most purposes, but it was terribly real all the same. Beston had gone through a painful period after Morton Smith's death, where he had felt as though he was the last surviving male of the family. Now that his brother and nephew were gone, however, the terrible loneliness and isolation he felt seemed almost unbearable. Letters from close friends such as the Days, the Neffs, David

McCord, and others were a solace but Beston continued to grieve over what he saw as "the ending of the line." Loving letters of consolation from his daughters were of some comfort, but it seems to have been impossible to divert his attention from his yearning for male companionship within his own family. He yearned for a link to his new son-in-law, Dick Barnes. When Barnes wrote Beston a "really distinguished and beautiful letter" after George's death, Henry thanked him graciously and included a plaintive plea for understanding: "I want to know you, so much, and I think you'll find me rather worth knowing." Unfortunately, the two seem to have had a fundamentally different view of things, particularly when it came to politics, and in the same letter Beston could not help but scold Barnes for an affront that had occurred at their last meeting: "When you were greeting all my attempts to discuss ideas with you with that snort, I did not want to see you for the snort is an ugly gesture of contempt, and that I take from no one . . . Robert Frost would have crowned you with the nearest potted geranium."[14]

The passing of his nephew was not only a personal blow to Beston but also seems to have redoubled his misgivings about the after effects from the Second World War. Beston's sense of male isolation within his family colored his view of post-war American society generally, as reflected in an exchange of letters with Lars Hallden, a Swedish student attending Bowdoin College. In a letter dated October 20, 1955, Beston frets, "I am troubled by the passivity of the American young. Their parents allow them to be slid downhill,—I had better write "tripped" downhill—into a brutal, foolish, and murderous war, and the young men themselves accept their own extinction with the passivity of corn cut by a scythe. I lay most of it, of course, to the over feminization of this culture."[15] Beston's comments to Hallden—which sound more like a reflection on America's entry into the First World War and the loss of a generation of young men in Europe, not America—may well have been more of an emotional backlash to George's death than anything else. More and more often he would launch into tirades about American women, and Elizabeth would listen in silence, understanding that the unspoken subtext to his frustration was, at least in part, the absence of a son. As Kate Beston Barnes later wrote in her poem "American

Women," "Right after/I was born,/my father had come/to my mother's bedside/in a storm of tears—/once again, no son."[16] For a long time the Bestons' marriage had been a happy one, but times and circumstances had changed; as Barnes recalled, "Was it a happy marriage? Yes, for a long time. There was a bad period at the end when HB grew disenchanted with the whole world—indeed, in a sort of lasting rage with it—and that very much included his wife. [By the 1950s] he was having some small strokes and was, I think, thrashing around angrily and unhappily during this process of loss, loss of himself and his powers."[17]

Both of the Beston daughters were now settled far from Maine, Kate and Dick Barnes in California and Meg in Colorado. Kate and Dick returned to Chimney Farm in July, bringing word that Dick had received a Ford Foundation Fellowship at Claremont College in California that was set to begin in the fall semester. Kate also had good news, having published a poem, "Cocktail Party," in the July 13 edition of *The New Yorker*; it is "brittle, modern, and good," her mother wrote approvingly.[18] Meg was considerably less eager to visit Maine it seems, content with the occasional letter or telephone call to her parents. Her relationship with her aunt Margaret, however, remained extremely close, and it was with her aunt that she first shared the news that she had fallen in love with a young man from Colorado, Dorik Mechau. Meg had met Dorik through her friend Vanni Mechau and was staying at the Mechau ranch in Carbondale that summer while he worked in Aspen, learning how to cook and "all the other responsible housewifely chores" from Dorik's mother. While Meg was not yet ready to reveal her plans to her parents, she was eager to share her joy with her aunt Margaret: "All in all I have never been so happy in my life or felt before a part of a living family group. Dorik and I are in love with one another and whether or not this will eventually lead to marriage is as yet unknown. My heart sings, my cup runneth over, the beauty of the country and the joy of living abound . . . I love you! Please love me despite my manifest transgressions. Am so happy!"[19] Meg believed that later that fall, probably at the family's annual Thanksgiving gathering at the Smith home in Hingham, that she and Dorik would be ready to announce their plans: "Of course, it will be difficult meeting old H.B. again but these things must be and will be easier now then later, although what in God's name will he say to old Dorik?"[20]

By MID-CENTURY Henry Beston had few peers in American nature writing. In the twenty-five years since the publication of *The Outermost House* Beston's literary reputation became more firmly established every year. Starting with Henry Chester Tracy's *American Naturists* (1930), which gave Beston a brief but glowing appraisal as a representative of the "great tradition" of American nature writing, Beston's work was nearly always featured in nature writing anthologies and critical studies of literary environmentalism. After the Second World War, when the emphases of the early conservation movement on preservation of wilderness areas, land use policies, and resources conservation were succeeded by more dramatic environmental issues such as nuclear war and the effects of radiation (soon followed by numerous other concerns such as chemical contamination, air and water pollution, and the fate of endangered species) there is a gradual but noteworthy shift in the critical response to American nature writing. Many of the preeminent nature writers of earlier eras were now seen as overly pastoral, even outdated or "quaint," and were superseded by writers whose emphasis on political or scientific themes in their nature essays was seen as more in tune with the modern temper and concerns. Beston was among a relative handful of writers such as Henry Thoreau and John Muir (later to include Aldo Leopold and Rachel Carson) whose work successfully bridged the mid-century divide between the nineteenth century and modern literary environmentalism.[21]

In Herbert Faulkner West's *The Nature Writers: A Guide to Richer Reading* (1939), which had its origins in a course called "The Nature Writers" that he taught at Dartmouth for many years (and which often featured Beston as a guest lecturer), West provides a wide range of about two hundred and fifty commentaries ranging from the ancient Greeks and Romans to contemporaries such as Beston, Dallas Lore Sharp, William Beebe and many others. While West makes no pretension to an encyclopedic completeness to his book, it is remarkably broad and diverse in its commentary but his choice of Beston to write the foreword to the study most likely indicates a shared emphasis on the poetic and spiritual aspects of the writing rather than only its usefulness as scientific communication. "The function of the writer on Nature," Beston writes:

> Is therefore akin to that of the poet. It is his task to give depth and colour to the adventure of human life, to touch the imagination of his readers, exalt their sense of beauty and mystery and fortify in their souls that power of intelligent awareness with which they look out upon their world. To this end, he properly studies the world first as an artist, finding a continuous delight in the vast and changing spectacle presented to his several senses: he is only secondarily a seeker after exact and material knowledge. He is an interpreter, not a dissector, and in the abandonment of the true path for the byway, his magic vanishes.[22]

What is at stake, however, is more than simply literary art and accomplishment, asserts Beston: "Nature is part of man's humanity. Torn from the earth and Nature, and put to dwell in a world of consciousness abstract as a kind of mathematical formula, man becomes unhuman, changing to something less than man or something more, and both are monsters, the last more dread." Coming just a few years before the Second World War and the development of the atomic bomb, Beston's cautionary statement is horrifically prophetic, and one he would later repeat in the foreword to the 1949 edition of *The Outermost House*.

Beston's mistrust of narrowly focused empiricism detached from the human spirit put him at arm's length from some of the more scientifically-minded of his literary contemporaries in nature writing. In 1944 William Beebe, a respected scientist and director of the Department of Tropical Research at the New York Zoological Society, published his own nature writing anthology, *The Book of Naturalists: An Anthology of the Best Natural History*. Given his scientific rather than literary background, Beebe's selections reflect an understandable bias toward accredited scientists (following Beebe's by-line on the title page was included a long list of his degrees and titles) although there are some curious exceptions such as Ernest Thompson Seton, who had been accused of falsifying his natural history during the "nature-faking" controversy of the early nineteenth century. On the other hand, Beebe's anthology did include as its final selection an essay entitled "Odyssey of the Eel" by a promising young writer named Rachel Carson. Beston was surprised to find that none of his work was included in the book, although considering what he had written about narrowly scientific approaches in the Foreword to Herbert Faulkner West's book on nature writing, perhaps he should not have been. Given that Beebe had included selections by Thoreau, Muir, and Burroughs, with whom Beston was usually linked as part of the American tradition in nature writing, it is entirely possible that Beebe's exclusion of any selection written by Beston was an intentional slight; maybe even one linked to their mutual interest in Elizabeth Coatsworth many years earlier. In any event, Beston noticed his banishment from the pages of Beebe's anthology, writing to Elizabeth:

> Our friend Beebe has brought out a book on naturalists in which *I* am not mentioned. I'm a little more than a naturalist I think, but tout de meme, I'm the only one of the gang who can really write. [Donald Culross] Peattie is in it, of course, for he writes book after book, but his prose is nothing but rhinestone jewelry and the thought in it a tray of stale buns. Mais assez, for why should Beebe (who is only good paste jewelry himself) know the really good and distinguished thing? I would have liked it only for the sake of the advertising.[23]

Inclusion in such collections, however, meant more to Beston than "advertising"; it also reflected his literary standing, something he cared about far more. When Rinehart included his chapter "The Headlong Wave" from *The Outermost House* in a new anthology, *Great American Nature Writing* (1950) edited by Joseph Wood Krutch, and then John Kiernan included "The Headlong Wave" in his *Treasury of Great American Nature Writing* (1957), Beston was pleased and probably a bit relieved after the omission from Beebe's book. Still, Beston was somewhat concerned that nearly all the anthologies and critiques of nature writing only referred to *The Outermost House*, and while he was gratified *that* book, at least, had secured a lasting place in American literature, he also feared that he would come to be known as "homo unum libris." As Beston felt old age closing in, he developed a sense of his place in American literature that was a mixture of pride and regret: "It pleases me to think that in my sixties my reputation as a scholar and man of letters is more and more recognized. (Alas, the coasts of the ocean of literature are strewn with wrecks and wreckage.) I had something to say to my generation which was important; I got a good deal of it on paper, but not as much as I should have."[24]

In recognizing that he had not written as much, perhaps, as he might have, it was probably impossible for Beston to avoid comparing his own literary oeuvre with that of that of his wife. Elizabeth Coatsworth had long been one of the most prolific poets and children's writers in the country, and she received a steady stream of literary honors beginning with the Newbery medal in 1931 for *The Cat Who Went to Heaven*. Her 1952 fantasy *The Enchanted* had been nominated for a Pulitzer Prize, and in January of 1955 she placed second in a poetry contest in which Robert Tristram Coffin had taken first prize and Allen Tate had won an award as well. The vast difference between her husband's literary output and her own did not go unnoticed by Elizabeth, and at one point she decided to take a hiatus from writing for a year to see if there was any way that might allow her to help Henry along with the pace of his writing. As his daughter Kate recalled, "It didn't seem to make the slightest difference and, on New Year's Day, she took to her desk with a huge (silent) sigh of relief."[25]

Along with *The Outermost House, Herbs and the Earth*, and *Northern Farm*, Beston was particularly fond of *American Memory* and remained puzzled about why the book had not received more recognition in its time. When David McCord wrote Beston a letter several years after the publication of *American Memory* stating how much he loved the book, Beston wrote a long, musing letter in return:

> I shall long treasure so kind and heart-sustaining a letter. I use the second adjective a'purpose for *American Memory* has long been a somewhat troubling memory to the Northern Farmer. I thought I had done something really new in spirit and historical approach (in literary design, too), and, moreover, had written (or edited) a book put together with sound scholarship . . . I still feel that the introductions are original and intelligent, and that the first of them all "The unknown land awaited them with power" says something no one else has said. And I like the introductory essays on Nature in America. "The American scene takes the imagination" etc . . .

The book did reasonably well . . . [but] the reviewers just did not *get* it. (Is it lack of imagination, David?) What it has served best for is as quarry for plagiarizers. Nevins and Comager of Columbia simply stole the whole idea the following year, even lifting the idea of certain given selections. I was the first, for instance, to show that the discovery of ether was one of the most important things to happen here. And others have swiped like roughnecks in an orchard by the tracks. I have really ceased to care. But I have always felt disappointed, and it is on this old sense of disappointment that your kind letter pours its healing balm. So I shall continue to hope that one understands America better after reading my book.[26]

He felt strongly that there were times in his later books when his writing reached the high level established in *The Outermost House*: "I have always had a particular liking for the paragraph on p.4 of Herbs and the Earth, beginning with 'it is only,' and going on to p.5 to close with the word 'joy.' And the close of the paragraph on p. 138 and the final sentence on the top of p. 139. This has always given me a sense of achievement. And the metaphor remains hard to forget."[27] Beston was particularly grateful when literary critics praised his entire body of work and not just *The Outermost House*, as Stanley Kunitz and Howard Haycraft did in their laudatory entry on Beston contained in their authoritative reference book *Twentieth Century Authors*. Beston sent them a cordial note of thanks: "your distinguished comment on me included with my biography has given me heart all my personal and writing life, and that I am deeply grateful for the accolade." [28]

As Elizabeth Coatsworth stated, Beston knew at once that *The Outermost House* was the finest thing that he had ever written; but it also set a personal standard for Beston that proved impossible to ever meet again, despite the literary quality of his later work. Beston was not the first writer, nor would he be the last, that would write a masterpiece in early to mid-career and never be able to quite capture the magic again. Indeed, some of the twentieth-century writers who suffered through this frustration—Ralph Ellison and Henry Roth, to name just two prominent examples—took decades to write another book. Perhaps Joseph Heller, author of *Catch-22*, had the best response to the conundrum of how to follow up on writing a literary classic. When a critic pointed out that Heller had been unable match the literary achievement of *Catch-22* since it was published in 1961, Heller retorted that neither had anyone else.

It was probably inevitable that *The Outermost House* would be compared to Henry Thoreau's *Cape Cod*, but as time went by Beston began to chafe at the comparison. In the first place a more apt comparison would probably be to *Walden*, but in the second place Beston saw key differences between his work and that of Thoreau and John Burroughs, the writers to whom he was most often compared. He told Professor Carl J. Weber from the English Department at Colby College that he "wasn't much of a Thoreauvian" and occasionally repeated that assertion; and Elizabeth Coatsworth stated that her husband did not think that Thoreau had much heart. And yet, when he was offered to write the introduction to the new Norton edition of Thoreau's *Cape Cod* in 1951 he was honored to do so.[29] His praise of Thoreau's "obstinate and unique genius" may have been somewhat restrained, but that may well have been due to a certain anxiety of influence as well as any perceived difference in philosophy or temperament. John Burroughs had felt much the same about comparisons of his work to that of Thoreau, complaining that Thoreau was always preaching and was so disdainful of his fellows that he "would rather open his door to a woodchuck than a man." Still, there is no doubt that Beston follows in the tradition of nature writing first developed by New England transcendentalists such as Emerson and Thoreau and then picked up and carried into the twentieth century by Burroughs and John Muir, among others.[30] Beston did reluctantly concede their influence on his own work—in a letter to Elizabeth Coatsworth in the 1920s he drolly referred to himself as the "ThoreauBurrough"—but he was also quick to claim that their influence on his own writing was rather minimal. In a sense, he may have been right—the two recurring phrases that Beston uses in referring to his own work were his assertions that he always tried to stand "on the side of life" and that humankind needed to rediscover the poetic sense of mystery and wonder in nature that is part of our human heritage. This, he believed, was where his work differed most from that of Thoreau and Burroughs, although his own self-description would serve nearly as well for a description of Thoreau or Burroughs: "As a philosopher, I remain something of a Virgilian, believing that creative work with the soil and the contemplation of nature make the two best pillars of our lives as human beings. Of the seasons in Maine, I prefer the beautiful and austere winter with its silences, its splendors of sky and snow, its tonic wholesomeness of cold. We live in a rather old-fashioned way, but, please God, we shall always have winter apples to bring up from the cellar, and another log of birchwood for the fire."[31]

In his later years, as a rising tide of literary honors swept in, Beston always retained a touching sense of pride mixed with wonder and humility at each acknowledgment that his work had reached people:

> The principal thing I stand for is, I suppose, not a "return to nature" which is a phrase capable of a quite childish interpretation, but the return to a *poetic relation to Nature*. Man is out of relation to his background, and his life has grown spiritually and psychically thin. His blood has grown thin. When man is in poetic relation to his background, he achieves a religious sense of life, and this is the sense that makes him man. Without a poetic relation to Nature and to the sense of his own destiny, he's no better than woodchuck . . . isn't as good! But you'll see what I wrote in the next to last ¶ of the life. Life has no significance in these years, it's only a battle of fierce and confused instincts . . . all the delightful quality of a street corner dog-fight. And I believe what I italicized in the last chapter of the O.H. "creation is here and now"—we are not living on a mechanism running down like a clock but on an earth sustained by an ever-creating outpouring stream of the divine imagination. I stand pretty much alone in teaching just this "wisdom", and that's why I have the "public" I seem to hang on to. But do stop me. That delightful parlour pastime about writing about ones self *is getting me*.[32]

When he was elected to the American Academy of Arts and Sciences in 1954, he wrote to Margaret Smith, "I haven't the slightest idea who saw me through the American Academy [it was apparently David McCord] and all I know about it from the other eminentissimi is that election to it is a very high honor. Its about 180 years old, being the second American society of intellectuals, the first being Franklin's philosophical foundation at Philadelphia. One honorary goes in with me, Dr. Albert Schweitzer, and I am honored by his presence on the list. We have each of us been saying somewhat the same thing."[33]

The Minotaur Downstairs

While there may have been some unfortunate repercussions to being famous primarily for *The Outermost House*, the evergreen nature of that work continued to attract a wide and devoted readership. He was particularly pleased whenever he received indications that it was still read and appreciated by the younger generation, and he frequently traveled to Dartmouth to speak to Professor Herbert Faulkner West's class on nature writing, which prominently featured his book as a modern classic. On June 1, 1950 West sent Beston a copy of the final exam that he had given the class, which concluded with an essay question on *The Outermost House*; on the exam West wrote, "Take a bow, Henry!" One of the most gratifying benefits of being so well-established as a passionate advocate for a physical and spiritual relationship with nature was that he had a chance to meet numerous like-minded people. In his earlier years that reputation brought him in contact with his poetic counterpart, Robert Frost. In later years, as he became more and more associated with rural life in Maine, many other kindred spirits, including the author Scott Nearing, and Carl Buchheister, director of the Maine Audubon Society, made their way to Chimney Farm to visit with the "Northern Farmer."

One of the most gratifying connections, however, was one that had been long delayed. In August of 1940 Rachel Carson, a thirty-three-year-old writer and editor employed by the United States Department of Fisheries, was spending her summer vacation on Cape Cod while undertaking the research for her first book, *Under the Sea-Wind*. Several years earlier, while she had been a graduate student in zoology at Johns Hopkins University, Carson had borrowed a copy of *The Outermost House* from the Pratt Public Library in Baltimore and was deeply moved by Beston's exquisite prose and his profoundly spiritual response to life on the great beach. Carson would later state that the two writers whose work meant the most to her were Henry Beston and Henry Williamson, writing to a friend that since discovering their books, "I have read and reread them more times than I can count; they are among the books that I have loved best and that have influenced me the most."[34] In search of literary inspiration she and two companions drove to Eastham one day that August to find the isolated dune shack where Beston had lived during his year on the great beach. When they got to the tiny cottage, as her friend Dorothy Hamilton recalled, "She seemed much impressed by the house when we finally found it. I remember her standing looking at it a long time, in complete silence."[35]

Published shortly before the attack on Pearl Harbor in 1941, *Under the Sea-Wind* received little attention. However, when Carson's second book, *The Sea Around Us*, won the National Book Award for non-fiction in 1952 and spent eighty-six weeks on *The New York Times* best seller list, her first book was reissued. One of the book reviewers for the 1952 edition of *Under the Sea-Wind* was Henry Beston, who wrote a glowing review of the book for *The Freeman*, a respected monthly magazine. In his review Beston wrote: "It is Miss Carson's particular gift to be able to blend scientific knowledge with the spirit of poetic awareness, thus restoring to us a true sense of the world." Deeply touched by this praise from a writer whose work had meant so much to her, Carson wrote a letter to Beston in 1954, one she said that she had meant to write long ago, to tell him how greatly she admired his work and how much *The Outermost House* had meant to her:

> Although this letter is a result of a telephone conversation with Carl Buchheister, it is, in a way, at least twenty years overdue. It was about that long ago That I discovered *The Outermost House* in a corner of the Pratt Library in Baltimore. I hesitate to guess how many times I have read the book since then, but I don't hesitate to say that I can think of few others that have given me such deep and lasting pleasure, or to which I can return with such assurance of a renewal of my original enjoyment.
>
> While I was writing *Under the Sea-Wind* I spent part of a summer at Woods Hole and one day drove to Eastham and walked down the beach to find the little house and the surroundings with which I felt so familiar through your pages. The daughter of one of your Harvard contemporaries, Mr. George Hamilton was with me. After that happy experience I wanted to write you, but procrastinated. Then, a year or more ago, some one sent me a clipping of your review of *Under the Sea-Wind* (I had missed the review on its appearance). Let me tell you now, though belatedly, that I found it the most beautiful, perceptive, and deeply satisfying one I had read, and because of my feeling about *The Outermost House*, I was so grateful it was you who had written it.
>
> Recently I acquired a bit of Maine coast at Southport and built a cot-

tage overlooking Sheepscot Bay; last summer we occupied it for the first time—my mother and I. Next week I am going to open the cottage and spend a few days there. When I was in New York earlier this week, I called Mr. Buchheister to ask whether veeries would be singing this early, and where. He immediately suggested I ask you about localities. To me the song of the veery is one of the most deeply moving of bird voices, and I should love to hear them again in Maine.[36]

Upon receiving Carson's letter, Beston invited her to visit him at Chimney Farm, which she and her friend Dorothy Freeman soon did. Beston gave Carson a copy of *Northern Farm* and sent her a copy of *The St. Lawrence* and *Henry Beston's Fairy Tales* a few months later.[37] The visit began a cordial friendship between Henry and Elizabeth Beston and Rachel Carson, and they exchanged regular letters and visits throughout the remainder of Carson's life.

Although he was nearing seventy, a constant stream of requests for lectures and other speaking engagements kept Beston busy. He was frequently invited to speak at numerous colleges, including Geneseo, Bowdoin, and Dartmouth, and had become a regular lecturer at the New York Historical Association's Seminar on American Folklore in Cooperstown, New York. The attention directed toward him at such events was truly gratifying to Beston and ameliorated his fears that his literary legacy would prove to be ephemeral. He wrote to Elizabeth after one such affair, "I am just home from Dartmouth. The visit was a gigantic success. No one could have been a more thoughtful host than Herbert West; I went to party after party; my lecture was highly approved of, and at the social gatherings I do think about everybody would have echoed Demetrius' cry in the Midsummer Night's Dream, 'Well-roared, lion!' I had a whole bevy of the most beautiful ladies gathered about me like lovely birds at a fountain."[38] A month later he was honored by Bowdoin College at their annual commencement ceremonies with an honorary Doctor of Humane Letters degree. As he wrote to his friend Rosalind Richards about the ceremony:

I found myself moved more deeply than I had expected. When the accolade was given me and the noble, austere hood of the doctorate passed over my head, I really felt a kind of new dedication stir the fire on the hearth of existence, and bring the consumed wood to a new glowing. When I was a whelp at Adams Academy in Quincy, I won the "Prize for Speaking" in my senior year, and the gold medal bore to one side a fine head of Cicero and the august Aceronian phrase "verbo animi proferre,"—to put forth the words of the soul." I really have tried to live by the beautiful phrase: I have never once been consciously false to it: I only wish I might have written more. Perhaps now there may come a late-arriving flourish.

I felt so grateful to be a part of an occasion in which the dignity of wisdom was honored with the beautiful symbols of the tradition of learning. More than ever am I convinced that "man" must have the sacramental as part of the life of the human spirit if "man" is to remain Man. We live by symbols; without them and the poets who give them to us, and restore them, our poor, troubled race can not grow the feather of a wing.[39]

Learning that *The Outermost House* would go into its eighteenth printing that year was a boost to Beston's spirits. In his notebook he wrote down a few lines that had a particular resonance for him, a quote from Rainer Maria Rilke's *Letters to a Young Poet*: "Works of art are of an infinite loneliness and with nothing to be so little reached as criticism. Only love can grasp and hold and fairly judge them."

Elizabeth spent much of the summer of 1956 in Claremont, California, helping out Kate and Dick, who were expecting their first child. When the Beston's first grandchild, Elizabeth Coatsworth Barnes, was born on August 7, 1956, Henry flew out to California to join the family. Henry and Elizabeth stayed at the Claremont Inn (which soon became a second home for them while in California) for another two weeks, reluctant to leave Kate, Dick, and Elizabeth's namesake grandchild. Meanwhile, Meg and Dorik Mechau, who had become engaged in March, were anxiously waiting to see if Dorik was to be inducted into the military. "I've met the brat," Henry wrote in his sardonic way; "he will do, so to speak, and I hope Meg will be illuminated by some idea of duty towards the poor lad. He is a Coloradan, half German, half Russian, one younger brother, two young married sisters. Name? Dorik Mechau. God help him!"[40] It was not until autumn they learned that he would not be drafted, upon which they decided for a November wedding. On November 10 they were wed in Nobleboro in a quiet ceremony with about twenty-five family and close friends in attendance.

The Minotaur Downstairs

The Indian summer flurry of activity in 1956 was followed by a much more measured pace at Chimney Farm following Meg's wedding. For the most part, Beston's days fell into a predictable and comfortable pattern at the farm—"People ring me up; people drop in; I work, I cook, I garden, I weed, I write." Exchanges of letters with friends such as Luther Neff now often focused on physical maladies. When Neff was hospitalized for a urinary tract problem, Beston wrote a sympathetic note to his old shipmate: "We are all so profusely troubled that you have been in the hospital and have been subjected to an operation. My blood chills at the thought of so beloved and honored a friend having to undergo the trial. I know of course, that such an operation is a life saver, and a great alleviator of pain; all the same it chills me that one so deeply loved as you should have to go through it."[41] Henry noted that he was himself bracing for a double operation for cataracts that summer, and would soon have to be fitted for a complete set

J. Luther Neff and Henry Beston at Chimney Farm, early 1950s. Beston met Reverend Neff, who was the chaplain on board the battleship U.S.S. *United States*, while Beston was a war correspondent in 1917.

of dentures as he was down to his last surviving tooth. "What fearsome things the poor body can let us in for!" wrote Beston. "Surely youth is the time to enjoy it, the time to sink one's teeth into a steak, the moment to seize upon a boiled lobster, the moment to slap a fair daughter of Eve upon the sitz-platz! (Wonderful Teutonic word). As one grows older one grows—so they say—a bit mellower and wiser, but you have to have help on the cellar stairs with the bag of potatoes."[42]

As the physical ailments of old age became more frequent, Beston sadly looked back at the past and mused,

> Alas what a troubled time is the onset of old age. All one's close and beloved friends are suddenly found to be ill and are carried off for an operation; or worse, vanish forever out of life leaving the world so much smaller. I was thinking the other day that nobody now alive remembers me as a college boy. They are all gone. I shall see no more, "the old, familiar faces." As for "the little window where the sun came peeping in at noon," . . . that's probably a garage or a filling station. So life renews itself, a necessary task and rather a cruel one in its procedure.[43]

Such *memento mori* served only to deepen Beston's occasional fits of melancholia, which were often accompanied by outbursts of frustrated fury. When Dylan Thomas had poetically urged his own father to "Rage, rage, against the dying of the light," perhaps he was fortunate that he did not get that for which he had wished. In late December of 1957, Elizabeth Coatsworth (*sans* Henry) traveled to California to help out Kate, who had just had her second child, Harold. "It is a joy a thousand times to have Mother here," Kate wrote, "She likes the house, she likes the baby. Our various friends are hailed in to tea or coffee to meet her—but not too many or too fast." Now that Kate was herself an adult, with a husband and children of her own, the close relationship she had with her mother had grown even closer, and apparently more frank. One night while Dick was working in his study, Kate wrote to her aunt Margaret, "we had a long discussion of home life—hers—brought on by me. Besides making my blood boil & filling me with awe & admiration, it made me thank goodness for *you*."[44] Some years later in an interview with Don Wilding, Barnes addressed the seeming paradox of her father, a writer who displays such confidence and serenity in his prose, being so irritable in his home life: "You see, all of us who write put our best selves into our writing, so that the reader's impression of the whole person is bound to be skewed. They say, you know, that people are often keen to meet a favorite writer, then are disappointed when they do—and they shouldn't be . . . there's a lot more to the living, whole person, and not all of it is happy."[45]

In January of 1958 Henry sailed to California by freighter to see his first male grandchild, and to go on a sailing cruise along the California coast. While Henry was sailing and observing the southward migration of the gray whales swimming to the calving lagoons of southern California, Elizabeth and Kate relished their time together with the children. "The household in the little stone house is *also* in bloom," wrote Elizabeth, "and my heart with it. Liz is such a dear independent little thing and the baby a blue-eyed bambino . . . Kate and I spent most of Saturday driving behind her steady saddle horse, in a two-wheeled cart along her favorite bridle paths, wide enough for such a conveyance, higher and higher into the uninhabited hills." Perhaps it was his time on the sea, or perhaps it was the birth of a grandson, but Henry seemed to be in particularly good spirits, and while he was sailing Elizabeth commented, "It will be lovely to have him here."[46] Dick Barnes was now teaching English at Pomona College, so Henry and Elizabeth roomed at the Claremont Inn at the campus, making frequent visits to Kate and Dick's little stone cottage in the hills before returning to Maine in April.

That June Meg and Dorik arrived at the farm, bringing along their first child, Clarissa. They stayed at the little writing cottage near the lake that Beston had built years earlier, and it seemed that much of the combativeness between Henry and Meg that had gone on for years was forgotten under the ameliorative influence of Dorik (whom Henry had come to like very much) and the baby. "Henry thinks that Clarissa can do no wrong," Elizabeth wrote to her sister; "Meg came into my room one afternoon & found him on his hands & knees with her. Meg is pleased and he is pleased and—so far so far! The atmosphere has been much better than one might expect. Dorik is brown with lots of canoeing and some swimming though the water has been colder than usual—today they are taking us for lobster at Pemaquid."[47] While Meg was visiting, Elizabeth and Henry received word that Kate was expecting again, something that concerned her mother: "third baby on the way and there are other things she'd like to do with her life . . . Meg, on the other hand, would be perfectly content with that." The visit went so well, in fact, that Meg and Dorik returned with Clarissa for a longer, ten-day stay at the farm in August, although Elizabeth never let her guard down: "Henry very tolerant, But always the sleeping volcano! (sleeping so far!)."[48]

Now seventy years old, Beston passed up the opportunity to once again serve as one of the faculty for the Cooperstown Seminar that summer, but other than that the yen for travel seemed to continue unabated. He received an honorary degree from the University of Maine at Orono in June and then went on a tour of Nova Scotia in September. While they now traveled more slowly, wrote Elizabeth to her sister, usually a hundred miles a day or less, Henry was once again in the mood to drive as his cataracts and energies had not permitted for some time: "The winds of the spirit blow and are still, and blow again."[49] After taking the car ferry across the Gulf of Maine—"an ocean voyage in miniature," commented Henry—they drove throughout the country in western Nova Scotia made famous by Longfellow's poem "Evangeline," before heading east to the Atlantic side where, wrote Beston, "The bays & estuaries there make their way long miles inland . . . it was a bit alarming to find a huge freighter apparently making its way through the great wilderness of spruce."[50] After leaving Nova Scotia they drove through Maine and New Hampshire to Vermont, where they stayed at the famed Trapp Family Lodge and visited the Sherburne Museum just south of Burlington before returning home.

Elizabeth stayed at the farm for only about a week, traveling to Buffalo to give a lecture at the University at Buffalo's Lockwood Library on September 28, 1958. Upon arriving in Buffalo Elizabeth felt extremely tired, but attributing that simply to all the traveling she and Henry had been doing, did not let that prevent her from giving her talk at the university—despite the fact that her fatigue was now accompanied by a sore throat and a fever of 104 degrees. After the talk she called her sister Margaret, who was so concerned by Elizabeth's description of the symptoms, drove to Buffalo the following day and took her to the hospital, where after undergoing a weeklong battery of tests, the doctors told Elizabeth she had leukemia. Upon learning of the diagnosis, Margaret and Elizabeth drove to Hingham, where Margaret could nurse her sister within a short distance of the Boston's excellent hospitals should they become needed. While Elizabeth took the news of her illness calmly, it would not be until November 12 that she felt well enough to return to Chimney Farm. The trip home was comfortable and uneventful, and Henry was waiting for her at the train station in Portland when she arrived. The one "untoward" moment she wrote, came when Henry—seemingly apropos of nothing—said to Elizabeth, "Well, you have a grave if you want it." "I don't" said I, "at this time, anyway."

Beston's remark was not coldly unfeeling or, as Elizabeth thought, simply a disconnected thought from out of the blue. In June, longtime friend Mary Cabot Wheelwright had visited the Bestons at Chimney Farm, "full of plans, interests, [and] affections"; but just a few weeks later she suddenly died. A woman staying with Wheelwright in her Northeast Harbor home on Mount Desert island reported that after complaining about a touch of indigestion, Wheelwright had gone upstairs to her room, lay down on her bed, opened a book, and soon slipped into a fatal coma.[51] Mortality was again foremost in Beston's mind, so now that Elizabeth was home Henry assumed the role of nurse, making certain that she took her medication at the proper times and sending her off to take a nap each afternoon regardless of whether she wanted one. "Henry is being very nice," Elizabeth wrote to Margaret, adding hopefully "After the first day or two, I think he'll relax."[52] Elizabeth's physician in Boston, Doctor Frank Gardner, gave Elizabeth a blood test shortly before her arrival home, and called with the encouraging news that the medication she was being given had driven her white cell count down from 140,000 to 28,000. That meant, as she wrote her sister Margaret, that the pills she was on "will do the business for the present at least."[53]

Henry Beston at Chimney Farm, 1961.

CHAPTER THIRTEEN

On the Side of Life
1959–1968

"No leaf is left
To rustle faintly,
No stream is left
To sing and flow,
In silence night
Darkens the woodlands.
In silence Orion
Shines over the snow.

ELIZABETH COATSWORTH
"Now Fall Asleep"
Country Poems (1942)

BY JANUARY 1959 Elizabeth was feeling strong enough to travel to California with Henry to see Kate, who had recently given birth to her third child. Kate and Dick named the baby Henry Beston Barnes, which touched Beston to his very core. At dinner one night he held forth on the topic of whether the baby should go to Harvard or Bowdoin, and where he should go to abroad for graduate work. "Henry is touchingly happy," Elizabeth wrote to Margaret, "[he] has stood outside the picture and now for the first time he's drawn into it and I am happy for him, and his 'plans' for the baby will do no harm, as they well might for a son."[1] Henry had become fond of staying at the Claremont Inn, which was conveniently close to the Barnes home, so he and Elizabeth spent the rest of the winter in California visiting with Kate and the grandchildren.

In late February, Henry took a short trip to Panama, so Elizabeth came to stay at the Barnes home. Kate was busy with the three children and Dick was trying to balance his teaching schedule at the University of California at Riverside with working on his doctoral dissertation for the graduate program at Harvard, so they were particularly glad to have Elizabeth's help. "The babies are most taken with her and she with them," wrote Kate to her aunt, "On school mornings I am always very busy making Dick's breakfast and his lunch and she feeds the little baby for me, a *great* help. Dick is overjoyed to have her here. With all her busyness she finds time to read his thesis and encourage him."[2] For her part, Elizabeth thoroughly enjoyed the chance to be a part of Kate's thriving family, and was tremendously impressed by how well Kate managed the household: "I've had a very happy time," Elizabeth wrote to her sister, "living along with the family & the babies and going on most wonderful expeditions, to the desert, to the mountains, to the missions . . . I'm quite expert at feeding and changing Hal. Kate is wonderful, feeding *everything*; babies, cat, dog, horse & as many as seven adults at the same time."[3]

Three weeks later, Henry returned from his trip and although Kate noted that he looked well upon his return, she also thought that he looked considerably older than he had the previous year—"although," she said, "I could be mistaken."[4] In mid-April the Bestons flew to Boston and then took the train up to Maine, but they spent relatively little time at Chimney Farm that summer, making excursions to Harvard to attend a memorial service for Ted Roosevelt Jr., a voyage through the Great Lakes, and a trip to Quebec. In mid-October, Henry and Elizabeth went to Cape Cod for the first time in several years. Beston drove out to check on the Fo'castle but he and Elizabeth opted for more comfortable quarters at a local inn. More of their time was spent visiting old friends like George and Yngve Rongner, Burton Kelley, and Kenneth Young's family than on the beach—although Beston still had a proprietary enough feeling about the Great Beach to point out in a letter to David McCord that "I do wish that the critics wouldn't say that H.T. [Henry Thoreau] invented the term 'the great beach.' That is the coinage of H.B."[5]

Harvard University's class of 1909 marked its fiftieth anniversary in 1959, and for the class report Beston, identifying himself as Henry Beston Sheahan so as not to confuse his former classmates, supplemented his biographical outline with a note that offers a concise summary of his out-look as he entered his seventies:

> Because I am a countryman by temperament, loathing the modern city with its violences and barbarities, I have spent my life in the country, having had the good fortune to be able to live winter and summer at my farm in Maine. It is some years since I have published a new book, but the duties of a literary career are unending; moreover, I have never lost my eager interest in the vast drama of nature and the forever changing spectacle on the tremendous stage. My friend David McCord has said that I am a "sky person" and that my literary work is always interested in the look of the sky, in the changing beauty and wonder of clouds and light, in the colours of the winds, and in the vast circlings of the great planets and the constellations as I watch them through the round of our country year. I confess that I do not find the rural life quite as easy to carry on as I once did.
>
> Both my daughters are married, the elder to a young mathematician working with the Harvard Observatory, the younger to a college instructor in California. My wife's children's books continue to maintain their high standing.
>
> Although I am not definitely associated with either the administration or the faculty of any college, my life is taking on more and more an academic quality. I lecture at Dartmouth every year where the manuscript of *The Outermost House* is in the treasure room of the Baker Library; I speak at various other institutions. The friendship of dear Bowdoin, from whom I had my first honorary degree, has meant worlds to me, and this very year the good University of Maine also gathered me into its honorary fold. The young people come to call at the farm, and we sit round the great open fire-place and discuss the world, the times, and the human spirit. The young American is a very good sort, and I like his contemporary good manners.
>
> Now as to my philosophy of life—for I have no doctrine. If something is wrong with man's world, something is wrong with man, and the something in this case is an alienation from Nature unexampled in human history. Nature is studied and analyzed, yes; the world's eye is busy with mathemat-ical formulae and the microscope, but the sustaining sense of beauty and wonder has largely vanished from heart and mind. The moon is no more the moon, but an astronomical subject at which we fire idiotic projectiles; the blessed sun is no more the great life-giving, life-ruling luminary. This

alienation is having an effect on human nature. In particular, something has gone awry with the power and warmth of emotion; the mass incinerations which the nations are preparing in case of war are the devices of fiends, not of human beings. In addition to this aridity of emotion, something very serious has happened to the sense of reality. Man no longer seems to know in what kind of a world he has been placed. It is only when man is part of the wholeness of Nature and regards Nature with the poetic spirit that he is really man. Are not all his religions merely great poems? Modern man has dismissed too great a part of himself.[6]

By that winter it was becoming more evident that Kate's observation about her father's condition was accurate. Beston had developed a chronic case of gout in his right foot, and after a heavy December snowfall went outside without his cane and fell. As the frustrated Elizabeth wrote to her sister, "Henry went out yesterday without his cane (*why?*) walked into a snowdrift (*why?*) fell & couldn't get up, yelled and yelled until at last Helen heard him, went out & had to pull him 3 times to his feet before he was able to keep them."[7] It wasn't until late January that they were able to get away from Maine and fly to California for their now annual winter stay near Kate and the children. Like Kate, Elizabeth was now convinced that Henry was slowing down, as chronic high blood pressure, hardening of the arteries, gout and a series of minor ailments took their toll. She wrote a letter to her sister that described a troubling dream she'd had: "Last night I dreamed that you were running down a corridor, crying, and that I ran after you, and put my arms about you and said that you must accept the fact of death. Then the dream stopped, but not my concern."[8]

Beston returned home to Chimney Farm in early April of 1960 to find a letter had arrived that completely rejuvenated his spirits. The American Academy of Arts and Sciences notified Beston that he would be the recipient in October of the Emerson-Thoreau Medal for Achievement in Literature. Beston was to be the third writer named as winner of the award—Robert Frost was the first in 1958 and T.S. Eliot the second in 1959. The award was particularly meaningful to Beston because it recognized his entire oeuvre, not just one work. When Elizabeth returned to Chimney Farm a few weeks later she was pleased to see how high her husband's spirits were—Henry was now using a foot vibrator in an attempt to alleviate the pain from his gout and he had entered into a daily walking regimen in an attempt to regain his strength after months of relative inactivity. In August Beston suffered a setback when he suffered a small stroke—one of many such "upsets" as Elizabeth called them, over the next several years. Within just a few weeks, however, he was steadier on his feet and surer of his words, and the trip to Boston to for the award ceremony in mid-October went off smoothly. Beston's old friend David McCord, himself a member of the Academy of Arts and Sciences, delivered the introductory remarks in which he praised Beston's "steadfast devotion to his art, his personal belief in 'the habitual vision of greatness,' the devotion of yourself, and the land and sea and sky which led to the award."[9] In his own remarks, Beston read passages from *The Outermost House*, *Northern Farm*, *The St. Lawrence*, and *Herbs and the Earth*, "emphasizing his relationship to nature, which is essentially religious," as the Academy reported in its *Bulletin* of November 1960.[10] After the trip home, Elizabeth wrote a letter of thanks to David McCord: "You know, through you, Henry will never now have the sense of not having had his work recognized. We stayed awake late Wednesday night and some time in the early hours I said 'Not asleep yet?' And Henry's voice came through the dark 'I'm too happy to sleep.'"[11]

Just a few days after returning to Maine, however, the excitement of the trip caught up to him and Beston suffered another stroke. "No more trips to Boston for Thanksgiving or Christmas," Elizabeth wrote to her sister, "even California looks dim to me but by January he may be very much himself. Day by day."[12] Elizabeth now served both as nurse and secretary, taking down Henry's letters by dictation as they responded to the many congratulatory letters that came in after the Emerson-Thoreau award ceremony. Given his uncertain health, Elizabeth was rather surprised when Henry insisted that not only should they travel to California for the holidays, but that the trip to a warmer climate might have a salutary effect on his health. Despite Beston's eagerness to travel, the journey took a great deal out of him; soon after arriving in Claremont he fell ill once again and spent much of the next four months shuttling between the hospital and their customary lodgings at the Claremont Inn. "When he's bad," fretted Elizabeth, "he stumbles and shuffles along on my arm & his cane & can scarcely walk up the inn. When he's good he wakes up feeling hungry for breakfast and has a much happier day."[13] The bad days, however, came with more frequency now, and Beston spent most of the February 1961 in the hospital resting and undergoing tests. His doctors believed that at least part of the cause for his now habitual unsteadiness when he stood was due to wild swings in blood pressure, so when he was finally released from the hospital in March he was given rubber stockings and an abdominal brace in the hope they would ameliorate the condition.

With all the medical issues Beston was dealing with, there was one rather unexpected change for the better during this time. Whether it was an unexpected side effect of the strokes, finally receiving attention for his literary accomplishments, or simply spending so much more time with his daughters and their families, all the anger and frustration that had smoldered over the past twenty years had almost magically disappeared. Political rants and frustration over what he might have written and didn't were no longer an issue and Beston became once again—albeit in a physically feebler form—the friendly, gregarious, optimistic person of his youth. His family noticed this as well, with the surprised Elizabeth noting that Henry didn't fight against his hospital visits as he once had and now seemed quite happy to be surrounded by friendly, attentive nurses and physicians. She noticed too that Kate, who along with her sister Meg had sometimes clashed with her father, "has been so loving and attendant upon him and he is so happy about it, and she, too, in making her peace with the past."[14] On April 8, 1961 Kate published a poem in *The New Yorker* that began with the line "Shake hands with Hector the dog," which became a catchphrase with Henry, who would hold out his hand and say "Shake hands with Hector the dog" whenever Kate visited. Relations between Henry and Meg had even noticeably approved. Meg and Dorik were now living in Cambridge, Massachusetts, with their three children, and when Beston was finally well enough to fly to Boston, Dorik cheerfully offered to drive him up to Maine.

The summer of 1961 was a very quiet one at Chimney Farm. Henry no longer read or wrote much as his cataracts made such pursuits difficult. He would often wander around the farm looking at whatever flowers were in bloom, or gazing out at the lake, sometimes mustering the strength to walk to the barn and ascend the stairs to his old study in the attic, the "Barnatheum," as he had dubbed it. His 73rd birthday on June 1st passed serenely; Elizabeth wrote: "Henry sits by the window, opening and enjoying his presents. He is delighted with the candy. When bears cease to love honey & Henry no longer cares for candy, the world will come to an end!"[15] Occasionally he would rouse himself to activity, but as often as not the result was inexplicable, as when he got it into his mind that they needed a new truck for the farm. He drove into Waldoboro and returned with a new International Harvester four-wheel drive light truck painted what Elizabeth called a "peacock green." It was a waste of money, she said, but "Anyway, it's a *fait accompli* and I don't try to spoil it for him though I tried to rouse his common sense beforehand (in vain)."[16] Knowing the precarious state of Beston's health, fewer visitors came to call at Chimney Farm other than family members such as Margaret Smith and nieces Marie and Joan Sheahan.

After months of slow physical improvement, Beston took a step backward in October when he suffered another stroke. The disappointed Elizabeth wrote to her sister, "After nearly eight months of slowly climbing up the ladder,—and so patiently and uncomplainingly!—Henry had another upset yesterday afternoon. Just how far this will put him back who can say?"[17] By December Beston was still unsteady on his feet but feeling well enough to insist that they take their annual trip to California to visit Kate—who was once again expecting—and her family for Christmas. The flight was a late one and they didn't get in to Claremont until one a.m. The strain was apparently too much for Henry, who had another stroke during the night and crawled to the bathroom on his hands and knees. He spent Christmas in a local hospital and was discharged on New Year's Day, 1962. Henry and Elizabeth spent much of the winter at the Claremont Inn, reading and enjoying visits from Kate and the children, although when they were alone Henry often sat at the window and talked of Chimney Farm, yearning for Maine and home. It was now apparent to Elizabeth that it was unlikely that they would be able to spend winters in California with Kate and her family as they had for the last several years, but as usual she stoically accepted the fact, keeping the disappointment to herself.

Since his trip to Cape Cod in the fall of 1959, Beston had been struggling with the issue of what to do with the Fo'castle. Since its last relocation, it no longer sat precariously atop the dunes, but was now nestled in the marshland—a somewhat safer, if less magnificent location. It was still a popular destination for artists and writers who could borrow the key to the cottage from Kenneth Young and stay at the famed dune shack: two of the visitors included poets Ted Hughes and his wife Sylvia Plath. On some of the paper, with a Chimney Farm letterhead, that Beston had left at the cottage years before, Plath wrote a tribute to him entitled "The Hermit at Outermost House" that is included in her *Collected Poems*. Despite his fondness for the Cape and his dune shack, Beston realized that it was probably time to let go of the beloved Fo'castle and pass it on. He contacted the Audubon Society in Wellfleet and offered to donate the Fo'castle and the land on which it was situated for the use of the Audubon Society and visiting artists, writers, and naturalists. The details were soon arranged and in the summer of 1961, after nearly thirty years, the beloved Fo'castle passed out of Beston's hands. Paradoxically, Beston's world on the great beach of Cape Cod seemed more vivid and alive in his mind than it had in many years. Eastham was celebrating its 300th anniversary as a township in 1963, and the Fo'castle became a central part of the celebration. A retired army colonel, Eugene Clark, a great admirer of *The Outermost House*, visited Chimney Farm on June 20, 1963 (just a day after the famed photographer Eliot Porter also visited), bringing audiotapes with greetings from seventeen of Henry's old friends at Eastham. Clark took numerous photos of Beston and recorded an interview with him to bring back with him to Cape Cod, understanding that the chance of Beston visiting his friends on the Cape ever again was slight.

The following year, however, brought a compelling opportunity for one final visit to Cape Cod and the Fo'castle for Henry Beston. On a crisp autumn day, October 11, 1964, at an amphitheater outside the headquarters of the recently created Cape Cod National Seashore in Eastham, Massachusetts, a coterie of dignitaries gathered on a makeshift stage flanking the frail, 76-year-old Beston and his wife. Elizabeth wore a black coat with a thick fur collar and had on a velvet hat. Henry wore a brown tweed sport coat and scarf, with a black basque cap on his head. Several hundred

[326]

people were packed into the amphitheater, which sat four hundred, and even more stood outside, close enough to see and hear the speakers who had gathered to pay tribute to Beston and *The Outermost House*. Governor Endicott Peabody of Massachusetts served as master of ceremonies for the event honoring Beston and designating the nearby Fo'castle as a national literary landmark. The idea of honoring Beston was the brainchild of Ivan Sandrof, literary editor of the *Worcester Telegram and Gazette* and had been enthusiastically advanced by Governor Peabody and his wife Toni. After an invocation delivered by Reverend Daniel Weck, pastor of the Eastham Universalist Church, Governor Peabody began the tribute to Beston. He lavishly praised the elegance of Beston's writing and its now widely recognized role in changing American attitudes toward the natural world: "We are here today partly because you have given the American people a heightened awareness of the outer beach as part of our way of life . . . *The Outermost House*, as a testament, has had immeasurable influence."[18]

After a brief tribute by Robert Gibbs, the superintendent of the Cape Cod National Seashore and Allen Morgan of the Massachusetts Audubon Society, the governor introduced George Palmer from the northeast regional office of the Department of the Interior. Palmer, who was on hand to represent Secretary of the Interior Stewart Udall, described the impact that *The Outermost House* had on the creation of the Cape Cod National Seashore. When the National Park Service was surveying the area with the idea of protecting it as a national seashore, said Palmer, they had compiled an enormous amount of information and written a voluminous report on the subject. He then read a short passage from *The Outermost House*: "Outermost cliff and solitary dune, the plain of ocean and the far, bright rims of the world, meadow land and marsh and ancient moor: this is Eastham; this the outer Cape. Sun and moon rise here from the sea, the arched sky has an ocean vastness, the clouds are now of ocean, now of earth." He paused for effect, then turned to Beston and said, "It seems to me, Mr. Beston, that it took several chapters of the report just to say this."[19] The overflow crowd responded with laughter and a wave of applause.

As the encomiums for Beston went on, Toni Peabody noticed that the guest of honor was becoming chilled and leaned over to wrap a woolen blanket around his thin legs. With some difficulty Henry stood and walked slowly to the lectern; as he did so, the crowd spontaneously rose to their feet and gave him a standing ovation. Beston quietly thanked the governor, his wife, and the other guests who had gathered to honor him and his work, saying, "We are all of one joy in knowing that the Great Beach where we stand has been set aside by our government. You have honored human awareness that perceives the nature about us and attempts to find words to give another kind of harmony, human, as well as that of the elements."[20] In closing his remarks, Beston read from his conclusion to *The Outermost House*, his voice gaining strength as he read:

> Whatever attitude to human existence you fashion for yourself, know that it is valid only if it be the shadow of an attitude to Nature. A human life, so often likened to a spectacle upon a stage, is more justly a ritual. The ancient values of dignity, beauty, and poetry which sustain us are of Nature's inspiration; they are born of the mystery and beauty of the world. Do no dishonour to the earth lest you dishonor the spirit of man. Hold your hands out over the earth as over a flame. To all who love her, who open to her the doors of their veins, she gives of her strength, sustaining them with her own measureless tremor of dark life. Touch the earth, love the earth, honour the earth, her plains, her valleys, her hills, and her seas; rest your spirit in her solitary places. For the gifts of life are the earth's and they are given to all, and they are the songs of birds at daybreak, Orion and the Bear, and the dawn seen over ocean from the beach.[21]

A short time later, five beach buggies carrying the Bestons and dignitaries from the ceremony—which Beston humorously referred to as "the coronation"—made their way from the amphitheater to the beach, where they traveled about a mile before stopping at the Fo'castle. Numerous reporters and other visitors followed along and watched as Elizabeth Coatsworth and Governor Peabody helped Beston from the car and supported him as he walked slowly up the steps to the dune shack. Ralph Hickok, a reporter for the New Bedford, Massachusetts *Standard-Times* wrote, "Mr. Beston looked around the larger room wordlessly, as one who meets an old dear friend after many years."[22] Some photographers asked Beston if they could get a picture of him at the kitchen pump, and the governor passed him a glass from the nearby cupboard. The pump was primed, and Beston worked the handle, pouring himself a glass of water and drinking from it as the photographers snapped away. A few minutes later the Bestons were taken back to park headquarters as the throng of visitors slowly filed their way into the shack. When the crowds cleared and dusk fell, the Bestons got back in their car for the long, slow drive back to Maine and Chimney Farm.

This would be Henry's last visit to the Fo'castle, and the "coronation" would be the last time he ventured so far from Chimney Farm. It was fortunate that Elizabeth's medication was keeping her leukemia in check, for she once again devoted a great deal of her energy to caring for Henry who, she told her sister, was now "so helpless—can't walk, talks with difficulty, hears with difficulty, scarcely reads, and even his food doesn't taste as it used to taste, and often he has little appetite. T.V.? No! even the Victrola which he enjoyed last year, he doesn't want this year."[23] When Henry felt up to it, Elizabeth took dictation to help him respond to some of the many letters he received after the October ceremony designating the Fo'castle a National Literary Landmark. Beston's correspondence regarding "the coronation" included congratulations from writers such as fellow Cape Cod naturalist John Hay and novelist Kurt Vonnegut, who wrote, "Fourteen years ago you wrote a friendly letter to me about my first book, which was called 'Player Piano.' I'm six books into life now. Yesterday I went to hear you speak at the Cape Cod National Seashore, was proud that our lives should have touched at some point, was moved by what your life has been and what you had to say. Your wife is lovely. Your park is lovely."[24] Beston's old friend Herbert Faulkner West wrote from Hanover, New Hampshire, to congratulate Henry and to say that the course at Dartmouth that Beston had so often visited was now discontinued: "Alas, the nature writers course is no more!! Emeritus professor now!!"[25]

On January 19, 1965, Beston woke with labored breathing and a high fever that worried Elizabeth sufficiently to call for an ambulance to take him to Miles Memorial Hospital in Damariscotta. He was diagnosed with pneumonia, but the doctors also found an inflammation around the heart. Even once the pneumonia was cleared up, Beston's heart condition, as well as his poor circulation and continuing fever, continued to be of concern. Elizabeth was so worried about his condition that she called to let the children know how sick their father was and was relieved to hear that Dorik Mechau planned to immediately drive up from Cambridge to help out. Elizabeth told her sister that she was going to keep his coming a secret, since it would be such a pleasant surprise for Henry: "I'm sure his coming will be a shot in the arm. He is just the right person for all of us."[26] Remarkably, Beston managed to recover sufficiently to return home to the farm by mid-February, although Elizabeth complained that he was often a challenging patient, slyly spitting out his medication when he thought she wasn't looking and shuffling around the house at all hours of the day and night. "It's not safe," she confided to Margaret, "but after all, nothing can stop him as he feels his means of locomotion returning."[27]

By April, as Henry got a little bit stronger and his night rambles continued unabated, Elizabeth gave in to the inevitable—she had already asked Ralph, the farm's hired hand, to watch over Henry during part of the day, and she now hired someone to help keep watch over him at night. When Beston heard that the theater department at Bowdoin College in Brunswick was staging three short Irish plays (one by Shaw and one by Beckett) in late April, he insisted that the four of them go to see them, so they rented a wheelchair for Henry and went to the theater. Elizabeth marveled that although Henry was so excited that he barely slept a wink that night after returning home from the performance, that he seemed perfectly fine the next morning. The experiment went off so well, that when a performance of Brecht's *Threepenny Opera* was staged at Bowdoin the following month they went to see that as well: "The boys did wonderfully. It was almost professional & Henry enjoyed every minute. He goes in a wheelchair, crawls up the steps, snails down the aisle & everyone is so gentle with him & he never complains against fate. His *will* to go to 'Live Theatre' is extraordinary. Nothing can stand in its way. Though he is sleepy this morning, there are no signs of ill effects."[28]

Now that Henry—and by extension Elizabeth—were no longer able to do any traveling, Chimney Farm was once again the center of their world, and visits from family and friends were social high points. During the remainder of 1965 they were treated to visits by Meg, Dorik, and their children; old friends Alva and Amy Morrison; Kate and her children; and Henry's nieces Marie and Joan Sheahan. Meg and Henry got along better than they had for years—age and infirmity having defused the "sleeping volcano"—and when the Mechaus stayed at the farm for a Christmas visit, it was evident how much he had changed. No longer was the tumult of a house full of children a distraction and annoyance; it was now a comfort: "Perky [the Bestons' dog] is beside herself with pleasure at having four little people more or less on her level, and likely to drop crumbs—Henry asks 'where are the children?' He likes to have them around, receives their kisses & then barricades himself quietly behind a book."[29]

Although Beston was no longer able to write, there were frequent cheering reminders that his work was still remembered and cherished. He regularly received letters from people—among them Nan Waldron, who would later write *Journey to Outermost House*—thanking him for the opportunity to stay at the Fo'castle through the Audubon Society. He also received

Henry Beston, Elizabeth Coatsworth, and their friend artist Maurice "Jake" Day, at a book signing in Maine, ca. 1965.

occasional inquiries from television producers and filmmakers interested in doing programs and films on *The Outermost House*, although none of these projects came to fruition. While he was unable to make the trip, Beston was pleased to receive an invitation from the Department of the Interior to attend as a guest of honor the dedication ceremony on May 30, 1966, formally establishing the Cape Cod National Seashore. It was no coincidence that the dedication of the Great Beach as a National Seashore helped drive a pronounced spike in sales of *The Outermost House*. Charles G. Bolte, who was now an editor at Viking Press, wrote to Beston in January 1966 to deliver the good news:

> I thought it might cheer your New Year if I told you that sales of *The Outermost House* in the Compass edition reached almost eight thousand last year. The progression here has been remarkable: the Explorer edition, published in 1961, sold three thousand that year, fifteen hundred the next, and we sold out the remainder to that first printing in 1963. We then transferred the title to the Compass imprint, which sold twenty-six hundred copies in 1963, 4300 in 1964, and, as indicated, almost double that last year. The book went briefly out of stock at the end of December, and a new printing is just in hand.[30]

A few months later, a laudatory article on *The Outermost House* written by a professor at Princeton University, Walter Teller, appeared in the July 31, 1966, edition of *The New York Times*. That article, wrote Bolte to Beston, "caused a great flurry of orders, and we have just put through a rush reprint."[31] Perhaps even more satisfying in its own way was a letter that Beston received from a woman on Long Island who had read the article in the *Times* and wanted him to know how much she loved *The Starlight Wonder Book*: "It may be heartening," she wrote, "to know that one's lesser-known book has also been deeply loved. It is satisfying to pay a warm debt of gratitude for the privilege of having loved it."[32]

By 1967 Beston was largely confined to bed, dogged by gout, recurring fevers, and a myriad of other health issues. By March he felt so restless and confined that Elizabeth tried something that Henry would never have countenanced in the past; she bought a Philco television and put it on a stand in his room. As she wrote to Margaret, "He longs so for the theatre, even for a movie like 'Khartoum'—so far it puts him to sleep (good in itself) we'll see as he gets stronger."[33] Much to Elizabeth's surprise, Henry— the philosophical arch-foe of the technological twentieth century—not only accepted the arrival of the television but seemed (at least in moderate amounts) to welcome it, particularly when classic plays or operas were telecast: "The T.V. is proving a blessing for us all, shortening the long afternoons. When not watching, it puts Henry to sleep, good either way."[34] Beston drifted in and out of awareness even when awake, receiving both good news—such as the possibility of an NBC television documentary on *The Outermost House*—and bad news, like the passing of his sister-in-law Marie Magee Sheahan, with an equanimity born in equal parts of a fading memory and a loosening of the "mortal coil," as Shakespeare had phrased it in *Hamlet*.

In early April of 1968, Truesdell Fife arrived at Chimney Farm for a visit. He was so shocked by how feeble Henry appeared that he expressed his concern to Elizabeth, who did her best to comfort him without making any pretensions that her husband was not, in fact, gravely ill. Four days later, on April 15, 1968, less than two months before his eightieth birthday, Henry Beston had another stroke and slipped quietly into a coma. As his daughter Kate Beston Barnes recalled, "He died quietly in his own bedroom at the farm, the place he loved so much, with my mother sitting on the bed for hours, stroking his hand and saying 'Go in peace, darling' over and over. At the moment of his death all the lights in the house blinked out. As usual, his daemon had timed it *just right*."[35]

Formal portrait of Beston, aged seventy-eight by John J. Fields, June 4, 1966. By this time
Beston had suffered several strokes, and was confined to a wheelchair.

Epilogue

I wish these houses had
More often at night
In the front rooms the glow
And gleam of light.
It's all in the kitchen now
By one rocking chair
Where the last of the family waits—
Receded there.

ELIZABETH COATSWORTH
"End of Time"
Country Poems (1942)

WHILE BESTON had outlived many of his old friends, several—Ray and Helen Nash, Truesdell and Carol Fite, and Henry's old college roommate Warren Butler—joined his family and neighbors at a little church in Newcastle before he was interred in the small burial ground at Chimney Farm under two great maple trees. After his burial Elizabeth wrote to their longtime friend David McCord, who was unable to attend the memorial service:

Henry was always himself, and with a word could bring to life the simplest and most overlooked thing. For me (as for others) he was always "opening windows." I'm glad Ray [Nash] wrote you about Henry's funeral. Even his death seemed right for him . . . he was in a coma yet knew that I was there. And it seems right that he is in the old farm burying ground. We're at work planning on an erratic left by the glacier near one gate (in reverse order of course!) for his stone. He never talked of death or even where he wished to be buried, but I think all this is suitable. There's to be that quotation about tomorrow's morning will be as heroic as any in the world in bronze under his name. Somehow all falls into place. I wanted to live to keep him master of his house to the end, and that's the way it was.[1]

As planned, the bronze plaque was soon attached to the glacial erratic at Beston's gravesite, with these lines from *The Outermost House*: "Creation is still going on, the creative forces are as great and as active to-day as they have ever been, and to-morrow's morning will be as heroic as any of the world." When Beston's will was produced, included among its provisions were bequests to his eight grandchildren and his godchildren, including namesakes Richard Beston Day, Ty Henry d'Alquen, Henry Beston Pearson, Henry Beston Oliver, and Henry Beston Barnes.

Starting in the early morning hours of Monday, February 6, 1978—fifty years after the publication of *The Outermost House*—perhaps the greatest winter storm to ever hit New England began its assault on Cape Cod. Heavy snows combined with strong winds from the northeast soon became a blizzard, and snow soon piled up in record-setting amounts throughout much of the region. Later that day, the storm front stalled just off the coast and the high seas combined with astronomical high tides to cause widespread flooding throughout coastal areas. On Cape Cod, hurricane-force wind gusts of up to ninety-three miles per hours were reported, and enormous swathes of the great beach were inundated by the storm surge. In the area near Eastham, the outbuildings and parking lot of coast guard beach, along with many beachfront houses were swept away by the storm—one of these casualties was Henry Beston's Fo'castle, the Outermost House. In his essay "A Beach for All Seasons," Robert Finch quipped that previous storms forcing the relocation of the Fo'castle may have made it "the only traveling National Literary Landmark in existence."[2] The blizzard of 1978 was the end of the Fo'castle, and one that would probably have struck Henry Beston—who had written in *The Outermost House* that to truly have a feel of the great beach as a scene of elemental wreck and disaster—as a fitting end for his sturdy little cottage. The house proved sturdy indeed, for after being swept off its foundation and pulled into Nauset Marsh, it remained intact, bobbing about, half-submerged in the water, until finally being swept out to sea and being pounded to pieces off Nauset Heights. On February 9, 1978, Wallace Bailey, director of the Massachusetts Audubon Society, wrote an open letter to his membership, opening with a simple declaration, "The Outermost House is gone." Some fragments were later recovered, including a chair and a portion of the outer wall that still held the plaque designating the house as a National Literary Landmark, reading "'The Outermost House' in which Henry Beston, author-naturalist, wrote his classic book by that name wherein he sought the great truth and found it in the nature of man." The Massachusetts Audubon Society still has the chair and plaque in its permanent collection.

DESPITE HER LEUKEMIA, Elizabeth Coatsworth Beston outlived her husband by nearly twenty years. She continued to write and by the end of her career had published over one hundred works, including a memoir entitled *Personal Geography: Almost an Autobiography* that came out in 1976. In that book she gives a succinct description of how her life changed after Henry's death: "Since Henry's death eight years ago I have had no desire to travel. I used to visit my sister in Hingham three or four times a year for a few days at a time, but since her death three years ago I take only relatively short drives. The long urge to write poetry has died almost completely away. And I live one day at a time."[7] In *Especially Maine* (1970), an anthology of Beston's work edited by Coatsworth, she writes that only when Henry "became part of a landscape could he write about it with what the Romans called filial piety," and concludes her introduction by saying: "Perhaps Henry's greatest gift was to call attention to things that had always been there, but whose significance had gone largely unnoticed until he spoke or wrote about them. He was a great opener of windows."[4]

When Elizabeth died in 1986, she was buried in the small farm graveyard, alongside Henry. Ten years later, the Beston's daughter, Kate Beston Barnes, author of *Crossing the Field* (1992), *Where the Deer Were* (1994), and *Kneeling Orion* (2004) was named the first poet laureate of the state of Maine. It was an honor that would have delighted both of her literary parents. In an issue of *Down East*, a monthly about Maine, she wrote a article entitled "Henry and Elizabeth—and Chimney Farm" that succinctly and poetically described life at Chimney Farm: "'The Farm' they called it, and now people ask what they raised. The answer is clear. Although they had flowers and herbs and vegetables in gardens, hay in the fields, apples and pears and cherries on the trees, their only real crop was words."[5]

Commonly Used Abbreviations

The following abbreviations have been used for frequently cited sources:

Books by Henry Beston [Sheahan]

BGV *The Book of Gallant Vagabonds*. New York: George H. Doran Company, 1925.

FFB *The Firelight Fairy Book*. Boston: The Atlantic Monthly Press, 1919.

FSA *Full Speed Ahead: Tales from the Log of a Correspondent with Our Navy*. Garden City, New York: Doubleday, Page and Company, 1919.

HE *Herbs and the Earth*. Garden City, New York: Doubleday, Doran and Co., 1935.

OH *The Outermost House: A Year of Life on the Great Beach of Cape Cod*. Boston: Houghton Mifflin, 1928.

TSL *The St. Lawrence*. New York: Farrar and Rinehart, 1942.

SWB *The Starlight Wonder Book*. Boston: The Atlantic Monthly Press, 1923. Published as Henry B. Beston.

AVP *A Volunteer Poilu*. Boston: Houghton Mifflin, 1916. Published as Henry Sheahan.

Books by Elizabeth Coatsworth Beston

EM Elizabeth Coatsworth, ed. *Especially Maine: The Natural World of Henry Beston from Cape Cod to the St. Lawrence*. Brattleboro, VT: Stephen Greene Press, 1970.

PG *Personal Geography: Almost an Autobiography*. Brattleboro, VT: Stephen Greene Press, 1976.

Archival Collections and Manuscripts

BFA Beston Family Archives. George A. Mitchell Special Collections. Bowdoin College Library.

Bibliography

Manuscript Sources

Beineke Rare Book and Manuscript Library. Yale University, New Haven, CT.

Beston Family Archives. George A. Mitchell Special Collections, Bowdoin College Library, Brunswick, ME.

Boston Athenaeum. Boston.

Eastham Historical Society. Eastham, MA.

Elizabeth Coatsworth Papers. Maine Women Writers Collection. University of New England, Portland, ME.

Elizabeth Jane Coatsworth Papers 1930–1968. Raymond H. Fogler Library, Special Collections. University of Maine at Orono.

Elizabeth Coatsworth Papers. Special Collections Department. University of Delaware Library, Newark, DE.

Elizabeth Coatsworth Papers. De Grummond Collection. McCain Library and Archives, University of Southern Mississippi.

Widener and Houghton Library Special Collections. Harvard University Library, Cambridge, MA.

Rauner Special Collections Library. Dartmouth College Library, Hanover, NH.

Kerlan Children's Literature Research Collection. University of Minnesota, Minneapolis, MN.

Walter Muir Whitehill Papers. Massachusetts Historical Society, Boston.

National Park Museum Collection. Cape Cod National Seashore, Eastham, MA.

Quincy Historical Society, Quincy, MA.

Thornton W. Burgess Museum, East Sandwich, MA.

Works by Henry Beston

Books (in order of publication date)

(unless otherwise indicated, published under the name Henry Beston)

A Volunteer Poilu. Boston: Houghton Mifflin, 1916. Published as Henry Sheahan.

Full Speed Ahead: Tales from the Log of a Correspondent with Our Navy. Garden City, NY: Doubleday, Page and Company, 1919. Published as Henry B. Beston.

Bibliography

The Firelight Fairy Book. Illustrated by Maurice Day. Boston: Atlantic Monthly Press, 1919. Published as Henry B. Beston.

The Starlight Wonder Book. Illustrated by Maurice Day. Boston: Atlantic Monthly Press, 1923. Published as Henry B. Beston.

The Book of Gallant Vagabonds. New York: George H. Doran Company, 1925.

The Sons of Kai: The Story the Indian Told. New York: Macmillan, 1926.

The Outermost House: A Year of Life on the Great Beach of Cape Cod. Boston: Houghton Mifflin, 1928.

Herbs and the Earth Garden City, New York: Doubleday, Doran and Co., 1935.

American Memory: Being a Mirror of the Stirring and Picturesque Past of Americans and the American Nation. New York and Toronto: Farrar and Rinehart, 1937.

The St. Lawrence. Illustrated by A.Y. Jackson. New York and Toronto: Farrar and Rinehart, 1942.

A Glimpse of the Indian Past. Cohasset, MA: South Shore Nature Club, 1946.

Northern Farm: A Chronicle of Maine. Illustrated by Thoreau MacDonald. New York and Toronto: Farrar and Rinehart, 1948.

White Pine and Blue Water: A State of Maine Reader. New York: Farrar, Rinehart and Straus, 1950.

Henry Beston's Fairy Tales. Illustrated by Fritz Kreidel. New York: Aladdin Books, 1952.

Previously Unpublished Contributions to Books

(unless otherwise indicated, published under the name Henry Beston)

Friends of France: The Field Service of the American Ambulance described by its members. Boston and New York: Houghton Mifflin, 1916. Includes accounts by Henry Sheahan, including "The Section at Verdun," 109–16; "Night," "Morning," and "Stray Thoughts," 203–5.

The Nature Writers: A Guide to Richer Reading. Edited by Herbert Faulkner West. Brattleboro, VT: Stephen Day Press, 1939. Foreword by Henry Beston, 5–6.

MacDougall, Arthur R., Jr. *Where Flows the Kennebec.* New York: Coward-McCann, 1947. Introduction by Henry Beston, ix–x.

Thoreau, Henry David. *Cape Cod.* New York: Bramhall House, 1951. Introduction by Henry Beston, 7–10.

Eastham, Massachusetts: 1651–1951. Eastham, MA: Eastham Tercentenary Committee, 1951. Introduction by Henry Beston.

Especially Maine: The Natural World of Henry Beston from Cape Cod to the St. Lawrence. Edited by Elizabeth Coatsworth. Brattleboro, VT: Stephen Greene Press, 1976.

Collaborations With Elizabeth Coatsworth:

Five Bears and Miranda. Illustrated by Frank Dobias. New York: Macmillan, 1939.

"Picnic Under a Pine." In *Picnic Adventures*, edited by Elizabeth Gilman, 166–77. New York and Toronto: Farrar and Rinehart, 1940.

Bibliography

The Tree That Ran Away. Illustrated by Fritz Eichenberg. New York: Macmillan, 1941.

"The Princess with the Long Nose." *Portal* (two parts) (August 9, 1941): 1–2,8; (August 16, 1941): 4–6.

Chimney Farm Bedtime Stories. Illustrated by Maurice Day. New York: Holt, Rinehart, and Winston, 1966.

MAGAZINE AND NEWSPAPER ARTICLES

(unless otherwise indicated, published under the name Henry Beston)

"Verdun." *Atlantic Monthly,* July 1916, 114–18. Article. Published as Henry Sheahan.

"The Vineyard of Red Wine." *Atlantic Monthly*, August 1916, 245–50. Article. Published as Henry Sheahan.

"Running Submerged: Special Correspondence from Henry B. Beston." *Outlook* September 18, 1918, 90–91. Article. Published as Henry B. Beston.

"On Night Patrol: A Tale of the American Destroyers." *Outlook*, October 2, 1918, 90–91. Article. Published as Henry B. Beston.

"Periscope on the Port Bow, Sir!: Being Torpedoed by a Submarine, and the Sinking the Submarine." *Ladies Home Journal*, November 1918, 8, 64. Article. Published as Henry B. Beston.

"With the American Submarines." *Atlantic Monthly*, November 1918, 688–97. Article. Published as Henry B. Beston.

"With the Convoy." *North American Review*, November 1918, 686–701. Article. Published as Henry B. Beston.

"With the Grand Fleet." *Country Life*, January 1919, 34–38. Article. Published as Henry B. Beston.

"An Old World House in a New World Lane." *House Beautiful*, August 1919, 80–81. Article. Published as Henry B. Beston.

"War and the Artist." *Living Age*, March 13, 1920, 679. No. Commentary. Unsigned.

"A World Revival of Handicrafts." *Living Age*, May 8, 1920, 368. Commentary. Published as H. B. B.

"Current Speech." *Living Age*, June 5, 1920, 616–17. Commentary. Published as H. B. B.

"Nationalism and Art." *Living Age*, June 19, 1920, 740–41. Commentary. Unsigned.

"Period Rooms." *Living Age* June 26, 1920, 772–73. Commentary. Published as H. B. B.

"Films and Plays." *Living Age*, July 24, 1920, 218–19. Commentary. Published as H. B. B.

"Jazz." *Living Age*, July 31, 1920, 280–81. Commentary. Published as H. B. B.

"Tough-Minded Novels." *Living Age*, August 14, 1920, 404–5. Commentary. Published as H. B. B.

"Turns and Films." *Living Age*, September 4, 1920, 590. Commentary. Published as H. B. B.

"A Novel of the Future." *Living Age*, October 9, 1920, 94. Commentary. Published as H. B. B.

"A Christmas Masque." *Living Age* December 25, 1920, 772–73. Commentary. Published as H. B.

Bibliography

"An Englishman Discusses American Folk Songs." *Living Age*, January 29, 1921, 280–81. Commentary. Published as H. B.

"The Young Men." *Living Age*, February 26, 1921, 528. Commentary. Published as H. B.

"Adventures and Houses." *House Beautiful*, April 1921, 281–84. Article.

"Adventures and Houses on the Eastern Sho'." *House Beautiful*, May 1921, 380–82. Article.

Review of *The Beautiful and Damned* by F. Scott Fitzgerald. "Atlantic's Bookshelf," *Atlantic Monthly*, June 1922, 897. Review.

"The Wonderful Tune." *Atlantic Monthly*, June 1923, 760–65. Children's story. Pre-published from *Starlight Wonder Tales* as Henry B. Beston.

"The Wardens of Cape Cod." *World's Work*, December 1923, 186–94. Article. Published as Henry B. Beston.

"The Fight for the Canal Zone." *Outlook*, March 5, 1924, 390–91. Article.

"The Navy's Oil Story." *Independent*, May 10, 1924, 247–49. Article.

"Stars of Romance." *Bookman*, December 1924, 470–72. Essay.

"The Real Master of Spain." *Outlook*, December 1924, 542–43. Article.

"Bullfight—Modern Style." *Independent*, December 6, 1924, 478–79. Article.

"The Flying Dutchman: The Wandering Jew of the Sea." *Mentor*, February, 1925, 61. Article. Published as H. B. Beston.

"The Real Wreck of the Hesperus: Being the True Story of the Famous Poem." *Bookman*, May 1925, 304–6. Article.

"The Season's Juveniles." *Independent*, September 26, 1925, 349–51. Review.

"The Pirate and the Poets: Glimpses of Edward John Trelawney." *Bookman*, October 1925, 132–36. Essay.

"Discoverers, Strange Lands, and Books." *New York Herald Tribune Books*, May 16, 1926, 8. Review.

"Children's Books of the Year." *Independent*, November 13, 1926, 550–51. Review.

"New Pages for Young Eyes." *Independent*, November 19, 1927, 512–13. Review.

"Night on a Great Beach." *Atlantic Monthly*, June 1928, 791–98. Essay. Pre-published from *The Outermost House*.

"New Books for Children." *Bookman*, December 1928, 491–93. Review.

"They Bossed the Clipper Ships." *New York Herald Tribune Magazine*, February 21, 1933 [clipping from Beston's scrapbook, BFA]. Article.

"Sound and Life." *Atlantic Monthly*, January 1933, 124–25. Essay.

"Good Reading." *New York Herald Tribune*, September 11, 1935. [clipping from Beston's scrapbook, BFA]. Review.

"Garden Escapes." *House Beautiful*, November 1936, 38–39, 93. Article.

"Farm Breakfast." *Christian Science Monitor*, October 24, 1939, 8. Poem.

"Aquarius." *Christian Science Monitor*, March 11, 1940, 12. Poem.

"The Young Philosopher's Song." *Christian Science Monitor*, September 5, 1940, 10. Poem.

"Letters from the Imaginary Animals in the Forest of Wonder." *Horn Book Magazine*, January 1941, 17–18. Children's story.

Bibliography

"To a Small Comic Dog." *Christian Science Monitor*, February 18, 1941, 8. Poem.

"Esther Wheelwright; Nun." *Catholic Digest*, March 1943 [Clipping from Beston's scrapbook, BFA].

"Franco-America's Growing Pains." *New York Times Book Review*, May 2, 1943, 7. Review of *The Shadows of the Trees* by Jacques Ducharme.

"Some Birds of a Maine Lake." *Audubon Magazine*, September 1943, 277–80. Article.

"Katherine Butler Hathaway." *Book-of-the-Month Club News*, October 1943, 5–6. Essay.

"France Out on a Limb." *Progressive*, May 1, 1944, 5. Article.

"'Sister Swallow,' Beloved Bird of Europe." *Audubon Magazine*, July 1944, 221–23.

"Passing the Buck for France's Defeat." *Progressive*, July 31, 1944, 9. Review of *Triumph of Treason* by Pierre Cot.

"Confusion in France." *Human Events*, September 27, 1944, 1–4. Essay.

"Country Chronicle." *Progressive* column appearing in each weekly issue from December 10, 1945 through December 30, 1946. Collected in *Northern Farm* except for eleven 1946 essays: January 7, 14, and 21; May 6; June 24; July 8 and 29; August 5; September 2; December 16 and 30.

"The Slav Has Won." *Human Events*, December 26, 1945, 1–4. Essay.

"The Crisis of the Peasant Civilization" *Human Events*, August 21, 1946, 1–4. Essay.

"Winds of Opinion." *American Affairs*, July 1947, 133.

"The Need of Belief as a Factor in Reconstruction." *Human Events*, October 29, 1947, 1–4. Essay.

"New England." Contribution to "The Mood of America: Regional Reports from the Progressive's Correspondents." *Progressive*, January 1948, 36–37. Essay.

"Spring Comes to the Farm." *Progressive*, May 1948, 35. Essay.

"The Northeast." Contribution to "The Mood of America: Regional Reports from the Progressive's Correspondents." *Progressive*, August 1948, 21–22. Essay.

"End of a Farm Summer." *Progressive*, October 1948, 27–28. Essay.

"The Farm Remembers." *Progressive*, January 1949, 23–24. Essay.

"Summer Regained." *Progressive*, June 1950, 24–25. Essay.

"Soliloquy on the Airplane." *Human Events*, October 18, 1950, 1–4. Essay.

"Season of Splendor." *Progressive*, November 1950, 22. Essay.

Review of *The Phasian Bird* by Henry Williamson. *Providence Sunday Journal*, November 26, 1950 [clipping from Beston's Scrapbook, BFA].

"Sound and Surf." *Reader's Digest*, August 1951, 94. Excerpt from *The Outermost House*.

"Orion Over the Cape Cod Dunes." *Christian Science Monitor*, August 20, 1954, 8. Excerpt from *The Outermost House*.

Comment on "Is America a Civilization?" *Shenandoah*, Autumn 1958, 23–26. Essay.

Bibliography

Selected Published Letters

"The Bombing of Berlin." *Christian Century*, March 21, 1945, 368–69.

"Condemnation." *Catholic Worker*, September 1945, 7.

Letter to the Editor against the atomic bomb. *Not Merely Gossip* (Supplement to *Human Events*), December 23, 1947.

"Jumping Towards the Moon." *Interpreter*, April 1, 1950, 3.

Other Bibliographic Material

Alexander, Ian. *Bergson: Philosopher of Reflection*. London: Bowes and Bowes, 1957.

Baker, Ray Stannard. *Woodrow Wilson: Life and Letters*. New York: Doubleday, Doran, 1936.

Barnes, Kate Beston. "Henry and Elizabeth—and Chimney Farm." *Down East*. May 1992, 50.

Barnes, Kate Beston. *Kneeling Orion*. Boston: David R. Godine, 2004.

Barnes, Kate Beston. *Where the Deer Were*. Boston: David R. Godine, 1994.

Barrus, Clara, ed. *The Heart of Burroughs's Journals*. Boston: Houghton Mifflin, 1928.

Barrus, Clara, ed. *The Life and Letters of John Burroughs*. 2 vols. New York: Russell and Russell, 1925.

Beebe, William. *The Book of Naturalists: An Anthology of the Best Natural History*. New York: Alfred A. Knopf, 1944.

Berry, Wendell. *The Unsettling of America: Culture & Agriculture*. San Francisco: Sierra Club Books, 1977.

Brooks, Paul. *The House of Life: Rachel Carson at Work*. Boston: Houghton Mifflin, 1972.

Brooks, Van Wyck. *From The Shadow of the Mountain: My Post-Meridian Years*. New York: E. P. Dutton and Company, 1961.

Burroughs, John. *Field and Study*. Boston: Houghton Mifflin, 1919.

Clarke, Ida Clyde. *American Women and the World War*. New York: D. Appleton and Co., 1918.

Coatsworth, Elizabeth. Introduction to *The Best of Beston*. Edited by Elizabeth Coatsworth. Boston: David R. Godine, 2000.

Coatsworth, Elizabeth. *Country Poems*. New York: The Macmillan Company, 1942.

Elizabeth Coatsworth, ed. *Especially Maine: The Natural World of Henry Beston from Cape Cod to the St. Lawrence*. Brattleboro, VT: Stephen Greene Press, 1970.

Coatsworth, Elizabeth. *Personal Geography: Almost an Autobiography*. The Stephen Greene Press: Brattleboro, VT, 1976,

Coatsworth, Elizabeth. *Compass Rose*. NEED INFO

Cowley, Malcolm. *A Second Flowering: Works and Days of the Lost Generation*. New York: The Viking Press, 1956.

Crowley, Sharon. *Composition in the University*. Pittsburgh: University of Pittsburgh Press, 1998.

Bibliography

Dalton, Elizabeth. Introduction to *Grimm's Fairy Tales*. New York: Barnes and Noble Books, 2003. First published 1869.

Ellis, Edward Robb. *Echoes of Distant Thunder: Life in the United States 1914–1918*. New York: Coward, McCann and Geoghegan, Inc., 1975.

Fallows, Marjorie R. *Irish Americans: Identity and Assimilation*. Englewood Cliffs, NJ: Prentice-Hall, Inc., 1979.

Federman, Donald. "Toward an Ecology of Place: Three Views of Cape Cod." *Colby Library Quarterly* 13 (1977): 209–22.

Ferro, Marc. *The Great War: 1914–1918*. New York: Routledge, 2001.

Finch, Robert. *Outlands: Journeys to the Outer Edges of Cape Cod*. Boston: David R. Godine, 1986.

Freeman, Martha, ed. *Always, Rachel: The Letters of Rachel Carson and Dorothy Freeman, 1952–1964*. Boston: Beacon Press, 1995.

Friends of France: The Field Service of the American Ambulance Described by its Members. Boston and New York: Houghton Mifflin, 1916.

Gallati, Stephen. "The Organization of the Service." In *Friends of France*. Page numbers? Boston: Houghton Mifflin, 1916.

Gardner, Joseph L. *Departing Glory: Theodore Roosevelt as ex-President*. New York: Charles Scribner's Sons, 1973.

Gibbs, Philip. *Now It Can Be Told*. New York: Harper and Brothers Publishers, 1920.

Gilbert, Martin. *The First World War*. New York: Henry Holt and Company, 1994.

Goldberg, Ronald Allen. *America in the Twenties*. Syracuse, NY: Syracuse University Press, 2003.

Hansen, Arlen J. *Gentlemen Volunteers: The Story of the American Ambulance Drivers in the Great War*. New York: Arcade Publishing, 1996.

Hathaway, Katharine Butler. *The Little Locksmith*. 1943. Reprint, New York: Feminist Press at CUNY, 2000.

Hay, John. *The Great Beach*. Garden City, NY: Doubleday and Company, 1963.

Hays, Samuel P. "Three Decades of Environmental Politics: The Historical Context." In *Government and Environmental Politics: Essays on Historical Developments Since World War Two*, edited by Michael J. Lacey. Page numbers? Washington, D.C.: The Woodrow Wilson Center Press, 1989.

Hinckley, Edward B. "Thoreau and Beston: Two Observers of Cape Cod." *The New England Quarterly* Volume IV (November 2, 1931): 216–29.

Holly, H. Hobart., ed. *Quincy's Legacy: Topics in Four Centuries of Massachusetts History*. Quincy, MA: Quincy Historical Society, 1998.

Jeffers, H. Paul. *Theodore Roosevelt Jr., the Life of a War Hero*. New York: Presido Press, 2002.

Kenny, Kevin. *The American Irish: A History*. New York: Pearson Education, Inc., 2000.

Khatchadourian, Raffi. "Neptune's Navy: Paul Watson's wild crusade to save the oceans." *The New Yorker*, November 5, 2007, 56–72.

Bibliography

Kiernan, John. *John Kiernan's Treasury of Great Nature Writing*. Garden City, NY: Hanover House, 1957.

Krutch, Joseph Wood. *Great American Nature Writing*. New York: William Sloane Associates, 1950.

Kurtz, Lester, *The Politics of Heresy; the Modernist Crisis in Roman Catholicism*. Berkeley and Los Angeles: University of California Press, 1986.

Lear, Linda. *Rachel Carson: Witness for Nature*. New York: Henry Holt, 1997.

Levin, Murray B. *Political Hysteria in America: The Democratic Capacity for Repression*. New York: Basic Books, 1971.

Lloyd, Allan. *The War in the Trenches*. New York: David McKay Company, Inc., 1976.

Lorenz, Clarissa ."Henry Beston: The Outermost Man." *The Atlantic Monthly*, October 1978, 108–9.

Lovell, S. D. *The Presidential Election of 1916*. Edwardsville, IN: Southern Illinois University Press, 1980.

Lyon, Thomas, ed. *This Incomperable Lande: A Book of American Nature Writing*. Boston: Houghton Mifflin Company, 1989.

McEntee, Girard Lindsley. *Military History of the World War: A Complete History of the Campaigns on all Fronts*. New York: Charles Scribner's Sons, 1937.

McCay, Mary. *Rachel Carson*. New York: Twayne Publishers, 1993.

Maier, Thomas. *The Kennedys: America's Emerald Kings*. New York: Basic Books, 2003.

Massie, Robert K. *Castles of Steel: Britain, Germany, and the Winning of the Great War at Sea*. New York: Random House, 2003.

Miller, Nathan. *Theodore Roosevelt: A Life*. New York: William Morrow and Company, 1992.

Neff, J. Luther. *Years of Memory*. Passaic, NJ: George Dixon Press, 1971.

Neff, John W. *Katahdin: An Historic Journey*. Boston: Appalachian Mountain Book Club, 2006.

Ousby, Ian. *The Road to Verdun: World War I's Most Momentous Battle and the Folly of Nationalism*. New York: Anchor, 2003.

O'Toole, Patricia. *When Trumpets Call: Theodore Roosevelt After the White House*. New York: Simon and Schuster, 2005.

Paul, Sherman. "Another Journal for Henry Beston." *North Dakota Quarterly* (Spring 1991): 92–111. Also included in *For Love of the World: Essays on Nature Writers*. Iowa City: University of Iowa Press, 1992.

Paul, Sherman. *For Love of the World: Essays on Nature Writers*. Iowa City: University of Iowa Press, 1992.

Payne, Daniel G. Introduction to *The St. Lawrence*, by Henry Beston, Wynford Edition. Toronto: Oxford University Press, 2012.

Payne, Daniel G. "Emerson's Natural Theology: John Burroughs and the 'Church' of Latter Day Transcendentalism." *ATQ*, September 2007, 191–205.

Phillips, Dana. *The Truth of Ecology*. New York: Oxford University Press, 2003.

Quinn, William P. *Shipwrecks Around Cape Cod*. Orleans, MA: Lower Cape Publishing, 1973.

Bibliography

Reynolds, Francis J. et al., eds. *The Story of the Great War: History of the European War from Official Sources*. New York: P.F. Collier and Son, 1916.

Richardson, Wyman. *The House on Nauset Marsh*. Riverside, CT: The Chatham Press, Inc., 1947.

Roosevelt, Theodore. *America and the World War*. New York: Charles Scribner's Sons, 1918.

Scheese, Don. *Nature Writing: The Pastoral Impulse in America*. New York: Twayne Publishers, 1996.

Scott, Winfield Townley. *Exiles and Fabrications*. Garden City, NY: Doubleday and Company, 1961.

Simo, Melanie L. *Literature of Place: Dwelling on the Land before Earth Day 1970*. Charlottesville, VA: University of Virginia Press, 2005.

Smith, Jean Edward. *FDR*. New York: Random House, 2007.

Smith, John. *The Complete Works of Captain John Smith (1580–1631) in Three Volumes*. Edited by Philip L. Barbour. Chapel Hill, NC: University of North Carolina Press, 1986.

Spencer, Maryellen. "Henry Beston (1868–1968): A Primary Checklist." *Resources for American Literary Study* (Spring 1982): 49–63.

Strachan, Hew. *The First World War*. New York: Viking, 2004.

Taubenberger, Jeffery et al. "Initial Genetic Characterization of the 1918 'Spanish' Influenza Virus." *Science* 21 (March 1997): 1793–96.

Thayer, William Roscoe et al. *The Harvard Graduates Magazine* 15 (1907) and 17 (1909).

Thoreau, Henry. *Cape Cod*. 1865. New York: Bramhall House, 1951.

Tracy, Henry Chester. *American Naturists*. New York: E.P. Dutton and Company, 1930.

Waldron, Nan. *Journey to Outermost House*. Bethlehem, CT: Butterfly and Wheel, 1991.

West, Herbert Faulkner. *The Nature Writers: A Guide to Richer Reading*. Brattleboro, VT: Stephen Day Press, 1939.

Wild, Peter. "Henry Beston's *The Outermost House*." *North Dakota Quarterly* (Winter 1987): 188–95.

Wilding, Don. *Henry Beston's Cape Cod*. Haverford, PA: Infinity Publishing, 2003.

Notes

INTRODUCTION

1. Beston, *AVP*, 192.
2. Beston, *AVP*, 189.
3. Beston, *AVP*, 209.
4. Strachan, *The First World War*, 189.
5. *Friends of France*, 205.
6. Hansen *Gentlemen Volunteers*, vii.
7. Beston, *AVP*, 89–90.
8. Beston, letter to J. Luther Neff, 12 August 1919, BFA.
9. Beston, letter to Jake Day, 13 November 1920, BFA.
10. Beston, letter to unidentified correspondent (probably Jake Day), 1 February 1921, BFA.
11. Beston, *OH*, 10.
12. Beston, *OH*, 121.
13. Brooks, *The House of Life*, 6.
14. Lyon, *This Incomperable Lande*, 83.
15. Coatsworth, *EM*, 72.
16. Beston, letter to Elizabeth Coatsworth, 7 January 1931, BFA.
17. Beston, *OH*, 5.
18. Coatsworth, *EM*, 6.
19. Beston, letter to Truesdell Fife, 5 September 1932, BFA.
20. Beston, *HE*, 4–5.
21. Beston, *OH*, 121.
22. Finch, *Outlands*, 78.
23. Beston, *OH* (Reprint: New York: Owl Books, 1992), xxxv. These lines were first published in Beston's foreword to West, *The Nature Writers*.
24. Paul, *For Love of the World*, 116.
25. Brooks, *From The Shadow of the Mountain*, 21.
26. Khatchadourian, "Neptune's Navy: Paul Watson's wild crusade," 67.
27. Beston, *OH*, 221–22.

Notes

Foreground: A Sense of Place

1. Coatsworth, *EM*, 48.
2. Beston, *HE*, 4.
3. Philip L Barbour, ed., *The Complete Works of Captain John Smith (1580–1631) in Three Volumes* (Chapel Hill: University of North Carolina Press, 1986), 1:341. In *Guns, Germs, and Steel*, geographer Jared Diamond makes the argument that environmental factors are at least as important, and often more so, than "eventfulness" in understanding history. As Adam Gopnik writes of Diamond's thesis, "there are no cultural legacies, just environmental stresses turning out new tools." "Decline, Fall, Rinse, Repeat: Is America Going Down?" *The New Yorker*, September 12, 2011, 40–47.
4. James R. Cameron, "Moswetuset Hummock," in Holly, *Quincy's Legacy*, 22.
5. William Bradford, *Of Plymouth Plantation, 1620–1647* (New York: The Modern Library, 1981), 39. At the time the *Mayflower* set sail, "New England" was commonly used to refer to a vast territory stretching from Pennsylvania to Canada. The Puritans originally intended to establish their colony in the Hudson River region, but the ship was blown off course and they revised their plan accordingly.
6. Bradford, *Of Plymouth Plantation*, 74–75.
7. H. Hobart Holly, "The Quincys' Homes in Quincy," in Holly, *Quincy's Legacy*, 41.
8. Fallows, *Irish Americans*, 37.
9. Fallows, *Irish Americans*, 247.

1. A New England Boyhood of Sea and Shore (1888–1915)

1. The family may have had their roots in The Pale, a part of eastern Ireland in the vicinity of Dublin that was part of the Norman conquest of 1169 and later passed to the nominal control of the English crown for a time in the Middle Ages. The Pale had a fairly significant number of French and English settlers during this period, and it is possible that the Beston side of the family line was among them.
2. In 2011 dollars this would have been the equivalent of approximately $68,000 (calculated using the Federal Reserve Bank's Consumer Price Index).
3. Kate Beston Barnes, telephone conversation with the author, December 17, 2011.
4. Cited in Maier, *The Kennedys*, 63.
5. *Boston Globe*, September 22, 1905.
6. Kate Beston Barnes, telephone conversation with the author, December 17, 2011.
7. Marie Louise Maurice was born on December 7, 1858.
8. Kate Beston Barnes, telephone interview with the author, December 17, 2011.
9. Kurtz, *The Politics of Heresy*, 182.
10. The origins of the Ancient Order of Foresters go back even further, to the society known as the Royal Foresters formed in Leeds in the eighteenth century. The name of the organization arose from the members' stated conviction that they had a duty

Notes

to assist their fellow men who had come upon hard times "as they walked through the forests of life." (Foresters Friendly Society website).

11. Marie Sheahan and Joan Sheahan Schwab, interview with the author, May 20, 2009, Quincy, MA, BFA.

12. Marie Sheahan and Joan Sheahan Schwab, interview with the author, May 20, 2009, Quincy, MA, BFA.

13. Lorenz, "Henry Beston: The Outermost Man," 108.

14. Lorenz, "Henry Beston: The Outermost Man," 108.

15. Harvard College Twenty-fifth Anniversary Report, Class of 1902 (1927), 594.

16. Lorenz, "Henry Beston: The Outermost Man," 108.

17. Lorenz, "Henry Beston: The Outermost Man," 108.

18. Elizabeth Coatsworth, typescript, February 1974, BFA.

19. Wilding, *Henry Beston's Cape Cod*, 7.

20. Henry Beston, interview by Pamela Bomhard, 1974, BFA. Also cited in Wilding, *Henry Beston's Cape Cod*, 8–9.

21. Elizabeth Coatsworth, Address to American Academy of Arts and Letters, 1954, BFA.

22. Marie Sheahan and Joan Sheahan Schwab, interview with the author, May 20, 2009, Quincy, MA, BFA.

23. Kate Beston Barnes, letter to the author, February 5, 2003. Joseph Sheahan married Mary L. Conway on February 10, 1902.

24. Henry Beston, letter to Elizabeth Coatsworth, February 10, 1929, BFA.

25. *Boston Globe*, September 22, 1905. His obituary in the *Boston Pilot* extolled both his medical abilities and his selflessness: "Skilled as a physician and surgeon, warm-hearted and generous, Dr. Sheahan established himself firmly in the affections of all. Almost every family in the city whom he attended can give instances of his devotion, which subordinated all regard for his own health and comfort. It mattered not what the conditions of weather or what time of day or night the call came, the doctor answered it. His charity was boundless, as the poor can tell." *Boston Pilot*, October 30, 1905.

26. Kate Beston Barnes, letter to the author, February 5, 2003.

27. Henry Beston, letter to Elizabeth Coatsworth, February 10, 1929, BFA.

28. Henry Beston, letter to Elizabeth Coatsworth, February 7, 1929, BFA.

29. Kate Beston Barnes, letter to the author, February 5, 2003.

30. In early 1940 Beston contacted John E. Wilson, an attorney with an office in Augusta, Maine, to inquire about changing his legal residence to Maine and changing his name to Beston. Wilson responded on April 16, 1940, writing, "As I have stated before, the common law of England and America is to the effect that a person can change his name at will, regardless of statutory enabling acts. You, of course, wish some memorial of your intention of the change. In view of the common law, I feel strongly that the State of Maine has no exclusive jurisdiction over the matter and that your memorial could come from any State in the Union (although if you proceed under the Maine statute, you must, of course, observe its terms and file the petition in the

county in which you reside). I feel, therefore, that the thing for you to do now that you are making the Mississippi River trip is to accomplish the change in the courts of Arkansas or Missouri or Ohio, and if you wish, I could undoubtedly dig up a Harvard Law School classmate in one of those States who could attend to the matter for you." This typescript letter is in the Beston Family Archives at Bowdoin College, and the notation "never done," written in Elizabeth Coatsworth's hand, is included on the letter. However, in his 1954 speech to the American Academy of Arts and Sciences commemorating his receipt of the Emerson-Thoreau Medal, Beston did claim that he had legally changed his name in the 1940s.

31. Thayer et al., *The Harvard Graduates Magazine*, Vol. 15, 1907.
32. Thayer et al., *The Harvard Graduates Magazine*, Vol. 17, 1909.
33. B. S. Hurlburt, letter to George Sheahan, October 30, 1908, BFA.
34. Hathaway, *The Little Locksmith*, 67.
35. Beston, "Katharine Butler Hathaway," 6.
36. Barrus, *The Life and Letters of John Burroughs*, 2:389–90.
37. Marie Sheahan and Joan Sheahan Schwab, interview with the author, May 20, 2009, Quincy, MA. Another version of this story was related by Francis Russell, who recalled Beston's telling him about a visit to the White House with Ted Jr. over the Christmas holiday: "One morning, during a visit, Henry woke early to eat breakfast alone. Then, recalled Russell, 'the President strode in, slapped him on the back and announced heartily, 'nothing wrong with a boy who gets up early and eat ham and eggs for breakfast!'" Wilding, *Henry Beston's Cape Cod*, 10.
38. Cited in Crowley, *Composition in the University*, 74. Crowley's finely researched work provides context and specific details of the development of composition studies both at Harvard and in American universities generally.
39. Crowley, *Composition in the University*, 77.
40. Henry Beston [Sheahan], letter to Mr. Wells, November 3, 1910, BFA.
41. Henry Beston, letter to Elizabeth Coatsworth Beston, October 15, 1931, BFA.
42. Harvard College Tenth Anniversary Report, Class of 1909 (1919), 594.

2. A Volunteer Poilu (1915–1916)

1. Gallati, "The Organization of the Service," 2–3.
2. Hansen, *Gentlemen Volunteers*, xiv–xiv.
3. Hansen, *Gentlemen Volunteers*, 5–7.
4. Hansen, *Gentlemen Volunteers*, 45.
5. Hansen, *Gentlemen Volunteers*, 20.
6. Mary Conway Sheahan, letter to Henry Beston [Sheahan], August 12, 1915, BFA. George Sheahan served as first lieutenant with the First Heavy Artillery, in the Massachusetts National Guard in 1915, then went overseas with Hugh Cabot's Third Harvard Unit, where he was cited for his skill with treating traumatic wounds. He

Notes

attained the rank of major with the BEF in France, then returned home before joining the US Army in September 1918. He served with the rank of captain until his discharge at Camp Lee, Virginia, in April 1919. After the war he returned to his practice in Quincy. Harvard Class of 1902, 50th report, 580.

7. William R. Hereford, letter to Henry Beston [Sheahan], July 17, 1915, BFA.
8. William R. Hereford, letter to Henry Beston [Sheahan], July 27, 1915, BFA.
9. William R. Hereford, letter to Henry Beston [Sheahan], July 27, 1915, BFA.
10. Beston [Sheahan], *AVP*, 2.
11. Beston, *AVP*, 7.
12. Beston, *AVP*, 10–11.
13. Beston, *AVP*, 14–15.
14. Beston, *AVP*, 182.
15. Beston, *AVP*, 186.
16. Beston, *AVP*, 186. Dreyfuss was finally exonerated in 1899. There is evidence that Zola's death in 1902 from carbon monoxide poisoning caused by a stopped chimney at his home was an intentional and politically inspired act arising from his defense of Dreyfuss. Dreyfuss was later reinstated in the army, from which he retired in 1907. Although he was in his late fifties when war broke out, he reenlisted in the army (as lieutenant colonel) and served with distinction. He was awarded the rank of Officer of the Legion of Honor in 1918.
17. Beston, *AVP*, 19.
18. Beston, *AVP*, 25.
19. Lloyd, *The War in the Trenches*, 43.
20. Gilbert, *The First World War*, 199.
21. Gilbert, *The First World War*, 199.
22. Ousby, *The Road to Verdun*, 37.
23. Gilbert, *The First World War*, 196.
24. Ousby, *The Road to Verdun*, 39.
25. Pierre Gouvy, letter to Henry Beston [Sheahan], August 22, 1915, BFA.
26. Beston, *AVP*, 30.
27. Beston, *AVP*, 30.
28. Reynolds et al., *The Story of the Great War*, 4:51.
29. Reynolds et al., *The Story of the Great War*, 65–66.
30. Beston, *AVP*, 32.
31. Beston, *AVP*, 35–36.
32. Strachan, *The First World War*, 181.
33. Gouvy, letter to Henry Beston [Sheahan], October 10, 1915, BFA.
34. Pierre Gouvy, letter to Henry Beston [Sheahan], October 27, 1915, BFA.
35. Beston, *AVP*, 51.
36. Beston, *AVP*, 61.
37. Beston, *AVP*, 64.

38. Beston, *AVP*, 76.

39. Beston, *AVP*, 64.

40. Henry Beston [Sheahan], unpublished diary, no date, BFA, Box 1, Folder 2, Item 4.

41. Beston, *AVP*, 86–87.

42. Beston, *AVP*, 84.

43. Beston, *AVP*, 165.

44. Beston, *AVP*, 147.

45. Henry Beston [Sheahan], unpublished diary, no date, BFA, Box 1, Folder 2, Item 4.

46. Lloyd, *The War in the Trenches*, 89.

47. Gibbs, *Now It Can Be Told*, 211.

48. Lloyd, *The War in the Trenches*, 67.

49. Beston, *AVP*, 134.

50. Beston, *AVP*, 133.

51. Clarke, *American Women and the World War*, 456.

52. Henry Beston [Sheahan], letter to Mabel Davison, November 1, 1915, BFA.

53. Henry Beston [Sheahan], letter to Mabel Davison, December 3, 1915, BFA.

54. Henry Beston [Sheahan], letter to Mabel Davison, no date, BFA, Box 1, Folder 3, Item 7.

55. Henry Beston [Sheahan], letter to Mabel Davison, December 3, 1915, BFA.

56. McEntee, *Military History of the World War* , 269–70.

57. Beston, *AVP*, 190.

58. Beston, *AVP*, 192.

59. Beston, *AVP*, 192.

60. Beston, *AVP*, 189.

61. McEntee, *Military History of the World War*, 273.

62. Reynolds, *The Story of the Great War*, 4:132.

63. Ousby, *The Road to Verdun*, 80.

64. Beston, *AVP*, 197.

65. Beston, *AVP*, 198.

66. McEntee, *Military History of the World War*, 279.

67. Beston, *AVP*, 199–200.

68. Henry Beston [Sheahan], "Be Merciful Frenchman! Kill Us!" *Boston Sunday Post*, May 7, 1916.

69. Beston, *AVP*, 203.

70. Beston, *AVP*, 203–4.

71. Beston, *AVP*, 209.

72. Strachan, *The First World War*, 189.

73. Ferro, *The Great War*, 75.

74. *Friends of France*, 205.

75. A. Piatt Andrew, letter to French Commissioner of Passports, March 20, 1916, BFA.

Notes

3. The Violence and Imbecilities of Men (1916–1919)

1. Massie, *Castles of Steel*, 689.
2. Beston, *AVP*, 101.
3. Miller, *Theodore Roosevelt*, 543–44.
4. Wilson did not choose this slogan as his primary reelection theme—indeed, there is evidence that he disliked the phrase and saw it as a naïve promise that he would continue to pursue a policy of strict neutrality no matter what might occur in the future. As he told the Secretary of the Navy Josephus Daniels, "I can't keep the country out of war. They talk of me as though I were a god. Any little German lieutenant can push us into the war at any time by some calculated outrage." Lovell, *The Presidential Election of 1916*, 56.
5. Baker, *Woodrow Wilson*, 6:296.
6. Sheahan, "Verdun," 114–18.
7. Sheahan, "The Vineyard of Red Wine," 245–50.
8. Coatsworth, *EM*, 1.
9. Beston, *AVP*, 100.
10. Sheahan, *Boston Sunday Post*, May 7, 1916, A1+.Print.
11. This account, which appeared on the front page of section C in the May 14, 1916 edition of the *Boston Sunday Post*, differed slightly from that related in *A Volunteer Poilu*, page 113. In *A Volunteer Poilu*, he wrote that someone else had related this scene to him.
12. Henry Sheahan, "Where Human Heart Fell From a Tree," *Boston Sunday Post*, May 14, 1916, A1. Print.
13. Harvard Class of 1909, 10th year report.
14. *Catholic World*, February 1917, 104:696.
15. *New Jersey Library Bulletin*, April 1917, 7.
16. *The Outlook*, December 20, 1916.
17. Hansen, *Gentlemen Volunteers*, 60–61. The same omission is made on websites: See, for example, www.firstworldwar.com/poetsandprose/ambulance.htm or www.angelfire.com/indie/anna_jones1/drivers.html.
18. Massie, *Castles of Steel*, 703.
19. Massie, *Castles of Steel*, 709.
20. Massie, *Castles of Steel*, 713.
21. Massie, *Castles of Steel*, 727–28. Coincidentally Queenstown, also known as Cobh, was the port from which Maurice and Catherine Sheahan had embarked on their journey to Boston in the late 1840s.
22. Ellery Sedgwick, letter "To whom it may concern," November 30, 1917, BFA.
23. After the war, Hughes was promoted to Admiral and subsequently served as president of the Naval War College (1923), and commander in chief of Naval Operations (1925).
24. J. Luther Neff, *Years of Memory*, unnumbered pages.
25. Beston, *FSA*, 40.

26. Gardner, *Departing Glory*, 388.

27. Gardner, *Departing Glory*, 391.

28. Beston, FSA, 180.

29. Beston, FSA, 180.

30. Lorenz, "Henry Beston: The Outermost Man," 108.

31. Beston, FSA, 83–84.

32. Beston, FSA, 60.

33. Beston, FSA, 204.

34. Beston, FSA, 119.

35. Beston, FSA, 174–75.

36. Beston, FSA, 245–54. In relation to the title of the chapter, Beston admitted, "Not that I am a sailor or ever was a sailor in Uncle Sam's Navy. All that I can claim to have been is a correspondent attached to the Navy 'over there.'" (246).

37. Henry Beston, letter to J. Luther Neff, January 15, 1920, BFA.

38. Henry Beston, letter to J. Luther Neff, January 15, 1920, BFA.

39. *American Library Association Booklist*, May 1919, 15:303.

40. *Springfield Republican*, May 25, 1919, 17.

41. *The New York Times*, unsigned review, April 6, 1919, 24:182.

42. Beston, FSA, 239.

4. WEARY OF ARMAGEDDON (1919–1923)

1. Wilson's Fourteen Points, as presented in his address to the United States Congress on February 11, 1918, consisted of the following: I. Open covenants of peace, openly arrived at, after which there shall be no private international understandings of any kind but diplomacy shall proceed always frankly and in the public view. II. Absolute freedom of navigation upon the seas, outside territorial waters, alike in peace and in war, except as the seas may be closed in whole or in part by international action for the enforcement of international covenants. III. The removal, so far as possible, of all economic barriers and the establishment of an equality of trade conditions among all the nations consenting to the peace and associating themselves for its maintenance. IV. Adequate guarantees given and taken that national armaments will be reduced to the lowest point consistent with domestic safety. V. A free, open-minded, and absolutely impartial adjustment of all colonial claims, based upon a strict observance of the principle that in determining all such questions of sovereignty the interests of the populations concerned must have equal weight with the equitable claims of the government whose title is to be determined. VI. The evacuation of all Russian territory and such a settlement of all questions affecting Russia as will secure the best and freest cooperation of the other nations of the world in obtaining for her an unhampered and unembarrassed opportunity for the independent determination of her own political development and national policy and assure her of a sincere welcome

into the society of free nations under institutions of her own choosing; and, more than a welcome, assistance also of every kind that she may need and may herself desire. The treatment accorded Russia by her sister nations in the months to come will be the acid test of their good will, of their comprehension of her needs as distinguished from their own interests, and of their intelligent and unselfish sympathy. VII. Belgium, the whole world will agree, must be evacuated and restored, without any attempt to limit the sovereignty which she enjoys in common with all other free nations. No other single act will serve as this will serve to restore confidence among the nations in the laws which they have themselves set and determined for the government of their relations with one another. Without this healing act the whole structure and validity of international law is forever impaired. VIII. All French territory should be freed and the invaded portions restored, and the wrong done to France by Prussia in 1871 in the matter of Alsace-Lorraine, which has unsettled the peace of the world for nearly fifty years, should be righted, in order that peace may once more be made secure in the interest of all. IX. A readjustment of the frontiers of Italy should be effected along clearly recognizable lines of nationality. X. The peoples of Austria-Hungary, whose place among the nations we wish to see safeguarded and assured, should be accorded the freest opportunity of autonomous development. XI. Rumania, Serbia, and Montenegro should be evacuated; occupied territories restored; Serbia accorded free and secure access to the sea; and the relations of the several Balkan states to one another determined by friendly counsel along historically established lines of allegiance and nationality; and international guarantees of the political and economic independence and territorial integrity of the several Balkan states should be entered into. XII. The Turkish portions of the present Ottoman Empire should be assured a secure sovereignty, but the other nationalities which are now under Turkish rule should be assured an undoubted security of life and an absolutely unmolested opportunity of an autonomous development, and the Dardanelles should be permanently opened as a free passage to the ships and commerce of all nations under international guarantees. XIII. An independent Polish state should be erected which should include the territories inhabited by indisputably Polish populations, which should be assured a free and secure access to the sea, and whose political and economic independence and territorial integrity should be guaranteed by international covenant. XIV. A general association of nations must be formed under specific covenants for the purpose of affording mutual guarantees of political independence and territorial integrity to great and small states alike.

2. *Journal of the American Medical Association*, December 18, 1918, 2174–5, 2154.

3. Taubenberger et al., "Initial Genetic Characterization of the 1918 'Spanish' Influenza Virus," 1793–96.

4. Molly Billings, "The Influenza Pandemic of 1918." http://virus.stanford.edu/uda /flubib.html. June 1997, modified RDS February 2005.

5. Levin, *Political Hysteria in America*, 29.

Notes

6. BFA, Box 1, File 6, American Field Service Medal.

7. Henry Beston, letter to J. Luther Neff, April 19, 1919, BFA.

8. Cressy Phinney, letter to Henry [Beston] Sheahan, March 25, 1919, BFA.

9. Henry Beston, letter to J. Luther Neff, April 19, 1919, BFA.

10. Cressy Phinney, letter to Henry [Beston] Sheahan, c. June 1919, BFA.

11. William Roscoe Thayer, ed., *The Harvard Graduates' Magazine*, unsigned review, June 1919, 616–17.

12. Henry Beston, letter to Mrs. W. C. Phinney, August 9, 1919, BFA.

13. Mrs. W. C. Phinney, letter to Henry Beston, August 15, 1919, BFA.

14. Mrs. W. C. Phinney, letter to Henry Beston, February 3, 1921, BFA.

15. Henry Beston, letter to J. Luther Neff, August 12, 1919, BFA.

16. *The New York Times*, April 11, 1918.

17. Henry Beston, letter to J. Luther Neff, April 19, 1919, BFA.

18. Henry Beston, letter to J. Luther Neff, August 12, 1919, BFA.

19. Henry Beston, letter to Jake Day August 19, 1919, BFA.

20. Dalton, "Introduction," *Grimm's Fairy Tales*, xv.

21. Beston, "Prince Sneeze," FFB, 70.

22. Beston, "Prince Sneeze," FFB, 81–82.

23. Beston, "Prince Sneeze," FFB, 87.

24. Beston, "Prince Sneeze," FFB, 88.

25. Beston, "The Lost Half-Hour," FFB, 107.

26. Beston, "The Lost Half-Hour," FFB, 109.

27. Beston, "The Lost Half-Hour," FFB, 114.

28. Beston, "The Seller of Dreams," FFB, 48–50.

29. Beston, "The Adventures of Florian," FFB, 21.

30. Beston, "The Enchanted Elm," FFB, 136.

31. Beston, "The Enchanted Elm," FFB, 139.

32. Ted Roosevelt Jr., letter to Henry Beston, December 2, 1919, BFA. The Roosevelts had four children: Grace Green Roosevelt (1911–1993), Theodore Roosevelt III (1914–2001), Cornelius V. Roosevelt (1915–1991), and Quentin Roosevelt II (1919–1948). The description of the lost reputation is in "The Lost Half-Hour," (112).

33. Theodore Roosevelt Jr., Foreword to FFB, by Henry Beston. Reprint, Eau Claire, WI: Cadmus Books, 1922. The United States senator to whom Ted Roosevelt refers is most likely Henry Cabot Lodge (R-Massachusetts), a close friend of the Roosevelt family.

34. Henry Beston, letter to J. Luther Neff, January 5, 1920, BFA.

35. Elizabeth Coatsworth, typescript, February 14, 1974, BFA.

36. This integrated system of parks and parkways was the first such design in America; it is now listed on the National Register of Historic Places.

37. Elizabeth Coatsworth, PG, 5.

38. Coatsworth, PG, 12.

Notes

39. Kate Beston Barnes, telephone conversation with the author, January 27, 2009. Depression may have run in the Coatsworth family, as two of Thomas Coatsworth's cousins also committed suicide.

40. Coatsworth, PG, 39.

41. Coatsworth, PG, 39.

42. Coatsworth, PG, 39.

43. Coatsworth, PG, 12.

44. Elizabeth Coatsworth, undated holographic notes (probably February 14, 1974), BFA.

45. Henry Beston, letter to Elizabeth Coatsworth, November 30, 1920, BFA. The Four Seas Publishing Company, located in Boston, was a publisher of literary and general interest titles. They were best known for their moderately priced series of popular classics, The International Pocket Library.

46. Henry Beston, letter to Elizabeth Coatsworth, December 21, 1920, BFA.

47. Henry Beston, letter to Elizabeth Coatsworth, December 21, 1920, BFA.

48. Henry Beston, letter to Jake Day, November 13, 1920, BFA.

49. Henry Beston letter to J. Luther Neff, October 17, 1920, BFA.

50. Marie Beston Sheahan, the eldest child of George and Marie Sheahan, was born on October 14, 1919.

51. The brilliant Rupert Hughes (1872–1956) was a novelist, soldier, and musician, who went on to became one of the most successful screenwriters of Hollywood's "Golden Age." His brother Howard Robard Hughes co-founded the Sharp-Hughes Tool Company; Rupert's nephew Howard R. Hughes Jr. inherited the company and went on to a remarkable public career as an industrialist and pilot before becoming a reclusive billionaire.

52. Henry Beston, letter to Elizabeth Coatsworth, January 28, 1921, BFA.

53. Henry Beston, letter to Elizabeth Coatsworth, January 28, 1921, BFA.

54. Henry Beston, letter to Elizabeth Coatsworth, January 28, 1921, BFA.

55. Henry Beston, letter to unidentified correspondent (probably Jake Day), February 1, 1921, BFA.

56. Henry Beston, letter to unidentified correspondent (probably Jake Day), February 1, 1921, BFA.

57. Henry Beston, letter to Elizabeth Coatsworth, February 16, 1921, BFA.

58. Henry Beston, letter to unidentified correspondent (probably Jake Day), May 23, 1921, BFA.

59. Henry Beston, letter to Bee Day, November 7, 1921, BFA.

60. Henry Beston, letter to unidentified correspondent (probably Jake Day), January 2, 1922, BFA.

61. Henry Beston, letter to unidentified correspondent (probably Jake Day), January 2, 1922. MS, BFA.

62. Henry Beston, letter to Elizabeth Coatsworth, January 10, 1923, BFA.

63. Henry Beston, letter to Elizabeth Coatsworth, January 7, 1923, BFA. Lowell died

suddenly from a cerebral hemorrhage in 1925 at the age of 51, leaving her sizable estate to her companion Ada Dwyer Russell. The following year she posthumously won the Pulitzer Prize for Poetry for her collection *What's O'Clock*.

64. Henry Beston, letter to Elizabeth Coatsworth, January 7, 1923, BFA
65. Henry Beston, letter to Elizabeth Coatsworth, April 10, 1923, BFA.
66. Kate Beston Barnes, letter to the author, February 5, 2003.
67. Beston, *SWB*, 4.
68. Beston, *SWB*, 8.
69. Beston, *SWB*, 93.
70. Beston, *SWB*, 108.
71. *Boston Transcript*, October 6, 1923, 8.
72. M. G. Bonner, *International Book Review*, November 1923, 62.
73. Everett McNeil, Review of *The Starlight Wonder Book* by Henry B. Beston. *New York Times (1857–Current file)* [New York, N.Y.] 14 Oct. 1923, BR4. *ProQuest Historical Newspapers The New York Times (1851–2005)*. ProQuest. Milne Library, SUNY College at Oneonta, Oneonta, NY. Accessed February 3, 2009, http://www.proquest.com/.
74. Harvard College Fifteenth Anniversary Report, Class of 1909 (1924), 76.
75. Henry Beston, letter, no salutation, c. April 1923, BFA.

5. A Gallant Vagabond (1923–1926)

1. Beston, "The Wardens of Cape Cod," 186–194, 186. Beston had visited the Cape with his family on several occasions during his childhood.
2. Beston, "The Wardens of Cape Cod," 186–194, 186.
3. Beston, "The Wardens of Cape Cod," 186–194, 186.
4. Beston, "The Wardens of Cape Cod," 186–194, 186.
5. Beston, "The Wardens of Cape Cod," 186–194, 186.
6. Henry Beston, letter to Jake Day, June 18, 1923, BFA.
7. BFA.
8. Henry Beston, letter to Elizabeth Coatsworth, August 8, 1923, BFA.
9. Henry Beston, letter to Bee Day, January 19, 1924, BFA. "Hoodoo" was 1920s-era slang for a financial trader whose luck had gone bad and who was now contagiously unlucky.
10. For a fuller account of the incident, see William P. Quinn, *Shipwrecks Around Cape Cod*, Orleans, MA: Lower Cape Publishing, 1973.
11. Born to a wealthy Boston family, Wheelwright met Beston sometime in the early 1920s. Tall and slim, with dark hair and "eyes like gooseberries," Wheelwright was an intelligent, independent woman with a commanding presence. She and Beston shared a love of the sea as well as a deep interest in the American Indians (in collaboration with Hastiin Klah, a Navajo elder, Wheelwright founded the Wheelwright Museum of the American Indian in Santa Fe, New Mexico, in 1937).

Notes

12. Henry Beston, no salutation, September 23, 1923, BFA.

13. Beston, *BGV*, x.

14. Henry Beston, letter to Jake Day, November 19, 1924, BFA.

15. Henry Beston, "Bullfight—Modern Style." *Independent*, 478–79.

16. Henry Beston, letter to Jake Day, October 23, 1924, BFA.

17. Henry Beston, letter to Jake Day, October 19, 1924, BFA.

18. Henry Beston, letter to Bee Day, December 31, 1924, BFA.

19. Coatsworth, *EM*, 2–4.

20. Wilding, *Henry Beston's Cape Cod*, 28.

21. Henry Beston, letter to Jake and Bee Day, November 24, 1924, BFA.

22. Henry Beston, letter to Jake Day, March 2, 1925, BFA.

23. Lease dated December 1, 1924, BFA.

24. Henry Beston, letter to Jake Day, March 2, 1924 BFA.

25. Jean Edward Smith, *FDR*, 691.

26. Beston, *BGV*, ix.

27. Beston, *BGV*, x.

28. Beston, *BGV*, 19.

29. Beston, *BGV*, 32.

30. Beston, *BGV*, 51.

31. Beston, *BGV*, 65.

32. Beston, *BGV*, 181–82.

33. Beston, *BGV*, 131.

34. Beston, *BGV*, 141.

35. Beston, *BGV*, 162.

36. Beston, *BGV*, 163.

37. Beston, *BGV*, 153.

38. Beston, *BGV*, 163.

39. Beston, *BGV*, 220.

40. Beston, *BGV*, 222.

41. Beston, *BGV*, 216.

42. Beston, *BGV*, 231.

43. Harrison Smith, *New York Tribune*, December 20, 1925, 7.

44. A. H. Gibbs, *Literary Review* of the *New York Evening Post*, December 5, 1925, 7.

45. Unsigned review, *New York Times*, December 6, 1925, 8.

46. Scott, *Exiles and Fabrications*, 174.

47. Henry Beston, letter to J. Luther Neff, November 20, 1925, BFA.

48. Beston, *OH*, 6–8.

49. Beston, *OH*, 6–7.

50. Henry Beston, letter, perhaps to J. Luther Neff, November 20, 1925, BFA.

51. Henry Beston, letter, probably to J. Luther Neff, November 20, 1925, BFA.

52. Henry Beston, letter, probably to J. Luther Neff, November 20, 1925, BFA.

53. Henry Beston, letter to Jake Day, December 20, 1925, BFA.
54. Henry Beston, letter to Jake and Bee Day, December 30, 1925, BFA.
55. Henry Beston, letter to J. Luther Neff, December 28, 1925, BFA.
56. Macmillan placed a Navajo swastika on the book's spine. As Dennis J. Aigner relates in *The Swastika Symbol in Navajo Textiles* (2000), the use of the swastika dates back thousands of years and has appeared in numerous cultures in Asia and the Americas. It was often used in Navajo sand-painting to represent the legend of the rolling log, in which a man cast out of his tribe seeks refuge in a hollowed out log which is swept down river; with the aid of helpful gods he finds a place of peace and prosperity. By the early twentieth century the symbol had become very popular on Navajo rugs and pottery designs coveted by tourists. When the symbol was appropriated by Hitler's Nazi Party and acquired its sinister connotations the southwestern tribes including the Navajo, Apache, and Hopi signed a proclamation renouncing its use and citing the desecration of the symbol by the Nazis.
57. Henry Beston, letter to Jake Day, January 16, 1925, BFA.
58. Henry Beston, letter to Bee Day, November 24, 1924, BFA.

6. ORION RISES ON THE DUNES (1926–1928)

1. Thoreau, *Cape Cod*, 20. Thoreau's own attitude toward the scene of the disaster was, if anything, even less sentimental: "On the whole, it was not so impressive a scene as I might have expected. If I had found one body cast upon the beach in some lonely place, it would have affected me more. I sympathized rather with the winds and the waves, as if to toss and mangle these poor human bodies was the order of the day. If this was the law of Nature, why waste any time in awe or pity? If the last day were come, we should not think so much about the separation of friends or the blighted prospects of individuals" (20–21). Thoreau's apparent lack of sympathy with the victims of the disaster might well be something of a pose, however—when the great Transcendentalist writer Margaret Fuller Ossoli was claimed by a shipwreck off the barrier beach of Long Island the following summer (July 1850), it was Thoreau, encouraged by Ralph Waldo Emerson, who traveled to Fire Island and spent days searching the coast for the body of his friend and her family.
2. Thoreau, *Cape Cod*, 115–16.
3. Cited in Wilding, *Henry Beston's Cape Cod*, 30.
4. Henry Beston, unpublished journal, September 18, 1926, BFA.
5. Henry Beston, unpublished journal, September 19, 1926, BFA.
6. Henry Beston, unpublished journal, September 19, 1926, BFA.
7. Henry Beston, unpublished journal, September 20, 1926, BFA.
8. Henry Beston, unpublished journal, September 21, 1926, BFA.
9. Henry Beston, unpublished journal, September 21, 1926, BFA. In an essay entitled "Landscape and Narrative," included in *Crossing Open Ground* (New York: Random

Notes

House, 1978), Barry Lopez makes a similar point regarding a Cree Indian's response to an anecdote Lopez had heard from the Nunamiut regarding insights into the nature of the wolverine that may not have been confirmable by his own experience: "You know...that could happen" (70).

10. Beston, *OH*, 10–11.
11. Henry Beston, unpublished journal, September 27, 1926, BFA.
12. Henry Beston, unpublished journal, September 22, 1926, BFA.
13. Wilding, *Henry Beston's Cape Cod*, 24.
14. Beston, *OH*, 16.
15. Henry Beston, unpublished journal, September 23, 1926, BFA.
16. Henry Beston, unpublished journal, September 25, 1926, BFA.
17. Henry Beston, unpublished journal, October 6, 1926, BFA.
18. Beston, *OH*, 20–21.
19. Beston, *OH*, 23.
20. Beston, *OH*, 25.
21. Lorenz, "Henry Beston: The Outermost Man," 107.
22. Wilding, *Henry Beston's Cape Cod*, 38.
23. Beston, *OH*, 95.
24. Alexander, *Bergson*, 7–8.
25. Barrus, *The Heart of Burroughs's Journals*, 272.
26. Bergson received a Nobel prize for his work in 1927, although it is telling that the award was granted in literature, not science. By the 1930s his work on "creative evolution" was no longer in vogue, although many of his concepts, such as that of the élan vital, which had added a mystical or spiritual element to the scientific theory of evolution, were still commonly referred to in various contexts.
27. Beston, *OH*, 95.
28. Henry Beston, unpublished journal, October 5, 1926, BFA.
29. Henry Beston, letter to Elizabeth Coatsworth, September 14, 1926, BFA.
30. Henry Beston, letter to Elizabeth Coatsworth, September 14, 1926, BFA.
31. Theodore Roosevelt Jr., letter to Henry Beston, September 16, 1926, BFA.
32. Henry Beston, unpublished journal, October 15, 1926, BFA.
33. Henry Beston, unpublished journal, October 15, 1926, BFA.
34. Henry Beston, unpublished journal, October 15, 1926, BFA.
35. Henry Beston, unpublished journal, October 15, 1926, BFA.
36. Henry Beston, letter to Mabel Davison, October 20, 1926, BFA.
37. Henry Beston, unpublished journal, October 15, 1926, BFA.
38. Wilding, *Henry Beston's Cape Cod*, 29.
39. Henry Beston, unpublished journal, October 16, 1926, BFA.
40. Beston, *OH*, 34.
41. Beston, *OH*, 36.
42. Beston, *OH*, 8.

43. Henry Beston, unpublished journal, October 22, 1926, BFA. "Death knowledge" is underlined in Beston's journal, evidently to emphasize its importance in his thinking; oddly enough, however, there is little on this topic in *The Outermost House*.

44. Beston, *OH*, 94–95.

45. Henry Beston, unpublished journal, October 1, 1926, BFA.

46. Henry Beston, unpublished journal, October 1, 1926, BFA.

47. Lyon, *This Incomperable Lande*, 82.

48. Beston, *OH*, 95.

49. Beston, *OH*, 91.

50. Beston, *OH*, 62.

51. Beston, *OH*, 68.

52. Beston, *OH*, 68.

53. Beston, *OH*, 82.

54. Henry Beston, letter to Mabel Davison, February 21, 1927, BFA.

55. Beston, *OH*, 89.

56. Beston, *OH*, 89–90.

57. Beston, *OH*, 119–20.

58. Beston, *OH*, 122.

59. Henry Beston, letter to Mabel Davison, February 22, 1927, BFA.

60. Beston, *OH*, 37–38.

61. Beston, *OH*, 144–45.

62. Beston, *OH*, 151–52.

63. Beston, *OH*, 158–59.

64. Beston, *OH*, 166–67.

65. Beston, *OH*, 195.

66. Beston, *OH*, 199.

67. Henry Beston, letter to Elizabeth Coatsworth, January 29, 1929, BFA.

68. Lyon, *This Incomperable Lande*, 82.

69. Bomhard, 6, BFA.

70. Coatsworth, *EM*, 4.

71. Theodore Roosevelt Jr., letter to Henry Beston, undated (summer 1927), BFA.

72. Theodore Roosevelt Jr., letter to Henry Beston, April 2, 1928, BFA.

73. Ellery Sedgwick, letter to Henry Beston, October 10, 1927, BFA.

74. Ellery Sedgwick, letter to Henry Beston, July 8, 1928, BFA.

75. Hays, "Three Decades of Environmental Politics," 22.

76. Beston, *OH*, 59.

77. Beston, *OH*, 165–66.

78. Beston, *OH*, 186–88.

79. Coatsworth, *EM*, 13–14.

80. Beston, *OH*, 100–103.

81. Federman, "Toward an Ecology of Place: Three Views of Cape Cod," 213.

Notes

82. Paul, "Coming Home to the World: Another Journal for Henry Beston" in *For Love of the World: Essays on Nature Writers*, 96.
83. Beston, *OH*, 220–22.
84. Henry Beston, letter to J. Luther Neff, January 29, 1934, BFA.
85. Henry Beston, letter to Elizabeth Coatsworth, August 30, 1928, BFA.
86. Henry Beston, letter to Mabel Davison, November 21, 1928, BFA.
87. Henry Beston, letter to Elizabeth Coatsworth, August 30, 1928, BFA.
88. Henry Beston, letter to Elizabeth Coatsworth, August 30, 1928, BFA.
89. Henry Beston, letter to Elizabeth Coatsworth, January 12, 1929, BFA.
90. Henry Beston, letter to Elizabeth Coatsworth, January 12, 1929, BFA.
91. Henry Beston, letter to Elizabeth Coatsworth, August 30, 1928, BFA.
92. Henry Beston, letter to Truesdell Fife, November 10, 1928, BFA.
93. Henry Beston, letter to Truesdell Fife, December 5, 1928, BFA.
94. Coatsworth, *EM*, 14.
95. Coatsworth, Introduction to *The Best of Beston*, 4.

7. Henry and Elizabeth (1929–1932)

1. "Orion" is from a series of poems Elizabeth Coatsworth wrote for Henry Beston to commemorate their first wedding anniversary.
2. Henry Beston, letter to Elizabeth Coatsworth, August 26, 1927, BFA.
3. Kate Beston Barnes, letter to the author, February 5, 2003.
4. Henry Beston, letter to Elizabeth Coatsworth, January 5, 1929, BFA.
5. Elizabeth Coatsworth, letter to Henry Beston, January 1929, BFA.
6. Henry Beston, letter to Elizabeth Coatsworth, January 9, 1929, BFA. In later years this statement would take on an ironic twist, for like the English monarch, Henry VIII, who yearned for a son and heir, Henry Beston too would be disappointed in having only daughters.
7. Henry Beston, letter to Elizabeth Coatsworth, February 6, 1929, BFA.
8. Bee Day, letter to Henry Beston, January 10, 1929, BFA.
9. Henry Beston, letter to Elizabeth Coatsworth, January 9, 1929, BFA.
10. Elizabeth Coatsworth, letter to Henry Beston, January 19, 1929, BFA.
11. Elizabeth Coatsworth, letter to Henry Beston, January 17, 1929, BFA.
12. Henry Beston, letter to Elizabeth Coatsworth, January 19, 1929, BFA.
13. Elizabeth Coatsworth, letter to Henry Beston, February 7, 1929, BFA.
14. Henry Beston, letter to Elizabeth Coatsworth. 29 January 1929, BFA.
15. Henry Beston, letter to Elizabeth Coatsworth, January 19, 1929, BFA.
16. Henry Beston, letter to Elizabeth Coatsworth, January 9, 1929, BFA.
17. Henry Beston, letter to Elizabeth Coatsworth, January 18, 1929, BFA.
18. Henry Beston, letter to Elizabeth Coatsworth, January 30, 1929, BFA.
19. Mary Cabot Wheelwright, letter to Henry Beston, January 18, 1929, BFA.

Notes

20. Corey Ford, letter to Henry Beston, January 25, 1929, BFA.
21. Henry Beston, letter to Elizabeth Coatsworth, March 6, 1929, BFA.
22. Henry Beston, letter to Elizabeth Coatsworth, March 10, 1929, BFA.
23. Henry Beston, letter to Elizabeth Coatsworth, March 17, 1929, BFA.
24. Henry Beston, letter to Elizabeth Coatsworth, March 23, 1929, BFA.
25. Henry Beston, letter to Elizabeth Coatsworth, March 23, 1929, BFA.
26. Henry Beston, letter to Elizabeth Coatsworth, May 8, 1929, BFA.
27. Henry Beston, letter to Elizabeth Coatsworth, May 8, 1929, BFA.
28. Henry Beston, letter to Elizabeth Coatsworth, May 8, 1929, BFA.
29. Henry Beston, letter to Elizabeth Coatsworth, May 2, 1929, BFA.
30. Henry Beston, letter to Truesdell Fife, May 29, 1929, BFA.
31. Elizabeth Coatsworth, typescript, February 14, 1974, BFA.
32. Elizabeth. Coatsworth, letter to Ida Reid Coatsworth, June 21, 1929, BFA.
33. Elizabeth Coatsworth, letter to Morton and Margaret Smith, June 21, 1929, BFA. Green heads are biting flies common to the Cape Cod area.
34. Henry Beston, letter to Ida Reid Coatsworth, July 1, 1929, BFA.
35. Henry Beston, letter to Morton and Margaret Smith, July 5, 1929, BFA.
36. Henry Beston, letter to Morton and Margaret Smith, July 25, 1929, BFA.
37. Elizabeth Coatsworth, letter to Morton and Margaret Smith, September 5, 1929, BFA.
38. Elizabeth Coatsworth, typescript, February 14, 1974, BFA.
39. Theodore Roosevelt Jr., letter to Henry Beston, March 11, 1930, BFA.
40. Henry Beston, letter to Elizabeth Coatsworth, April 1, 1930, BFA.
41. Henry Beston, letter to Elizabeth Coatsworth, April 2, 1930, BFA.
42. Henry Beston, letter to Elizabeth Coatsworth, April 1, 1930, BFA.
43. Henry Beston, letter to Elizabeth Coatsworth, April 1, 1930, BFA.
44. Henry Beston, letter to Truesdell Fife, April 25, 1930, BFA.
45. Beston, letter to Elizabeth Coatsworth, May 12, 1930, BFA.
46. Henry Beston, letter to Elizabeth Coatsworth, May 15, 1930, BFA.
47. Henry Beston, letter to Truesdell Fife, June 9, 1930, BFA.
48. Henry Beston, letter to Elizabeth Coatsworth, January 7, 1931, BFA.
49. Henry Beston, letter to Elizabeth Coatsworth, March 11, 1931, BFA.
50. Henry Beston, letter to Elizabeth Coatsworth, March 11, 1931, BFA.
51. Henry Beston, letter to Elizabeth Coatsworth, March 11, 1931, BFA.
52. Henry Beston, letter to Elizabeth Coatsworth, March 12, 1931, BFA.
53. Henry Beston, letter to Elizabeth Coatsworth, March 13, 1931, BFA.
54. Henry Beston, letter to Elizabeth Coatsworth, March 13, 1931, BFA.
55. Henry Beston, letter to Elizabeth Coatsworth, March 24, 1931, BFA.
56. Henry Beston, letter to Elizabeth Coatsworth, March 25, 1931, BFA.
57. Henry Beston, letter to Elizabeth Coatsworth, April 2, 1931, BFA.
58. Henry Beston, letter to Elizabeth Coatsworth, May 19, 1931, BFA.
59. Coatsworth, *EM*, 6.

Notes

60. Western Union Telegram, April 25 1931, BFA.
61. Henry Beston, letter to Elizabeth Coatsworth, September 12, 1931, BFA.
62. Henry Beston, letter to Elizabeth Coatsworth, September 17, 1931, BFA.
63. Henry Beston, letter to Elizabeth Coatsworth, September 28, 1931, BFA.
64. Henry Beston, letter to Elizabeth Coatsworth, September 29, 1931, BFA.
65. Henry Beston, letter to Elizabeth Coatsworth, September 29, 1931, BFA.
66. Henry Beston, letter to J. Luther Neff, December 24, 1931, BFA.
67. Henry Beston, letter to Truesdell Fife, April 29, 1932, BFA.

8. The Revelation of the Earth (1932–1935)

1. Henry Beston, letter to Elizabeth Coatsworth, April 1932 (undated), BFA.
2. Kate Beston Barnes, letter to the author, February 5, 2003.
3. Henry Beston, letter to Elizabeth Coatsworth, May 2, 1932, BFA.
4. Henry Beston, letter to Mabel Davison, May 3, 1932, BFA. The full letter reads:
   Marraine bien aimeé—
   It troubles me deeply to have to write this note but you leave me no alternative. If I am frank, I am sure that you would rather have it so. When I mentioned the other day that I was coming to Damariscotta, and you mentioned that you too might come, I tried to make it perfectly clear, in a way which would not wound you, that such a visit was unwise, and you got my meaning so unmistakably that you hastened to reassure me. Now Marraine, I have been through a tense year and lately through a tense experience ["I am tired" is crossed out] and I have come here for a change, a rest, new contacts, and (my family being in good hands) a complete freedom from added responsibility. Moreover, I have but eight days to get my house in order for my family, and there is a world to do. I now find that entirely without consulting me, in the face of my reasonable request, and in spite of your knowing perfectly well that any visit to Damariscotta must involve me, you have determined on coming, and are trying to engage rooms. Now, dear, do not come. If you do, I shall do the one thing open to me, I shall close the house instantly, cancel this little rest which means so much to me, and return to Hingham. I hardly need to say that I think your forcing this, in the face of my reasonable request, and at such a time and in such circumstances, is immeasurably short-sighted and unwise.
5. On 11 May 1932 Beston wrote to Elizabeth: "Marraine writes, and I reply, exactly as if nothing had occurred." BFA.
6. Henry Beston, letter to Elizabeth Coatsworth, May 13, 1932, BFA.
7. Henry Beston, letter to Elizabeth Coatsworth, May 17, 1932, BFA.
8. Henry Beston, letter to Elizabeth Coatsworth, May 6, 1932, BFA.
9. Henry Beston, letter to Elizabeth Coatsworth, May 11, 1932, BFA.
10. Elizabeth Coatsworth, letter to Margaret and Morton Smith, June 16, 1932, BFA.
11. Henry Beston, letter to Truesdell Fife, September 5, 1932, BFA.
12. Henry Beston, letter to Elizabeth Coatsworth, September 1932 [undated], BFA.

Notes

13. Elizabeth Coatsworth, letter to Morton and Margaret Smith, February 14, 1933, BFA.
14. Henry Beston, letter to Margaret Smith and Ida Reid Coatsworth, February 23, 1933, BFA.
15. Henry Beston, letter to Truesdell Fife, February 8, 1933, BFA.
16. *Quincy Patriot-Ledger*, February 1933. Clipping from Beston letter of February 5, 1933. BFA.
17. Henry Beston, letter to Truesdell Fife, April 11, 1933, BFA.
18. Henry Beston, letter to Truesdell Fife, July 20, 1933, BFA.
19. Goldberg. *America in the Twenties*, 85.
20. Henry Beston, letter to Truesdell Fife, February 8, 1933, BFA.
21. Henry Beston, letter to Truesdell Fife, November 5, 1932, BFA.
22. Henry Beston, letter to Truesdell Fife, March 16, 1934, BFA.
23. Henry Beston, letter to David McCord, February 13, 1934, BFA.
24. Henry Beston, letter to Morton Smith, July 12, 1933, BFA.
25. Henry Beston, letter to Truesdell Fife, October 21, 1933, BFA.
26. Kate Beston Barnes, letter to the author, February 5, 2003.
27. Henry Beston, letter to J. Luther Neff, June 20, 1932, BFA.
28. Elizabeth Coatsworth, letter to Margaret Smith, June 26, 1933, BFA.
29. Henry Beston, letter to Elizabeth Coatsworth, November 21, 1933, BFA.
30. Coatsworth, *EM*, 5.
31. Henry Beston, letter to Truesdell Fife, September 5, 1932, BFA.
32. Henry Beston, letter to Truesdell Fife, September 5, 1932, BFA.
33. Henry Beston, letter to Truesdell Fife, November 14, 1933, BFA.
34. Henry Beston, letter to Ida Reid Coatsworth, November 21, 1933, BFA.
35. Elizabeth Coatsworth, letter to Morton and Margaret Smith, August 1933 [undated], BFA.
36. Henry Beston, letter to J. Luther Neff, December 8, 1933, BFA.
37. Henry Beston, letter to Morton Smith, November 24,1933, Dartmouth College Archives.
38. Beston, *HE*, 21.
39. Elizabeth Coatsworth, letter to Margaret Smith. August 1934 [undated], BFA.
40. Coatsworth, *EM*, 7.
41. Kate Beston Barnes, "At Home," *Where the Deer Were* (Boston: David R. Godine, 1994), 26.
42. Henry Beston, letter to Truesdell Fife, November 1, 1934, BFA.
43. Henry Beston, letter to J. Luther Neff, July 5, 1935, BFA.
44. Beston, *HE*, 4–5.
45. Beston, *HE*, 11.
46. Beston, *HE*, 50.
47. *Christian Science Monitor*, March 22, 1935: 14.
48. David McCord, "Atlantic Bookshelf," *Atlantic Monthly*, June 1935.

Notes

49. Simo, *Literature of Place*, 141.

50. Simo, *Literature of Place*, 141.

51. Elizabeth Coatsworth, letter to Morton Smith, January 23, 1935, BFA.

52. Elizabeth Coatsworth, letter to Morton Smith, February 18, 1935, BFA. The Hotel Bella Vista would later make a cameo appearance in Malcolm Lowry's semi-autobiographical novel *Under the Volcano* (1947).

53. Elizabeth Coatsworth, letter to Margaret and Morton Smith, March 1, 1935, BFA.

54. Elizabeth Coatsworth, letter to Morton Smith, June 1935, BFA.

55. Henry Beston, letter to J. Luther Neff, August 12, 1935, BFA.

56. Henry Beston, letter to Truesdell Fife, September 13, 1935, BFA.

57. Elizabeth Coatsworth, letter to Morton Smith, November 24, 1935, BFA.

58. Henry Beston, letter to Morton Smith, November 30, 1935, BFA.

59. Elizabeth Coatsworth, letter to Margaret Smith, December 7, 1935, BFA.

9. The Divine Consciousness and the Soul of Man (1936–1940)

1. Henry Beston, letter to Truesdell Fife, January 2, 1936, BFA.

2. Henry Beston, letter to Truesdell Fife, January 2, 1936, BFA.

3. Elizabeth Coatsworth, letter [no salutation], March 1936, BFA.

4. Elizabeth Coatsworth, letter to Morton and Margaret Smith, January 15, 1936, BFA.

5. Elizabeth Coatsworth, letter to Morton and Margaret Smith, January 27, 1936, BFA.

6. Henry Beston, letter to Morton Smith, February 8, 1936, BFA.

7. Elizabeth Coatsworth, letter to Morton Smith, March 11, 1936, BFA.

8. Elizabeth Coatsworth, letter to Morton and Margaret Smith, June 1936, BFA.

9. Henry Beston, letter to J. Luther Neff, July 22, 1936, BFA.

10. Henry Beston, letter to Elizabeth Coatsworth, July 29, 1936, BFA.

11. Elizabeth Coatsworth, letter to Morton Smith, November 8, 1936, BFA.

12. Henry Beston, letter to Truesdell Fife, February 18, 1937, BFA.

13. Henry Beston, letter to Truesdell Fife, February 18, 1937, BFA.

14. Beston, Henry, letter to Truesdell Fife, January 1937, BFA.

15. Henry Beston, letter to David McCord, September 14, 1937, BFA.

16. Henry Beston, ed., *American Memory*, 43.

17. Henry Beston, interview by Pamel Bomhard, 1974 (8), BFA.

18. Beston, *American Memory*, 141.

19. Beston, *OH*, 216.

20. Elizabeth Coatsworth, letter to Morton and Margaret Smith, July 4, 1937, BFA.

21. Elizabeth Coatsworth, letter to Morton and Margaret Smith, July 12, 1937, BFA.

22. Elizabeth Coatsworth, letter to Morton and Margaret Smith, July 15, 1937, BFA.

23. Elizabeth Coatsworth, letter to Morton and Margaret Smith, August 9, 1937, BFA.

24. Elizabeth Coatsworth, letter to Morton and Margaret Smith, April 1937, BFA.

25. Henry Beston, letter to J. Luther Neff, August 10, 1937, BFA.

Notes

26. Elizabeth Coatsworth, letter to Morton Smith, October 11, 1937, BFA.

27. Elizabeth Coatsworth, letter to Morton Smith, October 18, 1937, BFA.

28. Elizabeth Coatsworth, letter to Morton Smith, September 1, 1937, BFA.

29. Elizabeth Coatsworth, letter to Morton Smith, September 1, 1937, BFA.

30. Henry Beston, letter to Truesdell Fife, November 19, 1937, BFA.

31. Of the stay with Mary Wheelwright, Elizabeth wrote, "We are nearly at an end of our marvelous week at Mary's old Spanish house on the Rio Grande. I love the pastoral feeling of the land—the plums in bloom, the Mexicans plowing, the Indian carts high with firewood, the sheep grazing, and beyond the high ring of snow-capped mountains. Yesterday we woke to find snow all over the ground; it had gone down to eighteen in the night, but the day is so warm that we sat in the sun against the wall with the eight little Thibetan dogs tumbling in and out of our laps like rag dolls. Every day we go adventuring to cliff dwellings, or Indian villages—today its to Taos, that lonely spot." Elizabeth Coatsworth, letter to Morton and Margaret Smith, April 3, 1938, BFA.

32. Henry Beston, letter to Morton and Margaret Smith, April 13, 1938, BFA.

33. Charles Bolte, letter to Henry Beston, May 12, 1938, BFA. Bolte went on to win a Rhodes Scholarship, and he enlisted in the British Army (despite his American citizenship) even before the United States entered the war. He lost a leg at the battle of El Alamein in North Africa, and in 1943 was the founder of the American Veterans Committee. He went on to work as an executive vice president at Viking Press and wrote several books, including *The Price of Peace: A Plan for Disarmament* (1956). He became a close friend of the Bestons and after retiring he moved to Maine, where he died in 1994 at the age of 74.

34. Henry Beston, letter to Morton Smith, June 22, 1938, BFA.

35. Elva Knight, letter to Elizabeth Coatsworth, August 4, 1938, BFA.

36. Elizabeth Coatsworth, letter to Morton Smith, July 16, 1938, BFA.

37. Henry Beston, letter to Truesdell Fife, June 24, 1938, BFA.

38. Henry Beston, letter to J. Luther Neff, July 21, 1938, BFA.

39. Henry Beston, letter to Elizabeth Coatsworth, September 19, 1938, BFA.

40. Henry Beston, letter to Elizabeth Coatsworth Beston, September 22, 1938, BFA.

41. Elizabeth Coatsworth, letter to Morton Smith, September 18, 1938, BFA.

42. Henry Beston, letter to Elizabeth Coatsworth, September 22, 1938, BFA.

43. Elizabeth Coatsworth, letter to Morton Smith, September 28, 1938, BFA.

44. George Sheahan, letter to Henry Beston, July 11, 1942, BFA.

45. Henry Beston, letter to Truesdell Fife, September 13, 1935, BFA.

46. Henry Beston, letter to Elizabeth Coatsworth, October 9, 1938, BFA.

47. Henry Beston, letter to Truesdell Fife, April 6, 1939, BFA.

48. Theodore Roosevelt Jr., letter to Henry Beston, April 3, 1939, BFA.

49. Henry Beston, letter to Elizabeth Coatsworth, August 24, 1939, BFA.

50. Henry Beston, letter to Truesdell Fife, August 31, 1939, BFA.

51. Henry Beston, letter to J. Luther Neff, June 23, 1939, BFA.

Notes

52. Henry Beston, letter to Morton Smith, October 14, 1939, BFA.

53. Elizabeth Coatsworth, letter to Morton Smith, August 29, 1939, BFA.

54. Henry Beston, letter to J. Luther Neff, September 11, 1939, BFA.

55. On October 7, 1939 Henry wrote to Elizabeth about the sinking of an American ship, the *Athenia*, by a German U-boat: "In the light of yesterday's headline "Berlin warns of plot to sink, etc." you must have thoughts of my attitude to the Lusitania affair. I am absolutely certain that some such terrible thing as the Germans announced has been prepared. There is first antecedent probability, to use the legal phrase. The Lusitania was so arranged that she would sink quickly. There followed some skullduggery connected with a change of course, and, then, the ship being torpedoes, there was no aid sent (from a region swarming with ships!) till the drowning had been of adequate horror. I discussed it with Ted, saying that the ship was pulled back and forth before the hidden submarine as a catnip mouse is pulled back and forth before a kitten hidden under the fringes of the sofa. They then covered the commander of the ship with honors, for having so well accomplished his hideous task.

The Athenia is patently bogus. As T. says, "there's something very queer about it." And to quote Huck Finn, "it just doesn't make sense." To sink a vessel returning full of tourists, is an absurdity, and the Germans are far too intelligent to do such a thing.

You now have the Iroquois. I'm sure something was planned for her. One sinking "framed" (beyond question to my rather skeptical mind) one sinking bogus (a sinking attended by complete absence of rational motive & by submarine behavior entirely out of the norm) and now one more, a sinking in intention, which a most responsible official signals, and the White House has sense enough to consider.

Its just too much, dear. To be tricked into war once by so hideous a stratagem is terrible enough, but to have it happen again, with that frightful cold bloodedness, is simply beyond human bearing. The whole thing is so appalling, so alien to our bones, that our incredulity is but natural. But the nation must think. For the allies, of course, it is salus populi suprema lex. Well, its certainly valus populi for us, too. But how really, in the full sense of the word, diabolical!

There is also a fair field for conjecture in the fact that these adventures are all connected with the presence at the admiralty of the Rt. Hon. Winston Churchill."

56. Henry Beston, letter to Elizabeth C. Coatsworth, October 17, 1939, BFA.

57. Henry Beston, letter to Elizabeth Coatsworth, late 1939, no date, BFA.

58. Henry Beston, letter to Elizabeth Coatsworth, March 2, 1940, BFA.

59. Henry Beston, letter to Henry Richards, December 28, 1940, BFA.

60. Henry Beston, letter to Elizabeth Coatsworth, September 31, 1940, BFA.

61. Elizabeth Coatsworth, letter to Margaret Smith, August 17, 1940, BFA.

62. Elizabeth Coatsworth, letter to Morton Smith, November 23, 1940, BFA.

Notes

10. A Naturalist Looks at War (1941–1945)

1. Henry Beston, letter to Henry Richards, December 18, 1940, BFA.
2. Elizabeth Coatsworth, letter to Pamela Bomhard, February 14, 1974. Cited in Bomhard (8).
3. Henry Beston, letter to Elizabeth Coatsworth, April [n.d.] 1941, BFA.
4. Henry Beston, letter to Elizabeth Coatsworth, April 12, 1941, BFA.
5. Henry Beston, letter to Elizabeth Coatsworth, May 5, 1941, BFA.
6. Henry Beston, letter to Elizabeth Coatsworth, May 10, 1941, BFA.
7. Henry Beston, letter to Elizabeth Coatsworth, May 10, 1941, BFA.
8. Henry Beston, letter to Elizabeth Coatsworth, June 3, 1941, BFA.
9. Henry Beston, letter to Elizabeth Coatsworth, June 18, 1941, BFA.
10. Elizabeth Coatsworth, letter to Morton and Margaret Smith, June 23, 1941, BFA.
11. Elizabeth Coatsworth, letter to Morton Smith, June 26, 1941, BFA.
12. Elizabeth Coatsworth, letter to Morton Smith, July 2, 1941, BFA.
13. Elizabeth Coatsworth, letter to Morton Smith, July 12, 1941, BFA.
14. Henry Beston, letter to J. Luther Neff, December 8, 1941, BFA.
15. Henry Beston, letter to J. Luther Neff, December 28, 1941, BFA.
16. Henry Beston, letter to Morton Smith, June [n.d.], 1942, BFA.
17. Elizabeth Coatsworth, letter to Morton Smith, July 1, 1942, BFA.
18. Elizabeth Coatsworth, letter to Morton and Margaret Smith, August 24, 1942, BFA.
19. Elizabeth Coatsworth, letter to Morton and Margaret Smith, August 27, 1942, BFA.
20. Elizabeth Coatsworth, letter to Morton Smith, November [n.d.], 1942, BFA.
21. Paul, *For Love of the World*, 116.
22. Beston, *The St. Lawrence,* ix.
23. Beston, *The St. Lawrence,* 107.
24. Beston, *The St. Lawrence,* 155.
25. Beston, *The St. Lawrence,* 108.
26. Henriette C. K. Naeseth, Review of *The Chicago* by Harry Hansen and *The St. Lawrence* by Henry Beston. *The Mississippi Valley Historical Review* 30, no. 1 (June 1943): 105–6.
27. Marine Leland, "French Canada: An Example of What America is Learning," *The Modern Language Journal*, 29, no. 5 (May 1945): 389–402.
28. Henry Beston, letter to Morton Smith, December 14, 1942, BFA.
29. Elizabeth Coatsworth, letter to Margaret Smith, December 14, 1942, BFA.
30. Henry Beston, letter to Elizabeth Coatsworth, January 10, 1943, BFA.
31. Henry Beston, letter to Elizabeth Coatsworth, January 12, 1943, BFA.
32. Henry Beston, letter to J. Luther Neff, January 25, 1943, BFA.
33. Charles Bolte, letter to Henry Beston, January 29, 1943, BFA.
34. Henry Beston, letter to Elizabeth Coatsworth, May 18, 1943, BFA.
35. Henry Beston, letter to J. Luther Neff, March 4, 1943, BFA.

36. Beston, *SL*, 172.
37. Henry Beston, letter to David McCord, May 8, 1943, BFA.
38. Henry Beston, letter to Elizabeth Coatsworth, May 10, 1943, BFA.
39. Elizabeth Coatsworth, letter to Morton and Margaret Smith, July 23, 1943, BFA.
40. Elizabeth Coatsworth, letter to Morton Smith, October 23, 1943, BFA.
41. Elizabeth Coatsworth, letter to Margaret Smith, October 29, 1943, BFA.
42. Henry Beston, letter to J. Luther Neff, November 29, 1943, BFA.
43. Henry Beston, letter to Elizabeth Coatsworth, June 10, 1943, BFA.
44. Charles Bolte, letter to Henry Beston, January 10, 1944, BFA.
45. Oswald Garrison Villard, letter to Henry Beston, January 19, 1944, BFA.
46. Henry Beston, letter to Elizabeth Coatsworth, April 27, 1944, BFA.
47. Henry Beston, letter to Elizabeth Coatsworth, May 2, 1944, BFA.
48. Henry Beston, letter to Elizabeth Coatsworth, May 2, 1944, BFA.
49. Henry Beston, letter to J. Luther Neff, June 6, 1944, BFA.
50. Henry Beston, letter to Elizabeth Coatsworth, June 5, 1944, BFA.
51. Henry Beston, letter to Elizabeth Coatsworth, June 7, 1944, BFA.
52. See Jeffers, *Theodore Roosevelt Jr., the Life of a War Hero*.
53. Henry Beston, letter to J. Luther Neff, July 14, 1944, BFA. The Bestons did not have a radio at the farm for several more years. They also did not yet have a telephone or electricity until after the end of the war.
54. Henry Beston, letter to Morton Smith, July 21, 1944, BFA.
55. Elizabeth Coatsworth, letter to Morton Smith, July 23, 1944, BFA.
56. Henry Beston, letter to David McCord, May 12, 1944, BFA.
57. Elizabeth Coatsworth, journal, August 4, 1945, Elizabeth Jane Coatsworth Papers, 1930–1968, Fogler Library, University of Maine at Orono, Special Collections.
58. Elizabeth Coatsworth, letter to Morton Smith, August 31, 1944, BFA.
59. Henry Beston, letter to Morton Smith, September 2, 1944, BFA.
60. Waldron, *Journey to Outermost House*, 18.
61. Henry Beston, letter to Elizabeth Coatsworth, September [n.d.], 1944, BFA.
62. Henry Beston, letter to Morton Smith, October 6, 1944, BFA.
63. Elizabeth Coatsworth, letter to Morton Smith, October 8, 1944, BFA.
64. Stanley M. Rinehart, Jr., letter to Henry Beston, October 10, 1944, BFA.
65. Stanley M. Rinehart Jr., letter to Henry Beston, October 16, 1944, BFA.
66. Henry Beston, "Confusion in France."
67. Henry Beston, Letter to the Editor, *The Christian Century*, March 21, 1945.
68. Henry Beston, letter to Elizabeth Coatsworth, January 8, 1945, BFA.
69. Henry Beston, letter to J. Luther Neff, February 1, 1945, BFA.
70. *Lincoln County News*, 12 November 1945. Clipping from BFA.
71. Henry Beston, letter to Elizabeth Coatsworth, May 7, 1945, BFA.
72. Henry Beston, letter to J. Luther Neff, June 30, 1945, BFA.
73. Elizabeth Coatsworth, letter to Morton Smith, August 19, 1945, BFA.

74. Harold E. Fey, letter to Henry Beston, August 23, 1945, BFA.
75. Henry Beston, letter to J. Luther Neff, December 8, 1945, BFA.
76. Elizabeth Coatsworth, letter to Margaret Smith, August 25, 1945, BFA.
77. Beston, letter to J. Luther Neff, December 8, 1945, BFA.
78. Henry Beston, letter to J. Luther Neff, June 30, 1945, BFA.
79. Henry Beston, letter to J. Luther Neff, June 30, 1945, BFA.
80. On one such occasion, in mid-May of 1945, Beston drove to Cape Cod to check on the status of the Fo'castle after another winter of storms. The house was fine but more sand had eroded from the dune, and Beston had to consider the possibility of moving the shack down from the crest of the ever-diminishing dune to a more sheltered location on the marsh side. Meg wrote a letter from school to the family inquiring about the Fo'castle, adding "Someday soon daddy and [I] will have to go down and spend some time, for I love the sea as well as he does." Meg Beston, letter to Beston family, May 22, 1945, BFA.
81. Henry Beston, letter to Elizabeth Coatsworth, November 16, 1944, BFA.

11. THE COSMIC CHILL (1945–1952)

1. Beston, *HE*, 5.
2. Henry Beston, letter to J. Luther Neff, December 30, 1946, BFA.
3. Morris Rubin, letter to Henry Beston, January 10, 1946, BFA. As Rubin said in the letter, "The response is uniformly excellent, and we are getting anywhere from a score to 30 letters a week, which is really a grand response."
4. Henry Beston, letter to J. Luther Neff, January 24, 1946, BFA.
5. Henry Beston, letter to Luther Neff, December [undated] 1946, BFA.
6. Beston, letter to Elizabeth Coatsworth, May 4, 1946, BFA.
7. Henry Beston, letter to Morton and Margaret Smith, June 6, 1946, BFA.
8. Henry Beston, letter to Elizabeth Coatsworth, May 27, 1947, BFA.
9. Henry Beston, letter to Elizabeth Coatsworth, May 27, 1947, BFA.
10. Beston, *OH*, xxxv. Beston first published the passage beginning, "Man can either be less than man" in the Foreword to Herbert Faulkner West's 1939 nature writing anthology *The Nature Writers: A Guide to Richer Reading*.
11. Elizabeth Coatsworth, letter to Morton and Margaret Smith, November 19, 1946, BFA.
12. Henry Beston, letter to Elizabeth Coatsworth, April 13, 1947, BFA.
13. As Henry wrote to Luther Neff in April, "Elizabeth has been in California these last two months, but is now on her way home. As I said before, it has been a kind of a dispiriting winter. Poor old Morton dying in September, Mother C. In December, and in February Uncle George, the elder of the two old uncles E. had in California, next to the last of the older order. As E. and her sister were next of kin, and there was absolutely nobody to take care of things, both sisters went out to do what was necessary." Henry Beston, April 22, 1948, BFA.

Notes

14. Henry Beston, letter to Elizabeth Coatworth, March 16, 1948, BFA.
15. Elizabeth Coatsworth, letter to Margaret Smith, June 4, 1948, BFA.
16. Elizabeth Coatsworth, letter to Margaret Smith, October 4, 1947, BFA.
17. Elizabeth Coatsworth, letter to Margaret Smith, October 11, 1947, BFA.
18. John Farrar, letter to Henry Beston, January 28, 1948, BFA.
19. Henry Beston, letter to J. Luther Neff, April 22, 1948, BFA.
20. Henry Beston, letter to Elizabeth Coatsworth, March 16, 1948, BFA.
21. Henry Beston, letter to Elizabeth Coatsworth, March 6, 1948, BFA.
22. Kate Beston Barnes, interview with Sarah Miller and Gary Lawless, March 16, 2005, Appleton, ME, BFA.
23. Henry Beston, letter to J. Luther Neff, December 19, 1948, BFA.
24. Henry Beston, letter to J. Luther Neff, December 26, 1949, BFA.
25. Henry Beston, letter to Elizabeth Coatsworth, September 10, 1948, BFA.
26. Henry Beston, *Northern Farm*, 4.
27. Beston, *Northern Farm*, 7.
28. Scott, *Exiles and Fabrications*, 180.
29. Beston, *Northern Farm*, 258.
30. Phillips, *The Truth of Ecology*, 219.
31. Beston, letter to J. Luther Neff, July 15, 1943, BFA.
32. H. L. Mencken, letter to Henry Beston, November 8, 1948, BFA.
33. H. L. Mencken, letter to Henry Beston, November 17, 1948, BFA.
34. David McCord, letter to Elizabeth Coatsworth, November 19, 1948, BFA.
35. George Sheahan, letter to Henry Beston, June 20, 1949, BFA.
36. Henry Beston, letter to Kate Beston, October 24, 1949, BFA.
37. Henry Beston, letter to J. Luther Neff, January 28, 1950, BFA.
38. Henry Beston, letter to Kate Beston, February 18, 1950, BFA.
39. Henry Beston, Introduction to *White Pine and Blue Water: A State of Maine Reader*, ed. Henry Beston, xxi.
40. Henry Beston, letter to Kate Beston, February 24, 1950, BFA.
41. Beston was also irritated when the dean of students at Wilson College informed the Bestons in February 1950 that Meg would be placed on academic probation until she made up a chemistry class that she had failed; not doing so would mean that she could not return to the college for her junior year the following fall.
42. Elizabeth Coatsworth, letter to Margaret Smith, February 23, 1950, BFA.
43. Henry Beston, letter to J. Luther Neff, September 13, 1950, BFA.
44. Kate Beston, letter to Margaret Smith, November 24, 1950, BFA.
45. Margaret Beston, letter to Henry and Elizabeth Beston, 1951 [n.d.], BFA.
46. Henry Beston, letter to J. Luther Neff, September 7, 1950, BFA.
47. Henry Beston, notes from "The Naturalist Concept of War," Lecture delivered at the Congregationalist Church, Rockland, ME, October 3, 1950, BFA.
48. Henry Beston, letter to Margaret Smith, March 14, 1951, BFA.

49. Henry Beston, letter to Lillian J. Bragdon, April 10, 1951, BFA.
50. Henry Beston, letter to Lillian J. Bragdon, April 28, 1951, BFA.
51. Henry Beston, letter to Lillian J. Bragdon, April 28, 1951, BFA.
52. Lillian J. Bragdon, letter to Henry Beston, August 9, 1951, BFA. Regarding the selection of Kreidel for the illustrations, on July 28, 1951 Beston wrote to Bragdon, "Fritz Kreidel sounds like just the man I want, and I do hope he will take the job...A beloved friend in Germany whose family I have tried to help out in every way has just named his new little son after me, so I have a "Heinrich" overseas. May heaven bless and guard him." The friends in Germany were Erica d'Alquen and her husband, to whom Beston had been sending relief packages after the war.
53. George Sheahan Jr., letter to Henry Beston, December 6, 1951, BFA.
54. Henry Beston, letter to David McCord, January 23, 1952, BFA.
55. George Sheahan Jr., letter to Henry Beston, September 19, 1952, BFA.
56. Lillian J. Bragdon, letter to Henry Beston, May 5, 1952, BFA. Overall, Beston was very pleased with how the book turned out, although as he wrote to David McCord, "In the earlier stories, some editor at the Aladdin broke up a number of my sentences, esteeming them, perhaps, too long, and leaving the last half of the sentence beginning with a "But" which is not Henry's way. But I soon put a stop to this very mistaken meddling. Alas, certain changes were already in the galleys, and I shrank from the huge expense of changing things back. 'Twill probably do no deep harm." Henry Beston. Letter to David McCord. 1 September 1952. BFA.
57. Henry Beston, letter to Margaret Smith, September 29, 1952, BFA.
58. Caroline Fife, letter to Henry Beston, May 13, 1953, BFA.
59. Elizabeth Coatsworth, letter to Margaret Smith, June 9, 1952, BFA.
60. Kate Beston, letter to Margaret Smith, June 22, 1952, BFA.
61. Kate Beston, letter to Margaret Smith, June 22, 1952, BFA.
62. Henry Beston, letter to J. Luther Neff, July 5, 1952, BFA.
63. Elizabeth Coatsworth, letter to Margaret Smith, September 25, 1952 BFA.
64. Henry Beston, letter to J. Luther Neff, July 5, 1952, BFA.
65. Henry Beston, letter to Lillian J. Bragdon, July 2, 1952, BFA.
66. Henry Beston, letter to J. Luther Neff, July 5, 1952, BFA.
67. Henry Beston, letter to Lillian J. Bragdon, July 2, 1952, BFA.
68. Frederick Rinehart, letter to Henry Beston, January 8, 1953, BFA.
69. Henry Beston, letter to David McCord, April 7, 1953, BFA.

12. THE MINOTAUR DOWNSTAIRS (1953–1958)

1. Henry Beston, letter to David McCord, August 21, 1953, BFA.
2. Henry Beston, letter to David McCord, August 21, 1953, BFA.
3. Henry Beston, letter to John and Rosalind Richards, September 25, 1953, Dartmouth.
4. Henry Beston, letter to John and Rosalind Richards, September 25, 1953.

Notes

5. Henry Beston, letter to David McCord, October 18, 1953, BFA.

6. Henry Beston, letter to Hans Ehlers, January 26, 1954, BFA.

7. Henry Beston, letter to Sharon Bannigan, April 29, 1955, BFA.

8. Henry Beston, letter to Kurt Wolff, April 28, 1955, BFA.

9. George Sheahan, Jr., letter to Henry Beston, October 6, 1954, BFA.

10. George Sheahan Jr., letter to Henry Beston, May 9, 1955, BFA.

11. *Quincy Patriot Ledger*, May 11, 1955, 1.

12. Joan Sheahan, letter to Henry Beston, May 19, 1955, BFA.

13. Henry Beston, letter to Dick Barnes, May 21, 1955, BFA.

14. Henry Beston, letter to Dick Barnes, May 21, 1955, BFA.

15. Henry Beston, letter to Lars Hallden, October 20, 1955, BFA

16. Kate Beston Barnes, "American Women," *Kneeling Orion*, 21.

17. Kate Beston Barnes, letter to the author, February 5, 2003.

18. Elizabeth Coatsworth, letter Margaret Smith, August 16, 1955, BFA.

19. Margaret Beston, letter to Margaret Smith, August 2, 1955, BFA.

20. Margaret Beston, letter to Margaret Smith, August [n.d.] 1955, BFA.

21. Tracy, *American Naturists*, 7.

22. Henry Beston, Foreword to *The Nature Writers: A Guide to Richer Reading*, by Herbert Faulker West, 5–6.

23. Henry Beston, letter to Elizabeth Coatsworth, November 14, 1944, BFA.

24. Henry Beston, letter to Margaret Smith, June 25, 1954, BFA.

25. Kate Beston Barnes, letter to the author, February 5, 2003.

26. Henry Beston, letter to David McCord, September 13, 1949, BFA.

27. Henry Beston, letter to Rosalind Richards, January 25, 1954, BFA.

28. Henry Beston, letter to Stanley Kunitz and Howard Haycraft, January 31, 1952, BFA.

29. Henry Beston, letter to Carl J. Weber, June 29, 1950, BFA.

30. See Payne, "Emerson's Natural Theology: John Burroughs and the 'Church' of Latter Day Transcendentalism."

31. Harvard Class of 1909, *Forty-fifth Anniversary Report*, 1954 (220).

32. Henry Beston, letter to J. Luther Neff, January 29, 1934, BFA.

33. Henry Beston, letter to Margaret Smith June 25, 1954, BFA.

34. Brooks, *The House of Life: Rachel Carson at Work*, 6.

35. Brooks, *The House of Life: Rachel Carson at Work*, 162.

36. Rachel Carson, letter to Henry Beston, May 14, 1954, Rachel Carson Papers, Beinecke Library, Yale University.

37. Freeman, Martha, ed. *Always, Rachel*, 54.

38. Henry Beston, letter to Elizabeth Coatsworth, May 24, 1953, BFA.

39. Henry Beston, letter to Rosalind Richards, June 21, 1953, BFA.

40. Henry Beston, letter to Luther Neff, March 24, 1956, BFA.

41. Henry Beston, letter to J. Luther Neff, January 1, 1957, BFA.

42. Henry Beston, letter to J. Luther Neff, March 23, 1957, BFA.

Notes

43. Henry Beston, letter to J. Luther Neff, April 23, 1957, BFA.
44. Kate Beston Barnes, letter to Margaret Smith, December 31, 1957, BFA.
45. Kate Beston Barnes, interview by Don Wilding, May 2004, BFA. See also henrybeston .org.
46. Elizabeth Coatsworth, letter to Margaret Smith, January 20, 1958, BFA.
47. Elizabeth Coatsworth, letter to Margaret Smith, June 28, 1958, BFA.
48. Elizabeth Coatsworth, letter to Margaret Smith, August 31, 1958, BFA.
49. Elizabeth Coatsworth, letter to Rosalind Richard, August 19, 1958, BFA.
50. Henry Beston, letter to David McCord, September 27, 1958, BFA.
51. Elizabeth Coatsworth, letter to Margaret Smith, August 1, 1958, BFA.
52. Elizabeth Coatsworth, letter to Margaret Smith, November 14, 1958, BFA.
53. Elizabeth Coatsworth, letter to Margaret Smith, November 16, 1958, BFA.

13. On the Side of Life (1959–1968)

1. Elizabeth Coatsworth, letter to Margaret Smith, January 14, 1959, BFA.
2. Kate Beston Barnes, letter to Margaret Smith, March 1959 [n.d.], BFA.
3. Elizabeth Coatsworth, letter to Margaret Smith, March 2, 1959, BFA.
4. Kate Beston Barnes, letter to Margaret Smith, March 20, 1959, BFA.
5. Henry Beston, letter to David McCord, December 1959 [n.d.], BFA.
6. Harvard University Class of 1909, *Fiftieth Anniversary Report*, 1959 (469).
7. Elizabeth Coatsworth, letter to Margaret Smith, December 31, 1959, BFA.
8. Elizabeth Coatsworth, letter to Margaret Smith, March 8, 1960, BFA.
9. David McCord, letter to Elizabeth Coatsworth, October 19, 1960, BFA.
10. *Bulletin of the American Academy of Arts and Sciences*, XIV, no. 2 (November 1960): 2.
11. Elizabeth Coatsworth, letter to David McCord, October 16, 1960, BFA.
12. Elizabeth Coatsworth, letter to Margaret Smith, October 18, 1960, BFA.
13. Elizabeth Coatsworth, letter to Margaret Smith, January 31, 1961, BFA.
14. Elizabeth Coatsworth, letter to Margaret Smith, April 25, 1961, BFA.
15. Elizabeth Coatsworth, letter to Margaret Smith, June 1, 1961, BFA.
16. Elizabeth Coatsworth, letter to Margaret Smith, June 25, 1961, BFA.
17. Elizabeth Coatsworth, letter to Margaret Smith, June 25, 1961, BFA.
18. *Cape Cod Standard Times*, Hyannis, MA, October 12, 1964, 1.
19. *The Cape Codder*, October 15, 1964, 3.
20. *Cape Cod Standard Times*, Hyannis, MA, October 12, 1964, 1.
21. Beston, *OH*, 218.
22. New Bedford, MA *Standard-Times*, October 18, 1964, 1.
23. Elizabeth Coatsworth, letter to Margaret Smith, January 17, 1965, BFA.
24. Kurt Vonnegut, letter to Henry Beston, October 12, 1964, BFA.
25. Herbert Faulkner West, letter to Henry Beston, October 13, 1964,BFA.
26. Elizabeth Coatsworth, letter to Margaret Smith, January 28, 1965, BFA.

Notes

27. Elizabeth Coatsworth, letter to Margaret Smith, February 27, 1965, BFA.
28. Elizabeth Coatsworth, letter to Margaret Smith, May 17, 1965, BFA.
29. Elizabeth Coatsworth, letter to Margaret Smith, December 29, 1965, BFA.
30. Charles Bolte, letter to Henry Beston, January 13, 1966, BFA.
31. Charles Bolte, letter to Henry Beston, August 31, 1966, BFA.
32. Adelaide Otis Santora, letter to Henry Beston, August 30, 1966, BFA.
33. Elizabeth Coatsworth, letter to Margaret Smith, March 20, 1967, BFA.
34. Elizabeth Coatsworth, letter to Margaret Smith, March 30, 1967, BFA.
35. Kate Beston Barnes, letter to the author, February 5, 2005.

Epilogue

1. Elizabeth Coatsworth, letter to David McCord, May 8, 1968, BFA.
2. Robert Finch, *Outlands: Journeys to the Outer Edges of Cape Cod*, 74.
3. Elizabeth Coatsworth, PG, 145.
4. Coatsworth, EM, 9.
5. Kate Beston Barnes, "Henry and Elizabeth—and Chimney Farm," *Down East*, May 1992, 50.

Index

Beston, Henry (*cont.*) "Country
Chronicle" in *The Progressive*, 270,
275–276; Dartmouth college visits,
235; death of, 333; death of brother
George Sheahan, 288–289; death of
Elizabeth in 1986, 337–338; death
of father, 13–14; death of F. Morton
Smith, 273–275; death of George
Sheahan, Jr., 298–300; death of Mary
Cabot Wheelwright, 317; death of
mother, 12–13; death of Ted Roosevelt,
Jr., 259–260; depression and strokes,
300–301, 322–323, 325; designation
of Fo'castle as literary landmark, xx,
326–329; editor for *The Living Age*,
82–83, 94–97; Elizabeth's diagnosis
with leukemia, 316–317; engagement
to Elizabeth Coatsworth, 166–170;
fairy tales, xix; farm life in Maine,
199–203; fashion sense, 112; Fo'castle,
xxix,121–124, 203–205; Fo'castle
destroyed by winter storm in 1978,
336–337; Fo'castle relocation, 261;
friendship with Rachel Carson,
309–311; genealogy of, 3–9; Great
Depression, 205–207, 230; great
hurricane of 1938, 239; growing mental
depression, 240–241; health worsens,
329–332; *Herbs and the Earth*, 212–218,
223; irritation over neighbor's shooting
range, 233–234, 237; Kate's wedding
to Richard Barnes, 296; leases land
on Cape Cod, 112–113; lecture on "A
Naturalist Looks at War," 285–286;
literary reputation, xxiii–xxv, xxvii,
xxviii, 302–308, 311; Margaret's
wedding to Dorik Mechau, 312–313;
marriage and children, xxi, 177–181;
marriage of brother George, 71–72;
Mary Cabot Wheelwright visit in New
Mexico, 124–125; meets Elizabeth

Coatsworth, 89–90, 92–93; moves
to Maine full-time, 250; opinion of
Hitler, 238, 242; *The Outermost House*
and Cape Cod, xix–xx, xxiii, 129–164
182, 203, 210, 212, 292, 294; Phi Beta
Kappa at Harvard, 281–282; plans for
second book on Cape Cod, 182–186,
188, 192, 196; returns to teach at
Harvard, 23–25; residence at Parson
Capen House, 8; struggles with
writing, 213–214; studies at Harvard
University, 14–21; submarine voyage
arranged by Theodore Roosevelt, Jr.,
108–109; summer stay on Jake Days'
houseboat in Maine, 189–191; teaches
at University of Lyon, 21–23; trip to
California for Kate's graduation, 290–
292; trip to England in 1929, 172–177;
trip to Germany in 1953, 295–296; trip
to Mexico in 1935, 218–219; trip to
Mexico in 1936, 224–226; trip to North
Carolina with Joe Wood, 246–247;
trip to Spain in 1924, 110–111; war
correspondence, 58–65; wins Academy
of Arts and Sciences Emerson-Thoreau
Medal, 322; wood alcohol poisoning,
220–221; war correspondent with U.S.
Navy, 68–71; *The World's Work* article
1923, 105–107

Beston, Margaret (Meg), xxi; birth of,
185, 187, 189, 192, 193, 194, 196, 197,
198, 203, 207, 208, 211, 215, 226, 230,
231, 233, 236, 237, 240, 241, 244, 246,
247, 248, 250, 255, 260; birth of first
child, Clarissa, 315, 316, 324, 330,
331, 376n. 80, 377n. 41; conflicts with
father, 266–267, 274, 277, 282, 284,
285, 288, 296, 301; engagement to
Dorik Mechau, 312; marriage to Dorik
Mechau, 313

Bethmann-Hollweg, Theobold von, 65–66

Index

Index

Index

Index

Index

Index

Index

*Set in Custodia types designed by Fred Smeijers and
Big Caslon types designed by Matthew Carter*

*Design and typography by Michael Russem at
the Cambridge Offices of Kat Ran Press*